P9-AOY-248

Teach Yourself®
Linux®

Date Due

12/15/02		
5/14/03		
12/17/05		
8/23/06		

BRODART   Cat. No. 23 233   Printed in U.S.A.

Teach Yourself®
Linux®

Steve Oualline and Eric Foster-Johnson

IDG Books Worldwide, Inc.
An International Data Group Company

Foster City, CA • Chicago, IL • Indianapolis, IN • New York, NY

Teach Yourself® Linux®

Published by
IDG Books Worldwide, Inc.
An International Data Group Company
919 E. Hillsdale Blvd., Suite 400
Foster City, CA 94404
www.idgbooks.com (IDG Books Worldwide Web site)

ISBN: 1-55828-598-9

Printed in the United States of America

10 9 8 7 6 5 4 3 2 1

1B/QY/QS/QQ/IN

Distributed in the United States by IDG Books Worldwide, Inc.

Distributed by CDG Books Canada Inc. for Canada; by Transworld Publishers Limited in the United Kingdom; by IDG Norge Books for Norway; by IDG Sweden Books for Sweden; by IDG Books Australia Publishing Corporation Pty. Ltd. for Australia and New Zealand; by TransQuest Publishers Pte Ltd. for Singapore, Malaysia, Thailand, Indonesia, and Hong Kong; by Gotop Information Inc. for Taiwan; by ICG Muse, Inc. for Japan; by Intersoft for South Africa; by Eyrolles for France; by International Thomson Publishing for Germany, Austria and Switzerland; by Distribuidora Cuspide for Argentina; by LR International for Brazil; by Galileo Libros for Chile; by Ediciones ZETA S.C.R. Ltda. for Peru; by WS Computer Publishing Corporation, Inc., for the Philippines; by Contemporanea de Ediciones for Venezuela; by Express Computer Distributors for the Caribbean and West Indies; by Micronesia Media Distributor, Inc. for Micronesia; by Chips Computadoras S.A. de C.V. for Mexico; by Editorial Norma de Panama S.A. for Panama; by American Bookshops for Finland.

For general information on IDG Books Worldwide's books in the U.S., please call our Consumer Customer Service department at 800-762-2974. For reseller information, including discounts and premium sales, please call our Reseller Customer Service department at 800-434-3422.

For information on where to purchase IDG Books Worldwide's books outside the U.S., please contact our International Sales department at 317-596-5530 or fax 317-572-4002.

For consumer information on foreign language translations, please contact our Customer Service department at 800-434-3422, fax 317-572-4002, or e-mail rights@idgbooks.com.

For information on licensing foreign or domestic rights, please phone +1-650-653-7098.

For sales inquiries and special prices for bulk quantities, please contact our Sales department at 650-762-2974 or write to the address above.

For information on using IDG Books Worldwide's books in the classroom or for ordering examination copies, please contact our Educational Sales department at 800-434-2086 or fax 317-572-4005.

For press review copies, author interviews, or other publicity information, please contact our Public Relations department at 650-653-7000 or fax 650-653-7500.

For authorization to photocopy items for corporate, personal, or educational use, please contact Copyright Clearance Center, 222 Rosewood Drive, Danvers, MA 01923, or fax 978-750-4470.

Library of Congress Cataloging-in-Publication Data

Oualline, Steve.
    Teach Yourself Linux / Steve Oualline and Eric Foster-Johnson.
        p. cm.
    ISBN 1-55828-598-9 (alk. paper)
    1. Linux 2. Operating systems (Computers) I. Foster-Johnson, Eric. II. Title.
QA76.76.O63 O834 2000
005.4'469--dc21   99–053979

Credits

Acquisitions Editor
David Mayhew

Development Editor
Valerie Perry

Technical Editors
Ed Hanley
Soren Harward

Copy Editors
Richard H. Adin
Timothy J. Borek

Project Coordinator
Linda Marousek

Graphics and Production Specialists
Amy Adrian
Brian Drumm
Angela F. Hunckler
Clint Lahnen

Doug Rollison
Brent Savage
Jacque Schneider
Janet Seib
Maggie Ubertini
Mary Jo Weis

Quality Control Specialists
Laura Albert
Corey Bowen
John Greenough
Marianne Santy

Book Designers
Daniel Ziegler Design
Cátálin Dulfu
Kurt Krames

Proofreading and Indexing
York Production Services

About the Author

Steve Oualline is the author of *Discover Linux.*

Eric Foster-Johnson is a software developer who works on Linux, UNIX, Windows NT, and a variety of other systems every day. An experienced author, Foster-Johnson's books include *Graphical Applications with Tcl and Tk*, *Perl Modules*, *UNIX in Plain English* (with Kevin Reichard), and *Linux: Configuration and Installation* with Patrick Volkerding and Kevin Reichard.

To Norma and Katya, and many years together

Welcome to Teach Yourself

Welcome to *Teach Yourself*, a series read and trusted by millions for nearly a decade. Although you may have seen the *Teach Yourself* name on other books, ours is the original. In addition, no *Teach Yourself* series has ever delivered more on the promise of its name than this series. That's because IDG Books Worldwide recently transformed *Teach Yourself* into a new cutting-edge format that gives you all the information you need to learn quickly and easily.

Readers told us that they want to learn by doing and that they want to learn as much as they can in as short a time as possible. We listened to you and believe that our new task-by-task format and suite of learning tools deliver the book you need to successfully teach yourself any technology topic. Features such as our Personal Workbook, which lets you practice and reinforce the skills you've just learned, help ensure that you get full value out of the time you invest in your learning. Handy cross-references to related topics and online sites broaden your knowledge and give you control over the kind of information you want, when you want it.

More Answers . . .

In designing the latest incarnation of this series, we started with the premise that people like you, who are intermediate to advanced computer programmers, want to take control of their own learning. To do this, you need the proper tools to find answers to questions so you can solve problems now.

In designing a series of books that provide such tools, we created a unique and concise visual format. The added bonus: *Teach Yourself* books actually pack more information into their pages than other books written on the same subjects. Skill for skill, you typically get much more information in a *Teach Yourself* book. In fact, *Teach Yourself* books, on average, cover twice the number of skills covered by other computer books — as many as 125 skills per book — so they're more likely to address your specific needs.

Welcome to Teach Yourself

...In Less Time

We know you don't want to spend twice the time to get all this great information, so we provide lots of time-saving features:

- ▶ A modular task-by-task organization of information — any task you want to perform is easy to find and includes simple-to-follow steps.
- ▶ A larger size than standard makes the book easier to read and more convenient to use at a computer workstation. The large format also enables us to include many more illustrations — hundreds of screen illustrations show you how to get everything done!
- ▶ A Personal Workbook at the end of each chapter reinforces learning with extra practice, real-world applications for your learning, and questions and answers to test your knowledge.
- ▶ Cross-references appearing at the bottom of each task page refer you to related information, providing a path through the book for learning particular aspects of the software thoroughly.

- ▶ The Find It Online feature offers valuable ideas on where to go on the Internet to get more information or to download useful files.
- ▶ Take Note sidebars provide added-value information from our expert authors for more in-depth learning.
- ▶ An attractive, consistent organization of information helps you quickly find and learn the skills you need.

These *Teach Yourself* features help you learn the essential skills about a technology in the least amount of time, with the most benefit. We've placed these features consistently throughout the book, so you quickly learn where to go to find just the information you need — whether you work through the book from cover to cover or use it later to solve a new problem.

You will find a *Teach Yourself* book on almost any technology subject — from the Internet to Windows to Microsoft Office. Take control of your learning today, with IDG Books Worldwide's *Teach Yourself* series.

Teach Yourself
More Answers in Less Time

> Search through the task headings to find the topic you want right away. To learn a new skill, search the contents, chapter opener, or the extensive index to find what you need. Then find — at a glance — the clear task heading that matches it.

Accounts and Packages

The next step is to define who you are by creating a user account and then to load on the system the software that you want to use.

You need to make an account for yourself so that you can safely play with Linux without worrying about wiping out anything vital.

Scroll up to the User Accounts item, and select Normal ⇨ User accounts. The accounts configuration window appears on the right.

Click Add to create a new account. Now fill in the Base info for the account. Put an account name in the Login name blank. This name should be all lowercase, with no spaces or special characters in it.

Under Full name enter your first and last names. Leave the group name blank. You don't have enough accounts on this system to benefit from group administration. Leave the Supplementary groups blank as well.

A home directory is a top-level directory where all a user's files are stored. This defaults to /home/account. Leave this blank empty because the default works just fine.

Linux lets you use different command interpreters. The one used in this book is the Bourne Again Shell (bash), so do not change the Command interpreter. Also leave the User ID blank.

Click the Accept button to create the account.

The configuration program asks for a password. Enter the initial password for this account and click Accept. Now type the password again and click Accept.

Click the Act/Changes button on the left side to commit the changes. Click the Activate the Changes button to actually make the changes. Click Quit (the one on the right) to exit Linuxconf.

During the installation process, you selected a default set of software to install. That was quick and simple. Now that you have Linux running, you can add the stuff you want and remove the stuff you don't want.

> Learn the concepts behind the task at hand and, more important, learn how the task is relevant in the real world. Timesaving suggestions and advice show you how to make the most of each skill.

① Select Config ⇨ User accounts ⇨ Normal ⇨ User accounts.

② Click the Add button to add a new account.

③ Enter the account information. Leave the home directory blank and select a shell. Leave the user ID blank (the system will select a good one for you).

④ Click the + next to Amusements to expand it.

⑤ Select Games. The currently installed packages are displayed.

⑥ Click one to select it.

⑦ Click Query to get detailed information.

> After you learn the task at hand, you may have more questions, or you may want to read about other tasks related to the topic. Use the cross-references to find different tasks to make your learning more efficient.

32

> Ultimately, people learn by doing. Follow the clear, illustrated steps presented with every task to complete a procedure. The detailed callouts for each step show you exactly where to go and what to do to complete the task.

x

Welcome to Teach Yourself

Go to this area if you want special tips, cautions, and notes that provide added insight into the current task.

The current chapter name and number always appear in the top right-hand corner of every task spread, so you always know exactly where you are in the book.

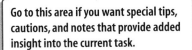

Getting On for the First Time

CHAPTER 2

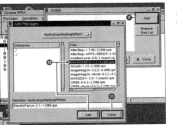

Software comes in bundles called packages. To start the package-handling program, select Foot ⇨ System ⇨ GnoRPM. The package manager displays a list of the package categories on the left. This list is limited to the installed packages. If we want to install a new package, we need to click Install to bring up the installation window.

Next, click Add to bring up a list of all the packages. Select the package that you are interested in and press Add. Continue selecting and adding until you get all the packages you want.

Click Close to return to the Install window.

If you want to find out more about a package, select it in the Install window and click Query.

Click Install to actually install the package.

To remove a package, use the tree on the left side of Gnome RPM to navigate through the package tree, and select the package from the right side of the window.

Click Uninstall to remove the package.

TAKE NOTE

WHAT IS RPM?

RPM stands for Red Hat Package Manager. The robust package management system that comes with Red Hat Linux is one of the major features which makes the Red Hat distribution of Linux the premier Linux distribution today.

It is the system that Red Hat uses to group related commands together to make them easy to install, upgrade, and remove. The Red Hat Package Manager does more than just installation and removal. It can also be used to build and create packages. (More on this can be found in Chapter 4.)

A full discussion of RPM would be a book in itself, but with a little playing around, you can discover the power of this tool for yourself.

- ⑧ *Click Install on the main window.*
- ⑨ *On the Install Window, click Add.*
- ⑩ *Select the packages to be installed and then click Add.*
- ⑪ *When finished, click Closed.*
- ⑫ *Select a package on the Install window to query.*
- ⑬ *Select Query for more information.*
- ⑭ *Click Close when done.*

33

Who This Book Is For

This book is written for you, an intermediate to advanced computer programmer who isn't afraid to take charge of his or her own learning experience. You don't want a lot of technical jargon; you *do* want to learn as much about the technology as you can in a limited amount of time. You need a book that is straightforward, easy-to-follow, and logically organized, so you can find answers to your questions easily. And you appreciate simple-to-use tools such as handy cross-references and visual step-by-step procedures that help you make the most of your learning. We have created the unique *Teach Yourself* format specifically to meet your needs.

Use the Find It Online element to locate Internet resources that provide more background, take you on interesting side trips, and offer additional tools for mastering and using the skills you need. (Occasionally, you'll find a handy shortcut here.)

xi

Personal Workbook

It's a well-known fact that much of what we learn is lost soon after we learn it if we don't reinforce our newly acquired skills with practice and repetition. That's why each *Teach Yourself* chapter ends with your own Personal Workbook. Here's where you can get extra practice, test your knowledge, and discover ideas for using what you've learned in the real world. There's even a Visual Quiz to help you remember your way around the topic's software environment.

Feedback

Please let us know what you think about this book, and whether you have any suggestions for improvements. You can send questions and comments to the *Teach Yourself* editors on the IDG Books Worldwide Web site at **http://www.idgbooks.com**.

Personal Workbook

Q&A

1. What two commands can you use to shutdown Linux?

2. How do you start the windowing system?

3. What must you do before you use your CD-ROM?

4. Can Linux read and write Microsoft Windows partitions? Can Microsoft Windows read Linux partitions?

5. What's root and why should you avoid using it?

6. What does the Linux equivalent of the Start button look like?

7. How do you start a terminal window?

8. What is a pager and how do you use it?

ANSWERS: 333

38

After working through the tasks in each chapter, you can test your progress and reinforce your learning by answering the questions in the Q&A section. Then, check your answers in the Personal Workbook Answers appendix at the back of the book.

Welcome to Teach Yourself

Another practical way to reinforce your skills is to do additional exercises on the same skills you just learned without the benefit of the chapter's visual steps. If you struggle with any of these exercises, it's a good idea to refer to the chapter's tasks to be sure you've mastered them.

Getting On for the First Time

CHAPTER 2

Read the list of Real-World Applications to get ideas on how you can use the skills you just learned in your everyday life. Understanding a process can be simple; knowing how to use that process to make you more productive is the key to successful learning.

EXTRA PRACTICE

1. Login as the user root and start the X Window System.

2. Create a user for your personal use. Use it to login as and start the X Window System.

3. Take a look at the directory /mnt/cdrom. Do an **ls /mnt/cdrom**. If there are files there, then your CD-ROM is mounted.

4. Check out some of the packages that you have installed.

5. Examine some of the packages that have not been installed yet.

6. Print a test page on your local printer.

REAL-WORLD APPLICATIONS

✔ Linux comes with a wealth of graphic manipulation tools. These can be installed to make Linux a powerful graphic manipulation engine. Steve Oualline uses it to store and enhance photographs from his digital camera.

✔ Linux comes with the Apache Web server. Install it and you have one of the cheapest and most popular Web server systems. (It's the server behind **http://www.oualline.com**.)

✔ Linux can be configured as a server for NFS, Novel, or Microsoft Windows networks. (There's advantages to not being controlled by a company interested in selling its own networking "solution.")

Visual Quiz

How would you fill out the blanks to the left for a user named Steve Oualline, account name steveo?

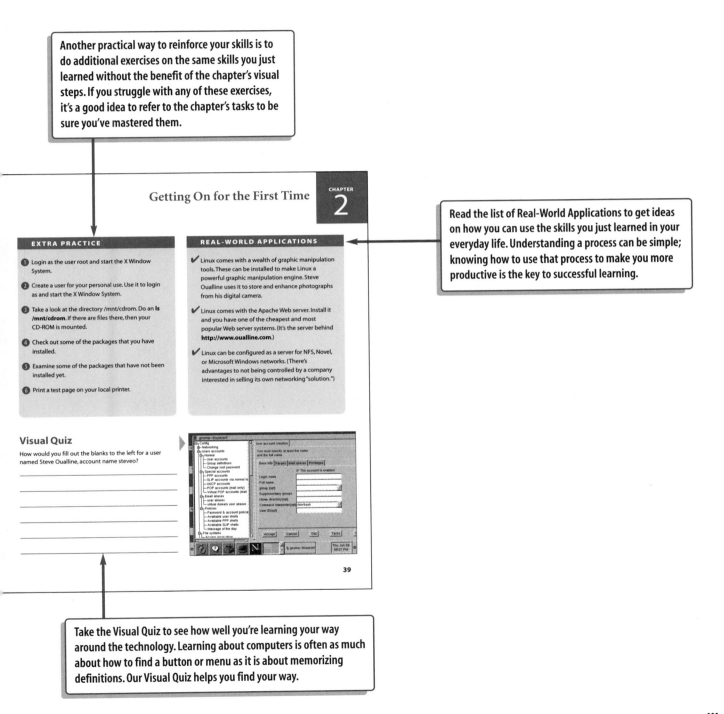

39

Take the Visual Quiz to see how well you're learning your way around the technology. Learning about computers is often as much about how to find a button or menu as it is about memorizing definitions. Our Visual Quiz helps you find your way.

xiii

Contents

Contents

Contents

Contents

Contents

What Is Linux?

Welcome to Linux. Linux is an operating system that runs on a variety of platforms, including most Intel-architecture PCs. As an operating system, Linux provides the basic infrastructure to run applications, and it's quite a lot different from Microsoft Windows, another operating system that runs on PCs that you may have heard about. Linux includes hundreds of applications, all on one CD-ROM. In this book, we teach you to use Linux, install it on your PC, configure it the way you want it, and to make use of its many applications.

Linux is available for downloading on the Internet — for free — or available on CD-ROMs such as the one that accompanies this book. Just about every program that runs on Linux, with the exception of some commercial applications, is available in source code form. That's great news, even if you are not skilled at programming yourself. There are thousands of people working on enhancing and fixing Linux software. Having the source code gives you an extra level of assurance that should problems arise, you have many options for getting the issues resolved. In short, the primary advantage of Linux is freedom of choice.

Linux is very similar to the much-maligned UNIX operating system. Most Linux commands mimic their UNIX counterparts, so if you have experience with UNIX, Linux makes a great home UNIX system. In fact, many Linux users started out trying to get more UNIX experience and found that Linux provides one of the cheapest entries into the world of UNIX.

For Microsoft Windows users migrating over, Linux also provides a number of helpful features. The Linux graphical desktops appear similar to the Windows look and feel. Linux can access Windows floppy disks, hard disks, and even the proprietary-formatted Joliet CD-ROMS. With an emulator called WINE, Linux can even run some Microsoft Windows applications directly.

Linux also includes its own set of applications, with more appearing every day because in the last few years, Linux has captured popular attention. More and more vendors are porting their applications to Linux, be it in the server space with the Oracle database or on the workstation side with Corel's WordPerfect word processor.

TAKE NOTE

HOW TO PRONOUNCE LINUX

You'd be surprised at how often this comes up, but yes, there is indeed a proper way to pronounce Linux. Say it *linn-ucks* and not *lih-nucks*. Linux inventor Linus Torvalds pronounces it something like *lee-nooks*. You can hear his pronunciation when you configure your sound card, as described in Chapter 10.

And, Linux systems can act as servers and workstations at the same time. The basic Linux installation includes server programs for e-mail servers, Web servers, file servers, and more. On the workstation side, you get a number of desktop environments to choose from, and a suite of applications. The same system — your PC — can act as both server and workstation. There are a number of things, though, that you can do to tune Linux for a particular task if you have specialized server or workstation needs. For example, many Internet Service Providers use Linux and tune it for Internet networking and Web serving. Other server systems may act as Microsoft Windows file and print servers (see the task on Samba in Chapter 15) and you may want to tune a system for that task.

Linux runs on most modern PCs that sport an Intel-compatible processor. It also runs on quite a few older

Introduction

386 and 486 systems. In general, Linux requires less processing power and less RAM than Microsoft Windows. In fact, its lower requirements are often how Linux gets in the door at many organizations. If you have an older 486 system lying around, you can load Linux on it and turn that system into a network router, Web server, e-mail server, print server, or other handy system. That's a plus with older hardware that is considered obsolete for running Microsoft Windows.

Linux runs on quite a few other architectures as well. Linux runs on SPARC (Sun), PowerPC (Macintosh and IBM RS/6000), 68K (older Macintoshes), ARM (NetWinders, Acorn RISC Machines), MIPS (SGI systems), Alpha (Compaq/Digital), and many other systems. Developers have ported Linux to the PalmPilot and Psion Series 5 handheld computers. Linux also scales up to huge systems sporting clusters of Linux systems running special software from the Beowulf project. (One such cluster, costing about $150,000, matched the best results of the leading system, a Cray supercomputer costing about $5.5 million on the POV ray benchmark.)

All in all, Linux means freedom. You are free to choose the hardware you want to run. You are free to choose the Linux distribution you want to run. You are free to choose the software to run without being locked into proprietary extensions to Internet protocols. You are free to choose the windowing system and desktop environment you prefer (the CD-ROM includes two desktops, GNOME and KDE). You aren't faced with strange bundling, such as being forced to run a certain Web browser if you choose to install a C++ compiler or word processor. In fact, you aren't locked into much at all. That's the main benefit of free software and open standards.

Linux history

Linux began with one person, Linus Torvalds, then a university student in Finland. Torvalds designed an operating system kernel that ran on Intel-based PC equipment. This was a big event, because at the time you could only purchase UNIX for PCs at a high cost. Early versions of Linux used some facilities from Minix, an operating system used in academic circles, such as the file system. The early versions didn't offer much, but each version added more and more.

After the very early versions, Linux distributions came into being. These distributions combined the Linux kernel with the GNU UNIX compilers and tools, along with Berkeley UNIX networking code, the X Window System, and a host of other free packages.

Linux distributions

So, now that you decided on Linux you face an even more difficult choice. You must choose between a plethora of Linux distributions. Technically, Linux is just the kernel. Linux distributors put together hundreds of other packages to make a complete distribution. These same distributors add installation programs and some aids for administering Linux systems.

Of the 20 or so Linux distributions, several stand out. We've chosen the Red Hat distribution because it is widely used and easiest to install. We also really like the Linuxconf program that ships with Red Hat Linux. Linuxconf handles most of the nasty chores of configuring your Linux system for you. Even more, it provides a Web interface, so that you can configure your Linux systems remotely.

Red Hat includes a reasonably good installation program and a way to manage add-on software — called *packages*. Red Hat's package manager, or **rpm**, provides a

Introduction

handy way to upgrade your system when new versions of programs come out.

Getting updates

This book contains a CD-ROM with the latest version of Red Hat Linux. Because Linux is under active development, you can expect new versions every six to eight months. This is a great thing, as you can get updated applications with more features, and every release fixes a number of bugs. Check the Red Hat Web page (**http://www.redhat.com**) for information on new versions and updates.

Linux applications and open source software

Linux is fueled by the free, or open source, software movement. By this, think free speech rather than free beer, although some of us might prefer the latter. Linux was developed by thousands of people, and it is available for free on the Internet. You can download the source code to virtually all of Linux.

Most Linux applications are also freeware. This leads to a few very good applications, including language compilers and the Apache Web server, which is listed as the number one Web server on the Internet.

With freeware, though, you also get a lot of applications that are not very good. It's hard to complain, because you get them for free.

Luckily, there are a number of very good applications in addition to Apache. These applications include The GIMP, a graphics program similar to Adobe Photoshop. Netscape Communicator is available for free on Linux. It provides Web browsing, e-mail, Usenet news, and HTML editing. The free source code Mozilla variant also runs on Linux.

Office software vendors such as Corel, Applix, and StarDivision support Linux. For many packages, you can download the applications for free.

Support for Linux

A question about Linux that is often asked regards support. We're always surprised by this, because we find basic OS support to be lacking in general. With Microsoft Windows, we all know to reboot our machine whenever there's a problem. If things get worse, you have the option of paying money to call Microsoft and ask for help. Chances are you'll be told that you can wait for the next NT service pack or load a current service pack that you already know may break a number of applications.

It is true that with Linux there are fewer trained administrators available for hire. In the Windows world, there are thousands and thousands of trained and certified administrators. The Linux situation is gets better with time, but you are likely to have a hard time hiring Linux experts, which may be an issue for your organization.

It is also true that with Linux, because you're typically dealing with fewer commercial products you get less formal support. To get around this, you can purchase support contracts from a number of third-party vendors such as LinuxCare, IBM, or Hewlett-Packard. You can also get support from distributors such as Red Hat.

Few hardware vendors support Linux. But then, we haven't found hardware support for Windows to be that great. For example, one of the authors called Compaq because a system experienced a BIOS (hardware) error that the hard disk was not found. Of course, this meant the system couldn't boot. After waiting an interminably long time on hold, the Compaq tech person insisted that we boot the machine and copy a Windows Registry file from the hard disk—for a system that could not detect the hard disk! We still can't believe it.

Supported versus free software

Steve Oualline writes a monthly programming column for PCI Communications. He decided to submit bug reports for supported software from Sun, HP, and SGI.

It took Sun about a week to take and register his problem report. This was followed by several months of waiting. Every once in a while he would do a problem report trace to make sure some progress was being made. Finally, an engineer investigated the problem and determined that it was valid, so a bug report was generated. Sun then looked at the bug report and decided that the problem wasn't big enough to change their software.

HP looked at the problem for a couple of weeks, then called Steve's system administrator and said something to the effect of, "This fellow appears to have problems with this type of programming. I suggest that he read a book on this subject." The system administrator responded, "He writes books on the subject himself."

The HP response was, "Oh. I guess I'll need to research this problem some more." We never heard from HP again.

SGI was reasonable. They pointed out that the bug was really a restriction in their software and it was documented. So, out of three bug reports for supported software, the most Steve got was a statement that it would not be fixed.

In another column, he described his experience with installing the GNU gcc compiler. Basically, he said it went smoothly except for running out of disk space five times. There was one minor problem with zero-length object files.

A few months later, the column was published. A short time later, Steve received an e-mail from the Free Software Foundation saying they were looking into his bug report.

That surprised him since he hadn't sent one in. They told Steve that they had read his column and described the reported problem. They supplied him with the solution.

So for three supported products, Steve received zero fixes. Steve *didn't* submit a bug report for *unsupported* software but received a fix. So, how supported is supported?

With Linux, at least you have the source code. This means that if you have the time, you can track down and fix many problems. Most of us don't have a lot of time, though. We've found that the Usenet newsgroups form a great source of support, particularly for hardware and configuration issues. Chances are that if you face a problem, someone else has already solved the problem and posted an answer to the Usenet.

And, there's a lot of support out there, particularly in informal channels. As Linux continues to grow, more and more support options will become available.

In the pages that follow, we teach you to install, configure, and make the most use of your Linux system. You'll be surprised at the rich set of applications available and how easy it is to set up.

We're not Linux evangelists. Linux is by no means perfect, and we expose its weaknesses as well as its strengths. We've both used Linux for years and we both independently chose Linux because it works. After reading this book and experimenting with the accompanying CD-ROM, you should have a good idea whether Linux will work for you.

Introduction

The changing nature of software

Linux is a moving target. It is constantly changing. We at IDG Books want you to have the latest version of both the text and the software. Sometimes this is rather difficult as new versions of the many Linux packages appear on an almost daily basis. Although we've tried to be as accurate as possible, we're only human. If you do find mistakes, please send us a note.

How to contact the authors

You can contact Eric Foster-Johnson at erc@pconline.com, and Steve Oualline at oualline@www.oualline.com. We welcome your messages, but be forewarned that we do not have every possible hardware combination should you face compatibility issues. Luckily, though, you'll find a huge selection of support help from free to commercial on the Internet.

Good luck, and welcome to Linux.

Teach Yourself® Linux®

PART

I

CHAPTER		
	1	Installing Linux
	2	Getting On for the First Time
	3	Linux Commands and the Shell
	4	Getting Help
	5	Text Editing
	6	Performing a Full Backup

Introducing Linux

Most PCs come with an operating system (OS) already installed, so few users ever need to go through the hassle of installing an OS. This first part teaches you how to turn the CD-ROM that accompanies this book into a full-blown working operating system on your PC hardware. After you get over disk partitioning, it really isn't that hard, as explained in Chapter 1.

Chapter 2 delves into the initial setup tasks you need to perform to get Linux ready to run and configured for your system.

After the initial setup, we discuss, in Chapter 3, the essential Linux commands that you need to know about. While Linux detractors point to the huge number of commands available, Linux actually relies on a few simple ones for most tasks.

When you learn the basics of the Linux commands, and especially the command-line interpreter — which is called a *shell* — you have all you need to tackle this great operating system.

Linux includes megabytes of documentation. A drawback, however, and one you'll face with other free software packages, lies in the different formats chosen for documentation. Chapter 4 covers the Linux commands for getting help and provides a number of examples.

Linux gets a lot of mileage out of plain old text files. Because of this, it's essential that you learn the Linux text editors discussed in Chapter 5.

After you have installed everything, back up. You don't want to lose your important work. Chapter 6 discusses performing this necessary task.

CHAPTER 1

MASTER
THESE
SKILLS

▶ Installation Overview

▶ Getting Ready to Install

▶ Understanding Disk Partitions

▶ Using FIPS to Split a Microsoft Windows Partition

▶ Starting the Installation Program

▶ Beginning the Install

▶ Disk Setup

▶ Finishing the Installation

Installing Linux

Linux is a major operating system and requires a little planning to install. Many people think Linux is hard to install, but the installation procedure has been greatly improved since Linux was first introduced. Now, Linux is easier to install than Microsoft Windows 98. (Unfortunately, most people buy computers with Microsoft Windows preinstalled and have no idea how hard it is to install.)

Part of Linux's "hard-to-install" reputation is a result of Linux's providing a lot of choices when it comes to installation methods. Like Microsoft Windows, you can install Linux from a local CD-ROM. But you can also install it over a network. In other words, one system running Linux with a CD-ROM can be used to install another. Linux can even be installed when the remote system is running MS Windows. For large installations, you can create a standard installation image and use the network to install it on all the machines at a single location.

But for now, let's limit ourselves to a simple, initial installation. In this chapter, I take you through the steps needed to make your Linux installation run smoothly. I start with planning, and lead you step-by-step through a simple install process that ends in your booting a fully functional Linux system.

The key to a smooth installation process is to plan and keep things simple. This chapter begins with the key planning steps. By taking a little time to plan before starting the install process, potential problems can be eliminated. Doing things right the first time avoids having to reinstall the system over and over again.

Once initial planning is complete, we can begin the installation. The process is quite simple. You only have to answer a few questions to get it underway.

Linux is not only an operating system, but hundreds of applications as well. One of the secrets to a good install is to *not* load the applications during the initial installation. Red Hat Linux comes with a great package system that can be used to install them later, after the core system is running. Deferring the installation of the applications gives you a safer and quicker install. Remember, keep things simple.

Once the installation is complete, you can proceed to the next chapter and begin the initial configuration and setup of your Linux system.

Installation Overview

Installing Linux is a major operation. Let's look at the major installation steps. First, you need to decide whether you want a Linux-only computer or a computer that can be booted with either Microsoft Windows or Linux. If you want to be able to still use Microsoft Windows, then you will want to create a startup Microsoft Windows disk. This disk is insurance against installation problems. This disk is also used in running the Linux installation tool FIPS (First Interactive Partition Splitter) and booting the Linux installation CD-ROM.

Linux requires its own disk space. It can be installed on it's own drive, or you can split the Microsoft Windows disk drive in two. This is done using your startup disk and the Linux FIPS utility, which is discussed later in this chapter.

Once disk space is created, you can start the Linux installation program. The easiest way to do this is to boot from your CD-ROM. Unfortunately, some computers won't let you do that. In that case, you can boot from the Microsoft Windows startup disk and then start the Linux installation program.

In some cases, you may not want to use Microsoft Windows at all. (If you never use it, you can return it for a refund. See the following Take Note section.) In that case, you must *NEVER* use Microsoft Windows. Not even to boot Linux. If you can boot directly from the CD-ROM, you can just insert the CD-ROM and start the installation.

If you can't boot from the CD-ROM, you'll have to boot from floppy disk. The CD-ROM contains utilities that can be used to create the boot disk you'll need to start the installation process. You'll have to find a working system (either Linux or Microsoft Windows) and use it to create the boot floppy. After that just boot and install.

TAKE NOTE

▶ THE MICROSOFT WINDOWS REFUND

It's next to impossible to buy a computer without Microsoft Windows preinstalled. One user wanted to run Linux (and Linux only) on his new laptop. Unfortunately, he was not able to buy a computer without Microsoft Windows preinstalled.

When he got his computer he did an unusual thing: he read the End User License Agreement that came with Microsoft Windows. In it was a clause stating that if he didn't agree to all the terms of the agreement, he could return the software to where he bought it for a full refund of the price of the software.

Because he didn't want to use Microsoft Windows, he returned the software. This proved a little more difficult than you might think. The computer company was not set up to process refunds. But after a flurry of letters and a little persistence, he succeeded in getting a refund.

If you want to get your refund (a) do not even boot your computer using the Microsoft Windows software, (b) return the software to the computer manufacturer, and (c) be prepared to fight.

CROSS-REFERENCE

The LILO (LInux LOader) program can be used to boot multiple operating systems. It is discussed in detail in Chapter 17.

FIND IT ONLINE

More information about Microsoft Windows refunds can be found at **http://LinuxMall.com/refund/**.

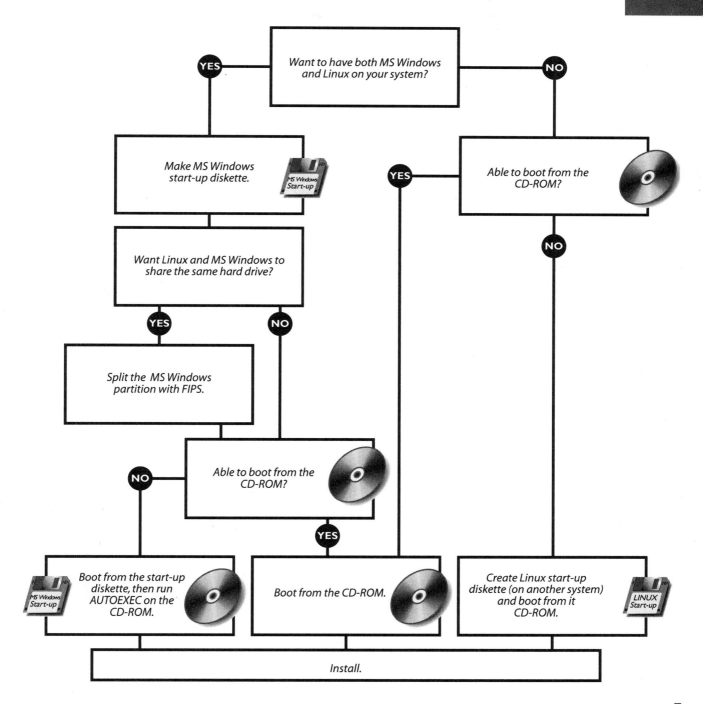

Want to have both MS Windows and Linux on your system? **YES** / **NO**

(YES →) Make MS Windows start-up diskette.

Want Linux and MS Windows to share the same hard drive? **YES** / **NO**

(YES →) Split the MS Windows partition with FIPS.

Able to boot from the CD-ROM? **NO** / **YES**

(NO →) Boot from the start-up diskette, then run AUTOEXEC on the CD-ROM.

(YES →) Boot from the CD-ROM.

(NO →) Able to boot from the CD-ROM? **YES** / **NO**

(NO →) Create Linux start-up diskette (on another system) and boot from it CD-ROM.

Install.

Getting Ready to Install

To install Linux, you have to know something about your hardware. If you are running Microsoft Windows (either Windows 95 or Windows 98), you can get this information from the operating system. If you are installing Linux on a new machine, you can get the hardware specifications from the documentation that comes with your system.

To get the hardware information out of Microsoft Windows, first select Start ⇨ Settings ⇨ Control Panel. Then double-click the System icon. Select the Device Manager tab and click Print.

When the Print window appears, select All devices and system summary and then click OK. You will get a detailed printout containing detailed information about your system. This information can be used to fill in the table on the opposite page.

Microsoft Windows startup disk

If you are running Microsoft Windows, the next step is to create a startup disk. First select Start ⇨ Setting ⇨ Control Panel. Double-click Add /Remove Programs. Select the Startup Disk tab. Insert a blank disk and click Create Disk. When the process is finished, write protect and label the disk.

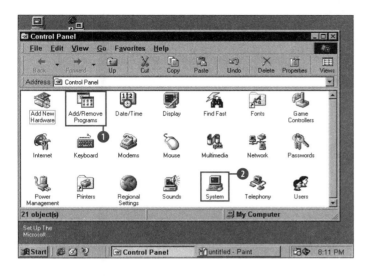

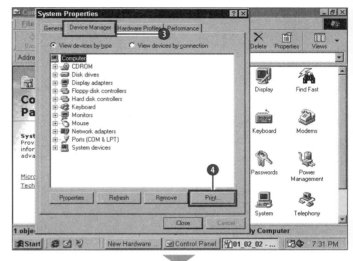

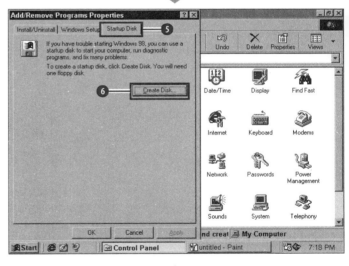

Table 1-1: SYSTEM INVENTORY FORM

Type of hard drive to be used for Linux

☐ IDE   ☐ SCSI

Type of CD-ROM for installation

☐ IDE   ☐ SCSI   Other _____

Mouse type

☐ Generic Serial ☐ Microsoft 2 button ☐ Mouse Systems

Mouse connection

☐ Serial port (COM _____)   ☐ PS/2 mouse

Type: _____

Network card

Type: _____ I/O Address: _____

Video card: _____

Monitor: _____

❶ Double-click Add/Remove Programs to create a startup disk.

❷ Double-click System to check your system resources.

❸ Select Device Manager to list the devices you have.

❹ Click Print to print an inventory report.

❺ Select Startup Disk.

❻ Click Create Disk to make the startup disk.

9

► Understanding Disk Partitions

To install Linux you have to set aside two disk partitions. A partition is a section of a disk drive. (It can be the entire disk drive, or a portion of it.) A physical disk drive is a single piece of hardware.

People frequently get drives and partitions confused. Microsoft hasn't helped things with their terminology. If you are using the Microsoft **fdisk** program, a physical disk drive is called a fixed disk drive. Disk drives are numbered 1,2,3, ... Partitions are called partitions and are numbered 1,2,3, ... All partitions are visible, even those that contain non-Microsoft file systems.

If you are running Microsoft Windows, partitions are called disk drives. Partitions (disk drives) are lettered starting with C. So C is the first partition, D the second, and so on. Partitions that contain non-Microsoft file systems are skipped.

Linux uses a simpler naming convention. The first disk is called /dev/hda, the second /dev/hdb, and so on. These are the names for the entire physical disk. The first partition on drive /dev/hda is /dev/hda1, the second /dev/hda2, and so on.

Linux requires two partitions. If you also want to use Microsoft Windows, you need one additional partition for that as well. Table 1-2 can help you plan your partition usage.

The first Linux partition is the swap partition, which is used by Linux for virtual memory. For most personal systems and other light Linux use, a 30MB swap partition will do just fine. Heavy usage, such as graphics manipulation or Web services, may require a 50MB swap partition. There are a few programs, such as **xanim** (a program that plays video files), that are real memory pigs and require lots and lots of memory, say 100MB.

Linux uses the second partition for its files. Installing the default system requires 250MB. Installing all the packages on the CD-ROM requires 1GB.

TAKE NOTE

► EXTENDED PARTITIONS

Originally, MS-DOS enabled you to divide your disk into one to four partitions. Partitioning was done for many reasons, not the least of which was to get around the space limitations of the old MS-DOS file system.

Soon people found that they wanted more than four partitions. But the space in the partition table was limited. So, a trick was devised: creating a partition containing more partitions. The new partitions are called extended partitions. The original four partitions came to be known as primary partitions.

A disk can have up to four primary partitions. One primary partition can be reserved for use by extended partitions. Fortunately, using the Disk Druid program that comes with Linux handles all this in the background, so we don't have to worry about such things.

► PARTITION RESTRICTIONS

Linux places no restrictions on which partitions it uses. The swap partition can be placed on any disk, and on any partition. No restriction is placed on the Linux file system partition.

Microsoft Windows is not so flexible. The Windows boot partition must be on the first IDE drive.

Table 1-2: DISK SPACE WORKSHEET

Space Requirements	Size	Drive
Legacy Operating System (Microsoft Windows)	MB	
Linux File System	MB	
Linux Swap	MB	

Table 1-3: TYPICAL WINDOWS SYSTEM — WINDOWS 95 USES THE ENTIRE DRIVE

Disk	Use	Linux Name	MS fdisk Name	MS Drive Name
First IDE	Entire Disk	n/a	1	n/a
	Windows Boot	n/a	1/partition 1	C:

Table 1-4: LINUX-ONLY SYSTEM WITH LINUX TAKING UP ONE DISK DRIVE

Disk	Use	Linux Name	MS fdisk Name	MS Drive Name
First IDE	Entire Disk	/dev/had	n/a	n/a
	Linux Swap	/dev/hda1	n/a	n/a
	Linux File System	/dev/hda2	n/a	n/a

Table 1-5: WINDOWS AND LINUX ON THE SAME DISK DRIVE

Disk	Use	Linux Name	MS fdisk Name	MS Drive Name
First IDE	Entire Disk	/dev/hda	1	n/a
	Windows Boot	/dev/hda1	1/partition 1	C:
	Linux Swap	/dev/hda2	1/partition 2	n/a
	Linux File System	/dev/hda3	1/partition 3	n/a

Table 1-6: WINDOWS ON THE FIRST DRIVE AND LINUX ON SECOND DRIVE

Disk	Use	Linux Name	MS fdisk Name	MS Drive Name
First IDE	Entire Disk	/dev/hda	1	n/a
	Windows Boot	/dev/hda1	1/partition 1	C:
Second IDE	Entire Disk	/dev/hdb	2	n/a
	Linux Swap	/dev/hdb1	2/partition 1	n/a
	Linux File System	/dev/hdb2	2/partition 2	n/a

Using FIPS to Split a Microsoft Windows Partition

Installing Linux on an existing Microsoft Windows system is a bit tricky. Windows usually uses the entire disk drive, leaving no space for Linux. You have to trick Windows into giving up some of its space, by using the **FIPS** program. **FIPS** is an MS-DOS-based program that splits a hard drive into two partitions.

Before you can use **FIPS**, you need to do some preparation. First, create a Windows startup floppy disk. Then copy the programs **FIPS.EXE** and **RESTORRB.EXE** to the disk. These utilities are found on the CD-ROM in the directory \DOSUTILS\FIPS20. Next, move all your Microsoft Windows data to the beginning of the partition by running the Microsoft disk defragmenter program. To run this program, select Start ⇨ Run and enter the command **defrag c:** in the box. (Force the program to run even if it reports the disk is not fragmented.)

The next step is to boot from the floppy and run the FIPS program. This program is designed to be as safe as possible. It performs a lot of checks on the system before enabling you to change the partition.

To be extra safe, the program makes a complete backup of the partition table before it changes anything. That way, if mistakes are made, you can use the **RESTORRB** program to restore it.

Next, the program goes into partition mode. The size of the old and new partitions is displayed. The program starts by setting the old partition (the one with Microsoft Windows on it) to the smallest possible size. You can increase this partition by pressing the left arrow (←). This transfers space from the new partition to the old. Using left arrow (←) and right arrow (→) you can adjust the sizes to the value you want. At this stage you are splitting off only one partition (the "New Partition") for Linux. Later during the installation, this new partition will be split into a Linux File System and Linux Swap partition.

Pressing Return locks the partition sizes in place and writes out your new partition table. To make sure that nothing went wrong, it is a good idea at this point to start Microsoft Windows and run SCANDISK on drive C.

If you run into trouble, or SCANDISK reports massive problems, you can use RESTORRB to restore the old partition table. *This can only be done if you've not modified any files on the partition since you first performed FIPS.*

CROSS-REFERENCE

Documentation for FIPS (and source code) can be found on the CD-ROM in the directory **/mnt/cdrom/ dosutils/fips20**.

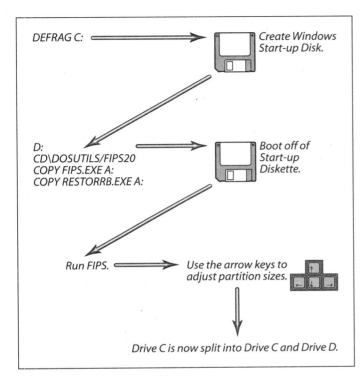

DEFRAG C: → Create Windows Start-up Disk.

D:
CD\DOSUTILS/FIPS20
COPY FIPS.EXE A:
COPY RESTORRB.EXE A: → Boot off of Start-up Diskette.

Run FIPS. → Use the arrow keys to adjust partition sizes.

Drive C is now split into Drive C and Drive D.

TAKE NOTE

DRIVE D

After running FIPS your Microsoft Windows drive C will be split into two drives C and D. Drive D will not be formatted, so do not try to use it.

Be aware that because you have a new drive D that the drive letters of your other drives will be changed. For example, if you had a CD-ROM on drive D, it will now be on drive E.

After you install Linux, Microsoft Windows will not recognize the existence of the new partition, and all your disk drives will revert to their former letters.

After you install Linux, Microsoft Windows will not recognize the existence of the new partition, and all your disk drives will revert to their former letters.

FIND IT ONLINE

For the latest information on FIPS, check out
http://www.igd.fhg.de/~aschaefe/fips/.

Starting the Installation Program

Once you are prepared for the installation, running the install program is next. This sounds simple, but because the Linux does not run under Microsoft Windows, there are some special steps that must be taken.

There are three ways to start the installation program:

▶ Boot from the CD-ROM.
▶ Boot from a Microsoft Windows Startup disk and run the AUTOBOOT program from the CD-ROM.
▶ Create a Linux boot disk and boot from the disk.

Booting from the CD-ROM

The easiest method of starting the installation is to boot from the CD-ROM. How to get your computer to use the CD-ROM varies from computer to computer. Usually there is an option in the CMOS setup that enables you to select the CD-ROM as the first boot device.

After enabling this feature, just insert the CD-ROM and reset your machine. The installation program will begin.

Warning: After you complete the installation, be sure and disable this feature. If you don't, you'll return to the installation program the next time you boot.

Booting from the Microsoft Windows startup disk

Unfortunately, the installation program cannot be run under Microsoft Windows. You can, however, boot from a startup disk and run the program from the MS-DOS command prompt.

Insert the Windows Startup disk and restart the computer. The startup disk will ask you what type of system to start. Choose "Start computer with CD-ROM Support."

Insert your Linux CD-ROM and make it your current drive by typing:

```
E:
```

where "E" is the letter of your CD-ROM drive. (Note: This may be a little different than what you expect because the startup disk creates a Ram drive and reletters drives D to Z.)

Next begin the installation with the commands:

```
CD \DOSUTILS
AUTOBOOT
```

Creating and booting from the Linux startup disk

If, for some reason, you can't run Microsoft Windows (it's not installed or you want to get your refund), then you can boot off the Linux startup disk. But first you have to make one. You'll need a machine with a working operating system and a blank floppy disk.

To create the Linux startup disk using Microsoft Windows, use the program **rawrite**, which is found in the \DOSUTILS directory on your CD-ROM. It copies disk images from the CD-ROM to floppy. You need to make a floppy disk that contains the \images\boot.img.

To start the installation, insert the Linux boot disk and reset your computer. The installation process begins. To create the disk using Linux, you can use the **dd** command to produce the disk. See the online documentation in the /mnt/cdrom/doc/rhmanual directory for details.

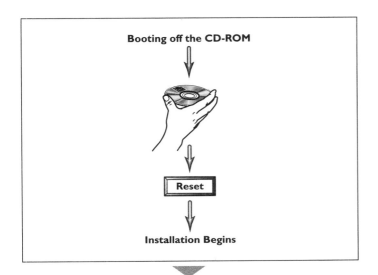

Booting off the CD-ROM

Reset

Installation Begins

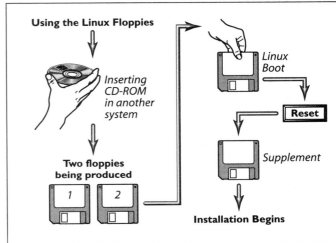

Using the Linux Floppies

Inserting CD-ROM in another system

Two floppies being produced

1 2

Linux Boot

Reset

Supplement

Installation Begins

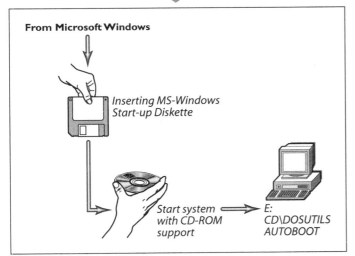

From Microsoft Windows

Inserting MS-Windows Start-up Diskette

Start system with CD-ROM support

E:
CD\DOSUTILS
AUTOBOOT

Beginning the Install

The installation program is used for installation, as well as for maintenance and other tasks. The initial screen enables you to select one of the many options. There are actually two installation programs. The default is a brand new X Windows System based program. Unfortunately this program is not reliable and crashes on many systems. The old text screen based program works just fine and is reliable, so we'll use that. When you get the initial **LILO:** prompt, just type **text** and **Return**.

`LILO: text`

The installation begins. The first screen displays a welcome message as shown in the top figure on the facing page. Near the bottom of the screen is an Ok button. It's highlighted, so you can "press" it by pressing Return.

The next screen asks you to select a language for use during the installation. Use the arrow keys to select an entry and then select it by pressing Space. Next, press Tab to move to the Ok button and then press Return.

Linux now asks you about the type of keyboard you are using. Select the correct entry and press Ok. This is followed by a question concerning the location of the installation media. For a simple installation, this will be a Local CD-ROM.

After a few more simple questions, you will arrive at the Installation Type question. Select "Install GNOME Workstation." (Unlike Microsoft Windows, there are several different desktops that you can use with Linux. The two most common are GNOME and KDE. We use GNOME throughout this book.)

The other choices (Server and Workstation) are special-purpose installations that you don't want.

The next few questions concern your hardware. If you created a system inventory in the "Getting Ready to Install" section earlier in this chapter, you can find the information there. Otherwise, you will have to get the information from other sources.

If you already have some Linux partitions on your primary hard drive, the installation program will give you a chance to erase them and replace them with your new Linux. The other choice is to handle your partitions manually. If there are Linux partitions you must partition manually as described in the next task. (FIPS creates two MS-DOS partitions, so manual partitioning is required if you used FIPS.)

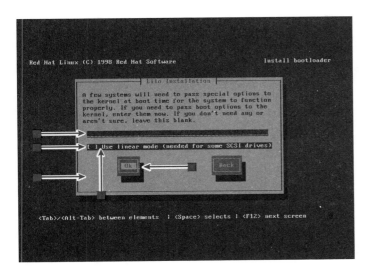

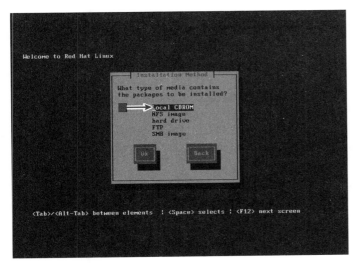

▶ **Space** *toggles checkboxes.*

▶ **Tab** *move from element to element.*

▶ **Enter** *"presses" the highlighted button.*

❶ *Select the "GNOME Workstation" installation.*

TAKE NOTE

▶ VIRTUAL TERMINALS

The Linux installation process provides several "virtual screens." The first, is the main install process. Pressing F1 switches to this screen.

The available virtual screens are

▶ **Alt+F1.** Main installation screen. Normally this is the only screen that you need for installation, but the others are interesting as well.

▶ **Alt+F2.** Shell prompt. If you are an advanced user, know what you are doing, and need to execute commands, use this screen.

▶ **Alt+F3.** Installation log. This screen contains detailed information about what's going on with your installation.

▶ **Alt+F4.** Kernel log. Messages from the kernel concerning device drivers and other system messages.

▶ **Alt+F5.** Other messages.

▶ SCREEN NAVIGATION KEYS

The following keys can be used to navigate around the installation GUI:

▶ **Tab.** Move to next element.

▶ **Up arrow (↑)/Down arrow (↓).** Select item from a scrolling list.

▶ **Space.** Toggles the value of checkboxes.

▶ **Return.** "Presses" the highlighted button.

▶ **F1.** Help.

Disk Setup

To install Linux, you must have at least two partitions. A typical screen partitioning GUI is shown here.

The disks are listed at the bottom of the screen. The first IDE disk drive is named hda, the second is named hdb, and so on. In this example, there is only one disk in the system, which is named hda.

The upper portion of the screen shows the partitions currently defined for that disk. In this example, there are two partitions already defined: hda1, a Windows 98 partition, and hda5, a Linux file system partition.

If you used FIPS to split your Microsoft Windows partition, then you will see two Microsoft Windows partitions at this point. The first partition contains your Microsoft Windows data. Leave this alone. The second partition contains nothing. Delete this one so that you can use the space for the two partitions that Linux requires.

The first task is to edit the Linux partition (hda5). To do this, highlight the hda5 line and press F3-Edit. The edit window appears as seen in the upper right illustration.

For this partition, change the mount point to / (pronounced root). On any disk, a partition can be marked Growable. This means that this partition can grow or shrink as needed to fill the remaining space after all the fixed-sized partitions are defined. In this example, we want to define a swap partition of a given size and let the root partition take up the rest of the space, so we mark this partition as growable.

We've not defined a swap partition for Linux yet, so press F1-Add to create one. (See the lower-left figure.) Leave the mount point blank; it's meaningless for a

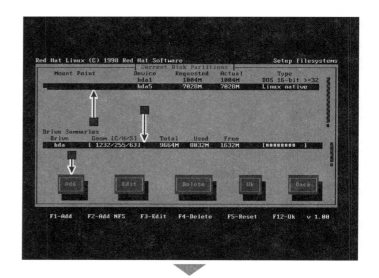

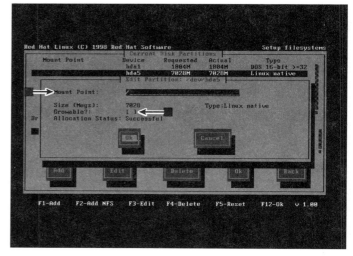

▶ List of partitions on the disk
▶ List of disks
▶ Adds a new partition to the disk

▶ **Mount point**
▶ Use / for Linux's file system partition. Leave blank for Linux swap partition.
▶ **Growable**
Indicates that the size specified is a minimum. This partition can grow to fill all free space. If more than one partition is marked growable, they get equal shares of the free space.

CROSS-REFERENCE

For information on Disk Druid, see the file /mnt/cdrom/doc/rhmanual/manual/doc033.htm.

18

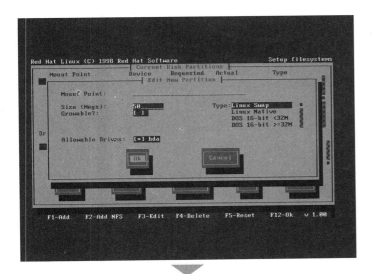

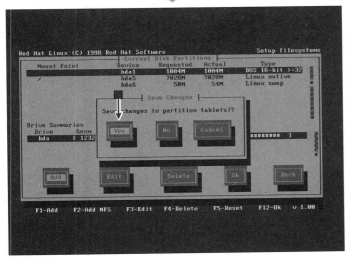

▶ *Make the Linux file system growable. Specify a size for the Linux swap partition.*

▶ *Linux swap partition. No mount point. Partition is 50MB and not growable.*

▶ *Commit the changes by pressing F12.*

swap partition. Set the partition type to Linux Swap and the size to the size that you defined in "Understanding Disk Partitions" and using Table 1-2, earlier in this chapter.

Finally press F12+Ok to accept these parameters and write your partition to disk.

TAKE NOTE

▶ PARTITIONING IS DANGEROUS

When you change the size of a partition, you lose all data in that partition. Misuse of partition editors is the quickest and most effective way of destroying all the data on an entire disk.

Do not repartition a disk drive on which you have data that you want to keep unless you have good, recent backups.

▶ LINUX AND FOREIGN PARTITIONS

Propriety software, such as Microsoft Windows, tends to be very myopic in its approach to things. With Microsoft Windows, the only disk formats recognized are those Microsoft invented.

Linux is different. The people who wrote Linux wanted something useful, not something that would lock you into their market.

The result is that Linux recognizes and handles many different types of file systems. This includes not only the FAT16 and FAT32 formats of Microsoft Windows, but also OS/2, Novell, Solaris, and many other formats.

Finishing the Installation

fter the partitioning is done, Linux initializes the disks that it will use. The swap partitions are initialized first, followed by the root file system.

The software installation now begins. A progress bar is displayed so that you can see the installation progress of each package and the progress of the install as a whole.

Next, the system asks about your mouse. Many of the programs that use the X Windows system work better if you have a three-button mouse. If you have a two-button mouse, you can configure Linux to emulate a three-button mouse. In this case, pressing both buttons simultaneously simulates pressing the middle button.

The next screen asks for a root password. This is the password assigned to the superuser. Anyone with this password can do anything they want on this system, so choose a good one.

Next you are asked to create some normal users for your system. This can be safely skipped at this point. Linux has a very nice user administration tool that you can use later to add users after you complete the installation.

The next step is the installation of the X Window system. You need to tell Linux about your video card and monitor. If your video card is not listed, you can always select Generic VGA, which enables you to limp along well enough to get Linux up and running. After that you can review some of the troubleshooting documents, such as /usr/doc/HOWTO/Xfree86-HOWTO. (This is in the package howto-6.0-4.noarch.rpm, which you need to install before taking a look at this file.)

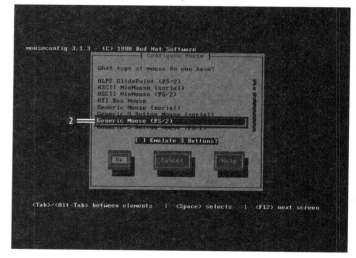

❶ Select mouse type.   ❷ Select time zone.

CROSS-REFERENCE

The directory /usr/doc/lilo-0.21 contains extensive documentation on the LILO (LInux LOader), which is used to boot Linux and other systems.

20

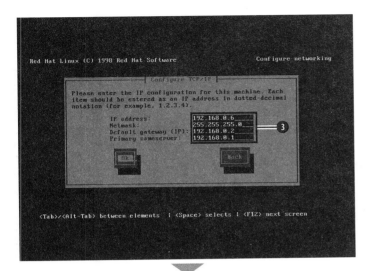

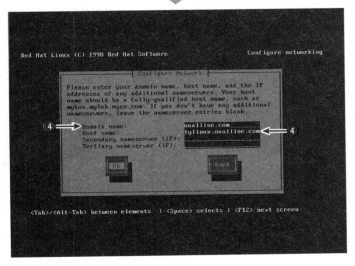

3 *Select video card type.* | **4** *The installation begins.*

Your installation is now complete. The next time your system starts a LILO prompt appears. You can then type **linux** to start Linux. If you type nothing, after a short timeout, Linux will start.

Note: If you have a Microsoft Windows partition on your disk, you can still get access to Microsoft Windows. You'll have to edit your /etc/lilo.conf file to tell LILO about windows as described in Chapter 17.

TAKE NOTE

HOW TO CHOOSE A PASSWORD

One of the problems with Linux, as well as with other UNIX systems, is that encrypted versions of the passwords are readable. This means that hackers can try and guess your password.

There are programs available that will try to crack your password by running every word in the dictionary through the password encryption algorithm and checking each against your password.

To foil these programs you need to choose a nonguessable password. One simple technique is to choose two random words from the dictionary and type them in using a symbol such as #$@$ to separate the words. Such a password is easy to remember and hard to crack.

Added security can be obtained by using nonstandard upper/lower case letters in your words. A password such as "ButtoN#KnowS" makes an excellent and secure password.

FIND IT ONLINE

Information on the windowing system XFree86 can be found at **http://www.xfree86.org**.

Personal Workbook

Q&A

1 Does your existing system have any data on it that you value?

_____

_____

_____

2 When was the last time you made a backup?

_____

_____

_____

3 How many partitions does Linux require?

_____

_____

_____

4 Where can the Linux partitions be located?

_____

_____

_____

5 How many partitions does Microsoft Windows require and where must they be located?

_____

_____

_____

6 What is _FIPS?_

_____

_____

_____

7 What is _LILO?_

_____

_____

_____

8 How would you determine how much disk space you need for each partition?

_____

_____

_____

ANSWERS: PAGE 333

EXTRA PRACTICE

1. Make a Microsoft Windows startup disk.

2. Use Microsoft Windows to produce a system inventory.

3. Press Alt+F1 through Alt+F4 to see what each does during an installation. (Always end with **Alt-F1** to return to the main install window.)

4. Take a look through the programs and documentation available in X:\DOSUTILS (X is the drive letter of your CD-ROM).

5. Take a look at the documentation in the X:\DOC directory on the CD-ROM.

REAL-WORLD APPLICATIONS

✔ Because Linux is free many people think that it is unsuitable for production-quality applications. Not true!

✔ Your Windows system crashes for the third time. You have been thinking about installing Linux for some time, but you are still hesitant. You think to yourself,"It's free. It can't be suitable for production-quality applications." You try Linux and are pleasantly surprised at how stable it is.

✔ "People ask me how I can afford to run Linux. I tell them my system has to be reliable; I can't afford not to!"

Visual Quiz

How would you configure this partition as the Linux file system?

_____

_____

_____

_____

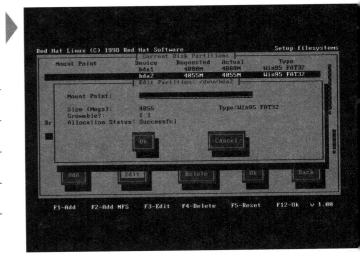

23

CHAPTER 2

MASTER
THESE
SKILLS

- ▶ First-Time Commands
- ▶ A Quick Tour of the Screen
- ▶ Initial Configuration
- ▶ Accounts and Packages
- ▶ Setting Up for Microsoft Windows and Networks
- ▶ Adding a Printer

Getting On for the First Time

Congratulations, you have installed Linux. Now you need to do a little configuration to get things going.

The first thing you need to learn is how to get in and out of Linux. Once you've signed on you can enter commands, such as **startx**, which starts the windowing system, and **halt** to shut down the system.

You should also know that Linux comes with a windowing system called X Window. The X Window System is highly modular. At the lowest level, there is the server. It is responsible for putting things on the screen (that is, drawing a black rectangle in the middle of the screen). On top of this is a window manager. It is responsible for the placement of windows and how they look. (It's the part of the system that draws things such as title bars and borders.) Finally, the applications are responsible for putting stuff in a window.

With Microsoft Windows, all these components are bundled. With Linux, they are separate, and you can configure your system to use different window managers depending on how you want your system to look.

By default, Linux installs a window manager that's part of a package called GNOME. GNOME is a collection of applications all designed to work together in a consistent manner to display a nice friendly desktop.

Linuxconf helps you configure your system. Unlike Microsoft Windows, Linux will not automatically give you access to the CD-ROM. You must "mount" it. The Linuxconf utility lets you do this. You can mount your Microsoft Windows partition as well. (Linux is very democratic. It will read other operating systems' disks.)

Linux comes with only one real account defined — the system administrator, root. The root account is a privileged, "superuser" account; normal protections do not apply to it. Experienced Linux users use the root account as little as possible. Instead, they create normal user accounts for the system. That's because if you make a mistake as a normal user, the Linux protection system will keep you from doing too much damage. On the other hand, if you make a mistake as a root user, you can kill your entire system.

Finally, Linux enables you to use your printer in "native" mode, or to use the PostScript emulator Ghostscript. In native mode, your print jobs are sent directly to the printer. If you decided to use Ghostscript, the printing system accepts PostScript data and translates it to native format for printing. This process is transparent to you because the printing system handles the details. As far as you're concerned, you have a PostScript printer.

First-Time Commands

If you've installed Linux correctly, you'll see the LILO: prompt when you boot. This program allows you to select the operating system you want to boot. Enter linux to start the program.

```
LILO boot: linux
```

As Linux starts, it displays a *lot* of diagnostic and information messages. These are useful to people doing device driver or kernel configuration work. (See Chapter 17, which discusses kernel configuration.)

After a short pause, Linux comes up and displays the login message. Enter the account name root. (At this stage, this is the only valid account name.) The system will ask you for the password. Enter the root password you setup during the installation.

Next the root prompt appears:

```
[root@ahostname /root]#
```

Because this prompt changes depending on things such as hostname and current directory, we use the generic root prompt (#) for the examples in this book.

Life at the command prompt

After you login you are presented with the command prompt. At this point you can type in commands (followed by Enter) to execute them.

For example the command:

```
# date
```

executes the **date** command.

There are a number of special characters available at this point. For example, the Delete key deletes the previous character. Pressing Ctrl+U erases the entire line.

The Ctrl+D key is the end-of-file (EOF) key. Typing it causes you to be logged out.

There is one more important key to remember. The Ctrl+C key aborts the current command. This is similar to the MS-DOS Ctrl+Break command and it works more consistently.

Now start the X Window System using the command **startx**.

① Enter the account name (root).

② Enter the password (it will not echo).

③ When the prompt appears you can type commands such as **date** and **startx**.

④ Enter the **date** command.

CROSS-REFERENCE

Chapter 7 describes how to configure your Linux system so that you get an X Window login instead of a text login.

Getting out of the X Window System

To get out of the X Window System, select the Foot icon (lower left), and the Log out command. (This won't actually log you out; it returns you to command mode.)

If you are stuck, you can use the emergency exit by pressing Ctrl+Alt+Backspace.

Shutting down

To shut down the system, login as root and execute the command:

halt

To reboot the system, login as root and execute the command:

reboot

⑤ Enter **stty –a** to display the terminal settings.

▶ The Delete (^?) key erases the previous character.

▶ The Ctrl+U (^U) key erases (kills) a line.

⑥ The **halt** command shuts the system down in an orderly manner and finishes with the System Halted message.

TAKE NOTE

▶ **WHY YOU SHOULD SHUTDOWN**

When Linux writes data to disk, the data doesn't actually get instantly written to the drive. Instead, it goes into a memory buffer. A daemon called update flushes things out to disk every so often.

When you shut down the system, all the disk information in memory is written out before the system halts. If you just press the reset button, this doesn't happen and data is lost.

Also when you start up, Linux will detect the improper shutdown and go through a long process to make sure that all the file systems on the disk are OK.

▶ **LINUX KEY NAMES**

Linux uses the carat (^) notation to indicate control characters. For example, if you see, "Type ^D to exit," that means that you should type Ctrl+D to get out of the program.

There's one other special key. That's the Delete key. The Linux notation for this character is ^?.

A Quick Tour of the Screen

After you start the X Window System with the **startx** command, a desktop called GNOME appears. At the bottom of the screen is a tool-bar called the GNOME Panel, which contains the tools described in Table 2-1.

Application windows

The area above the toolbar contains the application windows. The first time you start, you get two applications, the file manager and the GNOME help system. The file manager allows you to view and manipulate files. It acts much like the Microsoft Windows file manager.

The other window contains the GNOME help system, which presents you with a hypertext help system that gives you information on both GNOME and Linux. Just click away to explore the help system.

The title bar at the top of each window contains several icons that allow you to manipulate the window.

▶ *Clicking the Page button brings up a menu containing various window-related commands.*
▶ *Clicking the Minimize button lets you to shrink the window.*
▶ *Clicking the Maximize button lets you enlarge the window.*
▶ *Clicking the Close button lets you close the window.*

Table 2-1: TOOLS IN THE GNOME CONTROL PANEL

Tool	Description
Show/Hide Arrows	Click either one of these arrows and the panel slides into the side of the screen and only an arrow remains. Click the arrow again and it slides out.
GNOME footprint	This is the GNOME equivalent of the start button. It brings up a set of menus that enable you to run a variety of programs as well as configure your system.
The help button	The help button starts a help browser that gives you access to help on GNOME, the Linux man pages, and the GNU Info pages. (See Chapter 4 for more information.)
The GNOME configuration tool	This tool lets you change the way the GNOME desktop behaves.
Netscape	Starts the Netscape browser.
Pager	GNOME manages four pages. Each of these is the size of your screen so you can see only one at a time. Currently, you are viewing page 1, the upper-left page. If you click on one of the other four large rectangles in the pager, you will jump to that page.
	You may notice that the upper-left page has some small rectangles in it. These represent the windows that currently appear on that page.
Pager Information arrow	Pressing the pager information arrow displays a list of each page and the applications that are on them.
Pager Properties	Clicking this icon brings up a window which lets you configure the pager.
Application list	This is a list of all the applications that are running. Click on the application to jump to the page it is on and make it the active application.
Date/Time	Displays the current date and time.

Desktop icons

A number of icons appear on the desktop. The first icon is "Home directory." A home directory is the top-level directory for a user, which contains the user's personal files. It opens a file manager pointed to your home directory. These icons point to **http://www.redhat.com**: Red Hat Support, Red Hat Errata, Linux Documents, and GNOME Web Site. These are shortcuts to various places on the Web. Double-clicking any of these shortcuts starts Netscape and points to the given Web page.

The last icon, CD-ROM 0, mounts the CD-ROM drive and starts a file browser so that you can examine the contents of the drive.

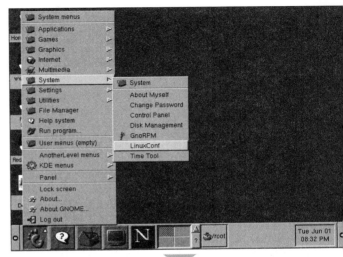

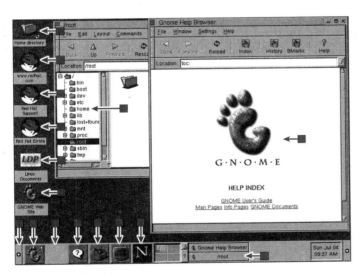

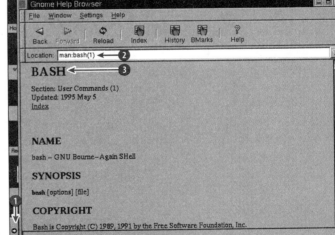

▶ *Opens a file browser to your home directory.*

▶ *Shortcuts to various useful places on the Web.*

▶ *Opens a file manager for the CD-ROM.*

▶ *Hide toolbar arrow.*

▶ *The GNOME equivalent of the Start button. Called the Foot button.*

▶ *Help.*

▶ *GNOME configuration toolkit.*

▶ *Terminal (opens up a window containing a terminal emulator).*

▶ *Netscape.*

▶ *Pager.*

▶ *Currently open windows.*

▶ *Help window.*

▶ *File manager.*

▶ *Start **Linuxconf** by selecting Foot ⇨ System ⇨ LinuxConf.*

① *Click the Help icon in Linuxconf to bring up the help system.*

② *Scroll down to the bottom and click man pages.*

③ *Scroll to the man page that you want to see and click it. (In this example, bash is used.)*

29

Initial Configuration

In this task, we go through the initial configuration tasks needed to get your system fully operational.

Mounting the CD-ROM

The first step is to mount the CD-ROM drive that contains your Linux CD. This is necessary to access the information and files that are on that CD. Your CD-ROM drive will be mounted in the directory /mnt/cdrom.

Start the Linuxconf program. Click the Foot button, by selecting Red Hat menus ⇨ Adminstration ⇨ Linuxconf. Linuxconf starts and displays a welcome screen. Click Quit to dismiss it. The main configuration window appears. The left column lists the various configuration tasks that are performed by this tool. Scroll down to File Systems and then click Access Local drive.

The right side of the tool displays the current file systems. Click /dev/cdrom to display the Volume Specification window.

Select the Options tab. Unset the Not mount at boot time option. If you want, select the User Mountable option. This option allows any user to mount and unmount the CD-ROM. Without this option, only root can perform mounts.

Click Mount to perform an immediate mount of the CD-ROM, then Accept to make the changes permanent.

Click Quit to get out of the Local Volume window.

Mounting the MS-DOS partition

If you have a Microsoft Windows/Linux system, your Linux system can access your Microsoft Windows partition. You mount the Microsoft Windows partition using the Linux Linuxconf ⇨ File System ⇨ Access local drive tool. Click the partition containing your Microsoft Windows file system.

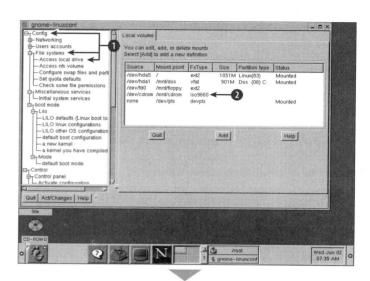

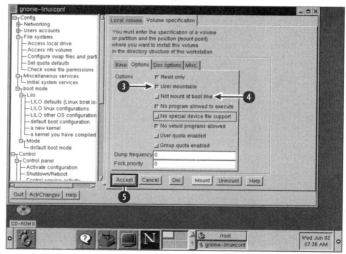

❶ Select the category Config ⇨ File Systems ⇨ Access Local Drive.

❷ Select the partition or device that you want to configure. In this case, it's the CD-ROM device (/dev/cdrom).

❸ Set User mountable if you want any user to mount or unmount the CD-ROM. This gives any user the power to change the CD.

❹ Clear Not mount at boot time to automatically mount the CD-ROM drive when the system starts.

❺ Click Accept to accept these values.

30

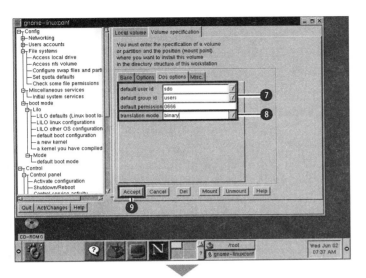

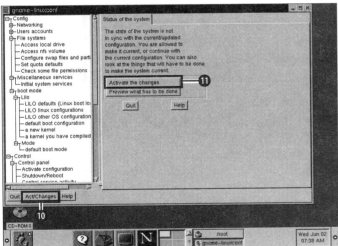

One of the problems with an MS-DOS file system is the question of who owns the files. Linux is better at protecting one user from modifying another's files. Linux lets you mount an MS-DOS file system, but you should tell it who the disk belongs to. To do this, click the DOS options and fill in the default user id with the name of the file's owner. You'll probably want to fill in the default group id, as well.

Linux and MS-DOS use different end-of-line characters. If you select the ASCII translate mode, Linux automatically edits any file you read or write to correct this problem. If you use the binary translation mode, no translation is done. In automatic mode, Linux chooses to translate or not based on the file's extension.

Committing the changes

Click the Act/Change button at the bottom of the first column to actually make the changes.

In the right panel click Activate the changes to make the changes. Click Quit to exit the Linuxconf utility.

⑥ *If you have an MS-DOS partition, select it.*

⑦ *Provide information about who owns the files on the partition and permissions. Code 0666 gives everyone read and write permission.*

⑧ *Set translation mode to binary.*

⑨ *Click Accept.*

⑩ *Click Act/Changes to activate the changes.*

⑪ *Click Activate the changes to make the changes real.*

TAKE NOTE

THE END-OF-LINE PUZZLE

One of the earliest I/O devices connected to computers was a printer/keyboard combination called a Teletype. The Teletype used a two-character combination (<carriage return><line feed>) to end a line.

Computer storage cost a lot back then and people discovered they could save money if they used only one character for end-of-line. Unfortunately, the various manufacturers couldn't agree on which character to keep. UNIX and Linux use <line feed> as the end-of-line character. Apple chose <carriage return>. MS-DOS and Microsoft Windows uses the original <carriage return><line feed> combination.

Accounts and Packages

The next step is to define who you are by creating a user account and then to load on the system the software that you want to use.

You need to make an account for yourself so that you can safely play with Linux without worrying about wiping out anything vital.

Scroll up to the User Accounts item, and select Normal ⇨ User accounts. The accounts configuration window appears on the right.

Click Add to create a new account. Now fill in the Base info for the account. Put an account name in the Login name blank. This name should be all lowercase, with no spaces or special characters in it.

Under Full name enter your first and last names.

Leave the group name blank. You don't have enough accounts on this system to benefit from group administration. Leave the Supplementary groups blank as well.

A home directory is a top-level directory where all a user's files are stored. This defaults to /home/*account*. Leave this blank empty because the default works just fine.

Linux lets you use different command interpreters. The one used in this book is the Bourne Again Shell (bash), so do not change the Command interpreter.

Also leave the User ID blank.

Click the Accept button to create the account.

The configuration program asks for a password. Enter the initial password for this account and click Accept. Now type the password again and click Accept.

Click the Act/Changes button on the left side to commit the changes. Click the Activate the Changes button to actually make the changes. Click Quit (the one on the right) to exit Linuxconf.

During the installation process, you selected a default set of software to install. That was quick and simple. Now that you have Linux running, you can add the stuff you want and remove the stuff you don't want.

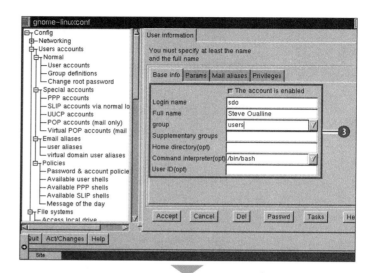

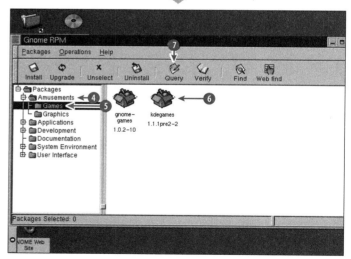

1. Select Config ⇨ User accounts ⇨ Normal ⇨ User accounts.

2. Click the Add button to add a new account.

3. Enter the account information. Leave the home directory blank and select a shell. Leave the user ID blank (the system will select a good one for you).

4. Click the + next to Amusements to expand it.

5. Select Games. The currently installed packages are displayed.

6. Click one to select it.

7. Click Query to get detailed information.

32

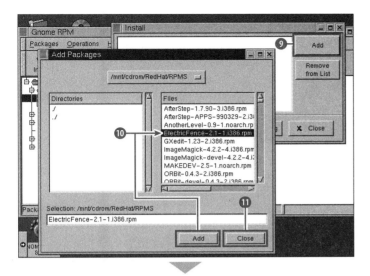

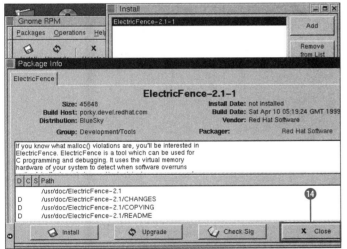

Software comes in bundles called packages. To start the package-handling program, select Foot ➪ System ➪ GnoRPM. The package manager displays a list of the package categories on the left. This list is limited to the installed packages. If we want to install a new package, we need to click Install to bring up the installation window.

Next, click Add to bring up a list of all the packages. Select the package that you are interested in and press Add. Continue selecting and adding until you get all the packages you want.

Click Close to return to the Install window.

If you want to find out more about a package, select it in the Install window and click Query.

Click Install to actually install the package.

To remove a package, use the tree on the left side of Gnome RPM to navigate through the package tree, and select the package from the right side of the window.

Click Uninstall to remove the package.

TAKE NOTE

▶ ### WHAT IS RPM?

RPM stands for Red Hat Package Manager. The robust package management system that comes with Red Hat Linux is one of the major features which makes the Red Hat distribution of Linux the premier Linux distribution today.

It is the system that Red Hat uses to group related commands together to make them easy to install, upgrade, and remove. The Red Hat Package Manager does more than just installation and removal. It can also be used to build and create packages. (More on this can be found in Chapter 4.)

A full discussion of RPM would be a book in itself, but with a little playing around, you can discover the power of this tool for yourself.

8 *Click Install on the main window.*

9 *On the Install Window, click Add.*

10 *Select the packages to be installed and then click Add.*

11 *When finished, click Closed.*

12 *Select a package on the Install window to query.*

13 *Select Query for more information.*

14 *Click Close when done.*

Setting Up for Microsoft Windows and Networks

This task shows you how to install LILO so that you can boot from either Linux or Microsoft Windows. It also tells you how to set up a network to communicate with the outside world.

Dual booting

Linux comes with a boot program that knows how to start both Microsoft Windows and Linux. If during the installation in Chapter 1 you preserved your Microsoft Windows partition, you can still run it. But you first have to tell Linux that it is still there.

The file **/etc/lilo.conf** describes the operating systems on your hard drives. When you begin, Linux is the only operating system described in the file. To get Microsoft Windows to work, you need to edit the**/etc/lilo.conf** file, adding the text in Listing 2-1 to the end of it.

Once this change has been made, run the command

    # /sbin/lilo

as root. This updates the boot sector of your hard drive. The next time you boot, you can enter **linux** or **dos**. (If you don't enter anything within 50 seconds, Linux will boot by default.)

Network configuration

Linux and networking go together well. In fact, many Internet service providers use Linux because of its strong networking capabilities. (If you do not have a network card, you can skip this section.)

To configure the network, you'll need to start the X Window System if you have not already done so. Next, start the **Linuxconfig** program by selecting Foot ⇨ System ⇨ LinuxConf. This brings up the Linux configuration tool. On the list of things to do, select Client tasks ⇨ Basic host information. You may need to click the + signs to expand the Config and Networking categories.

Enter the full name of your host in the Host name blank.

Next, click the Adaptor 1 tab to configure your first network interface. Make sure the Enabled checkbox is set.

A network card needs an IP address to work. You have three ways to get one:

- ▶ Manual — You tell the machine what IP address to use. If you are connected to an external network, you get this address from your network administrator. If you are on a private network (not connected to the Internet), you can use the numbers reserved for private networks — 192.168.0.1 through 192.168.0.253

- ▶ DHCP — DHCP stands for Dynamic Host Configuration Protocol. Using DHCP, your machine can ask a DHCP server for a network address, and the server will supply it. Your network administrator can tell you whether to use DHCP.

- ▶ BootP — This stands for Boot Protocol. It's another way your machine can ask a master server for an address. This protocol is being phased out, so only select it on instructions from your network administrator.

If you are unsure which method to use, choose Manual and use the IP address 192.168.0.1. (In the other two modes, you can leave this field empty.)

Enter the full name of your machine under Primary name + domain.

For the network device, choose eth0. (Adaptor 1 is eth0, Adaptor 2 is eth1, and so on.)

The system will attempt to choose the correct modules for the Kernel module section. If it does not, use the pulldown and select the driver that fits your device.

Press the Accept button to accept the values, and then click Act/Changes to activate the changes.

34

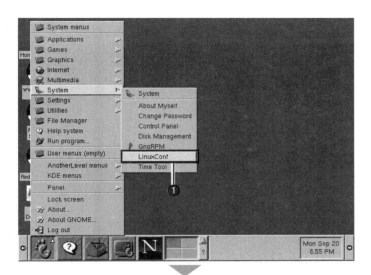

Listing 2-1: /ETC/LILO.CONF

```
boot=/dev/hda
map=/boot/map
install=/boot/boot.b
prompt
timeout=50

image=/boot/vmlinuz-2.2.5-15
        label=linux
        root=/dev/hda5
        read-only

other=/dev/hda1
        label=dos
        table=/dev/hda
```

▶ Add the lines below the underlined text.

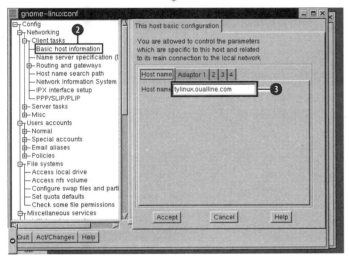

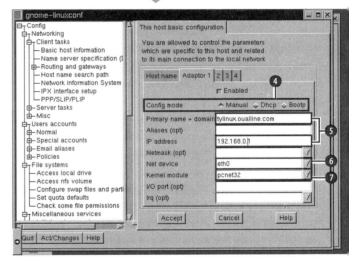

❶ Start the LinuxConf configuration tool, by clicking the foot icon ➪ System ➪ LinuxConf.

❷ Select Config ➪ Networking ➪ Client tasks ➪ Basic host information.

❸ Enter the host name.

❹ Select the configuration mode.

❺ Enter the host information.

❻ Select the device name eth0.

❼ Select a driver.

> **CROSS-REFERENCE**
>
> Chapter 18 discusses the LILO file in much more detail.

Adding a Printer

Start the Printer Tool, by selecting Foot ⇨ System ⇨ Control Panel. Then click the printer icon. The Printer Tool appears.

Click the Add button to create a new printer. If this printer is connected to your computer select the Local option and click OK. The other selections let you connect to another Linux/UNIX machine (Remote Unix Queue) and Microsoft Windows shared printer (LAN Manager Printer). Because remote printers are beyond the scope of this book, we assume that the printer is local.

An information screen appears listing the parallel printer ports detected by Linux. MS-DOS and Linux use different names and numbers for the printer ports as indicated below:

```
Linux  MS-DOS

/dev/lp0      LPT1
/dev/lp1      LPT2
/dev/lp2      LPT3
```

The next dialog lets you define and configure the printer. The Names blank lets you define a name for the printer. The name is used when you issue an **lpr** command. For example, the command:

```
$ lpr -Psam /etc/fstab
```

prints a file to a printer named sam. (If no name is specified, then the name lp is used.)

A single printer can have more than one name. For example, you may want to name your PostScript printer both ps and postscript. If you put more than one name in the Names blank they must be separated by the vertical bar (|). (Warning: There must be no spaces in this entry.)

The spool directory is where files for the printer are stored while they are waiting to be printed. By convention, this is a directory in /var/spool/lpd that is named the same as the printer. (That way it's easy for you to remember that the files in /var/spool/lpd/ps are for the printer named ps.)

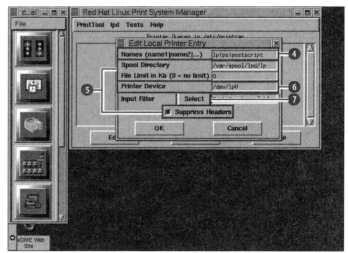

❶ Click Foot ⇨ System ⇨ Control Panel.

❷ Double-click the Printer and select Add.

❸ Click Local Printer, and then OK.

❹ Enter the name of the printer. If you want the printer to have more than one name, separate the names by vertical bar (|), but without spaces.

❺ Let these options default.

❻ This is the printer device.

❼ Click Select to select the printer.

36

TAKE NOTE

SERIAL PRINTERS

Serial printers are very tricky to setup. There are *lots* of configuration parameters (baud rate, stop bits, parity, flow control, and so on) that have to be configured right. Worse, configuration is a manual process involving editing the /etc/printcap file and putting in the right set of hexadecimal numbers.

In other words, it's a real mess. There are good, cheap, parallel printers out there. Use one of these instead.

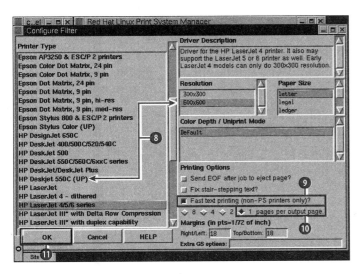

⑧ Select the printer type and printer-specific options.

⑨ Select this if you have a non-PostScript printer to print text in native mode.

⑩ Select 1 pages per output page. (The *mpage* command does multiple pages better than this system.) Select any other printer-specific options.

⑪ Click OK to install the printer.

The file limit parameter causes the **lpr** to reject files that are too large. If this is a personal system, leave this value at 0. (Thus, if you print a very large file, you just waste your own paper.)

The next blank lets you select an input filter, which converts text and PostScript into printer codes. Click Select to bring up a dialog that lets you select the correct filter for your printer.

Select your printer type from the scrolling list to the left. You can see information about the filter in the Driver Description box in the upper right. Options for the printer can be set in the Resolution, Paper Size and Color Depth boxes.

Some printers (mostly PostScript printers) expect each print job to end with an EOF (End of File) character. If you have one of these printers, set the Send EOF option.

Linux uses new-line, also known as line-feed, for an end-of-line character. If you send a raw text Linux text file directly to a printer

```
it will
        print like
                this
```

Set the Fix stairstepping option to correct this problem.

There are two ways of printing text on a text printer. The first is to send the text to the printer (fast text printing). The second is to turn it into PostScript, turn the PostScript into graphics, and print the graphics. This is a lot of work, but it does let you print multiple text pages on a single physical page. Because the **mpage** command does this (and lets you control the process a lot better), leave this option off.

The last option is Suppress Headers. A header is a single page printed at the beginning of a print job identifying what's printed and who printed it. You don't need headers for a personal system, so leave this set.

Once everything is defined, click OK to create the printer.

Personal Workbook

Q&A

1 What two commands can you use to shutdown Linux?

_____

_____

_____

2 How do you start the windowing system?

_____

_____

_____

3 What must you do before you use your CD-ROM?

_____

_____

_____

4 Can Linux read and write Microsoft Windows partitions? Can Microsoft Windows read Linux partitions?

_____

_____

_____

5 What's root and why should you avoid using it?

_____

_____

_____

6 What does the Linux equivalent of the Start button look like?

_____

_____

_____

7 How do you start a terminal window?

_____

_____

_____

8 What is a pager and how do you use it?

_____

_____

_____

ANSWERS: PAGE 333

EXTRA PRACTICE

1. Login as the user root and start the X Window System.

2. Create a user for your personal use. Use it to login as and start the X Window System.

3. Take a look at the directory /mnt/cdrom. Do an **ls /mnt/cdrom**. If there are files there, then your CD-ROM is mounted.

4. Check out some of the packages that you have installed.

5. Examine some of the packages that have not been installed yet.

6. Print a test page on your local printer.

REAL-WORLD APPLICATIONS

✔ Linux comes with a wealth of graphic manipulation tools. These can be installed to make Linux a powerful graphic manipulation engine. Steve Oualline uses it to store and enhance photographs from his digital camera.

✔ Linux comes with the Apache Web server. Install it and you have one of the cheapest and most popular Web server systems. (It's the server behind **http://www.oualline.com**.)

✔ Linux can be configured as a server for NFS, Novel, or Microsoft Windows networks. (There's advantages to not being controlled by a company interested in selling its own networking "solution.")

Visual Quiz

How would you fill out the blanks to the left for a user named Steve Oualline, account name steveo?

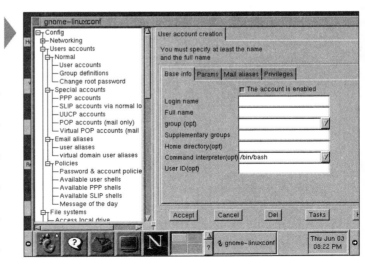

CHAPTER 3

MASTER THESE SKILLS

- ▶ Navigating Directories
- ▶ The Linux Command Line
- ▶ Listing Files
- ▶ Copying, Moving, and Deleting Files
- ▶ Viewing Files with More and Less
- ▶ Finding and Controlling Files
- ▶ Getting Information on the System
- ▶ The bash Shell
- ▶ Shell Scripts — A Whirlwind Introduction
- ▶ Shell Startup Files

Linux Commands and the Shell

Linux, built from its UNIX roots, relies heavily on the command line. Even with the graphical interfaces discussed in Chapter 7, Linux still requires many operations to be done from the command line.

The requirement for a command line, along with the cryptic set of UNIX commands, with names such as **cp** instead of *copy*, has led many to believe that Linux and UNIX are hard to use. Now, this isn't as bad as you may think. A powerful command line enables you to perform more easily tasks that are harder to do in a graphical environment. For example, if you want to back up all files ending in .c, .cc, and .h to a floppy disk, a command line proves much easier than selecting all these files in a graphical user interface. Even on the Macintosh, a premier graphical environment, the Macintosh Programmer's Workbench developer package added a command line to the Mac OS environment, precisely because many tasks, especially for software development, work better with a command line. A command line also enables you to batch together tasks, automating common commands. This type of work is typically harder to set up under graphical systems, where you're left with things like macros that simulate mouse clicks and menu choices.

While you are required to use a command line for many tasks, Linux doesn't lock you into a single type of command line. Windows users who run the MS-DOS prompt window with its limited functionality will be surprised to know that Linux supports many different command environments, which are called *shells*. Most Linux shells offer far more capability than any MS-DOS prompt window, and give you the freedom to choose which shell you prefer. These shells include scripting languages that enable you to automate many tasks. And, unlike DOS batch files, these scripting languages provide a rich set of functionality.

Shells read in the commands that you type, and then execute these commands. The trick is that Linux supports a rich set of commands as well as handy concepts, such as input redirection and wildcards.

This chapter tackles the command line and what you need to know to enhance your Linux experience. It covers the makeup of Linux commands, the bash shell, and the most common command-line commands.

Navigating Directories

Linux borrows heavily from its UNIX heritage. While Linux isn't based on any UNIX source code, Linux supports most of the key UNIX concepts, including that of directories.

The entire Linux file system is based on *directories,* or containers of files. The *root directory* resides at the top of the entire file system. All files that Linux can see then reside somewhere under the root directory, mostly in subdirectories. A *subdirectory* is merely a directory inside another directory. You can nest subdirectories within subdirectories and on and on.

Linux, like UNIX, uses a forward slash (/) as a directory separator. Linux indicates the root directory with a single slash, /. Thus, a directory name of /usr/bin indicates that usr is a subdirectory of the root directory, /. The directory bin, in turn, is a subdirectory of /usr. You can also see the Linux abbreviation factor at work here. The term usr is short for user and bin is short for binaries. The directory /usr/bin contains binaries, or applications. The table on the facing page shows some of the common Linux directories and what is found inside.

In addition to system directories such as /usr/bin, you have your own directory, which is allocated for your work. Every time you log in, you'll find yourself in your home directory. To see what directory is your home, type the **pwd** command, short for print working — or current — directory:

```
$ pwd
```

You'll see a response similar to this:

```
/home/erc
```

The environment variable named HOME also holds the name of your directory:

```
$ echo $H..OME
/home/erc
```

To change to a different directory, use the **cd** command:

```
$ cd /home
```

You can verify that the **cd** command worked by again entering the **pwd** command:

```
$ pwd
/home
```

When you navigate Linux directories, you can also take advantage of some shortcut names. The current directory has a shortcut name of ., a single period. The parent directory, that is, one directory up, has a short cut of .., or two periods. So, to change to one directory up, you can use the following command:

```
$ cd ..
```

When you get to the top directory (/), you cannot go any further up. Linux insists that all files, directories, and everything else that acts as a file appear somewhere under the root directory. This is quite different from Windows, where each drive, such as C: or D:, has its own root directory, which is \. Linux has only one root directory. Even so, Linux clearly supports more than one hard drive.

With Linux, you mount hard disks somewhere in the file tree starting at /. The place you mount a disk is called a *mount point.* For example, you may have two hard disks. You might use one for user home directories and want to mount that disk at /home. In this case, the second hard drive takes over beginning from /home and including all its subdirectories, such as /home/fred and /home/barney. The first hard drive holds all other files, that is, everything not under /home.

CROSS-REFERENCE
Chapter 2 covers creating user accounts.

FIND IT ONLINE
For more on working with directories, see **http://www. mathcs.duq.edu/unixhelp/tasks/index.html.**

TAKE NOTE

► CREATING DIRECTORIES

You can create a directory with the **mkdir** command, which is short for make directory:

$ mkdir reports

In the example, this command creates a directory named **reports** as a subdirectory of your current location. You can also create directories using the full path name, for example:

$ mkdir /home/erc/reports

► CHANGING TO YOUR HOME

To change back to your home directory, use the **cd** command alone or the ~ shortcut:

$ cd ~

► / VERSUS \

Linux and UNIX use a forward slash (/) to separate directories, whereas Windows uses a backslash (\). While it's easy to mix up the slashes, remember that the backslash has special meanings in Linux, and so will generally tell the operating system to do things you don't expect.

► WHERE'S THE C: DRIVE

Microsoft Windows assigns each disk drive a letter (A, B, C, and so on). This means that, as a user, you have to know which disk you are on.

Linux hides this information from you. All disks are seamlessly integrated in the file system using the mount command. So an ordinary user doesn't have to know anything about which disk he's using. A good system administrator can even add disks to a system without changing the file names of any files. Try doing that with Windows 98!

Table 3-1: LINUX SYSTEM DIRECTORIES

Directory	Holds
/	Root directory.
/bin	(Binary) commands, basic commands.
/boot	Used by the LILO boot loader.
/dev	Files representing devices like modems.
/dosc	Common location to mount MS-DOS C: drive.
/etc	Configuration files.
/home/fred	Home directory for user fred.
/lib	Libraries of prebuilt routines, including shared libraries; also kernel modules.
/mnt	Place reserved for mounting devices like disks and tapes.
/mnt/cdrom	Default location to mount a CD-ROM.
/root	Home directory for root user.
/sbin	System binaries, programs run by root or at system startup.
/tmp	Temporary storage.
/usr	Normally contains commands and support files that are part of the operating system. An upgrade will change files under /usr.
/usr/bin	(Binary) commands.
/usr/doc	Online documentation.
/usr/include	C programming include (header) files.
/usr/local	Place for you to store commands "local" to your site.
/usr/local/bin	Local applications.
/usr/man	Online manuals.
/var	System log files and things that are changed as the system runs. (Files in the other system directories are not expected to change often.)

...ıux Command Line

...scussed several Linux commands ...as **mkdir** and **pwd**. The time has ...me, though, to explain the Linux command line. The basic Linux command line has the following format:

command options parameters

The command line starts with a command, such as **mkdir**. After the command, you have a set of options that modify the behavior of the command. Finally, you have a number of parameters. Because most commands deal with files, the parameters are usually file or directory names. For example, the following command line has two parts:

`$ mkdir reports`

The command is **mkdir** and the parameter is *reports*, the name of the directory to create in this case.

You can expand the parameters using wildcards. A *wildcard* enables you to specify that you want all files that match a particular pattern. For example, the following wildcard requests all files ending in .txt: *.txt. The * indicates any text at all, or none, prior to the .txt. Thus, these filenames all match the pattern: report1.txt, Fred.txt, .txt, and Organization.2001.txt.

The UNIX and Linux philosophy aims at having many small commands each perform a single task. The way you get work done is by combining these small commands into powerful conglomerations. To aid with this, most Linux commands accept input from what is called *standard input,* typically the keyboard. Most Linux commands send their output to standard output, which defaults to the screen. Linux goes further and offers the capability to redirect the input and output of programs.

For example, the **cat** command merely concatenates a file and sends the results to standard output. You can concatenate a number of files together, and redirect the output into a single file. This file then will hold the entire contents of all the input files. For example:

`$ cat report1.txt report2.txt > report.bak`

This command concatenates report1.txt and report2.txt and stores the contents in the output file report.bak.

You can similarly redirect the input of a command. Use syntax similar to the following:

command < inputfile

To combine this with output redirection, use this syntax:

command < inputfile > outputfile

You can take advantage of wildcards, too:

`$ cat *.txt > report.bak`

This grabs all files ending in .txt and concatenates the files into the output file report.bak. Watch out, though. Don't redirect the output to one of the file names passed to **cat**. For example, the following command clears the file **a** first and then concatenates the empty **a** and **b** files, redirecting the output to **a**:

`$ cat a b > a`

Normal redirection sends the output of a command to a file, or reads the input from a file. Pipes extend this to enable you to send the output of one command to become the input of another. To indicate a pipeline, use the | key, called the *pipe key* in Linux:

`$ cat report1.txt | spell`

This command line sends the output of the **cat** command to the input of the **spell** command. You should then see the output of the **spell** command, a list of misspelled words, sent to the screen. You can also redirect this output:

`$ cat report1.txt | spell > badwords.txt`

CROSS-REFERENCE
Chapter 5 covers the **spell** and **ispell** commands.

FIND IT ONLINE
For more on the command line, see **http://www. mathcs.duq.edu/unixhelp/commanz/cmd2.html.**

TAKE NOTE

▶ REDIRECTION WITH > CLEARS OUTPUT FILE

When sending the output of a command to a file with >, any previous contents in the output file are deleted by issuing the command. To preserve the original contents of the output file, use >> in place of >. For example:

`$ cat report*.txt >> report.backup`

This command preserves any material that exists in report.backup.

▶ USING MORE SPECIFIC WILDCARDS

Sometimes, you want to have a more specific wildcard, to avoid grabbing too many files. For example:

`$ cat report*.txt > report.backup`

This just grabs files starting with *report* and ending with .txt.

▶ RUNNING COMMANDS IN THE BACKGROUND

You can run commands in the background by using an ampersand (&) after the command. For example:

`$ xclock &`

This runs the command **xclock** in the background, where it will not hog your prompt, so that you can immediately start entering other commands.

▶ REDIRECTING ERRORS

Errors go to standard error, which, like standard output, defaults to the screen. Errors are purposely separated so that when you are redirecting the output to a file, you can still see any errors. If you want to redirect errors, use the following syntax in **bash**:

`command 2> error_file`

Table 3-2: REDIRECTING INPUT AND OUTPUT

Command	Action
`command > filename`	Redirects output of *command* to *filename*; first truncates *filename*.
`command < filename`	Redirects input for *command* to come from *filename*.
`command >> filename`	Appends output of *command* to *filename*, does not truncate *filename* first.
`command < file1 > file2`	Redirects input for command from *file1* and sends output to *file2*, first truncates *file2*.
`command	command2`	Sends (pipes) output of *command* to become the input of *command2*.
`command 2> filename`	Sends errors to *filename*, in bash.

Table 3-3: WILDCARD EXAMPLES

Wildcard	Matches
*	Any text
*.txt	Any text ending in .txt.
A*.txt	Any text starting with A and ending with .txt.
[A-X]*.txt	Any text starting with an uppercase letter from A to X (not Y and Z) and ending with .txt.
report*.txt	All files starting with report and ending with .txt.
?	Any single character.
??	Any two characters, ??? matches any three characters, and so on.

Listing Files

The vast majority of Linux commands deal with files. That's only appropriate because Linux — like its estranged parent UNIX — abstracts most things to files. In Linux, a directory is a file, a printer is a file, a floppy disk is a file, as well as a sound device. Linux enables you to treat most devices as files. So, you'd expect to see a lot of commands that work with files.

One of the main things you need to do with files is list them. On Linux, the general purpose **ls** command — short for list — provides this function. To list the files in the current directory, type **ls**:

```
$ ls
1mchat.txt note.c    propsend.c  wind.txt
Makefile    primary.c  propstr.c
```

By default, **ls** sorts files based on the value of characters. This means that uppercase letters come before lowercase letters, and numbers before any letters at all.

ls supports a number of options that control how it displays the files in the current directory, shown in examples on the facing page.

To help DOS users move to Linux, you can run the **dir** and **vdir** commands. **vdir** acts like the **ls** command with the –l option:

```
$ vdir
drwxrwxr-x 3 erc erc 1024 Apr 17 11:41
tylin
-rw-rw-r— 1 erc erc 1502 Apr 14 20:13
ch3.txt
```

The **dir** command acts more like **ls**:

```
$ dir
1mchat.txt note.c    propsend.c  wind.txt

Makefile primary.c propstr.c
```

CROSS-REFERENCE

"Finding and Controlling Files," later in this chapter, covers file permissions.

Listing 3-1: LISTING IN ONE COLUMN

```
$ ls -1
1mchat.txt
Makefile
note.c
```

▶ *The -1 (one, not ell) option tells **ls** to output only one column.*

Listing 3-2: LISTING A DIRECTORY

```
$ ls /tmp
1dd.out.18955   nscomm40-erc/   winselection
```
▶ *You can pass a directory name to **ls** to list that directory.*

Listing 3-3: LISTING ALL FILES

```
$ ls -a
.          Makefile      propsend.c
..         note.c        propstr.c
```
▶ *By default, **ls** skips the "hidden" files, that is, any filename that starts with a period.*

Listing 3-4: LISTING WITH LONG OUTPUT

```
ls -al
total 3
drwxr-xr-x 2 erc eng 1024 Apr 6 20:11 .
drwxr-xr-x 3 erc eng 1024 Apr 6 20:17 ..
-rw-r-r— 1 erc eng 5872 Apr 6 20:04 1ch.txt
```

▶ *With the –l (ell) or long-form option, this shows, from left to right, the file permissions, number of links to the file (generally more for directories than normal files), the owner's name, the group name, the size of the file (in bytes), the time the file was last modified, and the name of the file.*

Listing 3-5: GETTING MORE INFORMATION

```
$ ls -CF
chap3/       eman*        ~chap3.txt
chap3.txt    fifoin|
```
▶ *The –F option displays a / appended to the file name for each directory, a * for an executable file, and a | after FIFOs, special first-in first-out files. It also displays @ for links and = for sockets.*

Listing 3-6: LISTING THE OLDEST FILES

```
$ ls -rt
chap3        eman         fifoin       chap3.txt
```

▶ *By combining –r (reverse order) with –t (sort by last-modifed time), you can list the oldest files first. This is useful when you need to clean your hard disk and want to find the oldest files for deletion.*

FIND IT ONLINE

Look for more on shells at **http://dir.yahoo.com/ Computers_and_Internet/Software/Operating_ Systems/Unix/Shells/**.

Copying, Moving, and Deleting Files

In addition to listing files, the most common operations are copying, moving, and deleting files.

To copy a file, use the **cp** command. The basic syntax follows:

```
cp source destination
```

For example:

```
$ cp report.txt report.bak
```

You can also copy a number of files using wildcards. In this case, the destination must be a directory:

```
$ cp report*.txt backup_dir
```

To move files, use the **mv** command:

```
mv source destination
```

You can also use **mv** to rename files.

```
$ mv oldname.txt newname.txt
```

If you enter a command such as the following:

```
$ mv fred barney
```

the **mv** command will merrily wipe out the original barney if a file of that name previously existed and replace it with the new barney, which was fred. With the –**b** option, **mv** will make a backup copy of barney before wiping it out. The backup file will have the same name, with a ~ on the end, barney~, for example.

To delete files, use the **rm** command, short for remove. (Do you get the feeling that the designers of these commands hated vowels?) The basic **rm** syntax is:

```
rm files_to_delete
```

For example:

```
$ rm *.txt
```

To avoid accidentally deleting files, you can use the –**i** option, short for interactive, with **rm**, as shown on the facing page. With –**i**, **rm** asks you to verify whether to delete each file. The **mv** and **cp** commands also support the –**i** option. See "The bash Shell" later in this chapter for how to set up aliases to always use the –**i** option.

The –**r** option to **rm** tells it to recursively travel down subdirectories and delete all files and subdirectories. In general, without the –**r** option, **rm** won't delete directories. Use **rmdir** instead.

The –**f** option to **rm**, short for force, overrides the –**i** option, so **rm** won't ask you to verify each file to be deleted.

TAKE NOTE

▶ DELETING FILES IS PERMANENT

There's no undelete command. When you delete a file, it's gone.

▶ THERE'S NO RENAME COMMAND

There's no specific command to rename an existing file; use **mv** instead.

▶ BE CAREFUL WITH THE RM COMMAND AND WILDCARDS

Watch out when using **rm** with wildcards. A simple error may result in the deletion of all files. For example, to delete all files ending in .txt, you could use a command like:

```
$ rm *.txt
```

If you accidentally put in a space, you could wipe out many more files than you expect. For example:

```
$ rm * .txt
```

removes all files in the current directory with the *, as well as a file named .txt, which is an unlikely name. To avoid mistakes, always use **rm –i** when you work with wildcards.

CROSS-REFERENCE

"Navigating Directories" earlier in this chapter discusses creating directories.

Listing 3-7: COPYING FILES RECURSIVELY

```
$ cp -r /usr/local/java /backup/java
```

▶ The *-r* option tells **cp** to copy the source files and all subdirectories; normally you pass a directory name with this option.

Listing 3-8: MAKING A BACKUP FILE WITH MV

```
$ mv -b fred barney
$ ls barney*
barney    barney~
```

▶ With the *-b*, or backup option, **mv** makes a backup copy of any file it replaces.

Listing 3-9: MOVING A NUMBER OF FILES

```
$ mv b* ../backup
```

▶ You can use wildcards with **mv** to move a number of files at once. The target must be a directory in this case.

Listing 3-10: ASKING BEFORE TRASHING FILES WITH RM

```
$ rm -i *.txt
rm: remove `barney.txt'? y
rm: remove `fred.txt'? n
$ ls *.txt
fred.txt
```

▶ To avoid clobbering files, use the *-i*, short for interactive, option to **rm**. In fact, we recommend that you alias **rm** to **rm** *-i*. Note that in the example, we did not delete the file fred.txt.

Listing 3-11: FORCING A DELETE

```
$ rm -if *.txt
```

▶ The *-f* option forces a delete, even if you specify *-i*, too.

Listing 3-12: DELETING A DIRECTORY AND ALL FILES IN IT

```
$ rm -rf tmp
```

▶ The *-r* option deletes recursively and is the way to get **rm** to delete a directory. (The *-d* option on the GNU **rm** command also deletes a directory.) This command deletes the tmp directory and all files and subdirectories within tmp. The *-f* option forces **rm** to delete files without asking.

Listing 3-13: DELETING DIRECTORIES WITH FILES

```
$ rmdir tmp
rmdir: tmp: Directory not empty
```

▶ The **rmdir** command deletes directories, but only if they are empty. Watch out for hidden files starting with a period.

FIND IT ONLINE

For help with copying and other basic commands, see
http://www.mathcs.duq.edu/unixhelp/tasks/files.html.

Viewing Files with More and Less

Because Linux uses text files in so many ways, you'll often need to view files. The **cat** command, mentioned previously, is one way to view a file. With **cat**, the file gets dumped to the screen. Long files stream past at breakneck speed. So, unless the file is relatively small, it's probably best to skip **cat** for viewing files.

While you can always call up a file with a text editor, sometimes it's just easier to launch a small, fast program like more or less.

The more program shows a file a screenful at a time. Press the spacebar to go forward another screenful, showing more of the file — get it? Press Enter to go forward one line. Type **q** to quit more. more also quits when you reach the end of the file or files you are viewing.

You can pass more than one file on the command line to **more**. more will show each file a screenful at a time. Type **:n** to jump ahead to the next file.

You can search with more, using /, the **vi** search command. Type / and the text you want to search for. For example:

/eth0

This tells more to search for the text *eth0*. Note that if more does not find your search text, it quits.

A friendlier program is called less, a pun on more. In general, less works like more but offers one great advantage: you can go backward in the file as well as forward. Type **U** in less to go up half a screen or **D** to go down half a screen; **W** goes up a full screen and **Z** goes down a full screen. Press the spacebar to go forward; **F** works as well.

One of the main differences of less is that when it reaches the end of the file, less stays put, printing (END). You need to press Q to quit. This is because even at the end of the text, you can still move backwards, so less isn't sure what to do.

The facing page shows less and more in action.

CROSS-REFERENCE
Chapter 5 discusses text editors.

50

Linux Commands and the Shell

Listing 3-14: VIEWING A FILE WITH MORE

```
$ more intro.txt
The Linux Phenomenon

All in all, Linux means freedom. You are
free to choose the hardware you want to
run. You are free to choose the Linux
distribution you want to run. You are
—More—(4%)
```

▶ *When more reaches a screenful of data, it displays the — **more**— prompt. Press the spacebar or F to move forward.*

Listing 3-15: PIPING A COMMAND TO MORE

```
$ dmesg | more
Memory: sized by int13 0e801h
Console: 16 point font, 400 scans
Console: color VGA+ 80x25, 1 virtual
console (max 63)
Probing PCI hardware.
Memory: 127776k/131072k available (748k
—More—
```

▶ *You can pipe the output of a command to **more** or **less.***

Listing 3-16: VIEWING MULTIPLE FILES WITH MORE

```
$ more chap3*.txt
::::::::::::::
chap3a.txt
::::::::::::::

Filename Completion

To work with filename completion, type in
a command as you normally would. As you
—More—(16%)
```

▶ *When you view multiple files with **more** (or **less**), the program lists the name of each file as it starts to display it, chap3a.txt in this case.*

Listing 3-17: VIEWING A FILE WITH LESS

```
$ less intro.txt
The Linux Phenomenon

All in all, Linux means freedom. You are
free to choose the hardware you want to
run. You are free to choose the Linux
distribution you want to run. You are
:
```

▶ *With **less**, you can go backwards. This is quite useful when viewing online information. **less** just displays a : as its prompt. Press the spacebar or F to move forward, or B or U to move backward.*

FIND IT ONLINE

For more on **vi**, see
http://www.cs.vu.nl/~tmgil/vi.html.

Finding and Controlling Files

To search for files, use the **find** command. Once you've found your files, you may want to control access to these files.

Finding files

Find searches from some directory on down, including the root directory, looking for files that match a certain test. For each file found, **find** performs an action on that file. For example, one of the simplest finds to run is the following:

```
$ find / -type f -name core -print
```

This command tells **find** to start searching at the root directory (/) and look for files that are named **core**. (The name **core** usually means that a program crashed and output a potentially large core dump debugging file. There is at least one entry under /usr/src that is a valid use of the term core.) The **-name core** part is the test **find** performs on each file it finds. Finally, the **-print** action tells **find** to print out all file names that pass the test. (Technically, **-print** isn't needed.)

The **whereis** command also helps find files:

```
$ whereis fvwm
fvwm: /usr/X11R6/bin/fvwm /usr/bin/X11/fvwm
```

After you've found files, you may want to search the contents. To do so, use the **grep** command, short for globally search for regular expression and print, or just a general regular expression parser. **grep** searches files and prints lines of text from the files that match a particular pattern. For example:

```
$ grep find *.txt
chap3f.txt:use the find command.
```

In this case, **grep** searches all files ending in .txt for the text *find*. **grep** looks for any match, so *find*, *finding*,

and *finder* all match, but *Find* does not. (The -i option tells **grep** to ignore case.)

You can ask **grep** to search for more than just words. **grep** supports a pattern language that enables you to use regular expressions to control the search. For example, a pattern of [fRk]ind tells **grep** to search for all text starting with *f, R,* or *k* and ending with *ind*. Thus, *find, Rind, finder,* and *kinder* would all match.

Controlling files

UNIX files support three types of permissions: read, write, and execute. A user with *read permission* for a file, as you'd expect, can read the file. With *write permission*, you can modify or delete a file. *Execute permission* is special. If marked, the file is treated as an executable command, covered later in this chapter under "Shell Scripts — A Whirlwind Introduction." For directories, execute permission means that you can use the **cd** command to make that directory your current directory.

Each file has three sets of these three permissions. The three sets apply to the user or owner of the file, to the group, and to everyone else — the entire universe of users on your system. For example, *groups* can enable all people in the accounting department to access certain files while keeping out all the engineers.

To control file permissions use the **chmod** command. This command can accept either numeric parameters or use symbolic names that are easier to remember. The facing page shows examples of **chmod**.

TAKE NOTE

NO NEED FOR –PRINT
The GNU version of **find** used on Linux does not require the **–print** option. Because most versions of UNIX find *do* require **–print**, you may want to train your fingers now.

CROSS-REFERENCE
An excellent book on regular expressions is *Mastering Regular Expressions* by Jeffrey E.F. Friedl. See Appendix B.

Listing 3-18: FINDING FILES

```
$ find / -name core -print
find: /etc/uucp: Permission denied
find: /var/spool/at: Permission denied
find: /var/spool/cron: Permission denied
/proc/sys/net/core
find: /root: Permission denied
find: /usr/doc/dhcpcd-0.70: Permission
denied
find: /usr/doc/procps-1.2.9: Permission
denied
/usr/lib/rhs/control-panel/core
/usr/src/linux-2.0.36/net/core
```

▶ *Finding files named core. The errors mean that you don't have permission to view some directories.*

Listing 3-19: GIVING PERMISSIONS NUMERICALLY

```
$ chmod 666 barney
```

▶ *This gives all users permission to read and write the file. Add together the octal values from Table 3-4 as follows: 400 owner can read, 200 owner can write, 40 group members can read, 20 group members can write, 4 all other users can read, 2 all other users can write. Add them up and you get 666.*

Listing 3-20: GIVING EXECUTE PERMISSION

```
$ chmod u+x barney
```

▶ *Marks the barney file as executable by owner (u for user).*

Listing 3-21: GIVING EXECUTE PERMISSION TO EVERYONE

```
$ chmod a+x barney
```

▶ *Marks the file barney as executable by all users (a for all).*

Table 3-4: NUMERIC FILE PERMISSIONS

Octal Value	Meaning
400	Owner can read the file.
200	Owner can write and modify the file.
100	Owner can execute the file.
040	Group members can read the file.
020	Group members can write and modify the file.
010	Group members can execute the file.
004	Everyone else can read the file.
002	Everyone else can write and modify the file.
001	Everyone else can execute the file.

Table 3-5: SYMBOLIC VALUES FOR CHMOD

Value	Meaning
u	File's owner
g	Group
o	Users not in group (all other users)
+	Add permission
-	Remove permission
r	Read permission
w	Write permission
x	Execute permission

FIND IT ONLINE

The **man find** command and the **info find** command both explain more about **find.**

Getting Information on the System

Because so many Linux commands work with files, it's important to have certain information, such as the available disk space for storing files. As you'd expect, Linux includes a number of commands in this area as well.

The basic command to see how much disk space is available is called **df**, short for disk free. By default, **df** lists the space used and available on all file systems. The facing page shows a system with /, /boot, and /home2 mounted.

To see how much space a directory uses, such as your home directory, use the **du** command, short for disk usage. With the **–s** (summary) option, **du** just provides the total amount of disk used for the current directory and all subdirectories with one line of output.

To get a listing of the about of free memory, use the **free** command.

The **uptime** command lists the amount of time your Linux system has been running, as well as the system loads:

```
$ uptime
  3:17pm  up 202 days, 23:29,  3 users,
  load average: 0.01, 0.02, 0.00
```

The **uptime** command outputs the current time, how long the system has been running (for 202 days, 23 hours, and 29 minutes in this example), how many users are currently logged on (3), and the system load averages (the number of jobs waiting to run over a given time period) for the past 1 (0.01), 5 (0.02), and 15 (0.00) minutes.

The **top** command, shown on the facing page, takes over your screen and lists the top processes — the processes that are using the most CPU time. If your system slows, this is a utility that can help you determine what is happening. Use Q to stop **top**.

The /proc file system

Linux provides a special pseudo file system, /proc. Inside this file system are entries for each running process (by process number), as well as special entries that tell you about your hardware and operating system. This data is displayed as a set of what looks like text files. These really aren't files, but act as such, so that you can run commands like **cat** and **ls** on the items in /proc. For example, the /proc/net/dev file lists all networking devices or interfaces, including the loopback device lo, Ethernet cards such as eth0, and dial-up links such as ppp0.

The file /proc/cpuinfo describes your CPU, while /proc/meminfo lists information on available memory. Files such as /proc/dma and /proc/interrupts describe your system's hardware.

TAKE NOTE

▶ **TRY W AND WHO**

The **w** command lists information on all users logged in, as well as load information provided by **uptime**. The **who** command lists all the users logged in at the present time. You can try **whoami** (who am I) to see what user you are logged in as.

▶ **GNOME**

From the GNOME desktop, the Utilities menu offers a number of neat programs for getting system information, including System info, System monitor, and GNOME disk free.

CROSS-REFERENCE

Chapter 7 covers the GNOME desktop.

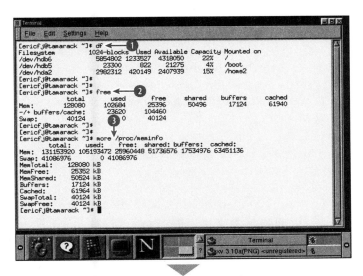

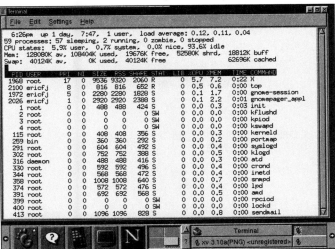

1 The **df** command lists the amount of space free on each file system.

2 The **free** command lists the amount of free memory.

3 The /proc/meminfo file shows infomation on memory as well.

▶ The **top** command displays information on the top processes using your CPU.

Listing 3-22: LISTING DISK USAGE

```
$ du
1           ./tylinux/fig/t2
130         ./tylinux/fig
236         ./tylinux
237         .
$ du -s
237         .
```

▶ The **du** command lists the amount of disk space used by a directory and all its subdirectories.

▶ With **-s**, you get just one line of output for each parameter, or just one line with no parameters.

Listing 3-23: GETTING CPU INFORMATION

```
$ more /proc/cpuinfo
processor       : 0
cpu             : 686
model           : Pentium II (Deschutes)
vendor_id       : GenuineIntel
```

▶ Look in /proc/cpuinfo for more on your CPU.

FIND IT ONLINE

For information on monitoring processes, see **http://www.mathcs.duq.edu/unixhelp/shell/jobz4.html.**

The bash Shell

The main Linux shell is called bash, short for Bourne Again Shell. For most users, unless you or your system administrator has changed things, bash is the default Linux shell.

At its most basic, a shell merely provides a prompt and awaits your commands. The bash prompt lists your user name, system name, and current subdirectory in a form of a long prompt similar to the following:

`[ericfj@tamarack ericfj]$`

In our examples, though, we just display the final $ to indicate the bash prompt.

As you'd expect, you enter commands at the prompt and press Enter. In addition to entering commands, bash offers a number of features, including the handy *filename completion*. With filename completion, the shell fills out filenames for you, which is especially helpful for long file names. All you need to do is type in the first part of a file name and then press Tab to have bash fill out the name, as explained on the facing page.

shadow password file, or NIS, the Network Information System. You can use the About Myself choice from the AnotherLevel Administration menu from the GNOME desktop to change your shell.

You can also use the **chsh** command to change your shell:

```
$ chsh -s /bin/tcsh
Changing shell for ericfj.
Password:
Shell changed.
```

This changes your default shell to /bin/tcsh. You will be prompted for your password.

▶ RUNNING ANOTHER SHELL

No matter what your shell is, you can run a different shell from the command line. If your shell, say, is tcsh and you want to run bash, simply run the **bash** command at the tcsh % prompt:

```
% bash
```

Your shell is now bash until you exit the shell:

```
$ exit
```

▶ CONTINUING A COMMAND ON MULTIPLE LINES

With most Linux shells, you can use a backslash (\) at the end of a line to indicate that the command is continued on the next line. For example:

```
/usr/local/bin/DailyUpdate.pl \
 -na -i $HOME/daily/tmpl.txt \
 -o $HOME/public_html/daily.htm
```

TAKE NOTE

▶ WHAT SHELL ARE YOU RUNNING?

Check the SHELL environment variable to find your default shell:
```
$ echo $SHELL
/bin/bash
```

▶ CHANGING YOUR SHELL

The /etc/passwd file contains one line per user account. Near the end of the line for your account, you'll see your default shell, typically /bin/bash. Only the root user can edit this file. And, some systems don't use /etc/passwd; instead, they use a

CROSS-REFERENCE
"The Linux Command Line," earlier in this chapter, discusses input and output redirection.

Other shells

The original UNIX shell, developed long ago, was sh, or the Bourne shell, and named for Steven Bourne, its creator. But, UNIX did something that was then quite revolutionary: UNIX split the shell from the operating system. This differs from older OSes such as VMS, as well as Windows, all of which tightly integrate the command shell.

Soon, various other shells became popular, including the C shell, or csh, developed by Bill Joy as part of the Berkeley UNIX projects. The C shell offered many new features to the Bourne shell, and provided a syntax vaguely similar to that of the C programming language, hence its name. After a while, David Korn of AT&T, then the owners of UNIX, brought back some of the C shell features and placed them in an enhanced Bourne shell, now called the Korn shell, or ksh.

The Korn shell offered some great features and maintained compatibility with the Bourne shell syntax — a big plus. The Korn shell, though, was a commercial product. Because of this, freeware developers created their own shell, bash, called the Bourne Again Shell as a pun on the original Bourne shell. bash adds many features of both the Korn and C shells, so it is not fully compatible with either, although it is more like the Korn shell than the C shell.

On Linux, you can run bash, tcsh — an extended C shell, or pdksh, a freeware Korn shell, as well as a lot of other shells, including ash and zsh. There's even a shell called the adventure shell.

Filename completion

With filename completion, when typing the name of a file or directory, type in just enough to identify the file, and then press Tab. bash will fill in the rest of the name. For complicated directories, you may need to type a few characters, press Tab, type a few more, press Tab, and so on. For example, to list a directory under /usr/local, you could start typing the following:

```
$ ls /usr/lo
```

After getting to lo, press Tab, and watch bash fill out /usr/local/. (Don't press Enter yet.) If you know about a subdirectory further down, start typing that name. On our system, for example, Java is installed in /usr/local/java. So, if we type **ja** and then press Tab:

```
$ ls /usr/local/ja
```

we see the following:

```
$ ls /usr/local/java/
```

If you don't have a subdirectory starting with ja, bash will beep or flash at you. Also, if you have more than one file or directory that begins with ja, bash will also flash or beep at you. You must type in enough to uniquely identify one name.

In place of Tab, you can also press Esc+/, that is the Esc key and then the forward slash key (/). (If you are a Korn shell user, watch out, as the Korn shell uses Esc+\ instead of Esc+/.)

bash will also complete environment variables with Esc+$. Try it with the following command:

```
$ ls $HOM
```

Now press Esc+$ and see whether the command expands to:

```
$ ls $HOME
```

Continued

FIND IT ONLINE

Find **pdksh**, a free Korn shell, on the CD in the RPM file
pdksh-5.2.13-3.i386.rpm.

The bash Shell
Continued

A history of commands

Another neat feature bash offers is called a *history,* that is, a list of the commands that you've executed. To see the history of your previous commands, type **history**:

```
$ history
    1  cd ~/mp3
    2  pwd
    3  fc -l
    4  ls
    5  history
```

You'll see a lot of history even if you haven't done much, as bash on Linux, by default, saves the history to files between sessions. Like the Korn shell, you can enter **fc –l** to list the history, too; **fc** is short for fix command.

When you see the output from the **history** command, each previous command is numbered. To execute one of the commands in the history, use **!** with the number of the command in this history. So, to reexecute the command listed as number 4, use the following command:

```
$ !4
```

You can also use **!** to reexecute the most recent command that starts with a word or text. For example, to reexecute the most recent command that started with **ls**, enter:

```
$ !ls
```

By default, Ctrl+P will show the previous command in the history and Ctrl+N the next command (once you go back a few).

Command-line editing

Another feature to make it easier to enter commands is called *command-line editing.* This gives you the ability to edit a command, fix typos, or just change a similar command to what you really want to do.

bash provides two styles of command-line editing, based on the two primary Linux text editors, vi and emacs. Generally, you'll want to turn on the mode that matches whichever editor you prefer. To turn on vi editing mode, use the following:

```
$ set -o vi
```

bash defaults to emacs editing mode. If for some reason you need to switch to it, type

```
$ set -o emacs
```

In the default **emacs** mode, you can use Ctrl+B to move to the left and Ctrl+F to the right. Ctrl+A moves to the start of the line and Ctrl+E to the end.

In vi mode (discussed in Chapter 5), press Esc to exit insert mode and enter command mode. In command mode, entering **k** moves to the previous command in the history, while entering **j** moves forward in the history.

TAKE NOTE

▶ **NO R COMMAND**

bash was originally created to be a free version of the Korn shell. If you are a Korn shell user, you'll feel right at home with many bash features, but note that bash does not support the **r** command to reexecute the previous command. In **bash**, use **!!** instead.

▶ **NO !$ EITHER**

In addition to providing many of the features of the Korn shell, bash provides a number of features from the C shell, too. But, bash does not support the **!$** notation that, in the C shell, refers to the last parameter of the last command.

CROSS-REFERENCE

Chapter 4 covers online documentation to get more on bash, and Chapter 5 covers emacs and vi.

Creating aliases

Continuing on in the aim of making it easy to enter commands, bash — as well as many other shells — provides the capability to provide a name — called an *alias* — for another command. You can use aliases to help you out in a number of ways, including:

▶ Making the OS more forgiving of easily mistyped commands, such as maek for **make**

▶ Carrying over commands that you are used to on another system, such as copy for **cp** for Windows users

▶ Creating safeguards for dangerous Linux commands, such as **rm –i** for **rm**

▶ Providing short cuts for very long commands, such as a complicated backup command

With bash, the basic form for making an alias is:

alias *alias_name=command*

For example:

$ alias rm='rm -i'

This command aliased **rm**, which is used to delete files, to the safer **rm –i**. The task on copying, moving, and deleting files explains this option.

To get a list of your aliases, use the **alias** command with no parameters:

$ alias
alias which='type —path'

Other versions of bash use the **alias –p** command to list aliases.

Remove an alias with the **unalias** command:
$ unalias rm

Table 3-6: COMMON VI COMMAND-MODE EDITING COMMANDS IN BASH

Command	Action
h	Move left one character (same as left arrow).
j	Move down in history (same as down arrow).
k	Move up in history (same as up arrow).
l	(Ell) Move right one character (same as right arrow).
x	Delete character under the cursor.
dw	Delete word.
dd	Delete whole line.
^	Move to start of line.
0	(Zero) Move to start of line.
$	Move to end of line.
e	Move to end of current word.
w	Move to next word.
b	Move to previous word.
a	Append text by going into edit mode (use Esc to return to command mode).
i	Insert text by going into edit mode (use Esc to return to command mode).
~	Convert character under cursor to uppercase.
I	Begin inserting at the beginning of the line.
A	Begin inserting at the end of the line.

FIND IT ONLINE

See **http://www.faqs.org/faqs/by-newsgroup/comp/ comp.unix.shell.html** for frequently asked questions on shells.

Shell Scripts — A Whirlwind Introduction

A *shell script* is simply a text file containing a number of commands as you could type them at the prompt. The main purpose of shell scripts lies in automating common tasks. You can save time typing in long commands, and if you repeat the same tasks over and over, you have a great reason for automation. For example, enter the following commands into a file:

```
#!/bin/sh
# rpminfo filename.rpm
# Prints out information on an rpm file.
rpm  -qilp $* | more
```

Save the file under the name **rpminfo** and then run the following command:

```
$ chmod a+x rpminfo
```

The **chmod** command marks the script as an executable file. More on that later.

You now have a new command, **rpminfo**, which prints out information on a .rpm file (Red Hat package), to give you a better idea what the package contains. Run this command as follows:

```
$ rpminfo filename.rpm
```

where filename.rpm is the name of a rpm package file.

The first line tells the shell to run /bin/sh to execute the script (more on that ahead). The next two lines are comments to help you figure out what to do. The fourth line runs the **rpm** command with a number of command-line parameters telling it to output information on a .rpm file, adding any command-line parameters that you pass with the $* special syntax. The results of the command are then piped to the **more** command.

In your scripts, any line that starts with a # is a comment. All the text after the # will be ignored.

To hold data, you can use variables. The basic syntax is:

```
variable=value
```

Don't put a space between the variable, =, and the value. You can then read the value of a variable using the $variable syntax, the same as for environment variables such as HOME and SHELL.

To get input, use the **read** command:

```
read variable
```

Read accepts input from the user and places the data entered into the given *variable*.

The **for** command loops for a given number of iterations. If you want to do tasks such as modify every file in a directory or something like that, you can use a **for** loop. The facing page shows an example of a **for** loop that is used in Listing 3-27.

The **if** and the **case** commands enable you to test variables against values and then make decisions on those values.

Usually, you use the **if** command with the **test** command. **Test** tests files and values and forms a great way to set up the condition used for the **if** command. See Listing 3-26 for an example of the **test** command.

TAKE NOTE

▶ **TAKE ADVANTAGE OF HISTORY AND PASTING**

The command history, discussed earlier in this chapter, provides a great source of commands that you can use for help in creating shell scripts. Combine the history with the ability to paste selected text into a window — covered in Chapter 9 — and you'll find it a lot easier to build your scripts.

CROSS-REFERENCE

Teach Yourself UNIX, also published by IDG Books Worldwide, covers more on shell scripting. See Appendix B.

Table 3-7: SPECIAL VARIABLES FOR ACCESSING COMMAND-LINE PARAMETERS IN SCRIPTS

Variable	Holds
$0	The name of the script as run on the command line.
$1	The first command-line parameter or option.
$2 ... $9	The second through the ninth parameter or option. There is no $10 for the tenth or beyond parameters.
$*	All command-line parameters or options. Use this to access more than nine parameters.
$#	The number of command-line parameters or options.

Listing 3-24: FIRST SHELL SCRIPT

```
echo -n "Your Linux version is "
cat /etc/redhat-release
```
▶ The *-n* option tells echo *to print without a new line.*

Listing 3-25: GETTING INPUT FROM THE USER

```
echo -n "Enter filename: "
read filename
```

echo "Your name is $filename"
▶ *Use the* **read** *command to get input from the user.*

Listing 3-26: USING IF

```
os=`uname -s`

if (test $os = "Linux") then
  echo "Your OS is Linux"
else
  echo "What are you doing?"
fi
```
▶ *The backquotes (called back ticks) tell the script to execute the* **uname –s** *command and place the results of the command into the variable named os.*

▶ *The test command compares the variable os with Linux. If there is a match, one message is displayed. Otherwise, the script displays the other message.*

Listing 3-27: WRITING A LOOP

```
echo -n "Enter pattern: "
read pattern
for filename
  in $pattern
do
    echo "$filename"
done
```
▶ *This script takes in a wildcard pattern from you, and then prints out all files that match the pattern.*

Continued

FIND IT ONLINE

For more on shell scripting, see **http://www.mathcs. duq.edu/unixhelp/scrpt/scrpt2.html.**

Shell Scripts — A Whirlwind Introduction *Continued*

Windows depends on certain filename extensions being registered with the command that runs those files. Thus, you can configure a Windows system to run files ending in .CGI with a particular script interpreter. In general, .BAT files are DOS scripts and .EXE files are executable commands. Linux, on the other hand, doesn't bother with filename extensions for commands. For example, the **cp** command is literally a file named cp (typically stored in /bin). In Windows, such a program would need to be named cp.exe, and you'd type **cp** only at the command line. In Linux, the filename and what you type match. The shell knows cp is an executable file because it is marked with the execute permission, and cp is a compiled program.

Shell scripts, though, make things more complex. Because shell scripts are just plain-text files, how does Linux tell that a shell script is a script and not a plain old file of text? You need to tell Linux by doing two things: First, you need to mark the script as executable with the **chmod** command. The **chmod** command changes the permissions of the file, so that the shell will accept the file as executable. Listing 3-29 on the facing page shows this.

Second, you need to insert a special magic comment into the very first line of the shell script.

The **chmod** command changes the permissions of the file, so that the shell will accept the file as executable (see Listing 3-29). This comment tells bash which shell should execute the shell script. Which shell? Well, because Linux supports so many shells, including bash, tcsh, ash, and zsh, you need to specify exactly which shell should run the commands. This is very important, as the C shell, for example, interprets commands differently than bash.

Many scripts use the plain old Bourne shell, sh, as the scripting engine. This is partially for historical reasons but also because sh should be available on all Linux and UNIX systems. You cannot say the same about the other shells, including bash. While bash is the default shell on Linux, it can be an optional package, so users may not have it. Furthermore, on UNIX systems, bash is not found anywhere near as often as on Linux. Hence the use of sh.

The magic comment to have sh interpret your script is:

```
#!/bin/sh
```

The # indicates this is a comment. On the slight chance that a shell does not understand this syntax, the shell will ignore the directive because it starts with a comment marker. The ! tells the shell that this is a special comment. The full path of the desired shell then follows, /bin/sh in this case. To have bash interpret the shell script, use the following instead:

```
#!/bin/bash
```

> **TAKE NOTE**
>
> ▶ **OTHER SCRIPTING LANGUAGES**
> The #! syntax is used by other scripting languages such as Perl and Tcl. You might see comments such as #!/usr/bin/perl, which indicates a Perl script, #!/usr/bin/wish for a Tcl script, or #!/usr/bin/python for a Python script.

CROSS-REFERENCE

"Finding and Controlling Files," earlier in this chapter discusses the **chmod** command.

62

Executable files

When you run a script, your shell needs to determine which shell to launch to run it. To determine this, the shell reads in the first few bytes of a file, usually about 16 bytes (although this can vary). The #! helps give away a shell script's identity. Other files have a magic number in the first few bytes. The file /usr/share/magic (often /etc/magic on UNIX systems) keeps a list of the magic numbers Linux knows about.

Table 3-8: SHELL LOCATIONS

Shell	Location
bash	/bin/bash, may be installed in a different place on UNIX
csh	/bin/csh, really tcsh on Linux
ksh	/bin/ksh, not always available on Linux
sh	/bin/sh
tcsh	/bin/tcsh

Listing 3-28: A SAMPLE SHELL SCRIPT

```
#!/bin/sh
case $SHELL
in
/bin/bash)
  echo "You run bash."
  ;;
/bin/tcsh)
  echo "You run tcsh."
  ;;
*)
  echo "You run the $SHELL shell."
  ;;
esac
```

❶ The **case** statement checks a value, held in $SHELL in this case, against a set of predefined values, shown here as /bin/bash and /bin/tcsh. Using this test, the script can determine your default shell.

❷ The ***)** case captures all nonmatching entries.

Listing 3-29: MARKING A FILE EXECUTABLE

```
$ ls -l s1
-rw-rw-r—  1 erc eng 141 Apr 19 21:25 s1
$ chmod a+x s1
$ ls -l s1
-rwxrwxr-x  1 erc eng 141 Apr 19 21:25 s1
```

❶ Before running **chmod**, the script file s1 has no execute permission.

❷ After running the **chmod** command, as shown here, s1 supports execute permission for all users, indicated by the x in the long listing.

FIND IT ONLINE

See **http://language.perl.com/versus/csh.whynot** for why csh is not good for shell scripts.

Shell Startup Files

When bash starts up, it reads in a number of files that can customize its settings, modify command paths, and set up aliases. These startup files — really special shell scripts — set up the environment bash runs in on your system. By editing these files, you can set up a custom bash environment that better fits your needs.

When bash starts, it looks for — and executes — the following files, many in your home directory (indicated with a $HOME/):

▶ /etc/profile for login shells, that is the default shell run when you first log in. These settings carry over to other shells launched from bash.
▶ $HOME/.bash_profile, for login shells.
▶ $HOME/.profile, for login shells if $HOME/.bash_profile is not present. The Korn shell uses .profile, too. Thus, if you're a Korn shell user, you may want to continue using a .profile file.
▶ $HOME/.bashrc, for interactive (nonscripting) shells that are not login shells. That is, all other instances of bash you launch that are not used to execute scripts.
▶ $ENV, this variable may name a file. If set, bash always runs it.

When the bash login shell exists, assuming bash is your default shell, it will run a file named $HOME/.bash_logout, if it exists.

The best place to customize bash is in a file such as .bash_profile in your home directory. You generally don't want to edit systemwide files such as /etc/profile.

TAKE NOTE

▶ **SET UP ALIASES IN .BASHRC**

The .bashrc and .profile files are a great place to set up aliases. (The official location for aliases is .bashrc, but if you're moving from UNIX, you may be more familiar with the .profile file.) For example, we recommend aliasing **rm** to **rm –i** to avoid accidentally deleting files. (The **–i** option tells **rm** to ask you before deleting each file.) We also set up some aliases to help forgive common misspelled words, such as maek for **make**. Listing 3-30 shows some common aliases.

▶ **ENVIRONMENT VARIABLES**

You may need to set up environment variables in your .bash_profile or other startup file. For example, you may need to set your default printer, or other special settings that pertain to your site. Again, a file such as .bash_profile is the perfect place for these settings.

CROSS-REFERENCE
Appendix B lists a number of books that contain more information on shell scripts and startup files.

FIND IT ONLINE
The bash frequently asked questions list is at http://www.faqs.org/faqs/unix-faq/shell/bash/.

Linux Commands and the Shell

Listing 3-30: A .PROFILE FILE FOR DOS COMMANDS

```
# A set of aliases for MS-DOS Users

# You can use the predefined dir,
# or define this alias.
alias dir='ls -F'

# Copying files.
alias copy=cp

# Deleting files.
# This alias asks for confirmation.
alias del='rm -i'
alias erase='rm -i'

# Directories
alias md=mkdir
alias rd=rmdir

alias type=less
# Or "alias type cat" if you
# don't want paging

# Printing.
alias print=lpr
# Or "alias print lpr -Plpxx"
#   where "lpxx" is your
#   favorite printer.
```

▶ *This file sets up a number of aliases that are handy for users more familiar with DOS than Linux.*

Table 3-9: SHELL STARTUP FILES

Shell	Startup, Login, and Logout Files
bash	/etc/profile, $HOME/.bash_profile or $HOME/.profile (login shells); $HOME/.bashrc (interactive); $ENV; .bash_logout (logout)
csh	.cshrc; .login (login); .logout (logout)
ksh	.profile (login); $ENV
sh	.profile (login)
tcsh	.tcshrc or .cshrc; .login (login); .logout (logout)

Table 3-10: SOME GOOD STARTUP BASH ALIASES

Alias	Use
alias rm='rm -i'	Makes it harder to remove files by accident.
alias ls='ls —color= auto -CF'	Provides more information on which files are directories, and so on, on listings.
alias ll='ls -l'	Fast alias for long listings.
alias h=history	Fast alias for history.
alias maek=make	Takes care of common typo.
alias emasc=emacs	Takes care of common typo.
alias nec='/usr/local/ bin/nc -noask'	Launches nedit text editor without prompting; see Chapter 5. The **nc** command conflicts with the name of another Linux command and hence the **nec** alias and the full path to the real command to avoid the conflict.

Personal Workbook

Q&A

1 Does Linux lock you into one command shell?

_____

_____

_____

2 How can you tell which shell is your default?

_____

_____

_____

3 Which commands can you use to view files?

_____

_____

_____

4 Which command can you use to change your default shell?

_____

_____

_____

5 What is an *alias*?

_____

_____

_____

6 What is the magic syntax for the first line of a **bash** shell script?

_____

_____

_____

7 What does this syntax do?

_____

_____

_____

8 Name one of the files executed by bash when it starts.

_____

_____

_____

ANSWERS: PAGE 334

Linux Commands and the Shell

EXTRA PRACTICE

1. Look at the online manual information for bash with the **man bash** command. You'll see quite a lot of material.

2. Jump ahead to Chapter 4, which describes the **info** command. There's a lot of material on bash available from the **info** command.

3. Try **tcsh** from within bash, and then exit **tcsh** to return to bash.

4. Go through the files under /proc to learn as much as you can about your system.

5. Use the **top** command to determine which processes are using the most of your CPU resources.

6. Verify that Linux records the proper amount of RAM for your system by looking in the files in /proc.

REAL-WORLD APPLICATIONS

✔ You've come to Linux with other UNIX experience. Change your shell to tcsh, which is more familiar to many UNIX users.

✔ The file system with /tmp seems to be filling up, which causes problems for programs that need temporary space. Use the **ls** command with the long output to check the size of the files in /tmp.

✔ You're one cool dude and you introduced Linux to your organization. Now all these UNIXheads at your site are complaining about how bash isn't the same as the Korn shell that they are used to. Download the pdksh and set that up for these users.

✔ You want to set bash to say "Hello" and print the date and time whenever someone logs in. Add shell commands to do this to your .bash_profile file.

Visual Quiz

What command is running here?

_____

_____

_____

_____

_____

_____

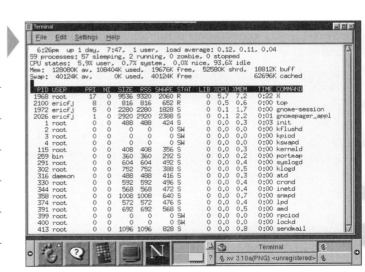

67

CHAPTER 4

MASTER
THESE
SKILLS

▶ **Documentation Formats and Locations**
▶ **Finding Documentation**
▶ **Using the man Pages**
▶ **Reading GNU Info Files**
▶ **Using PostScript and HTML**
▶ **Handling Compressed Files**
▶ **TeX and Source Files**

Getting Help

One of the nice things about Linux is the amount of documentation that comes with the system. It comes not only with reference documents, but also practical advice in the form of "HOWTOs" written by people who know what they are doing.

That's the good news. The bad news is that Linux supports many different documentation formats and people use them all (and then some). Reading the documentation can be a little difficult, especially if you don't know what you are doing.

In the early days of computers, online documentation was limited to text. That's because that was all that the printers and displays could handle. Also storage costs were so high that it didn't pay to store formatting information along with the documentation.

Later, with the creation of UNIX, the man pages (short for manual pages) were created. These documents contain embedded formatting instructions. The documents could then be run through the **nroff** command for printing on text devices or the **troff** command (the Linux version of this command is **groff**) for printing on a typesetter. This form of documentation is still widely in use today and provides the backbone of the Linux system documentation.

The man system is rather primitive. There have been many attempts to improve it and to provide a better documentation system. One of these is the TeX formatter, which is a next-generation text-formatting tool similar to **troff**. This format is not very useful for online documentation, so a specialized TeX format called texinfo was created by the Free Software Foundation. You can view texinfo documents using the Linux **info** command, or you can use the **tex** command to turn the files into printed documentation.

So the bad news is that Linux uses lots of different documentation formats. The good news is that you've got tools to handle them all. In the next few pages, we introduce you to the different documentation formats and how to get information out of them.

Whatever you want to do, there's probably a Linux document to help you. The trick is finding it and figuring out how to view it.

Documentation Formats and Locations

Documentation used to be the weakness of free software. In the past, you'd get little if any at all. But over the past few years, people have been producing manuals, guides, help text, and other documentation, which has become a part of Linux.

There are many different forms of documentation available to the Linux user. Table 4-1 lists some of the common places where documentation is kept and the various formats used.

The original online UNIX documentation was called the manual pages, or man pages for short. However this format was rather limited, so the Free Software Foundation devised the texinfo format. The texinfo form of online documentation could be run through one program, turned into online help in another, and turned into a printed manual. Thus, you could benefit in two ways from one source.

Some people don't bother with advanced formatting and just write text files. Text is simple, universal, and requires no processing to view or print. Its main limitation is that it does not contain any formatting. Monospaced font is all you get.

For formatted documents, many people use the text processor TeX. It enables you to embed typesetting commands inside a text file. When the file is run through the TeX program, you get a nicely formatted printed document.

A newer form of documentation is HTML. Netscape and Microsoft Internet Explorer are making this format popular. The nice thing about the HTML format is that it can easily be viewed on many different systems.

For people who absolutely must use propriety documentation systems (that is, Microsoft Word), there is the PostScript format. PostScript is a page-layout language output by almost all the word processors on the market today. Linux has tools that allow you to view and print PostScript files.

Linux also comes with a form of document rarely found in the Microsoft Windows world — the program's source code. If you're a programmer, you can examine in detail the files and code that make up a command to figure out what it's really doing.

Linux has tools to view and print all these forms of documentation as well as a few other formats. In the next few tasks, you'll see how to shake Linux and get a lot of information to fall out.

The GNOME help system

When you first start the X Window System, the GNOME desktop displays a help viewer. This viewer is also available by clicking the question mark icon on the toolbar at the bottom of the screen.

The help viewer gives you a hypertext display with access to the GNOME User's Guide, the man pages, the info files, and other GNOME documents.

The GNOME User's Guide is a complete manual for the GNOME desktop. The man pages link contains a list most of the standard Linux man pages converted to HTML. The Info Pages link gives you access to most of the info pages, also converted to HTML. The GNOME Documents contains documentation for the various GNOME tools, written in GNOME's own formatting language, DocBook.

The help system is simple and provides a nice, easy-to-use display. Unfortunately, it is rather limited. A big drawback is that there is no search system. It's a good start, but there are other ways of getting information out of Linux such as the man pages, the GNU texinfo system, as well as the **find** and **grep** commands.

Table 4-1: COMMON DOCUMENTATION FORMATS AND LOCATIONS

Extension	Type	Related Commands	Typical Locations
.txt	Text	more, less	/usr/doc
.1 through .8 or .1.gz through .8.gz	Man	man, groff + manxman	/usr/man
.info, .info.gz	GNU Info	info	/usr/info
.html, .htm	Hypertext	Netscape	/usr/doc, /usr/share/doc/HTML
.tex	TeX	tex	/usr/doc
.texi	texinfo	makeinfo, info	/usr/doc
.ps	PostScript	gs (GhostScript), gv	/usr/doc, /usr/src/linux/pcmcia-cs-3.0.9/doc
.rpm	RedHat Package	rpm	/mnt/cdrom/RedHat/RPMS (binaries) /mnt/cdrom/RedHat/SRPMS (sources)

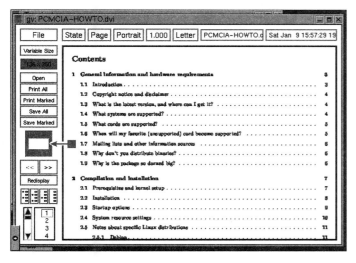

❶ Open a terminal window.
❷ Go to the directory containing the postscript file.
❸ Enter the command **gv** filename to display the file.
▶ Scrolling window

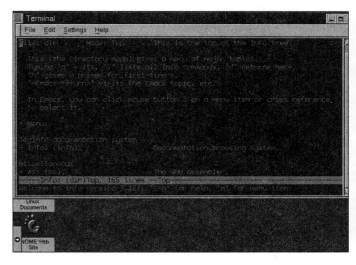

❶ Type **info** subject to start the information viewer.

Finding Documentation

Before you can read any documentation you need to find a file to read. If the file is in any of the well-known documentation directories, then you're lucky. But if it is stashed in an obscure location, you need to do a little work to get it. Suppose you know the filename, but not where the file is. How do you find it? One method is to use the locate command to find the file. The general form of the command is:

```
$ locate name
```

where *name* is the filename or part of the filename.

The locate command is fast because it searches an online database that contains the names of all the files on the system. This database is updated nightly. (That means that any files you added to the system today will not be found by the locate command.)

The **find** command is also useful locate files. The first example to the right shows how to use a simple find command to locate all the files containing the word disk in the directory /usr/doc and it's children.

But suppose you don't know the name of the file that you are looking for. The **fgrep** command searches through a list of files looking for a given string. The second example shows how to use the command to search a set of text files for the word *disk.*

The **fgrep** command can be combined with the find command to search the entire disk for any file that contains a given word. See Listing 4-3 for a demonstration.

Sometimes you get too much information. For example, you may want information on disk formatting, but instead you get a lot of information on disk partitioning. The **fgrep** command has a –v option that lets you *exclude* all lines that contain a given string.

So the solution to the too much information problem is to execute your search, and pipe the results to

fgrep –v. Also if the information scrolls off the screen fast, you can add another pipe to the **more** command. See Listing 4-4 for details.

If you know which RPM package a certain command belongs to, you can list the contents of the package using rpm -ql | less to look for documentation files. Look for files in /usr/doc, /usr/man, or /usr/doc — that's where the documentation usually is.

With these commands, you can easily find almost any documentation file that you want. But once found, you'll need to view it and that's covered in the next few tasks.

Listing 4-1: USING THE LOCATE COMMAND

```
$ locate disk
  !!!!!! +++++ -> Name or name fragment of
  !!!!!!            the file to look for.
  ++++++------> The "locate" command

$ locate disk
/dev/ramdisk
/etc/CORBA/servers/diskusage_applet.gnorba
/sbin/mkbootdisk
..... and so on.
```

Listing 4-2: FINDING ALL FILES WITH "DISK" IN THEIR NAME

```
$ find /usr/doc -name "*disk*" -type f -print
  !!!! !!!!!!!!! !!!!! !!!!!!!!! !!!!!!!! ++++++ -> What to do when the file is
  !!!! !!!!!!!!! !!!!!!!!!!!!!! !!!!!!!!                found — print the name.
  !!!! !!!!!!!!! !!!!!!!!!!!!!!! +++++++ ——-> Limit search to type
  !!!! !!!!!!!!! !!!!!!!!!!!!!!!                        f (file) things (excludes
  !!!! !!!!!!!!! !!!!!!!!!!!!!!!                        directories, special files)
  !!!! !!!!!!!!! +++++++++++++ ————-> Look for files that are named
  !!!! !!!!!!!!!                                        "*disk*" (wildcards allowed)
  !!!! ++++++++ —————————> Directory where the search
  !!!!                                                  starts (/usr/doc).
  ++++ —————————-> The "find" command

$ find /usr/doc -name "*disk*" -type f —print
/usr/doc/util-linux-2.9o/README.cfdisk
/usr/doc/util-linux-2.9o/README.fdisk
/usr/doc/util-linux-2.9o/sfdisk.examples
```

Listing 4-3: FINDING ALL THE FILES THAT END IN ".TXT" WITH "DISK" IN THEIR CONTENTS

```
$ find /usr/doc -name "*.txt" -type f -exec fgrep disk {} /dev/null \;
  !!!! !!!!!!!!! !!!!!!!!!!!!!! !!!!!!!! !!!!! !!!!!!!!!!!!!!!!!!!!!!!!!! ++ -> End
  !!!! !!!!!!!!! !!!!!!!!!!!!!! !!!!!!!! !!!!! !!!!!!!!!!!!!!!!!!!!!!!!!!    of cmd.
  !!!! !!!!!!!!! !!!!!!!!!!!!!! !!!!!!!! !!!!! +++++++++++++++++++++++ -> Command
  !!!! !!!!!!!!! !!!!!!!!!!!!!! !!!!!!!! +++++ -> Execute command on the file (1)
  !!!! !!!!!!!!! !!!!!!!!!!!!!! +++++++ -> Limit search type f (file) entries
  !!!! !!!!!!!!! +++++++++++++ -> Search for all files named "*.txt"
  !!!! ++++++++ ——-> Place to start the search
  ++++ -> The find command itself

Note 1:

The command is:
    fgrep disk {} /dev/null
    !!!!! !!!! !! +++++++++ -> This is a second file to search. It actually is
    !!!!! !!!! !!              the null file containing nothing. It's here to
    !!!!! !!!! !!              give fgrep two things to search. That's because
    !!!!! !!!! !!              fgrep will not print the file name if it is given
    !!!!! !!!! !!              only one file to search. So we give it two, the
    !!!!! !!!! !!              second containing nothing, but we trick fgrep
    !!!!! !!!! !!              into printing the file name (of the first file).
    !!!!! !!!! ++————> find replaces {} with the actual file name
    !!!!! ++++ ————> The string to search for
    +++++ ——————-> The searching command "fgrep"

$ find /usr/doc -name "*.txt" -type f -exec fgrep disk {} /dev/null \;
```

Using the man Pages

The man pages provide good, concise documentation on almost all of Linux's commands, system calls, library functions, and file formats. They provide good reference material. However, their terseness limits their usefulness in a learning environment. As one person put it, "They are a good way of finding out what to do if you already know what to do."

The basic **man** command is:

```
$ man name
```

where *name* is the name of the command or system call about which you want information. The top of the opposite page shows the results of a typical **man** command.

The man pages are divided into several different "sections," which are listed in Table 4-2. Some things, such as "open," are both a command (section 1) and a system call (section 2). If you execute the command:

```
$ man open
```

you get the first manual page found, the one for the command. If you want the system call, you need to explicitly specify a section number.

```
$ man 2 open
```

But what if you don't know what command that you want? The

```
$ man -k subject
```

prints the title of all man pages with *subject* in their title.

The **xman** command is an X version of the man command. It gives you a little better output than the original **man** command.

The man pages are stored in a variety of places such as /usr/man, /usr/X11R6/man and /usr/lib/perl5/man.

The **man** command uses the locations listed in the file /etc/man.config to locate these directories.

If you want to print a typeset version of a man page it will take a little work. The "source" for the man pages is /usr/man. To print a man page, for example cp(1), use the commands shown at the lower-left of the opposite page.

Table 4-2: MAN SECTION NUMBERS

Section	Contents
1	Commands
2	System Calls
3	Library Calls
4	Special Files
5	File formats and conventions
6	Games
7	Macro packages and conventions
8	System management commands

Listing 4-4: A TYPICAL MAN COMMAND TO GET INFORMATION ON THE CP COMMAND

```
$ man cp
CP(1)                    CP(1)
NAME
      cp - copy files
SYNOPSIS
      cp [options] source dest
.....
```

▶ Using **groff** to typeset a manual page and then view it using **gv**.

❶ Go to the man directory by using the command cd /usr/man.

❷ Typeset the document with groff –man man1/cp.1 >/tmp/cp.ps. The result is a file named /tmp/cp.ps.

❸ Use the **gv** command to view the file by typing **gv /tmp/tmp.ps**.

Listing 4-5: USING THE MAN –K COMMAND TO LIST THE TITLES OF ALL MAN PAGES WITH THE WORD "DISK" IN THEIR TITLES

```
$ man —k drive
3c574_cs (4)         - 3Com 3c574 Etherlink XL 10/100 PC Card device driver
3c575_cb (4)         - 3Com 3c575 Etherlink XL 10/100 CardBus device driver
3c589_cs (4)         - 3Com 3c589 Etherlink III device driver
....
```

Reading GNU Info Files

To get around the limitations of the old-style man format, the people at the Free Software Foundation invented the info format. This format is better suited to today's computers. It provides the reader with both hyperlinks and searching capability. Using it is not that hard. Just type

    $ info

and you are thrown into the top level of the system. You can use the arrow keys to move about the screen or use the commands listed in Table 4-3.

The Tab key moves the cursor from link to link. Pressing it repeatedly tabs you through the various subjects. When you find one you're interested in, press Enter to jump to it.

The info system presents it's documentation in a hypertext-like format. Tab jumps to the next link, Enter selects it. If you want to go up a level, use the **u** (up) command. **n** moves you to the next node or page in the info file, and **p** move you to the previous node. To get out, type **q**.

The **info** command has a search mode that starts when you press Ctrl+S. It works a little differently than the search commands that you are used to. It is an incremental search and starts searching after you type the first character after the Ctrl+S. For example, suppose you want to search for the word information. You type Ctrl+S and **i**, and immediately the command locates the first *i* in the file. Type **n** and it will now find in. After you complete Ctrl+S **infor**, it will locate the string infor. All you have to do is type enough of the string to get you where you want to go to locate the information that you want. To end the search, press Enter. To cancel the search, press Ctrl+G.

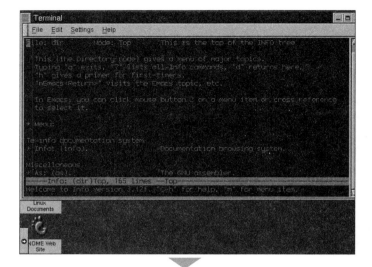

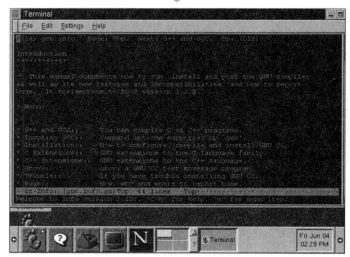

❶ *Use Tab to jump to the next link.*

❷ *Press Enter to select a topic.*

❸ *Enter **q** to exit the system.*

❹ *The **u** command goes up a node.*

❺ *The **space** command goes down a page.*

76

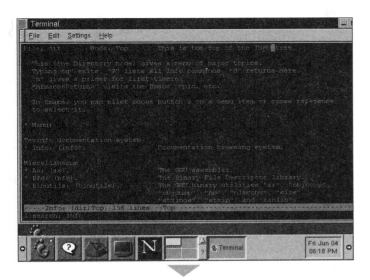

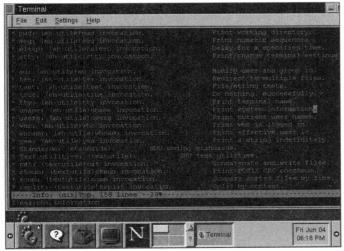

People familiar with emacs will recognize that this is the same command that is used for searching in emacs. In fact, info and emacs are very similar. Many of the commands used in emacs also work with info, and emacs even has a mode where you can view info files in the editor itself.

The info files are kept in /usr/info. If you know the name of the file that you want to look it, the command:

```
$ info name
```

will read it. (Do not include the extension .info.gz.)

Finally, sometimes you find info files in nonstandard places. To read these files use the command:

```
$ info -f filename
```

where *filename* is the name of the info file (which ends in .info or .info.gz).

The info format is a big improvement over the older man format. It's not only much easier to read and search, but it's also easier to write. Even though info is more modern, many people still like to stick with the older man format.

Information on info

To get a complete command list of all the info commands, start with the command:

```
$ info
```

and then select the Info link, which enables you to browse the documentation for the info system.

⑥ *Use Ctrl+S to start an incremental search.*

⑦ *Enter the string to search for (in this example, info). The search begins when the first character is entered.*

⑧ *To search for the next occurrence of info, press Ctrl+S again.*

⑨ *To terminate the search, press Enter.*

⑩ *To search for a longer string (while in search mode), just enter the string. In this example, we are looking for information.*

Using PostScript and HTML

Postscript is a page-layout language that enables you to define exactly how a page is to look. Most word processors and text formatters can write PostScript files, and Linux has tools that can display and print them. So, people who use non-Linux word processors can still produce nicely formatted Linux-readable documentation by using PostScript files.

The gv program displays Postscript files on the X screen. The program is very simple. To display a file, use the command:

    $ gv *file*

The PgUp and PgDn keys can be used to move from page to page.

At the top of the screen is a menu bar. The scale menu can be used to zoom in or out of the document.

The **gv** program has a unique way of handling scrolling. Most programs use scroll bars to handle data that's larger than the window. The **gv** command uses a small view window inside a larger page window. To scroll, use the left mouse button to drag the view window to section of the page that you want to see.

A PostScript file can be printed using the normal Linux printing commands. For example:

$ lpr gawk.ps

prints the document file on the default printer.

HTML

HTML stands for Hypertext Markup Language. This is the format used by most of the documents on the World Wide Web. But HTML can be used for more than just Web pages; you can write documents in it as well.

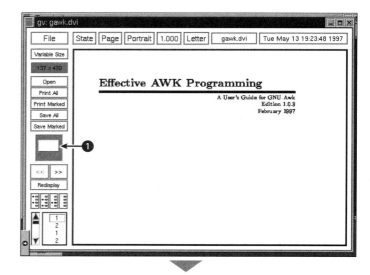

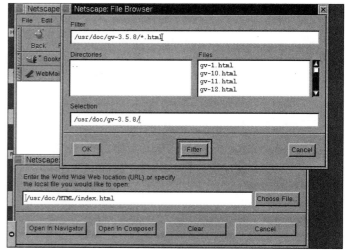

❶ Move the small window around in the bigger one to scroll. The small window is what you can see, the big one is what's on the page.

❶ Open a file using the File ➪ Open Page menu item.

❷ Click Browse to open a file browser.

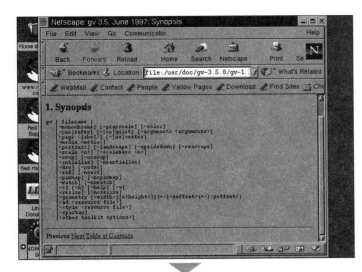

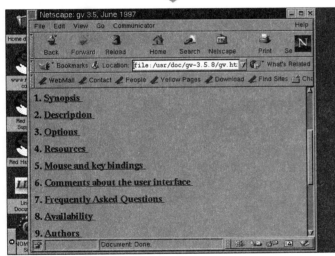

Files ending with .htm and .html are hypertext files. These can be viewed using the Netscape program. To view a file simply use the command:

```
$ netscape file
```

You are now in Netscape and can use the hyperlink environment that you are familiar with.

To open a file, use the File ⇨ Open Page menu item. Selecting it brings up the open file dialog. Click Choose File to bring up a file browser.

TAKE NOTE

▶ HOW TO GET WORD TO OUTPUT POSTSCRIPT

To get Microsoft Word (or any Microsoft program) to print PostScript, you must install a new printer. This printer won't print on paper; instead, it will print to a file.

Begin by clicking Start ⇨ Settings ⇨ Printers. Then double-click Add Printer. Define a new Local Printer. For printer type, choose Apple, Apple LaserWriter.

When the system asks you which port the printer is connected to, select FILE.

Now when you print, a window will pop up asking you for an output filename. The resulting PostScript file can then be read on any Linux system with **gv.**

❸ *Hyperlinks such as Table of Contents can be followed by clicking them.*

❹ *Type **file:/usr/doc/gv-3.5.8/gv.html** to view the documentation for the gv command.*

Handling Compressed Files

To save space, document files are frequently compressed. Anything ending with .gz is a compressed file. For example, a compressed Postscript file might be named pam.ps.gz.

These files cannot be used directly. Instead, they must be decompressed, and then used. The **gunzip** command decompresses files. For example:

```
$ gunzip pam.ps.gz
```

decompresses pam.ps.gz, and in the process changes the name to pam.ps. The file can now be viewed using the Linux postscript viewer gv.

The zcat command decompresses files and writes them to standard output. For example, to view a compressed text file, type these commands:

```
$ zcat ChangeLog.gz | more
```

In the task Finding Documentation earlier in this chapter, we saw how to use **fgrep** to search files for a given string. The **zgrep** function performs the same service for compressed files. For example, to search for the word disk in all the files in /usr/doc/HOWTO, use the command:

```
$ zgrep "disk" \
        /usr/doc/glibc-2.1.1/*.gz
```

The **zgrep** command can also be combined with find to search an entire directory tree. For example, to search every document in /usr/doc, no matter what directory, for disk, use the command:

```
$ find / -type f -name "*.gz" \
    -exec zgrep disk {} /dev/null \;
```

Listing 4-7: ZCAT/ZGREP SESSION

```
[root@idglinux /root]# cd /usr/doc
[root@idglinux doc]# cd glibc-2.1.1/
[root@idglinux glibc-2.1.1]# zcat ChangeLog.gz | more
1999-04-16  Ulrich Drepper  <drepper@cygnus.com>

    * nscd/cache.c (prune_cache): Only disable file checking for
    future if the file does not exist.
    Update file_mtime if cache was flushed.


—More—
[root@idglinux glibc-2.1.1]#
[root@idglinux glibc-2.1.1]# zgrep strcat Change*
ChangeLog.2.gz:      * string/string.h (strcat): Parameters names were swapped.
ChangeLog.5.gz:      * sysdeps/i386/i486/strcat.S: Correct some more 8bit operation
ChangeLog.5.gz:       * sysdeps/i386/strspn.S, sysdeps/i386/i486/strcat.S: New files.
ChangeLog.6.gz:      * sysdeps/alpha/strcat.S: Likewise.
ChangeLog.6.gz:      * sysdeps/alpha/strcat.S: Likewise.
ChangeLog.6.gz:      * sysdeps/i386/i486/strcat.S: Likewise.
ChangeLog.6.gz:      * sysdeps/i386/i486/strcat.S: Likewise.
ChangeLog.6.gz:      * sysdeps/alpha/strcat.S: New file.
ChangeLog.6.gz:      advice: Use `stpcpy' instead of `strcat' if possible.
ChangeLog.7.gz:      * sysdeps/powerpc/strcat.c: New file.
ChangeLog.7.gz:      (hesiod_to_bind): Avoid using strcat and extra strlen calls, use
ChangeLog.7.gz:      * sysdeps/generic/strcat.c: Likewise.
ChangeLog.7.gz:      Crusade against strcat.
ChangeLog.7.gz:      * nis/nss_nisplus/nisplus-publickey.c: Remove uses of strcat.
ChangeLog.7.gz:      * sysdeps/i386/i486/strcat.S: Likewise.
ChangeLog.7.gz:      * sysdeps/generic/strcat.c: Likewise.
ChangeLog.8.gz:      * sysdeps/i386/i486/bits/string.h (__strcat_c) [__i686__]: Correct
ChangeLog.9.gz:      * manual/string.texi: Add optimization examples for strcat and strchr.
ChangeLog.gz:* sysdeps/sparc/sparc32/strcat.S: Avoid using register g6.
ChangeLog.gz:* sysdeps/sparc/sparc32/sparcv9/strcat.S: New file.
ChangeLog.gz:* sysdeps/sparc/sparc32/strcat.S: New file.
ChangeLog.gz:* sysdeps/sparc/sparc64/strcat.S: New file.
[root@idglinux glibc-2.1.1]#
```

TeX and Source Files

The **groff** (originally called **troff**) format was one of the original UNIX documentation formats. Later, a new documentation formatter called TeX was created. Many of the newer Linux documents are written in TeX.

Sometimes you will encounter things that are not documented at all. Fortunately, Linux is an open-source package, so you can look at the source to find undocumented information.

TeX

The TeX text processor takes text files with typesetting information in them and produces typesetting output. TeX can typeset not only documents written for TeX, but also the GNU texinfo format files. These files are designed so that you can process them through the command **makeinfo** and create an .info file, and by using TeX, turn the files into printed manuals.

TeX is extremely powerful, but a little hard to run. The actual printing of a document is a three-part process. First, you run TeX to typeset your document. Because this is the first time you have run the program, vital information needed to construct items such as the table of contents is written out. (Because this information was not written out previously, the table of contents produced on this run will be invalid.)

TeX produces lots of output while it is being run. You can safely ignore all of it, unless your run ends in an obvious fatal error.

Next, you run TeX again. It uses the information gathered during the first pass to properly typeset the entire document. The output of this process is a device-independent (dvi) data file that contains the typeset results.

To print this you need to turn the .dvi file into PostScript. This is accomplished using the **dvips** command. If you have a printer that uses the PCL language instead of PostScript (LaserJet-compatible printers use PCL), you can create a PCL file by using the command **dvilj** instead.

The source

Red Hat Linux comes with the rpm package system. This system not only enables you to install and remove packages, but it also can find out information about packages.

In Chapter 2, we discussed how to use **GnoRPM** to manipulate binary packages. Using **GnoRPM** you can find out information about both installed and uninstalled packages.

But suppose you run across a command or file and want to find out where the package came from? The command:

    $ rpm -qf file

prints out the name of the package containing *file*. If you want to find out more about the package or its contents, typing

    $ rpm -qi package

lists information about the package and its description, and

    $ rpm -ql package

lists the contents of the package.

One of the problems with almost all programs is that they're not completely documented. How many times have you seen an obscure error message like:

    Error: data packet phase high.

while running a program? Looking the error message up in the manual doesn't work because it's not listed. So what do you do?

If you have Linux, you take a look at the source code for the program. If you know how to understand programming languages such as C or PERL, you may be able to figure out what's going wrong. For most people, however, reading through several thousand lines of cryptic computer code is not going to be a lot of help.

The source packages are contained in the directory **/mnt/cdrom/SRPMS**. To install a source package, execute the following commands as root:

```
# cd /mnt/cdrom/SRPMS
# rpm -i package-name
```

This installs sources in /usr/src/redhat. Unfortunately, they are installed as raw, packed sources, which aren't too useful.

You need to unpack the sources. First go to the /usr/src/redhat/SPECS directory. It contains a spec file that tells rpm how to unpack and build the sources.

The **rpm –bp** *spec-file* command can now be used to unpack the sources. The results are stored in /usr/src/redhat/BUILD.

Once these commands are executed, you can go browse the source and hopefully find out what this strange error message means.

TAKE NOTE

FREE SOFTWARE AND RELIABLITY

One of the myths about free software is that it is unreliable. Nothing could be further from the truth. People who have a stake in its reliability use free software. When something goes wrong they fix it and then publish the fix so that everyone can use it.

Listing 4-8: SAMPLE BUILD SESSION

```
[root@idglinux ~]# cd /mnt/cdrom/SRPMS
[root@idglinux SRPMS]# rpm -i adjtimex-
1.3-6.src.rpm
[root@idglinux SRPMS]# pwd
[root@idglinux SRPMS]# cd
/usr/src/redhat/SPECS
[root@idglinux SPECS]# rpm -bc
adjtimex.spec
Executing: %prep
+ umask 022
+ cd /usr/src/redhat/BUILD
+ rm -rf adjtimex-1.3
+ /bin/gzip -dc
/usr/src/redhat/SOURCES/adjtimex-1.3.tar.gz
+ tar -xf -
...
+ cd adjtimex-1.3
+ CFLAGS=-O2
+ ./configure
creating cache ./config.cache
checking for gcc... gcc
checking whether we are using GNU C... yes
...
creating Makefile
+ make
cc -O2 -o adjtimex adjtimex.c
+ exit 0
[root@idglinux SPECS]#
```

Personal Workbook

Q&A

1 What do the following commands do?

```
$ man man
$ info info
```

_____

_____

2 When you use the **info** command's search feature, you can stop the search with either Ctrl+G or Enter. What's the difference between these two commands?

_____

_____

_____

3 How many times must you run **groff** before you get a good output file? How many times must you run **TeX** to get a good output file?

_____

_____

4 How would you view a file named pam.ps.gz? How would you print it?

_____

_____

_____

5 How would you find all the files in /usr/doc that contain the word LILO?

_____

_____

6 Which command would you use to list the names of all the HTML files on the CD-ROM?

_____

_____

7 You are running a program and you get an error message that you've never seen before. After searching all the documentation and not finding any help, what can you do?

_____

_____

_____

8 You've just installed your system, and for some reason the **man –k** command doesn't work. What might be the trouble?

_____

_____

_____

ANSWERS: PAGE 335

EXTRA PRACTICE

1. Find the documentation files for the **LILO** command.

2. Typeset the man page for tcsh and view it on the X screen.

3. Using the **info** command, find the documentation on the common commands available in this program.

4. Find all the HTML documents on the CD-ROM.

5. View a document in /usr/doc/HOWTO.

6. Search all the HOWTO documents for information on RAID.

REAL-WORLD APPLICATIONS

✔ After calling up any manual pages that **man –k** describes, look in /usr/doc for information on ppp.

✔ You're curious and start exploring the /usr/doc directory. You discover the HOWTO subdirectory and find a wealth of information on how to set up Linux for various tasks. After discovering the PPP-HOWTO document, you can now provide even more help to your colleagues in setting up dial-up networking.

✔ You want to have a system that boots both Linux and Windows 95 or 98. Look in /usr/doc/HOWTO/mini for the mini-how-to documents and see if you can find any information on dual booting.

Visual Quiz

The viewer shows only the middle of the page. How would you view the top of the page? The bottom? How would you view the next page?

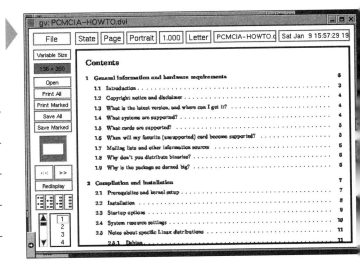

CHAPTER 5

MASTER THESE SKILLS

▶ The vi Survival Guide
▶ Moving a Little Faster
▶ Getting Help
▶ Editing Faster
▶ Visual Mode and Multiple Windows
▶ The : Commands
▶ Simple Commands for Programmers
▶ The vi Cookbook
▶ emacs, the Wonder Editor
▶ Editing Files with emacs
▶ Other Text Editors
▶ Spell-Checking Files

Text Editing

Linux relies heavily on simple text files. Most configuration files are stored as plain ASCII text, unlike the Windows Registry. Because of this, to succeed with Linux, you must know how to edit files.

While you can use nice graphical text editors, such as gedit or gnotepad+, you often need to get started from a plain text-based login. In fact, to configure the X Window System, which gives you the capability to run Linux graphics, you may need to edit configuration files. So, you need to learn some of the more primitive Linux text-editing tools.

There is a great religious debate going on in the Linux community concerning which editor is better, vi or emacs. The vi editor is the original UNIX full-screen editor. It comes standard on every UNIX and Linux system. It is designed to be fast and efficient. You can edit things quicker in vi than in any other editor — if you know how to use it. That's where **vi** has a problem. It's difficult to learn. Part of the problem comes from its choice of commands, making it hard to learn and remember, at first. For example, the keys h, j, k, and l, are used for left, up, down, and right, respectively; characters are deleted with x; and y and p are used for copy and paste. However, after you get used to it, these commands are fast.

The other problem with vi is that it is a *modal editor*. That means that it has a command mode, an insert mode, and some other minor modes. This can easily confuse a novice. Frequently, someone will type **3dd** to delete three lines, only to find that he or she was in insert mode and just added 3dd to the document.

emacs on the other hand is a *mode-less editor*. (emacs does have something called modes but they are very minor compared to the major modes of vi.)That means that it is much easier to use and learn. It's also takes more keystrokes to do things.

But emacs is much more than just a text editor. With it you can do things such as run a command window, read your mail, take a look at the Usenet news, and many other things. There are some people who can spend their whole life inside an emacs window.

The vi Survival Guide

The vi editor is efficient and fast — if you know how to use it. The problem is that the program has a steep learning curve, and thus requires some practice and drilling to learn.

This task teaches you the minimum vi commands that you need in order to edit. You must learn these commands before you can proceed to the other tasks, which teach you how to do things faster and more efficiently.

To start the editor use the command:

```
$ vi first.txt
```

The parameter first.txt is a filename. If this file exists it is edited. If it does not, then it is created.

When you start vi with an empty file, you see three things: your cursor in the top-left corner, a column of ~ along the left side, and some status text in the bottom-left corner. The cursor is where you begin typing; the ~ indicate that all those lines are empty; and the status text at the bottom is telling you that you are editing first.txt, which is a new file.

vi always starts in command mode. To begin inserting text, type I. The bottom left of the screen now shows -- INSERT --, which indicates that you are now in insert mode. Enter some text. Press Enter to end lines, as this is not a word processor and lines do not wrap automatically. If you make a typing mistake, don't worry, just continue on. Note: If you really screw up an editing session, there's a way to tell vi to forget the whole thing. That's the :q! command. This causes vi to exit without saving any changes to the file.

When you are done press Esc. The mode indicator is now blank indicating that you are in command mode again.

Now exit the editor by typing ZZ.

Editing the file

To edit the file you just created enter the command:

```
$ vi first.txt
```

Get used to the cursor movement keys listed on the following page.

Warning: You can use the arrow keys to move around, but if do, you'll never learn the H, J, K, and L keys explained at the beginning of this chapter and your editing will be significantly slower. Also, on some other UNIX systems, the arrow keys don't always work. If you will only use Red Hat Linux, this isn't a major concern, but you should use h, j, k, and l if you truly want to master vi.

Adding a line

Suppose you want to add another line at the bottom of the file. First, use the j key to move the cursor to the bottom line.

Next "open" up a new line *under* the current one with the **o** command. Notice that this command throws you into insert mode. You can now type in an additional line as seen in the example to the right. When you're done press the Esc keyto exit insert mode.

If you want to open a line *above* the cursor use the **O** command.

Deleting stuff

To delete a character, make sure you are in command mode, and then position the cursor over the character and press x. (This command comes from the old typewriter days where you would obliterate mistakes by typing xxxx over them.)

To delete a line type **dd**.

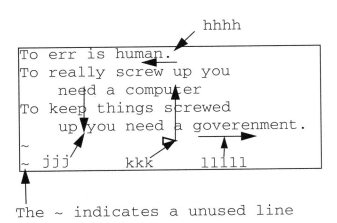

```
                                    hhhh
To err is human.
To really screw up you
    need a computer
To keep things screwed
    up you need a goverenment.
~
~  jjj       kkk       lllll
```

The ~ indicates a unused line

```
To err is human.
To really screw up you
    need a computer
To keep things screwed
    up you need a goverenment.
~
~
```

o(Boy is this
true)**Escape**

```
To err is human.
To really screw up you
    need a computer
(Boy is this true)
To keep things screwed
    up you need a goverenment.
~
```

goverenment ———x——▶ goverment

The a command

The **a** (append) command acts just like **i** except that **i** starts inserting before the character under the cursor and **a** inserts after. For example, if you wanted to add the word *Front* at the beginning of the line, you would position the cursor at the start and enter the command **iFront Escape**. If you wanted to add the word End at the end of the line, position the cursor at the end of the line and use the command: **aEnd Escape**.

Table 5-1: VI CURSOR MOVEMENT KEYS

Cursor Movement	Command	Meaning
k	i	Insert (end with Esc).
∧	a	Append (end with Esc).
|	x	Delete character.
h <-+-> l	ZZ	Save file and exit.
|	:q!	Exit and throw away changes.
v	dd	Delete line.
	o	Create line below.
	O	Create line above.

Moving a Little Faster

One of the more useful commands is the undo (**u**) command. This command undoes the last change. Multiple **u** commands can be used to reverse multiple changes. The Ctrl+R is the "redo" command. It undoes the result of the last undo. For example, if you want to undo the last two changes, and you type uuu (u three times), you can correct the problem, by typing a single Ctrl+R.

Every command in vi can be preceded by a number. Most commands use this as a repeat count. For example, **5k** moves you five lines. Similarly, the command **64i=Escape** inserts 64 equal signs in your document, and 5dd deletes 5 lines.

The basic cursor movement keys move one character at a time. To move a word at a time, use the **w** command. The **b** command skips backward over words.

Two of the most useful commands are the two that search for single characters. At first it may sound like searching for only one character is extremely limited and somewhat useless, but as you edit you'll find these commands extremely useful. The **f**x command searches for the character x on the current line. For example, if the cursor is positioned at the start of the line:

```
Linux is cheaper than Microsoft Windows
```

then the command **fc** jumps to the beginning of cheaper. Type **fW** and the cursor jumps to the beginning of "Windows." (This search is case sensitive.) Now enter **Fs** and the cursor backs up to the s. In vi, oftentimes an uppercase command does the reverse of a lowercase command, such as f and F.

Now we can remove the s with the **x** command and then add a $ using **i$Escape** and we get:

```
Linux is cheaper than Micro$oft Windows
```

Searching

To search for a string use the command /*string*. For example, to search for the string Linux, use the command /**Linux** and press Enter. Searches are case-sensitive, so /Linux /linux, and /LINUX will all find different things. When you type / to start the search, you'll notice that the cursor jumps to the bottom of the screen, where you enter the search string.

Searches are actually made using regular expressions, so be careful using characters such as [,], {, }, ^,$,., and *. The search starts at the current cursor location and continues on for the rest of the file. If it still does not find what it's looking for, it will start at the top of the file and search up to the cursor.

To search backward through the file use the **?** command. (The connection between / and **?** may not be obvious until you realize that they are on the same key.)

The **n** command repeats the previous search. The **N** command reverses the search direction and repeats the previous search. For example, suppose you are looking through a document for information about disks. You start by searching for the word disk, typing /**disk** and then pressing Enter. The first occurrence of the word is no help, so you search again using the command **n**. Using the **n** command you jump through the file looking for disks.

Say you accidentally use the **n** command one too many times. Realizing your mistake, you decide that what you really wanted was the previous occurrence of the word. So, you reverse direction using the **N** command. Remember that case matters.

Scrolling up and down

The Ctrl+D command scrolls down a half page. The Ctrl+U command scrolls up a half page. These commands can be used to move up and down quickly in a file.

The **G** command causes vi to jump to the bottom of the file. The *<number>***G** command moves the cursor to the line indicated by *<number>*. (To go to the top of the file use the command **1G**.)

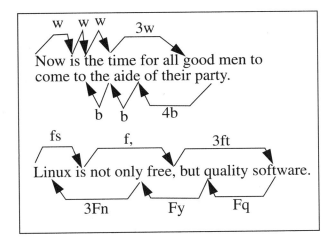

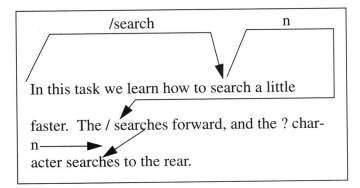

Table 5-2: EDITING COMMANDS

Command	Meaning
<number><cmd>	Repeat the command *<number>* times.
u	Undo the previous change.
Ctrl+R	Redo a previous change (after an undo).
w	Forward one word.
b	Backward one word.
f*<char>*	Search for *<char>* on the current line (forward).
F*<char>*	Search for *<char>* on the current line (backward).
/*string*	Search for *string* forward.
/	Repeat last search forward.
?*string*	Search for *string* backward.
?	Repeat last search in the backward direction.
n	Repeat last search.
N	Reverse direction and repeat last search.
Ctrl+D	Scroll down half page.
Ctrl+U	Scroll up half page.
G	Go to the bottom of the file.
*<number>*G	Go to the indicated line.

Getting Help

The standard UNIX version of the vi editor is limited and has remained basically unchanged for many years. Linux does not come with the standard vi editor. Instead Linux uses a souped-up version of vi, called VIM, that has been expanded and augmented with many very useful additional features.

One of the most useful new features is the **help** command. To get help type **:help** followed by Enter, and a help window appears. You can move through this window using the normal vi editing commands. To dismiss the window and return to editing type **:q** and then press Enter.

There are a few tricks to navigating the help screen. The text enclosed in vertical bars (for example, |intro|) denotes vi tags. (Tags are discussed in the task "Simple Commands for programmers," later in this chapter.) If you position the cursor inside the bars and press Ctrl+] the screen will jump to text discussing that subject.

If you want to go back to where you were before the jump, type Ctrl+O. To exit the help system and return to the editing, type **ZZ**.

The **:help** command by itself gives you general help. If you want help for a specific subject, such as "intro" use the **:help intro** command.

The help system contains entries for all commands. For example, if you want help on the **ZZ** command, enter **:help ZZ**.

Modes in the vi editor

The vi editor has several modes. You are already familiar with insert mode and command mode. In addition, there is replace mode, which is similar to insert mode except that characters are overwritten, and visual mode, which is discussed later in this chapter.

Some commands have different meanings depending on which mode you're in. For example, in command mode, Ctrl+T jumps to the previous tag. (See "Simple Commands for programmers" later in this chapter for details.) In insert mode, this command increases the indentation of the current line.

To get help for the command mode version of Ctrl+T type **:help CTRL-T** and then press the Enter keyIf you want the insert mode of the command, type **:help i_CTRL-T** and press Enter.

Help pages

There are several very useful help pages available to the vi user, including:

:help howto This section is a good starting point for find help on a wide variety of subjects.

:help quickref A quick reference of all the **vi** commands. Be aware that because **vi** has a *lot* of commands the quick reference is over 1000 lines long.

:help regular-expression A section that describes how to use regular expressions. Regular expressions are used by the search commands to define the string to search for. (Many other UNIX commands use regular expressions as well.)

FIND IT ONLINE

An organization has grown up to enhance and support the improved vi editor (vim). Visit their site at **http://www.vim.org**.

Table 5-3: VIM HELP COMMANDS

Command	Meaning
:help	Open a general help window.
:help *Subject*	Get help on a given subject.
:help *key*	Get help a given key.
Ctrl+]	Follow a hyperlink. (Actually jump to the "tag" under the cursor.)
Ctrl+O	Jump to the previous tag.
ZZ	Close the current window.

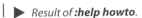

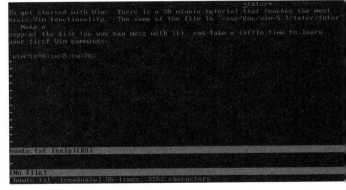

▶ Result of **:help** command. | ▶ Result of **:help howto**. | ▶ Result of following the "tutor" link.

Editing Faster

When you reach the point where you have learned the basic editing commands and are beginning to be annoyed by their slowness, you can start learning the faster editing commands.

As you learned, the delete line command is **dd**. To delete a word use the command **dw**. (See example at right.) Remember that **w** moves the cursor to the end of a word. In fact, you can use the **d** command followed by any cursor movement command.

For example, you can combine **d** with the **fq** command to delete all characters up to and including the next **q** on the command line.

Now let's get fancy and combine numeric prefixes with **d**. For example, to delete five words, use the command **5dw** (or **d5w**). To delete to the third occurrence of q, use the command **3dfq** or **d3fq**.

Changing text

The change command (**c**) acts just like the **d** command except that it leaves you in insert mode. For example, to change a word, enter the command **cw***new-word***Escape**.

To change an entire line, use the **cc** command.

If you want to change an individual character, position the cursor over the character and type **r***newcharacter* to replace it.

Replace mode

Replace mode functions a lot like insert mode. All of the commands are the same, but instead of adding text, the existing text is overwritten. To enter replace mode, type **R** while in insert mode.

Repeat last edit

One of the most simple and powerful editing commands is the **.** command. This command repeats the last edit. For example, if the last editing command you type was **dw** (delete word) then typing **.** will delete the next word.

This doesn't sound especially powerful, but as you use it, you will learn how useful it is. Here's a short example: Suppose you want to change all occurrences of the word bug to feature. To do this, enter the following commands:

1. Use the / search to find the word bug.
2. Change it to feature using the **cwmanager** and Esc command.
3. Find the next bug using the **n** command.
4. Change it using **.**.
5. Keep using the **n.** commands until all bugs are features.

The ^ and $ commands

The ^ command moves the cursor to the beginning of the line. This is also the magic character that matches the beginning of a line in a search pattern. For example, the command

```
/^Disk
```

searches for the word Disk at the beginning of a line.

The **$** command moves the cursor to the end of the line. Like ^, the **$** can be used in a search command to match the end of a line. For example, the search

```
/data\.$
```

matches any line that ends with the word data. (The backslash is needed in front of the dot because the dot is another magic character in a search. The \ tells vi to take away the magic from dot and make the dot just a dot.)

> **CROSS-REFERENCE**
> The vi editor has a list mode which tries to make all the text in the file visible. See "The vi Cookbook," later in this chapter.

94

~~A man called technical support to~~ complain that the coffee cup ~~holder~~ on his ~~computer was broken.~~

He didn't know who made it, but the label read 6x.

dd -- removes line
dw -- delete word
dfn -- delete to the frin "n"

A man ~~called technical~~ support to complain that the coffee cup holder on his computer was broken.

He didn't know who made it, but the ~~label~~ read 6x.

the case read 6x.

d3fl -- delete to the third "l" (3dfl works)
cwcaseEscape -- Change word to "case"

Table 5-4: TEXT MODIFICATION COMMANDS

Command	Meaning
u	Undo.
Ctrl+R	Redo the previous undo.
dd	Delete a line.
dw	Delete word.
dfq	Delete up to and including the first q on the line.
3dfq	Delete up to and including the third q on the current line.
d$<cm>$	Delete based on a cursor movement command. In this case $<cm>$ denotes a cursor movement command such as **w**, **b**, fx, Fx, and so on.
cc*text*Esc	Change the current line.
cw*text*Esc	Change word.
c$<cm>$*text*Esc.	Change based on cursor movement.
•	Repeat last editing command.

The computer when down today and we had to think.
dw -- delete word
The computer down today and we had to think.
. -- dot -- repeat last command (dw)
The computer today and we had to think.
. -- dot -- repeat last command (dw)
The computer and we had to think.
u -- undo list change
The computer today and we had to think.
Ctrl-R -- Redo last change (undo last undo)
The computer and we had to think.

Visual Mode and Multiple Windows

The improved **vi** that comes with Linux contains a visual mode. This mode is ideal for dealing with moving, deleting, or doing other things to large amounts of text. To enter visual mode, type **v**. The character under the cursor is displayed in reverse video. Also a -- VISUAL -- indicator appears at the bottom of the screen. The cursor movement keys can now be used to extend the video selection.

To delete the highlighted text, press **d**. The text is deleted and you return to command mode.

When text is deleted, vi stores it in a clipboard. You can paste this text in your file by using the **p** command.

Putting together all these commands, we can move a paragraph from one location to another.

The **y** (yank) command acts just like the **d** command except that it just puts the text on the clipboard and does not delete it. For example, **yw** puts a word on the clipboard. The **yy** command will yank an entire line.

The **y** command also works in visual mode, yanking the highlighted text on to the clipboard.

Suppose you make a spelling mistake such as typing *teh*. To correct it, simply position the cursor over the *e* and enter the **xp** command. The **x** deletes the character under the cursor (the *e*), and the **p** pastes it after the character under the cursor (the *h*). These two simple commands provide a quick way to flip characters.

Multiple windows

The standard vi editor forces you to deal with a single editing window. The improved Linux version of **vi** lets you use multiple windows.

The **:split** command splits the current window in two and displays the current file in both windows. By default, you are in the top window. You can move around as much as you want in the top window independent of what's being displayed in the bottom one. If you make changes to the file however, they will show up in the bottom window.

To change windows, use the Ctrl+Wj command to go down one window. The Ctrl+Wk command lets you go up one. (Remember our cursor movement commands: **j** = up, **k** = down.)

To close a window, use the **ZZ** command.

Suppose you want to edit two different files at once. The

```
:split file
```

command splits the window, and starts editing *file* in the new window. Because you are editing two files at once you can do such things as cut text out of one file and paste it into another.

The size of a window can be decreased using the Ctrl+W– command. The Ctrl+W+ increases it.

Normally vi keeps the edited file in an internal buffer. This buffer is written to the file when you type the **ZZ** command. If you want to explicitly write the file use the **:w** command. The **:q!** command quits throwing away the data in the buffer. Any changes before the last write are committed and will not be thrown away.

If you are editing a file, and want to switch to another file, use the **:vi** *file* command.

① *Move to the beginning of the text to be moved.*

② *Enter visual mode with the **v** command.*

③ *Move to the end of the text to be moved.*

④ *Cut it and place it on the clipboard with the **d** command.*

▶ *Move to where the text is to go and paste it in using the **p** command.*

Table 5-5: WINDOWING AND CLIPBOARD COMMANDS

Command	Meaning
v	Enter visual mode.
v<*move cursor*>d	Delete the highlighted text.
p	Paste after cursor.
P	Paste before cursor.
yy	Yank current line onto the clipboard.
y<*cw*>	Yank the text up to the location specified by the cursor movement on to the clipboard.
xp	Correct typo. (Move the character under the cursor over to the right one.)
:split	Split the current window in two. The current file appears in both windows.
:split *file*	Spilt the current window and begin editing the file named *file* in the other window.
Ctrl+Wj	Move to next window down.
Ctrl+Wk	Move to next window up.
ZZ	Close window.
Ctrl+W+	Increase the size of the current window.
Ctrl+W–	Decrease the size of the current window.

The : Commands

The original vi editor was built on top of a line-oriented editor called ex. The vi editor still lets you enter **ex** commands by typing : and the command.

The most useful : commands are those used to set options. For example, by default searches in vi are case sensitive. In other words, a search for FOO will not find the string foo. If you want vi to do case-insensitive searches (foo = Foo = FOO) then issue the command:

`:set ignorecase`

(**ignorecase** can be abbreviated **ic**)

If you want to turn this option off, use the command:

`:set noignorecase`

To find out what options are set, use the command:

`:set`

This list is limited to the options that do not contain their default values. If you want a list of all options, use the command:

`:set all`

Some other options that you may want to set are:

`:set nowrapscan`

Normally when vi performs a forward search it will search to the end of the file, then start from the beginning and search up to the cursor. This option prevents the search from wrapping at the end of file.

Normally vi starts searching after you enter the search string. With:

`:set incsearch`

It starts searching when you type the first character in the string. Each time you type another character, the search location will be updated.

Replacing one word with another using one command

Suppose you're deluged with marketing speak and you want to make all bugs into features and you don't need to review your changes. Execute the command:

`:1,$s/bugs/features/g`

The colon (:) indicates the execution of an **ex** type command. All **ex** commands begin with range of line numbers on which the command operates. Here, we've chosen the whole document, from line **1** to the last line (**$**).

The **s** command performs a substitution. The old text follows enclosed in slashes (**/bugs/**). The replacement text comes next, also delimited by the slash (**/features/**). The **g** command tells the editor that this is a global change and so if the word bugs appears more than once on a line, change them all. Be careful, because the text contained within the first set of slashes is actually treated as a regular expression. Characters such as (,), *, ., [,], \, and / don't behave like normal text.

The initialization file: .vimrc

You can customize the way **vi** works by entering commands into a .vimrc file. When **vi** first starts, it looks for a file in your home directory called **.vimrc** and reads the commands in it. This is so you can place your favorite options in it and have them automatically set when you start the program. See Listing 5-1.

TAKE NOTE

THE VIRGIN WHAT!?

A church had just bought its first computer and was learning to use it. The church secretary set up a form letter to be used in a funeral service. Where the person's name was to be, she put in the word<*name*>. When a funeral occurred she would change this word to the actual name of the departed.

One day, there were two funerals, first for a lady named Mary, then later one for someone named Edna. So the secretary used global replace to change <*name*> to Mary. Next, she generated the service for the second funeral by changing the word Mary to Edna. That was a mistake!

Imagine the minister's surprise when he started reading the part containing the Apostle's Creed and saw, "Born of the Virgin Edna."

Listing 5-1: A SAMPLE .VIMRC

```
1.      :syntax on
2.      :set autoindent
3.      :set autowrite
4.      :ab #d #define
5.      :ab #i #include
6.      :ab #b
/*****************************
7.      :ab #e
*****************************/
8.      :ab #l /*———————————*/
9.      :set sw=4
10.     :set notextauto
11.     :set cindent
12.     :set incsearch
```

▶ *Line 1 turns syntax coloring on. (See the section "Simple Commands for Programmers" for details.)*

▶ *Line 2 turns on auto indent. Each line will be indented the same as the previous one. (See the section "Simple Commands for Programmers" for details.)*

▶ *Line 3 sets autowrite. The **vi** editor will automatically write out files changing files. Normally, you have to write the file manually, then change the file.*

▶ *Lines 4-8 define the abbreviations that are used to make the creation of programming easier. (See the section "Simple Commands for Programmers" for details.)*

▶ *Line 9 sets the "shift width" to 4. The shift width is used by the indentation-related command to determine how much to indent.*

▶ *Line 10 turns off intelligent sensing of end of line types. MS-DOS and UNIX use a different format for text files. The only difference is in how they handle end-of-line. With this feature enabled, **vi** hides these differences. With it off, MS-DOS files are not automatically handled.*

▶ *Line 11 turns on C-style indentation.*

▶ *Line 12 turns on incremental searches.*

Simple Commands for Programmers

The vi editor contains a number of very useful commands for programmers. The most useful of these is the **%** command. It finds matching {}, (), or [] characters. The example at the right shows how the **%** command can be used to jump between matching curly braces. This command is especially useful when you have a program, such as the second example, in which you've made a mistake. In this example, a brace has been accidentally omitted. So, what the programmer thinks are matching braces are not. The **%** command is tremendously useful when it comes to locating problems such as this.

The Linux vi has improved the **%** command somewhat. Not only will it detect matching (), {}, and [], but it will also detect matching #ifdef/#else/#endif statements. So, if you put the cursor on a #ifdef and press **%**, it will jump to the matching #else or #endif.

Indentation plays a big role in programming. Proper indentation can make the difference between a totally unreadable mess and an understandable program.

The << and > commands shift the current line left or right one shiftwidth. (The shiftwidth defaults to eight but can be changed, as we will see later.)

Like the **d** and **c** commands, the < and > commands are followed by a cursor motion command.

The default shift width is eight characters. Studies have shown that programs are most readable when the indentation is four characters.

To change the shift width used by vi execute the command:

`:set shiftwidth=4`

(You can use the shorthand version **:set sw=4**.)

When autoindent is set, the editor automatically indents each new line the same as the one before it. But what happens if autoindent gives you more indent than you want? For example, if you are doing a block such as

```
if (flag) {
    do_part1();
    }
```

The last } should be at one level less than the do_part1(); line, but autoindent places it at the same level. The Ctrl+D command comes to the rescue. It causes the cursor to backup one shiftwidth after an autoindent.

Better than autoindent is cindent. When you issue the command:

`:set cindent`

the vi editor automatically performs indentation for your C or C++ program.

The improved version of vi can perform syntax coloring. That's where different parts of the program — comments, keywords, strings, variables, and so forth — are displayed in different colors. To enable this option, use the command:

`:set syntax=on`

Syntax coloring works great on the raw Linux terminal (the one you get before you start the X Window System). However, in an xterm shell window it doesn't work so well. To correct the problem you need to tell vi that you are using a color-xterm. This is accomplished by entering the shell command:

`$ export TERM=linux`

If you want to make this change permanent, you can add the lines:

```
if [ $TERM == xterm ] ;
    export TERM= linux;
fi
```

to your .bash_profile file.

Warning: Spacing is very important.

Continued

100

```
#ifdef LINUX
#include "asm/scsi.h"
#endif LINUX

int main()
{
    int flag = 0;

    set_flag(&flag, "This is a flag");
    if (flag) {
        printf("Flag is set\n");
    }
    return (0);
}
```

```
int main()
{
    if (flag)
    {
    printf("Flag");
    }
    printf("Normal");

int main()
{
    if (flag)
        {
        printf("Flag");
        }
    printf("Normal");
```

▶ *Use of the % command*

▶ *Using >% to shift a block*
▶ *(Shiftwidth is set to 4.)*

Table 5-6: VI EDITOR SIMPLE COMMANDS

Command	Description
%	Find matching {}, [], (), #ifdef/#else/#endif.
<<	Shift line left.
>	Shift line right.
<*cm*	Shift lines from current location to result of cursor movement, left.
>*cm*	Shift lines from current location to result of cursor movement, right.
>%	Shift all text to a matching (), {}, or [] right.
<%	Shift all text from here to a matching (), {}, or [] left.
:set shiftwidth=4	Set the number of spaces to shift for the < and > commands.
:set autoindent	Turn on auto indent. Each new line will be indented the same amount as the previous ones.
Ctrl+D	When autoindent is set, backup up over one indentation level.
:set cindent	Turn on intelligent C-style indentation.
:set syntax=on	Turn on syntax coloring.

Simple Commands for Programmers *Continued*

Abbreviations

The vi editor lets you define abbreviations using the

```
:abbreviate abbr string
```

command. (**:abbreviate** can be abbreviated as **:ab**.)

So why is this command in the programming section? Well here are some useful abbreviations:

```
:ab #d #define
:ab #i #include
```

After entering these commands, when you type **#i**, vi will put #include in your file.

One interesting use of these commands is for boxed comments. Here are the abbreviations:

```
:ab #b /*******************************
:ab #e *******************************/
```

Now when you type **#b**, you get the top of a boxed comment and **#e** gives you the bottom. Note that the length of the starred lines is carefully selected to so that the end of the line matches a tab stop.

Tags

The ctags command (provided by the ctags package and unrelated to VIM) produces a short database containing the names of all the procedures in a set of files. For example, the command:

```
$ ctags *.c
```

finds all the procedures in all the C files in your current directory. The database it produces is stored in a file called tags.

The vi editor uses this to locate procedures. For example, if you want to edit the procedure get_data you can use the command:

```
$ vi -t get_data
```

The vi editor sees that you want to edit based on a tag (the –t option) and looks in the database for get_data. It then opens the file containing this procedure and positions you to it.

You can jump to any procedure while editing in vi using the

```
:ta procedure
```

command.

The tag feature is nice for browsing through source files. For example, suppose you want to figure out what's happening in get_data. You use the vi **–t get_data** command to examine that procedure. The get_data procedure calls read_header and you want to see what's going on there.

Position the cursor over the read_header name and press Ctrl+]. The editor will jump to the read_header procedure (even if it is in another file.)

Make and vi integration

When programming you go through a cycle of edit, make, edit, make, and so on. The vi editor has an extension that short circuits this process. When you execute the command

```
:make
```

the editor runs the program make to compile your program. (Note that you must have created a **Makefile** before using this command for things to work properly.) But the editor does more than just run **make**, it captures any compilation errors that occur. The cursor is then positioned on the line with first error.

After you correct the problem, you can go to the next error using the **:cn** command. Related commands include **:cc** to jump to the current error and **:cp** to go to the previous one.

These commands let you jump through the program and fix all the errors. When you've done, you can try to compile again using the **:make** command.

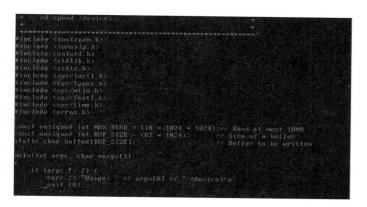

Table 5-7: COMMANDS

Command	Meaning
:abbreviate abbr. string	Define an abbreviation.
:ab abbr. string	Short version of abbreviate.
$ ctags *.c	Generate a "tags" file containing a list of the locations of all the procedures in the *.c files.
$ vi –t proc	Edit starting at the tag (procedure name) indicated by proc.
:ta proc	A way of jumping to a procedure from inside of **vi**.
:make	Run the **make** program and capture the errors.
:cc	Jump to the location of the current error message.
:cn	Jump to the location of the next error.
:cp	Jump to the location of the previous error.

▶ *Result of :make command.* ▶ *File positioned at the first error message.*

▶ *Using :cn to position to the next error line.*

The vi Cookbook

In this task, we provide step-by–step instructions for performing many useful operations in **vi**.

Moving text

To move a paragraph from the top of the document to the bottom, follow these instructions:

1. Move the cursor to the top of the paragraph you want to move.
2. Enter the **ma** command to place a mark named **a** at this location.
3. Move the cursor to the bottom of the paragraph to be moved.
4. Enter the command **d'a**, which deletes to mark **a**. This places the deleted text on the clipboard.
5. Move the cursor to line where the text is to go. The paragraph will be placed after this one.
6. Use the **p** command to paste the text in below the cursor.

Copying a block of text from one file to another

To copy a block of text between files, follow these instructions:

1. Edit the first file.
2. Go to the top line to be copied.
3. Enter the **ma** command to mark this line as mark **a**.
4. Go to the bottom line to be copied.
5. Use **'ay** to place the text from mark a (**'a**) in the "yank" buffer (**y**).
6. Use the command **:vi** *other-file* to edit the other file.
7. Go to the line where the insert is to occur. The text will be place after this line.
8. Use the **p** command to paste the text below the cursor.

Sorting a section

Frequently, you will edit a file with a list of names in it, such as a list of object files that make up a program similar to this:

```
version.o
pch.o
getopt.o
util.o
getopt1.o
inp.o
patch.o
backupfile.o
```

This list would be nice in alphabetical order, or at least ASCII order. To alphabetize this list, follow these instructions:

1. Move the cursor to the first line to be sorted.
2. Use **ma** to mark the first line as mark a.
3. Move to the bottom of the text to be sorted.
4. Enter **!'asort**. The **!** command tells vi to run text through an external shell command and to replace the lines run with the results of the command. The **'a** tells the editor that the text to be worked on starts at the current line and ends at mark a. The command that the text is to go through is **sort**.

The result is:

```
backupfile.o
getopt.o
getopt1.o
inp.o
patch.o
pch.o
util.o
version.o
```

In actual practice, what you see in most *Makefiles* (files used by UNIX to control compilation) looks more like this:

```
OBJS = \
        version.o           \
        pch.o               \
        getopt.o            \
        util.o              \
        getopt1.o           \
        inp.o               \
        patch.o             \
        backupfile.o
```

The backslash (\) is used to indicate a continuation line. After sorting this list looks like:

```
OBJS = \
        backupfile.o
        getopt.o            \
        getopt1.o           \
        inp.o               \
        patch.o             \
        pch.o               \
        util.o              \
        version.o           \
```

The names are in order, but the backslashes are wrong. You need to fix them using normal editing before continuing.

```
OBJS = \
        backupfile.o        \
        getopt.o            \
        getopt1.o           \
        inp.o               \
        patch.o             \
        pch.o               \
        util.o              \
        version.o
```

Dealing with *Makefile* and other mean files

One problem with the file format used by the UNIX **make** command is that it's extremely fussy.

For example, the following is correct:

```
prog: prog.c
        cc -g -o prog prog.c
```

The following is not:

```
prog: prog.c
        cc -g -o prog prog.c
```

At first glance, these two lines appear to be exactly the same. But look closer. The cc line of the first one begins with a Tab. The second one begins with eight spaces. So how are you supposed to tell them apart especially when one the screen (or the printed page) they look exactly the same? The answer is you can't. You might think that's a bit unfair. Especially when **make** works on the first one but not the second. Fortunately, vi has a mode — list mode — that tells you exactly what's in your file. Executing the command

`:set list`

puts you in list mode. When the display is set into "list mode" all characters print. Tabs show up as "^I" and the end of line shows up as $. So in list mode, our two examples look like this:

```
prog: prog.c$
^Icc -g -o prog prog.c$
```

and

```
prog: prog.c$
        cc -g -o prog prog.c$
```

From this it's easy to see which line has the Tab.

Continued

105

The vi Cookbook

Continued

The vi editor is not a word processor. However, there are a couple of things that you can do to make things better for you when editing text.

Word processors automatically wrap when you type a line that's longer than the margins. The vi editor lets you make a line as long as you want. Executing the command:

```
:set textwidth=70
```

tells vi to automatically break lines when the line runs longer than 70 characters. (You can adjust this number to whatever line length you want.) This makes entering text much easier. It doesn't solve the problem of editing. If you enter a paragraph and then decide to delete half the words on the first line, **vi** will not reformat the text.

You can force a reformat of a paragraph by following these instructions:

1. Move to the top of the paragraph.
2. Enter **!}**. The **!** command tells **vi** to pipe a section of text through a filter. The **}** tells **vi** that the section of text for the pipe command is a single paragraph.
3. Next comes **fmt –70. Enter**The UNIX command **fmt** is a primitive formatter. It performs word wrapping well enough for text documentation. The –70 tells **fmt** to format lines for 70 characters per line.

Reading a man page

You can use the vi editor to browse through text files. Very useful files to browse through are the man pages. Getting the man pages into **vi** involves the Linux equivalent of a four-corner billiards shot. Start with:

```
$ man subject | ul -i >tmp.txt
$ vi tmp.txt
```

You are now in the vi editor looking at your man page. All the normal vi cursor movement commands can be used to browse the file.

Removing carriage returns from MS-DOS file

In an MS-DOS file, each line ends with a ^M character. This is caused by the funny way that MS-DOS treats the end-of-line.

To remove the ^M characters from a MS-DOS file, enter the command:

```
:1,$s/Ctrl+VCtrl+M//
```

This command starts with a colon (:) to tell **vi** to enter ex mode. All **ex** commands start with a line number range, in this case its from the first line (**1**) to the last (**$**). The slash indicates the start of the "from text." The Ctrl+V tells vi to treat the next character as a regular character, even if it's a special one.

The next character is Ctrl+M. (Without the Ctrl+V, this would be treated as Enter.) The next slash ends the "from text." What follows is the "to text" enclosed by slashes. In this case, it's nothing (//).

Trimming the blanks off an end of line

Some people find spaces and tabs at the end of a line useless, wasteful, and ugly. To remove white space at the end of every line, execute the command:

```
:1,$s/\s*$//
```

The colon (:) tells **vi** to enter **ex** command mode. All **ex** commands start with a line range, in this case, the entire file (line **1** to the last line: **$**). The first set of slashes encloses the "from text." The \s is the special regular-expression code for any white space, which

106

matches either tabs or space. The asterisk (*) means that the previous character specification (space or tab) can be repeated any number of times. The dollar ($) indicates an end-of-line. So, \s*$ tells **vi** to look for any number of spaces or tabs followed by an end-of-line. These are then replaced by the text in the next set of slashes. This text is nothing, so the spaces and tabs are effectively removed.

Oops, I left the file write protected

The **vi** editor enables you to edit a write-protected file with little or no warning. The only trouble is that when you try to exit using **ZZ** you get the error:

```
file.txt         File is read only
```

and **vi** doesn't exit. The trick is to execute the **:shell** command. This command takes you out of **vi** by starting a command processor (shell) running under **vi**

You can then write enable the file:

```
$ chmod u+w file.txt
```

and get out of the shell:

```
$ exit
```

returning to **vi**. Finally, you need to force **vi** to write the file using the command:

```
:w!
```

(It still thinks the file is write protected, so we need to use the force option (!) to convince it to write to it.)

Changing "Last, First" to "First Last"

You have a list of names in the form:

    Last, First

that you want to change to:

    First Last

It can be done with one command:

```
:1,$s/\([^,]*\), \(.*$\)/\2 \1/
```

The colon (:) tells **vi** that this is an **ex** style command. The line range for this command is the whole file, as indicated by the range **1,$**. The **s** (substitute) tells vi to do a string substitution. The old text is a complex regular expression. The \(... \) delimiters are used to inform the editor that the text that matches the regular expression side is to be treated special.

The text in the first \(... \) is assigned to **\1** in the replacement text. The second set of text inside \(... \) is assigned **\2**, and so on. In this case, the first regular expression is any bunch of characters that does not include a comma. The [^,] means anything but a comma, the * means a bunch of characters (zero or more).

The second expression matches anything (.*) up to the end of line ($). The result of this substitution is that the first word on the line is assigned to **\1** and the second to **\2**. These values are used in the end of the command to reverse the word.

> **TAKE NOTE**
>
> ▶ **EDITING FILES CONTAINING A GIVEN WORD**
>
> Editing files containing a given word involves the **fgrep** command, as well as the special shell character back tick (`).

emacs, the Wonder Editor

If there ever was a text editor that could do every-thing you could imagine — and then some — it's emacs. emacs is a formidable editing system and much more. It has a built-in programming language that is based on LISP, so you can create new extensions to emacs by writing short snippets of LISP code. You can also redefine the keys on the keyboard to perform any emacs commands. Many users have already written extension packages for programming, editing special file types, such as Java or HTML files, and for doing tasks such as reading e-mail and Usenet news, and even browsing the Web.

emacs also comes with an extensive online help sys-tem, which is necessary because of the large number of commands available.

To start emacs, simply enter the emacs command. If you're running the X Window System graphics, you'll see an emacs window similar to that shown on the facing page. If you're running from a terminal console, you'll get a non-X version of emacs. Both versions work similarly. It's a lot easier to start learning with the X Window ver-sion, mainly because of the menus provided.

emacs supports hundreds of commands, most of which start with the Ctrl or Meta keys. To get going, use the menus until you learn a few of the commands. Then you can start working from the keyboard. We've found this to be a great way to learn emacs.

Once you start emacs, you can begin typing immedi-ately. Unlike vi, emacs doesn't use modes for entering text or running commands. Normal characters that you type go in the current window, which is called the cur-rent buffer. Because there's no command or input modes, you need special keys to tell emacs when you are entering a command. These commands start with the Ctrl or Meta keys.

There's no Meta key on your keyboard. In typical emacs fashion, this key is bound to either the Esc or Alt key. On Red Hat Linux, both Esc and Alt work the same as the Meta key. In the emacs documentation, keyboard short cuts are described as C-x or M-x, which translates to Ctrl+x or Meta+x (Alt or Esc). For example, the command **C-h t** means you type Ctrl+H and then press T. This is important because **emacs** has extensive online references to keys like this.

For another example, to save your work and exit **emacs**, type **C-x C-c**. That's Ctrl-x Ctrl-c. You're now ready to tackle the most extensive text editor in exis-tence. Table 5-8 lists some of the most important com-mands to get started with **emacs**.

> **TAKE NOTE**
>
> ▶ **XEMACS VERSUS EMACS**
> There are two main branches in the emacs family: GNU emacs, described here, and xemacs, which presents a slightly different interface under the X Window System. There is no text mode version of xemacs though; you must run the X Window System.

CROSS-REFERENCE
See the "The vi Survival Guide" earlier in this chapter for discussion of another editor.

Table 5-8: BASIC EMACS COMMANDS

Command	Action
C-x C-s	Save text in current buffer under current filename (save-buffer).
C-x C-c	Save text in current buffer and exit emacs (save-buffers-kill-emacs).
C-x C-w	Save text in current buffer under a different name (write-file).
C-x C-f	Open file (find-file).
C-g	Cancel command, used when emacs seems hung on something (keyboard-quit).

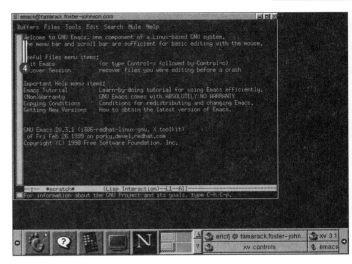

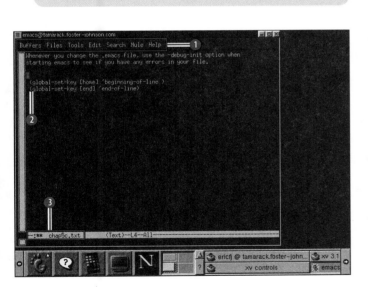

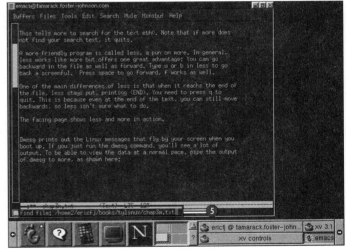

❶ *While learning emacs, select commands from the menu bar.*

❷ *Edit text in the main editing buffer window.*

❸ *Enter commands in the minibuffer.*

❹ *The introduction screen in GNU emacs helps you get going.*

❺ *When you issue a command that requires input, you enter the input in the minibuffer area.*

FIND IT ONLINE

The **xemacs** home page resides at **http://www.xemacs.org.**

Editing Files with emacs

Editing with emacs is easy. You just type. You don't need to remember to go into insert mode as you do with vi. And, you can execute hundreds of emacs commands.

emacs supports extensive commands to move about a file, as shown in Table 5-9 (the long commands are listed in parentheses, which can be run by typing **M-x** and the long command). For newcomers, the PgUp and PgDn keys do what you'd expect, and to move about on a line, use the arrow keys. Use C-**a** to move to the beginning of the line and C-e to move to the end.

emacs supports the Delete key for deleting text. By default, the Delete and Backspace keys act the same — as most users would consider the backspace function. You can also use **C-d** to delete the character to the right of the cursor, which is what the Delete key does in many editors. M-d deletes and entire word, while M-Delete deletes the word to the left. Tables 5-10 and 5-11 list a number of deleting and editing commands with the long commands listed in parentheses. You can run any of these long commands with the M-x command. Just type M-x followed by the long command.

emacs supports extensive searching capabilities. **C-s** starts a forward incremental search, searching from your current position onward in the file. As you type characters, emacs searches for the next occurrence of that pattern. So, if you type *b*, emacs searches for the first *b* going forward. If you then type an *e*, emacs searches for the first *be* going forward, and so on until you type in your word. In many cases, emacs will have already found the word you are looking for long before you type in the whole word. **C-r** searches backwards.

And, like most text editors, emacs supports copy and paste. emacs predates the current interface standards of Ctrl+X for cut, Ctrl+C for copy, and Ctrl+V for paste,

which became popular with the Macintosh. Instead, emacs uses C-W, M-W, and C-Y.

You can see a number of cut items from the Select and Paste choice on the Edit menu. Unlike other editors that support only one clipboard, emacs lets you paste data that was cut in previous operations.

If you edit multiple files, each file is considered a buffer. Thus, you can call up a number of documents in emacs and switch between them. emacs goes further, though. You can split your current window between a number of buffers. Use the **C-x 2** command to split the current window and **C-x 1** to restore to one buffer for the full window. To switch windows, enter **C-x o**. You can also call up a file into a new window using the **C-x 4 f** command.

Continued

CROSS-REFERENCE

Chapter 9 covers copy and paste under the X Window System.

110

Table 5-9: COMMANDS TO MOVE ABOUT

Command	Action
C-F	Jump forward one character, like the right arrow (forward-char).
C-B	Jump backward one character, like the left arrow (backward-char.)
C-N	Jump down one line, like the down arrow (next-line).
C-P	Jump up one line, like the up arrow (previous-line).
M-F	Jump forward one word (forward-word).
M-B	Jump backward one word (backward-word).
C-A	Jump to beginning of line (beginning-of-line).
C-E	Jump to end of line (end-of-line).
Home	Jump to beginning of file (beginning-of-buffer).
End	Jump to end of file (end-of-buffer).
M-<	Move to beginning of the file (beginning-of-buffer).
M->	Move to the end of the file (end-of-buffer).
PgUp	Scroll *text* down one page; seems weird but acts like you'd expect (scroll-down).
PgDn	Scroll *text* up one page; seems weird but acts like you'd expect (scroll-up).
C-V	Move forward one screen (scroll-up).
M-V	Move backward one screen (scroll-down).
C-L	Clear screen, move cursor to center, and redraw (recenter).
C-S	Search forward (isearch-forward).
C-R	Search backward (isearch-backward).

Table 5-10: EDITING COMMANDS

Command	Action
Insert	Toggle overwrite mode (overwrite-mode).
Delete	Delete character to left (delete-backward-char).
C-D	Delete character to right (delete-char).
M-D	Delete word (kill-word).
M-Delete	Delete word to left (backward-kill-word).
C-k	Delete to end of line (kill-line).
C-t	Transpose two characters (transpose-chars).

Table 5-11: BUFFER COMMANDS

Command	Action
C-x 2	Split window (split-window-vertically).
C-x 1	Return to one window (delete-other-windows).
C-x b	Jump to next buffer (switch-to-buffer).
C-x b *buffer*	Jump to named *buffer* (switch-to-buffer).
C-x 4 b	Jump to next buffer and create new window for it (switch-to-buffer-other-window).
C-x C-f *filename*	Load file into buffer (find-file).
C-x 4 f *filename*	Load file into new window (find-file-other-window).
C-x C-s	Save current buffer to current filename.
C-x C-b	List buffers (list-buffers).

FIND IT ONLINE

The emacs home page is located at **http://www.emacs.org.**

111

Editing Files With emacs

Continued

Getting help in emacs

With its hundreds of complicated commands, using Ctrl and Meta shortcuts, new users would be lost in emacs if not for its extensive online help. From the keyboard, C-h is the basic prefix for emacs help commands. From the window, the Help menu provides a front-end to most emacs help commands.

To get going, try the **C-h t** command, which starts the emacs tutorial.

Table 5-12 lists the emacs commands for getting help. Again, the long commands are listed in parentheses. You can run any of these long commands with the **M-x** command. Just type **M-x** and then command, such as *help-with-tutorial.*

Customizing emacs

emacs includes a built-in LISP interpreter, as well as an online manual on the LISP dialect used by emacs. You can write extensive add-ons, or create simple customizations.

To begin, let's use the online help to find information on customizing emacs, and then change the bindings for the Home and End keys so that these keys move the cursor to the beginning and end of the current line.

To figure out how to do this, we need to look in the emacs manual, which is formatted in a primitive hypertext system called info, and find some examples for redefining keys. From the *Help* menu, call up the emacs manual. You'll see a bunch of topics, most having nothing to do with emacs. The **m** command can call up topics — called menus. Type **m** followed by the name of the topic. We want to find three topics: *Emacs*, *Key Bindings*, and *Init Rebinding*.

In this section of the manual, there are some calls to the global-set-key command. We can test this command with the **M-x** command. Type **M-x** and at the prompt, enter *global-set-key*. This will then prompt you for the key. Press the Home key. Then, at the prompt for the command, type in *beginning-of-line* (which we got from Table 5-9). You should now be able to press the Home key and have the cursor go to the start of the line rather than the start of the document.

We now just have to enter the commands into the .emacs file, as shown in Listing 5-2. The format for these commands comes from the examples in the emacs info manuals. With emacs, you do a lot of copying of examples. If you want to change something, chances are someone has already done something similar. You just have to find it.

Whenever you change the .emacs file, use the **–debug-init** option when starting emacs to see if you have any errors in your file.

CROSS-REFERENCE
Chapter 4 covers getting help in Linux.

Table 5-12: GETTING HELP

Command	Action
C-h i	Browse emacs manuals in info — a primitive hypertext — mode (info).
C-h a *text*	List commands containing *text* (command-apropos).
C-h b	List key bindings (describe-bindings).
C-h c *key*	Name commands bound to *key* (describe-key-briefly).
C-h C-h C-h	Show help on help.
C-h k *key*	Show help on a given *key* (describe-key).
C-h t	Run the emacs tutorial (help-with-tutorial).
C-h x *command*	List the keys that run a given *command* (where-is).

Listing 5-2: AN .EMACS FILE

```
(global-set-key [home] 'beginning-of-line)
(global-set-key [end] 'end-of-line)
```

▶ *When emacs starts up, it executes the commands in the .emacs file stored in your home directory. These commands redefine the Home and End keys.*

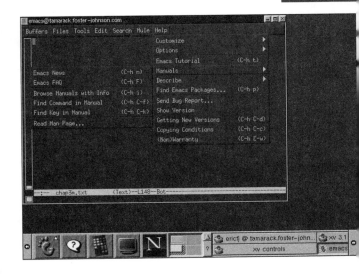

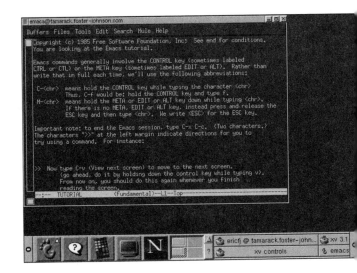

▶ *Find information online from the Help menu.*

▶ *Start the emacs tutorial with the **Ctrl-h t** command. This i... an excellent way to get started.*

FIND IT ONLINE

You can download the Windows version of emacs from **ftp.cs.washington.edu/pub/ntemacs/docs/ntemacs.html.**

Other Text Editors

Your choice of editors is largely based on your personal preferences. No two people agree on the exact same things, which is OK. vi and emacs form the mainstay of Linux text editing, but they certainly aren't pretty or all that easy to learn. If you'd like a simple editor more in tune with the Windows Notepad editor, Linux offers a number of choices.

Both the GNOME and KDE desktop environments offer simple GUI text editors. In GNOME, you can use gedit, a small lightweight text editor. A related text editor is gxedit, which requires the GTK toolkit (upon which GNOME is also built), but not the full GNOME desktop.

In KDE, the kedit application provides a simple text editor. You can use this to edit most text files. kwrite, another text editor, automatically recognizes a number of programming languages and highlights the syntax accordingly.

For non-X environments, one of the most popular "simple" text editors is pico, which comes with the Pine mail program. To start pico and edit a text file, type

```
$ pico [filename]
```

All of the basic pico commands (and there are far fewer than in emacs or vi) are listed at the bottom of the screen.

One of the best GUI editors for software development is called nedit, short for Nirvana editor, which you can download from the Internet. nedit presents a simple interface similar to that shown in the third figure on the facing page. In general, nedit supports the common cut, copy, and paste commands as you'd expect if you have experience with Windows (as do gxedit, gedit, kedit, and kwrite). This is a far cry from emacs, which supports its own standards.

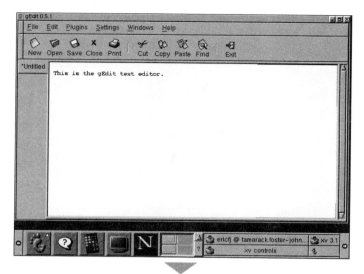

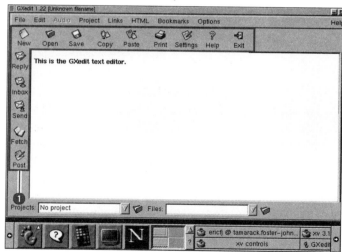

▶ Gedit acts as the text editor for the GNOME desktop.

❶ Select a gxedit editor icon for quick access to common commands.

CROSS-REFERENCE
Chapter 7 covers the GNOME and KDE desktops.

FIND IT ONLINE
The home page for the excellent nedit text editor is located at **fnpspa.fnal.gov/nirvana/nedit.html**.

114

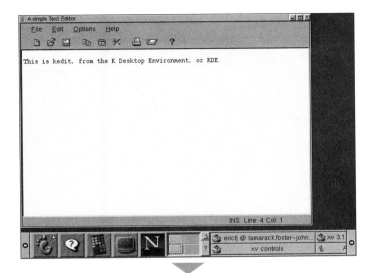

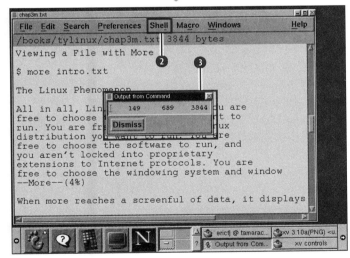

▶ *The kedit text editor provides a simple interface for the KDE desktop.*

❷ *Run commands from the nedit Shell menu, such as **wc** (word count).*

❸ *The output of the **wc** command appears in its own window.*

nedit supports a number of handy things, such as connections to Linux utilities like wc, which you can use to count the number of words in the document. The fourth figure on the facing page shows this in action.

Another great feature of nedit lies in its server mode. Through the **nc** command, you can tell nedit to open a new file. This makes it rather easy to call up the editor, without all the expense in memory and CPU cycles to launch the whole program. Instead, you get just another window in the one instance of the nedit program. Note that the **nc** command conflicts with a network utility program, which is why we usually alias it to **nec** instead, as shown in Chapter 3.

For example, to start a new nedit window — whether or not **nedit** is currently running — type:

```
$ nc filename
```

The **nc** command, short for nedit client, starts nedit in server mode (after asking you) and then calls up an nedit window to edit the passed-in *filename*. You do not have to run this command in the background, as it will soon quit, once having started an nedit session. To avoid being asked each time whether to start nedit, we often alias **nec** to **nc –noask**:

```
$ alias nec='/usr/local/bin/nc –noask'
```

The **–noask** option tells the **nc** that comes with nedit (and we assume that it is installed in /usr/local/bin) to automatically start nedit if needed.

TAKE NOTE

▶ TEXT-BASED EDITORS

Linux offers a number of editors that don't require X Window graphics, including joe and jed, which are both on the CD-ROM.

Spell-Checking Files

In true Linux (and UNIX) fashion, spell checking is not part of some large monolithic application. Instead, spell checking is a separate command that you can call.

Traditional UNIX just supports a **spell** command. When run, **spell** spits out all the words in a text file that it thinks are misspelled. This isn't very helpful.

Linux goes further and supports the more extensive **ispell** command, which will prompt you to change misspelled words. **ispell** also will list near misses, if for example, you misspelled a word by a few letters.

As it detects a misspelled word — really a word that is not in its dictionary — **ispell** will highlight the word, as shown in the first figure on the facing page. You can then type **a** to accept the word as is — that is, don't change it — or a number to select one of the numbered alternatives **ispell** displayed, such as 0 for the first alternative or 1 for the second. **ispell**, like many Linux computer programs, starts counting at 0. Just get used to it.

If you want to accept a spelling of a word in just one instance, press the spacebar instead of a. Pressing a accepts the word for the entire run of the spell-checker. Pressing the spacebar accepts the word once. **ispell** will also flag other occurrences of the word.

Whenever you're done, choose x for exit and save, or q for quit with no save. If you don't save, all your spelling changes will be lost.

Spell-checking in emacs

emacs also supports a spell-check option. From the Edit menu, choose the Spell submenu and then select the Check Buffer choice to check the spelling of all words in the current buffer — normally used to hold a file. This launches a process much like **ispell**.

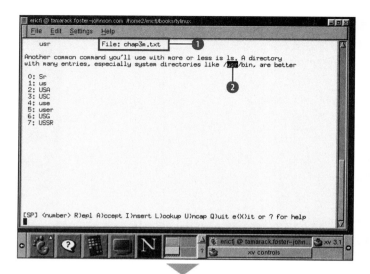

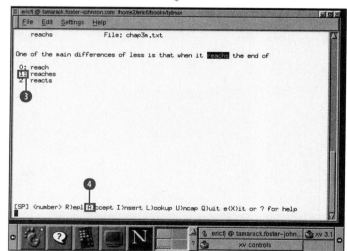

❶ Check the spelling of words in text files with *ispell*.

❷ Words *ispell* doesn't like are highlighted.

❸ Select a number to accept the spelling recommended by *ispell* for a given alternative; for example, 1 for reaches in this case.

❹ Type *a* to accept the word as is.

CROSS-REFERENCE

See "emacs, the Wonder Editor" earlier in this chapter.

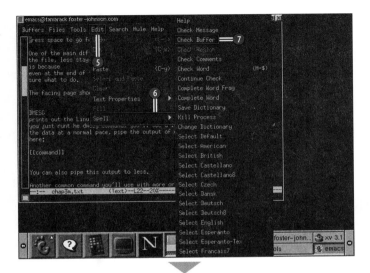

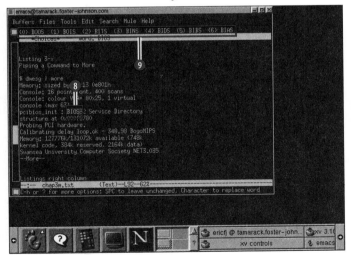

In emacs, the commands you type are essentially the same as for **ispell**. To accept a word without changing it, press the spacebar. To change a word, type in the number of the option that matches which change you want.

To quit the emacs spell checking, use **C-g**, the generic **emacs** cancel command.

If you have a region of text selected, you can choose the Check Region choice from the Spell submenu. This just checks the spelling of the selected words.

> **TAKE NOTE**
>
> ▶ **LINUX SPELL IS NOT UNIX SPELL**
>
> In UNIX, you type the following command to check the spelling of words in a file:
>
> `$ spell `*`filename`*
>
> This won't work in Linux, and the command will seem to hang. What's happening is that the spell command really calls the **ispell** command and **ispell** is waiting for input. Instead, use the following command:
>
> `$ spell < `*`filename`*
>
> This will act like the traditional UNIX **spell** command.

5 Select the Edit menu in emacs.

6 Choose Spell.

7 Choose Check Buffer to call the spell-checker from emacs to check the current file.

8 emacs highlights the word to correct.

9 Select from the choices at the top, or type **a** to accept the word.

> **FIND IT ONLINE**
> For more on **ispell**, see **http://www.gnu.org/software/ispell/ispell.html**.

117

Personal Workbook

Q&A

1 Which command exits vi?

_____

_____

_____

2 Which command exits emacs?

_____

_____

_____

3 How do you search for text in vi?

_____

_____

_____

4 How do you search for text in emacs?

_____

_____

_____

5 How do you get out of insert mode in vi?

_____

_____

_____

6 What can you use to check the spelling of words in a file?

_____

_____

_____

7 How can you call this from emacs?

_____

_____

_____

8 Which commands can you use to read online manual pages with vi?

_____

_____

_____

ANSWERS: PAGE 335

118

EXTRA PRACTICE

1. Call up the emacs tutorial and run through the examples.

2. Call up an info file from emacs. You've now started down the path of performing more commands from within emacs. You will only be happy when you do everything possible from emacs. There is no turning back!

3. The keys H, J, K, and L, are used for left, up, down, and right in vi. Originally, these key bindings were created because terminals didn't have arrow keys. Even so, try out these retro keys and see how easy it is to move about the screen. Especially if you can touch-type, you may find these keys help make vi a much more productive editor.

REAL-WORLD APPLICATIONS

✔ You normally use the **vi** text editor, but you now have a massive text file that's too big for your favorite text editor. Call up the file in emacs to view it.

✔ The spell checker tells you that you made a mistake with a word that you know is correctly spelled. Look the word up in a dictionary just to prove to yourself that automated tools are not perfect — at least not yet.

✔ After looking at all the handy improved features of vim, you may never want to go back to the traditional vi used on UNIX systems. Look up the vim home page and download the source code, so that you can use vim on UNIX systems, too.

Visual Quiz

Which editor is shown here?

_____

_____

_____

_____

_____

_____

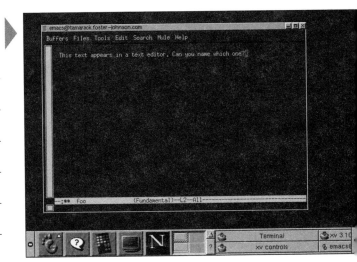

CHAPTER 6

Performing a Full Backup

The most expensive part of a computer to replace is not the disk drive, the CPU, or the other hardware. The most expensive part of the computer is the data stored on it. Computers cost "only" thousands of dollars. The data you put on it is priceless. If you want to keep your data, you must back it up. Most computer professionals backup their systems religiously.

There are many different backup tools distributed with Linux. The most commonly used backup tool is the **tar** command. This tool is available on all UNIX systems and is pretty much the standard when it comes to making tapes for transport from machine to machine.

The **tar** command was followed by the **cpio** command, which was an attempt by AT&T to replace the old **tar** command with something better. It didn't work. People stayed with **tar**. The result is that **cpio** backups are rarely used.

Another standard backup system is the **dump/restore** command pair. These tools are frequently used for system backup. One problem with **dump** is that it places severe limitations on what you can dump. On most systems, the smallest unit you can specify for backup is not a directory but a *partition*. The Linux version of this command has been updated so that you can select individual files or directories to be dumped. But the historical limitations of this program mean that it's rarely used to produce interchange tapes.

In addition to the UNIX standard tools, Linux comes with a lot of homegrown tools, such as taper. This is a GUI-based backup system. However, because it does not come with any standard UNIX system, it's not commonly used. There are many other tools such as BRU, AMANDA, and DIBS, available to the Linux user.

Most of the backup tools are network aware. In other words, you can use the tape on one Linux system to backup the disk on another. This is ideal for small networks such as an office environment where you would like everyone's machine to be backed up to a central server.

Although Linux comes with many different backup systems, we only discuss **tar** in detail. That's because the **tar** command is the most commonly used UNIX backup utility. Also the **tar** command reliably does the backup and recovery operations needed for simple backups.

The Care and Feeding of tar

The **tar** command takes a bunch of files and stores them in an archive. It can also extract the files from an archive.

The parameters of the **tar** command take a little getting used to. The first letter tells **tar** what to do. In this case, the letter **c** indicates that tar is to create an archive.

This is followed by a series of option letters. The first option, **v**, causes **tar** to issue verbose output containing the name of each file as it's added to the archive. If this option is not present, **tar** does its work silently.

The second option, **f**, tells tar that the next argument is the name of the archive file. If this is omitted, **tar** uses the default tape drive as an archive.

Extracting files

To extract files from the archive use the command:

```
$ tar xvf archive
```

If you want to extract particular files, use the command:

```
$ tar xvf archive files
```

The names of the files must exactly match the names of the files in the archive.

Tar and compression

By default the **tar** command only handles archives, it does not perform compression unless we add a -- **gzip** flag.

For example:

```
$ tar cvf /tmp/file.tar .
```

creates an uncompressed archive of the current directory. The command:

```
$ tar cvf /tmp/file.tar.gz -- gzip .
```

creates a compressed archive. (We've used the standard extensions .tar and .tar.gz in this example, but **tar** doesn't care about the extension. It's looking for the -- **gzip** flag only.)

There's one special file that **tar** can read and write. That's the file named "-" which stands for standard in or standard out (depending on whether you are reading or writing).

For example instead of using the command:

```
$ tar tf /tmp/file.tar
```

You can use the command:

```
$ tar tf - </tmp/file.tar
```

To move directories from one place to another, we use one **tar** to create an archive, and pipe it to another **tar** residing in the other directory. For example, let's suppose that we want to move all the files in /mnt/source to /mnt/dest. We would use the command:

```
$ cd /mnt/source
$ tar cf - . | (cd /mnt/dest; tar xvf -)
```

The first command puts in the source directory. The first tar command creates an archive of the current directory (.). This output is sent to the standard output (–). We do not use a **v** option because we don't want to write anything but archive data to the standard out.

The second part of the command is enclosed in (). The cd /mnt/dest changes directory to the destination directory. (Because this command is inside the parentheses, it affects only the commands that follow inside the parentheses.) The **tar xvf –** command extracts files from the standard input. (This is the output of the previous **tar** command.)

Listing 6-1: USING TAR TO CREATE A SIMPLE ARCHIVE

```
$ tar cvf /tmp/cd.tar .
./
cd-speed.cc
Makefile
cd-speed
```

Listing 6-2: GETTING THE TABLE OF CONTENTS OF THE ARCHIVE

```
$ tar tf /tmp/cd.tar
./
cd-speed.cc
Makefile
cd-speed
```

Listing 6-3: EXTRACT THE FILES FROM THE ARCHIVE

```
$ tar xvf /tmp/cd.tar
./
cd-speed.cc
Makefile
cd-speed
```

Listing 6-4: CREATING A COMPRESSED ARCHIVE

```
$ tar cvf /tmp/cd.tar.gz —gzip .
./
cd-speed.cc
Makefile
cd-speed
```

Notice that the size of archive went way down!

```
$ ls -l /tmp/cd.*
-rw-r—r— 1 sdo users 40960 May 2 13:23
/tmp/cd.tar
-rw-r—r— 1 sdo users 10347 May 2 13:24
/tmp/cd.tar.gz
```

Listing 6-5: EXTRACT FILES FROM THE COMPRESSED ARCHIVE

```
$ tar xvf /tmp/cd.tar.gz —gzip
./
cd-speed.cc
Makefile
cd-speed
```

TAKE NOTE

TAR VERSUS CP

There is a recursive copy command **cp –r** that will copy directory trees. But this command does not understand symbolic links or hard links. Symbolic links are changed to actual files in the destination. A file with two hard links is turned into two separate files.

The **tar** command knows all about symbolic links and hard links. These are preserved across a **tar/tar** copy.

DO NOT ARCHIVE THE ARCHIVE

A common mistake that novices make is to issue a **tar** command that inadvertently attempts to include the archive in the archive. For example:

```
$ tar cvf dir.tar .
```

The problem is that dir.tar is in the current directory so **tar** tries to put dir.tar inside dir.tar.

Magnetic Tape Basics

To make the best use of your tape drives, you need to understand how Linux treats them. UNIX has a long history and was invented when standard magnetic tape was a ½-inch reel that stored only a few megabytes. Today, tapes have changed a lot, but the basic tape concept remains the same.

To write a magnetic tape, the drive moves the media across a write head. Electronics in the write head change the magnetic charge on the tape. The data on the tape is written in groups called records. An end-of-record maker follows the record. (On ½-inch tapes, this is a small section of blank tape at the end of the record. Modern tapes use other methods.)

The smallest unit of data that you can read or write on a tape is a record. There is a special record called an end-of-file (EOF) mark. This indicates the end of a tape file. Note: Tape files do not have filenames, instead they have positions (first file on the tape, second file on the tape, etc.) Two EOF marks in a row indicate the end of the data on the tape, called end-of-media or (EOM).

Tape drives pull a little trick when writing tape files. When the file is closed, the driver writes two EOF marks (indicating EOM) and backspaces over one of them. That way if you don't write another file on the tape then the EOM is in it's proper place. If you do, then the first record of the new file will wipe out the EOM and when that file is closed a new EOM will be written on the tape.

Linux does *not* use this trick by default. You must enable it by using the **mt** command:

```
# mt —f /dev/st0 stsetoptions \
two-fms can-bsr
```

The format of the **mt** command is:

```
mt —f device command [count].
```

Device name

Linux supports many different types of tape. Each tape drive has two names, one for the rewinding device, the other the nonrewinding device. (See table at right.)

For example, the first SCSI tape is named /dev/st0 (rewinding) and /dev/nst0 (nonrewinding). When the rewinding device is closed, the tape is rewound. If you use the nonrewinding tape, then when you're done, nothing happens to the tape.

TAKE NOTE

HOW *NOT* TO MOVE A TAPE FORWARD

A common mistake that people make is to use the command:

```
$ mt —f /dev/ftape fsf 1
```

to forward space one file on the tape. The problem is that they are using the rewinding device. The result is that the tape is fast-forwarded one file, and then the device is closed and rewound. The result is that the spacing operating is completely useless. The proper command is:

```
$ mt —f /dev/nftape fsf 1
```

Table 6-1: MT COMMANDS

Command	Description
status	Display the status of the tape drive.
rewind	Rewind command.
offline	Place the tape "offline" and eject the tape
fsf *count*	Forward space files by *count* number.
stoptions **two-eofs** **can-bsr**	Set options (in example, tell the drivers to write two-eofs and backspace over one when the file is closed; can-bsr tells the driver that the drive can execute a backspace record command)
eod	Space to the "end" of data (if two-eofs is set, this will space past the second eof).

Table 6-2: TAPE DEVICES

Name	Description
/dev/ftape	Rewinding floppy tape drive (includes Colorado backup tape drives and other internal tape drives connected to the floppy controller)
/dev/nftape	Nonrewinding floppy tape
/dev/rtf0	Rewinding floppy tape #0 (same as /dev/ftape)
/dev/nrft0	Nonrewinding floppy tape #0
/dev/st0	Rewinding SCSI tape #0
/dev/nst0	Nonrewinding SCSI tape #0
/dev/st1	Rewinding SCSI tape #1
/dev/nrst1	Nonrewinding SCSI tape #1
/dev/ht0	Rewinding IDE tape #0
/dev/nht0	Nonrewinding IDE tape #0
/dev/ht1	Rewinding IDE tape #1
/dev/nht1	Nonrewinding IDE tape #1

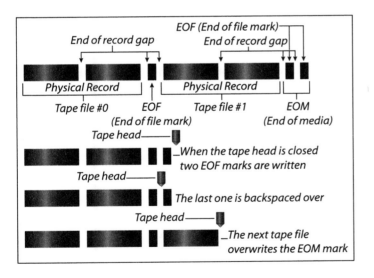

FIND IT ONLINE

The file /usr/doc/HOWTO/Ftape-HOWTO contains information on different kinds of tape drives.

tar and Magnetic Tapes

The tar program was designed to work with tape drives. To write a tar tape, just use a tape device as an output file.

For example to write a tar file containing all the files in the current directory to the floppy tape drive, use the command:

```
$ tar cvf /dev/ftape .
```

This command uses the rewinding tape drive. After the **tar** command finishes the tape is rewound.

To extract the files from the tape, use the command:

```
$ tar xvf /dev/ftape
```

Again, the rewinding tape drive is used.

Multiple tape files

It's possible to put multiple tar archives on a single tape by using the nonrewinding tape device to write multiple tape files. Each tape file contains a single tar archive.

For example:

```
$ cd ~/dir1
$ tar cvf /dev/nftape .
$ cd ~/dir2
$ tar cvf /dev/nftape .
```

Because we are using the nonrewinding tape, the tape is left positioned at the end of the data and not rewound. If we want to use it, we need to rewind it. This is accomplished using the **mt** command:

```
$ mt -f /dev/nftape rewind
```

The **mt** command can perform a variety of positioning commands. The "rewind" command rewinds the tape.

Now let's take a look at what's on the tape. It's obvious to get a table of contents all we need is commands:

```
$ mt -f /dev/nftape rewind
$ tar tf /dev/nftape
$ tar tf /dev/nftape
WRONG WRONG WRONG
```

This example fails. That's because tar is a funny program. When it takes the table of contents of a tape, it knows exactly how much data is on the tape file and stops after it has read all the data. Unfortunately, this is right before the EOF mark. If we do nothing, the next **tar** command will try and read a file, hit the EOF mark, and get nothing.

What we must do instead is:

```
$ mt -f /dev/nftape rewind
$ tar tf /dev/nftape
$ mt -f /dev/nftape fsf 1
$ tar tf /dev/nftape
```

The fsf 1 command tells **mt** to "forward space file" one file. This moves the tape to the beginning of the next tape file and past the EOF.

But note: When **tar** is used to produce compressed archives by adding the --**gzip** option (see below) this bug does *not* occur.

> **TAKE NOTE**
>
> ▶ **STANDARD TRANSFER FORMAT**
> The most common method of transferring data between UNIX and UNIX-like (Linux) systems is a tar tape.

Listing 6-6: MT AND TAR EXAMPLES

```
$ mt —f /dev/nst1 status
SCSI 1 tape drive:
File number=0, block number=0.
Tape block size 1024 bytes. Density code
0x0 (default).
Soft error count since last status=0
General status bits on (41010000):
 BOT ONLINE IM_REP_EN
```

```
$ mt -f /dev/nst1 rewind
$ tar cvf /dev/nst1 ./cd-speed
./cd-speed/
./cd-speed/cd-speed.cc
./cd-speed/Makefile
./cd-speed/cd-speed

$ tar cvf /dev/nst1 ./puzzle
./puzzle/
./puzzle/square.cpp
./puzzle/lamp.p
./puzzle/puzzle.cpp

$ mt -f /dev/nst1 rewind
$ tar tf /dev/nst1
./cd-speed/
./cd-speed/cd-speed.cc
./cd-speed/Makefile
./cd-speed/cd-speed

$ mt -f /dev/nst1 fsf 1
$ tar tf /dev/nst1
./puzzle/
./puzzle/square.cpp
./puzzle/lamp.p
./puzzle/puzzle.cpp
```

Using tar for Tape Backup

This task describes how to construct a shell script to perform nightly backups.

We start by constructing a shell script that contains a simple **tar** command:

```
#!/bin/sh
mt -f /dev/nftape rewind
cd /
tar cf /dev/nftape .
```

This script works well enough, but it would make things a lot easier to maintain if we used a shell variable for the name of the tape device.

```
#!/bin/sh
TAPE=/dev/nftape
mt -f $TAPE rewind
cd /
tar cf $TAPE .
```

The **tar** command dumps everything on the root file system. Including /proc. Because /proc is generated by the operating system and contains nothing that needs to be backed up, let's drop it from the archive by using the --**exclude** command to omit it (notice the dot at the beginning of ./proc):

```
tar cf $TAPE --gzip --exclude ./proc .
```

We want to compress our archive. This is accomplished by adding the --**gzip** option to the **tar** command:

```
tar cf $TAPE --gzip --exclude ./proc .
```

One of the problems with backup tapes is knowing what is on them. A solution is to write the backup script on the tape as the first file.

The **tar** command does a mean thing when the --**gzip** option is specified. Through the use of background processes, the command finishes a little before it frees the tape. That means that if you try to use the tape immediately after the **tar** command finishes, your command will fail because the tape is busy. The solution is to do a **sleep 30** (a command that waits 30 seconds) just after the **tar** to let things settle out.

This is done with the **dd** command. This command can precisely control the way data is read and written. In this case, we want to write out 1K physical records because that's what almost all tape drives accept.

Our **dd** command looks like:

```
dd if=$0 of=$TAPE bs=1k conv=sync
```

(This is explained in detail to the right.)

Testing the script

To test the script, as root, execute the command:

```
# sh -x /root/dump/full.sh
```

The **sh -x** command tells the shell (**sh**) to execute the script with echo on (–**x**). With echo enabled, the shell writes out each command in the script before executing it. The tape should spin and things should be backed up.

Let's now write-protect the tape and take a look at it. (Write protection prevents a mistake from erasing a tape.) When looking at a tape, make sure you start at the beginning by rewinding the tape:

```
# mt -f /dev/nftape rewind
```

Next, look at the first tape file. That's the script that wrote the tape. To extract and view it, use the commands:

```
# dd if=/dev/nftape of=/tmp/script.txt
bs=1k
# more /tmp/script.txt
```

The next tape file is the first **tar** file. The **tar tf** gets the contents of the tape:

```
# tar tf /dev/nfstape --gzip
```

If things went well with the backup, you will get a directory of all the files that were backed up. You will also see a warning:

```
gzip: stdin: decompression OK, trailing
garbage ignored
tar: Child returned status 2
tar: Error exit delayed from previous errors
```

This is caused by the data being written to the tape in fixed-size blocks. It can safely be ignored.

Listing 6-7: FULL.SH

```
#!/bin/sh
#
# Performs a full backup
#
TAPE=/dev/nst0
mt -f $TAPE rewind
#
# Create a timestamp file for future
# incremental backups
#
touch /root/full_timestamp
# Backup the backup script
dd if=$0 of=$TAPE bs=1k conv=sync
# Backup the system
cd /
tar cfl $TAPE --gzip .
```

Listing 6-8: SAMPLE BACKUP AND TEST RUN

```
# sh -x /root/dump/full.sh
+ TAPE=/dev/nst0
+ mt -f /dev/nst0 rewind
+ touch /root/full_timestamp
+ dd if=/root/dump/full.sh of=/dev/nst0
bs=1k conv=sync
0+1 records in
1+0 records out
+ cd /
+ tar cfl /dev/nst0 --gzip --exclude ./proc
.
+ sleep 30
# mt -f /dev/nst0 rewind
```

```
# dd if=/dev/nst0 of=/tmp/full.tmp bs=1k
1+0 records in
1+0 records out
# tar tf /dev/nst0 --gzip
./
lost+found/
mnt/
mnt/floppy/
etc/exports
etc/group
....
```

```
gzip: stdin: decompression OK, trailing
garbage ignored
tar: Child returned status 2
tar: Error exit delayed from previous errors
```

Table 6-3: PARAMETERS TO THE DD COMMAND

Parameter	Description
if=*file*	The name of the input file (default=stdin).
of=*file*	The name of the output file (default=stdout).
bs=*size*	Size of the block to be read or written. On disks, size does not matter. On tape drives, this is the size of a physical record. Some tape drives limit the physical record size allowed. A size of 1K works for almost all tape drives.
conv=sync	Conversion specification. There are a variety of conversions allowed. The sync conversion tells **dd** to pad any short blocks to make them fill a complete block.

Incremental Dumps

A full backup copies all the files on your system to tape. It's the simplest and most complete form of backup. It's also the one that takes the longest and uses the most tape.

Many times you may want to do an incremental backup. That's where you back up only the files that have changed since a certain date, such as the time you did your last full backup.

Doing an incremental backup is a more work because you need to first find the set of files that need to be backed up, and then copy them to tape.

The **find** command has options that enable you to find all the files that are newer than a given file. This is useful in incremental backups.

A little preparation is needed. You need to change your full backup script to change the modification date of a timestamp file just before doing the **tar**. That way you can use this file as a marker so that you can backup all files that were changed since your timestamp.

The **touch** command makes the system think that a file has been modified. The file is not changed, but the system doesn't know that, so it changes the modification date. So to create a timestamp file whose modification date indicates the time the last full backup was done, put the line:

```
touch /root/full_timestamp
```

in full.sh just before the **tar** command.

Now when you want to do an incremental dump, you can ask the **find** command to locate all the files that have been modified since /root/full_timestamp.

The actual **find** command is

```
find . —type f \
—newer /root/full_timestamp \
-print
```

This command prints out, one per line, the names of all files modified after (–newer) than /root/full_time-stamp.

Now, for a case of extreme weirdness: There is a bug in this code. It doesn't properly handle the case where a file name has a newline in it. Believe it or not, Linux allows you to put control characters (including newline) inside filenames. No one sane ever does it, but we want our backup to be bulletproof and handle insane cases.

The **find** command has an option (—**print0**) that uses the null character instead of newline to separate names. This solved our problem because null is one of the two characters not allowed in a Linux filename. (The other one is slash.)

The output of **find** can be piped to a **tar** command. We need to tell **tar** that it's going to receive a list of files from the standard input. That's done with the" --**files_from** – option.

Another option (--**null**) tells **tar** that this is a null-terminated list. So our backup command is

```
find . —type f \
-newer /root/full_timestamp \
-print0 | \
tar cf /dev/nftape —files_from - \
--null --gzip
```

You'll be happy to know that this works — almost. There is one little problem that remains to be solved. The problem is that **tar** doesn't like to create an archive with nothing in it. So, if you don't change any file, the **tar** will break.

The solution is simple: make sure you modify a file between backups. One way to do that is to use the **touch** command to modify a file just before you do the **tar**:

```
# touch /tmp/dump.me
```

The full incremental script can be seen in Listing 6-9.

Listing 6-9: SAMPLE TEST RUN OF BOTH FULL AND INCREMENTAL BACKUPS

```
sh -x /root/dump/full.sh
+ TAPE=/dev/nst0
+ mt -f /dev/nst0 rewind
+ touch /root/full_timestamp
+ dd if=/root/dump/full.sh of=/dev/nst0
bs=1k conv=sync
0+1 records in
1+0 records out
+ cd /
+ tar cfl /dev/nst0 --gzip --exclude ./proc
.
+ sleep 30
sh -x /root/dump/inc.sh
+ TAPE=/dev/nst0
+ mt -f /dev/nst0 eod
+ dd if=/root/dump/inc.sh of=/dev/nst0
bs=1k conv=sync
0+1 records in
1+0 records out
+ touch /tmp/dump.me
+ cd /
+ find . -type f -newer
/root/full_timestamp -print0
+ grep -v ^\./proc
+ tar cf /dev/nst0 --gzip --null --files-
from -
+ sleep 30
```

▶ Rewind the tape and get the table of contents for the full backup.

```
# mt -f /dev/nst0 rewind
# dd if=/dev/nst0 of=/tmp/full.tmp bs=1k
1+0 records in
1+0 records out
# tar tf /dev/nst0 --gzip >/tmp/full.toc
```

```
gzip: stdin: decompression OK, trailing
garbage ignored
tar: Child returned status 2
tar: Error exit delayed from previous
errors
```

▶ Now we do a sleep 30 to wait for the **tar** command to release the tape.

```
# sleep 30
```

▶ Now get the table of contents for the incremental dump.

```
# dd if=/dev/nst0 of=/tmp/inc.tmp bs=1k
1+0 records in
1+0 records out
# tar tf /dev/nst0 --gzip
```

```
gzip: stdin: decompression OK, trailing
garbage ignored
tar: Child returned status 2
tar: Error exit delayed from previous
errors
# sleep 30
```

Scheduling the Backup

Let's now plan a weeks' worth of backups. For Monday, we do a full backup so our mon.sh script looks like this:

```
#!/bin/sh
# Do a full dump
/home/root/dump/full.sh
```

Tuesday through Saturday we do an incremental dump. The scripts look like this:

```
#!/bin/sh
# Do a incremtal dump
/home/root/dump/inc.sh
```

To make administration a little easier, we create five scripts called tue.sh, wed.sh, thur.sh, and fri.sh.

Sunday, we do an incremental dump, but also we eject the tape:

```
#!/bin/sh
# Do a incremtal dump
/home/root/dump/inc.sh
# Eject the tape
mt -f /dev/nftape off
```

Scheduling the script

Now that we have a backup script, the next step is to schedule it. Start the linuxconf program by selecting Foot ⇨ System ⇨ LinuxConf. Select the Control ⇨ Configure superuser schedule item.

Click Add to add a new entry to the list of scheduled jobs. We'll now fill in the entry for Monday. Enter the name of the command to run in the Command blank. You should use the full path of the command to be run. In this case, it's /usr/root/dump/mon.sh.

The Months entry determines which months this script is to run. You can select *, in which case the script will run all months. In this case, we want backups to run all the time, so we leave the entry as *.

The Day of the Month entry selects which day of the month to use. Again, this does not matter for a weekly full backup, so leave it *.

The Day of the Week does matter. For Monday we want this entry to be a 1. (If you want a script to run multiple days you can enter multiple days separated by a slash, such as 1/3/5, or a range of days 2–5.)

The script should run at 2:00 a.m., so put 2 in the Hours and 00 in the minutes.

Click Accept to accept this entry.

This process is repeated for the script for each of the other days of the week. When you are done, click Act/Changes to install the changes and exit.

Now when 2:00 a.m. comes, a script is automatically started. Any output is saved and sent to root as a mail message. If all goes well, you'll get a mail message each morning telling you how well your backups went.

132

Listing 6-10: MON.SH

```
#!/bin/sh
/root/dump/full.sh
```

Listing 6-11: TUE.SH

```
#!/bin/sh
/root/dump/inc.sh
```

Listing 6-12: WED.SH

```
#!/bin/sh
/root/dump/inc.sh
```

Listing 6-13: THUR.SH

```
#!/bin/sh
/root/dump/inc.sh
```

Listing 6-14: FRI.SH

```
#!/bin/sh
/root/dump/inc.sh
```

Listing 6-15: SAT.SH

```
#!/bin/sh
/root/dump/inc.sh
```

Listing 6-16: SUN.SH

```
#!/bin/sh
/root/dump/inc.sh
mt -f /dev/nftape off
```

▶ *Some of these scripts are the same so as to illustrate their flexibility. You can easily add different daily tasks to the scripts without having to change the schedule.*

TAKE NOTE

▶ **THE BACKUP TORTURE TEST**

A while ago a system administrator for a major university tested a variety of UNIX backup systems under extreme conditions. The most difficult thing for some systems to handle was files with "holes" in them — files written out by some strange programs that look like they have a lot of data in them. What they really have is a little data at the beginning of the file, a little data at the end, and nothing in-between.

Files that contain holes are very difficult to deal with. If you copy them, the copy command fills the hole, causing the amount of disk space consumed by the file to skyrocket. Most backup programs have trouble with them, too. It's next to impossible to tell the difference between a file full of nothing and a file with a hole in it.

The result of the testing was that all backup systems failed. Not one could handle all the test cases correctly. The GNU **tar** program did fairly well and was able to backup and restore most of the files. At that time it could not handle file names with newlines in them and some of the longer filenames.

Since that time GNU **tar** has been augmented and enhanced. Even today, however, it would probably not pass the backup torture test (the test is very extreme), but it should be capable of handling all of your backup and restore needs.

Backup Comparisons

Linux comes with a variety of backup tools. In this task, we compare the features of the various programs.

tar

The **tar** command is the old UNIX standard. It is a command-line only utility; there is no GUI version available.

One of the nice things about Linux is its capability to do networking. **tar** makes use of this through its capability to use a tape drive on another system over the network. For example, if you specify the tape name /dev/ftape, the tape on the local machine is used, but if you specify a name such as zabbar:/dev/ftape, then the program will use the tape device on the zabbar system.

The Linux version of **tar** can also handle large backups that span multiple tapes. When the first tape fills up, **tar** prompts for the next tape. The **tar** command can even be configured to run a script when the tape gets full. This is useful when you have an autoloader that can change tapes automatically.

The **tar** command can perform compression while backing up. Frequently the compression system used by **tar** (**gzip**) performs better than the hardware compression built into most modern tape drives.

One disadvantage of **tar** is the way it writes files on tapes. The general format of the tape is:

```
file header, file data
file header, file data
file header, file data
...
```

To get a table of contents or restore a file, the entire tape must be read.

cpio

The **cpio** command was an attempt by AT&T to create a better **tar**. One of the major problems with the **cpio** program is its limited functionality. To use it to do real backups, you must not only know the **cpio** command, but also the **find** command.

Like tar, the **cpio** command handles both local and remote tapes. A big drawback of **cpio** is that it does not handle multiple tapes.

Compression is not built into **cpio**, but it's possible to use **cpio** and **gzip** to create compressed tapes.

Finally, **cpio** writes tapes using the header/data format like **tar** does. This means that getting files or getting a table of contents requires scanning the entire tape.

Another big drawback of **cpio** is that it uses a nonstandard format. Actually, **cpio** takes the term nonstandard to new levels. It's not even compatible with itself. There are several **cpio** formats, each created by a different manufacturer. Also, there is a compatibility mode, which generates yet another different format. The result is that unless you know exactly how a **cpio** tape was created, you are going to have a lot of fun trying to read it.

dump/restore

Programs such as **cpio** and **tar** use the same program to read and write tapes. With the **dump/restore** programs, one program, **dump**, writes the tape and the other, **restore**, reads it.

134

The **dump** program is another UNIX standard backup program. It was designed back in the days of ½-inch tape and is still in love with this type of tape. Many of the parameters used by dump are based on this format, so adjustments must be made if you are using other types of tapes.

The **dump** program can write multiple tapes, but you must estimate the size of the tape before writing it. If your estimate is too small, you waste tape. Too big, and **dump** runs out of tape and aborts. Getting the size right is difficult especially with the compression that is built into most modern drives.

The **dump** program does not compress the data on the drive.

Although the **dump** command is extremely difficult to use, the **restore** command is just the opposite. The "interactive" restore mode gives you a minishell in which you can browse the file system and select the files to restore.

Also, because the **dump** program writes a table of contents at the beginning of the tape, getting a table of contents, or starting a **restore** is fast because the **restore** program does not have to scan the entire tape to find out what's on it.

taper

The **taper** program is an interactive backup program. It provides a nice, easy-to-use interface. It comes with all the features you could want in a backup system — compression, multiple tapes, and other features.

It keeps the list of files on the tape in a database on disk. This makes getting the content of a tape or restoring a single file extremely fast. If a tape is not in the database, the tape must be scanned before it can be used. This can take some time.

There is a major drawback to this program, however: it is not as mature and reliable as other backup system. As a result, its reliability is not as good as **tar**, **cpio**, or **dump**.

Table 6-4: BACKUP PROGRAM COMPARISONS

Tool	Ease of Use	Reliability	Remote Tapes	Multiple Tapes	Compression	Table of Contents
tar	B	A	Yes	Yes	Yes	File headers
cpio	C	C (format problems)	Yes	No	No (can use gzip externally)	File headers
taper	A	B	No	Yes	Yes	Disk database
dump/restore	C/A	A	Yes	Yes (badly)	No	Beginning

Personal Workbook

Q&A

1 What does the **v** option mean in the following command?

```
tar cvf /dev/nst0 /home/sdo
```

_____

_____

2 How do you get a table of contents of a tape using **tar**?

_____

_____

3 What's the difference between a tape file and a disk file?

_____

_____

4 Which option to **tar** turns on compression?

_____

_____

5 The following commands are used to backup two different directories.

```
$ mt —f /dev/nftape rewind
$ tar cf /dev/nftape ./first
$ tar cf /dev/nftape ./second
```

How would you extract all the files in the directory "second"?

_____

_____

_____

6 A system administrator decided to use the following two commands to position the tape at the beginning of the second tape file. But he did something wrong. What?

```
$ mt —f /dev/ftape rewind
$ mt —f /dev/ftape fsf 1
```

_____

_____

_____

7 If you write a compressed archive and try to read it without the **--gzip** option, will it work?

_____

_____

8 Why should you avoid the **cpio** program?

_____

_____

ANSWERS: PAGE 336

136

EXTRA PRACTICE

1 Backup a directory tree to a file using tar. Take the table of contents of the archive and restore it to a temporary directory.

2 Backup a directory tree to a file using tar, only this time use a compressed archive.

3 Write three tar archives to a tape. Get the table of contents of each archive.

4 Execute an info tar command and review the online documentation for tar.

5 Write a backup script and try it out.

6 Use cron to schedule regular backups.

REAL-WORLD APPLICATIONS

✔ A company keeps its business records on the computer. To make sure that everything is safe in case the building should burn down, the company makes two copies and stores one at an offsite location.

✔ The help desk got a call from a student who couldn't find his files. After a little investigation, the help desk found out that the last time the student logged in was *more than five* years ago. Since that time, the computing center had gone to a different type of backup media (three times) and switched to a different backup program (twice). Yet the senior administrator who was a fanatic about keeping old backup programs and tape drives around was able to restore his data.

Visual Quiz

What command is being scheduled and when will it run?

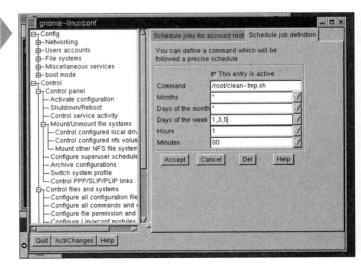

PART II

The Linux Desktop

Linux is based on UNIX, an operating system famous for short, quirky commands. Even so, today's Linux sports a modern graphical user interface. This part covers the Linux desktop and how you can make the most of it.

As discussed in Chapter 7, Linux graphics come from the X Window System. This generic windowing interface doesn't lock you into any particular user interface; you can layer just about any interface on top of X.

Two such interfaces include the GNOME and KDE desktop environments. Each aims to provide a complete user-friendly interface on top of Linux. Red Hat Linux, discussed in this book, supports both KDE and GNOME, but the default environment for Red Hat is GNOME.

Chapter 8 covers the productivity applications that come with the GNOME and KDE desktops, along with applications that aren't connected to either interface. Linux lets you freely choose the programs that you want to run regardless of the desktops they support.

Even with a desktop environment, you'll still need to enter Linux commands. Chapter 9 covers the special windows that wrap the Linux command-line shells.

No desktop would be complete without the capability to play music and sounds. Chapter 10 covers how to do this from Linux.

Chapter 11 covers working with that other major operating system that runs on PCs. You can share files, read disks, and even run some applications with a special program called **wine**.

Chapter 12 rounds out the desktop by covering the after-hours fun you can have with Linux by playing games.

CHAPTER 7

MASTER
THESE
SKILLS

▶ Introducing the Desktop
▶ Configuring the Red Hat Desktop
▶ Resources and Resource Files
▶ Window Managers
▶ Screen Savers and Backgrounds
▶ Setting Up an X Login

The X Window System

In a computing galaxy long ago and far away, each UNIX workstation vendor invented its own incompatible windowing system. Organizations that had systems from multiple vendors were left in the cold when it came to writing applications in these windowing systems. Developers had to write software for each separate system, and no system was like another. At the time, vendors probably thought this form of customer lock-in was a great thing. Then along came the X Window System. Developed by the Massachusetts Institute of Technology, X provided a windowing system that ran on workstations from a number of vendors. This, and the fact that it was released for free, meant that X caught on like wildfire. When Linux came on the scene and needed graphics, it only made sense to port X.

X reverses the usual concept of client and server. The server resides on your desktop, controls the windows on the display, and accepts input from the keyboard and mouse. Clients, or X applications, communicate with the X server and request that the server draw images and send keystrokes to the application. These clients can run on your Linux system or on any other system on the network. This network transparency means that you can run X applications on other systems—taking advantage of their computing power—and display them on your desktop.

Another key feature of X is the strict devotion to the idea that X provides the mechanism to get things done, but not the policy that dictates how you have to do things. This is especially true in the area of user interfaces.

On top of the relatively low-level X programming APIs, you can layer any type of user interface you want. This is a freedom you simply don't have on Windows or Mac OS systems.

Today, X, in the form of XFree86, provides the graphics on Linux. Red Hat chose the GNOME environment to form the default desktop. The GNOME environment includes quite a few new applications that sport a much better user interface than older X programs such as xman or xterm.

You get this environment when you log in and enter the **startx** command:

```
$ startx
```

Don't run this command if you already have a graphic environment displayed. (For example, after reading the "setting up an X login" task, you may have a graphics environment from the moment Linux boots. In that case, you don't need to run **startx**.)

Introducing the Desktop

The desktop is what you see when you start X via the **startx** command. Starting with Release 6.0, the default Red Hat desktop is provided by GNOME, short for the GNU Network Object Model Environment. GNOME provides a desktop like that shown in the first figure on the facing page. Some users run an alternate desktop, the K Desktop Environment, or KDE. (By default, the Red Hat install program will not install KDE. If you want KDE, be sure to install it.) Some users don't run a big environment at all, because both GNOME and KDE require a lot of RAM and computing power.

Whether or not you use GNOME, the techniques described in this chapter apply to all X environments. You may need to call up a different dialog under KDE to configure something, but the actions are very similar.

The basic desktop starts out pretty empty, with the GNOME help program and file manager. The first thing you are likely to do is start a program or two. You can start programs from the desktop by clicking the launch icons at the bottom of the screen or from the main menu on the taskbar. You call up this menu by clicking the GNOME footprint icon on the taskbar at the bottom of the screen. One of the best features of GNOME is that it also shows the menus from AnotherLevel (yet another desktop environment) and KDE.

Once you have a few programs on the screen, you'll notice that one window is highlighted differently from the rest. This is the window with the keyboard focus. Any text that you type at the keyboard goes to this window. To switch the keyboard focus to another window, click the mouse in that other window. That window should rise to the top and display the special highlighting. Only one window at a time can accept keyboard input.

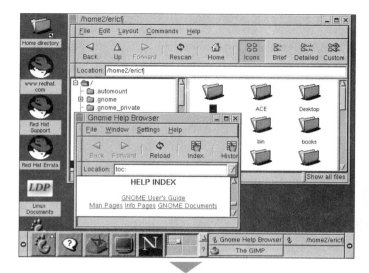

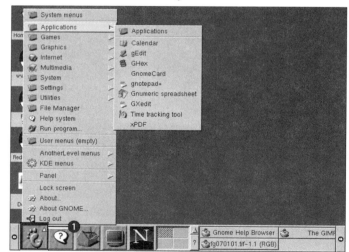

▶ *Run the **startx** command to see this initial GNOME desktop.*

❶ *Click the GNOME menu icon to see all these applications and submenus. These menus provide convenient access to a huge number of applications.*

CROSS-REFERENCE

Chapter 8 covers the major desktop applications.

142

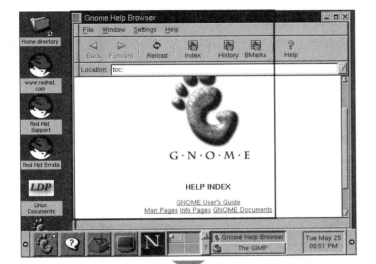

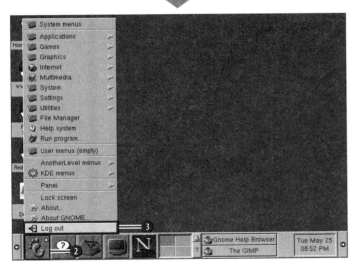

Much of your interaction with the system comes from the mouse. X assumes that you have a three-button mouse. With a two-button mouse, you can emulate the middle mouse button by clicking both mouse buttons simultaneously.

In most cases, the leftmost mouse button does most of the work of selecting things and making windows active. The rightmost mouse button will often pop up a menu, just like on Windows. Also like Windows, you can double-click or triple-click a mouse button.

Continued

TAKE NOTE

► LEFTIES UNITE

To reverse the left and right mouse buttons, use the following command:

```
$ xmodmap -e "pointer = 3 2 1"
```

To restore the mouse buttons to the original order, use this command:

```
$ xmodap -e "pointer = 1 2 3"
```

► QUITTING GNOME

We discovered a bug when trying to quit GNOME — many times it simply won't quit. If you face this, press the Ctrl+Alt+Backspace keys and X should exit.

► *Call up online help documents normally served up by the **info** and **man** commands from the GNOME help window.*

❷ *Select the GNOME footprint icon to call up the menu.*

❸ *Choose Log out to exit the GNOME desktop and X. GNOME will prompt you to confirm your choice.*

FIND IT ONLINE

The KDE project home page is **http://www.kde.org.**

Introducing the Desktop
Continued

You can launch X applications from the GNOME desktop, or from the command line. Many programs provide a command line window, sporting your default shell (typically bash). From the shell prompt, you can also launch X Window applications.

Furthermore, most X programs accept a similar set of command-line parameters. Not all do, but most X programs support the options shown in Table 7-1.

One of the best features of X lies in its capability to run a program on one system and display the results on another. You do this by telling the program the name of the X display — the X server — it should connect to. You can set this name in the DISPLAY environment variable, or pass it with the **-display** command-line parameter. The basic format is:

```
-display hostname:server.screen
```

The *hostname* is the name of the system with the X server. The *server* number identifies which X server on the *hostname* you want. In most cases, there is only one X server on a given machine, so this number is almost always 0. (The counting starts with zero instead of one.) The *screen* number identifies which screen — usually a physical monitor — to display on. The vast majority of X servers have a single monitor, so, again, this number is almost always 0. As of this writing, the XFree86 X servers do not support multiple screens, but commercial X servers from companies such as Xi Graphics, do. For example:

```
$ xclock -display tamarack:0
```

tells the xclock program to display on machine tamarack on the first X server. Most X servers are set by default not to accept connections from clients running on other hosts or by different users. To find out how to set up X to allow clients to run over the network, read the Remote X Apps mini-HOWTO.

Setting window size and position

The X coordinate system starts out at 0,0 at the upper-left corner of the display. X values increase going across the screen, and Y values increase going down. Most X applications accept a **-geometry** command-line parameter, which you can use to set the size or position (or both) of a window. For the position, you provide the X and Y values for the upper-left corner of the window. For example, the following command starts the **xclock** application at 200 pixels across the screen and 350 pixels down:

```
$ xclock -geometry +200+350
```

If you want to control the starting size of the window, pass the width and height — as pixel values — first:

```
$xclock -geometry 100x120+200+350
```

This sets the starting size at 100 pixels wide by 120 pixels high, with the position the same as last time. You can skip the position if you just want to set the starting size:

```
$xclock -geometry 100x120
```

Table 7-2 covers the strange 0,0 positioning that indicates the four corners of the display.

CROSS-REFERENCE
Chapter 9 covers the GNOME terminal program.

FIND IT ONLINE
Find Xi Graphics at **http://www.xig.com**.

TAKE NOTE

SECURITY ISSUES WITH MULTIPLE DISPLAYS

When you try to connect to another X server, you may get a security error. The xhost program enables you to turn on access to your display from programs running on a particular host. To enable access for a host named nicollet, use the following command on your display:

```
$ xhost +nicollet
nicollet being added to
access control list
```

To enable access from any host, which is a security risk, use this command:

```
$ xhost +
access control disabled,
clients can
connect from any host
```

To disallow access for a particular system, use a minus instead of a plus. For example:

```
$ xhost -nicollet
nicollet being removed
from access
control list
```

The xauth program sets up an authorization key that X applications must present to connect.

LOCATIONS OF X PROGRAMS

Most X programs are stored in the /usr/X11R6/bin directory. GNOME programs reside in /usr/bin, as do KDE programs.

In general, programs that are window managers have *wm* in their name, and programs that provide a shell window have *term* in their name.

Table 7-1: COMMON X COMMAND-LINE PARAMETERS

Parameter	Usage
–geometry *WidthxHeight+X+Y*	Sets the starting size and position of the window with *Width* by *Height*, at *X, Y*.
–display *hostname*: *server*.screen	Start X program displaying on X *server* and *screen* on *hostname*.
–fg *color*	Set program's foreground *color*.
–bg *color*	Set program's background *color*.
–foreground *color*	Set program's foreground *color*.
–background *color*	Set program's background *color*.
–rv	Reverse video, that is, swap the foreground and background colors.
–iconic	Starts window as an icon.
-help	Provides help for a GNOME application.
–xrm "X resource value"	Sets a given X resource value. See the task on X resource files for more on this.

Table 7-2: SPECIFYING THE CORNERS OF THE DISPLAY

Value	Which Corner
+0+0	Upper-left corner
+0-0	Lower-left corner
-0+0	Upper-right corner
-0-0	Lower-right corner

Configuring the Red Hat Desktop

If you're running the GNOME desktop, you can configure much of the desktop from the handy GNOME Control Center, shown on the facing page. From this panel, you can set up screen backgrounds, choose a theme for the GNOME look, adjust keyboard and mouse parameters, and more.

When you quit GNOME, it saves the location of the windows on your display, if desired. GNOME tries to restore these windows the next time you enter the GNOME desktop (that is, the next time you run the **startx** command).

GNOME supports multiple virtual desktops, screen-sized areas that help you organize your work. Each desktop displays the GNOME taskbar and its own set of windows. By default, GNOME provides four areas shown in the pager in the first figure on the facing page. (This may sound confusing. If so, try switching between virtual areas and it should become clear very fast.)

By selecting the *Panel* submenu and the choice for *This panel properties*, you can control where the GNOME taskbar goes, as well as whether it should show the hide buttons at the far ends of the taskbar.

The *Settings* menu provides a large number of choices for controlling the desktop, from sounds to the menu editor, shown in the last image on the facing page.

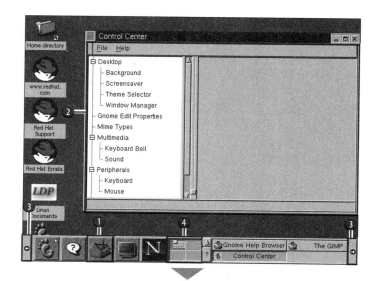

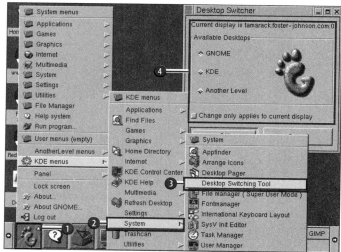

❶ Click the configuration tool icon.

❷ Change settings from the GNOME Control Center.

❸ Click the hide button to shrink the taskbar.

❹ Click in the pager to switch the virtual desktop.

❶ Select the GNOME footprint icon.

❷ Call up the KDE System menu.

❸ Choose the Desktop Switching Tool.

❹ From this window, select GNOME, KDE, or AnotherLevel, the older Red Hat desktop.

CROSS-REFERENCE

The task, "Window Managers," later in this chapter shows how to change the number of virtual desktops.

146

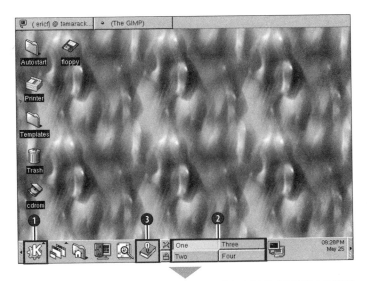

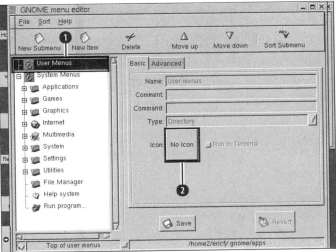

❶ *From the K icon, you can call up menus to select applications.*

❷ *KDE supports multiple desktops, defaulting to the four shown here.*

❸ *Select the KDE help icon for help.*

❶ *Call up the GNOME menu editor from the taskbar Settings menu. (This menu provides a plethora of ways to configure your desktop.) Modify the menu from the menu editor.*

❷ *To pick an icon for your new menu choice, click the icon button, currently labeled No Icon because you haven't selected one yet.*

TAKE NOTE

▶ INSTALLING KDE

If you prefer to run the KDE environment, you can install the KDE RPM files when you install Red Hat Linux. If installed, you will see the KDE menus under the GNOME menus. To switch to KDE from GNOME, select the KDE *System* menu from the GNOME taskbar and select the Desktop Switching Tool. You can now select from GNOME, KDE, or the AnotherLevel (from Red Hat 5.2) desktops.

After switching the desktop, you need to quit the desktop and restart X for the changes to take effect.

To switch back to GNOME from KDE, you can run the program switchdesk-gnome. This displays the same window you used to switch to KDE in the first place. Now, you can switch back to GNOME. Again, you need to exit X and restart — but from KDE this time.

▶ .XINITRC VERSUS .XCLIENTS

If you choose not to run GNOME or KDE, you can use the older Red Hat desktop. On this desktop, you can control the starting applications by editing a file named .Xclients-default in your home directory. This file is a shell script, and you can simply add in the commands to run, ensuring that all commands — except for the last — have an ampersand (&), which indicates that the commands are run in the background. If you do run GNOME or KDE, you'll see short commands in this file, exec gnome-session for GNOME and startkde for KDE.

The rest of the world — Linux and UNIX — uses a file named .xinitrc to store the X Window applications to start when you run the startx command. Red Hat Linux chose .Xclients-default for some bizarre reason. However, .xinitrc will run perfectly fine.

FIND IT ONLINE

The main GNOME home page is http://www.gnome.org.

Resources and Resource Files

Most X programs — but not all — get configuration information from settings stored in X resource files. As with most things on Linux, X resource files are text files that contain individual resources and values for those resources.

A resource file contains resource-setting commands, and each command has the following format:

`resource_to_set : value_to_use`

For example:

`*background: maroon`

This sets the background resource to the value maroon. As you'd expect, this tells X applications to use maroon for the background color. The * has special significance. The * acts as a wildcard, much like with directory listings. What really happens inside an X application is that a particular widget — such as a menu choice, or push button, or toggle — looks for its background resource. If nothing more specific is set, then this wildcard setting applies.

A more specific setting uses a dot notation to specify an exact entry, such as the following:

`xfm.viewport.toggle.background: white`

This also sets the background resource, to white in this case, but only for a particular named widget, xfm.viewport.toggle. The last part of the name is the resource to set, and the first part names the particular part of the interface.

In general, you won't set the values of particular widgets unless you're writing graphical programs. For most applications, you can start with the application's name and a resource value. For example, this setting states that any application looking for **emacs** resources should use an orange background, which takes precedence over the more general *background setting shown previously:

`emacs*background: orange`

Resource files

Applications look for resources in X resource files. A common general purpose file is .Xdefaults, which is found in your home directory. (Note the leading dot, which makes this a "hidden" file.)

Applications also support their own class-based X resource files. Each application has a name and a class name, which you can find from the handy **xprop** command:

`$ xprop | grep WM_CLASS`

Enter this command and then when the cursor changes to a cross, select the window you are interested in. You'll see output such as the following:

`WM_CLASS(STRING) = "xclock", "XClock"`

Use the second, capitalized value as the class name. Once you have the class name, you can create an X resource file of that name, XClock in this case, in your home directory. The online documentation for X applications should cover any resources supported.

The facing page shows examples with the xclock and xterm applications.

TAKE NOTE

WORK THROUGH THE DESKTOP IF POSSIBLE

Both the GNOME and KDE desktops permit a lot of menu-based configuration. Use these where available, because GNOME and KDE applications tend to ignore X resource files and use their own mechanisms, such as the GNOME themes, for setting values like colors and fonts.

CROSS-REFERENCE

For more on resources, see the UNIX Administrator's Guide to X, listed in Appendix B.

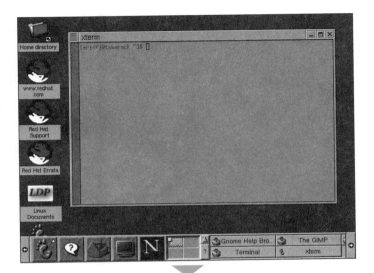

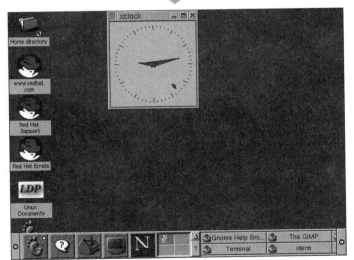

▶ Save this file under the name **XTerm** in your home directory. Then run the xterm program. Note how the colors change from the defaults.

▶ The effects of the resource file in Listing 7-1 on the **xterm** program.

▶ Save this file under the name **XClock** in your home directory. Then run the xclock program. The resources are described in the xclock online manual page.

▶ The changes to the xclock program appear when you next run the application.

Listing 7-1: THE XTERM FILE

```
! The ! indicates a comment.


! Default for xterm is black on white,

! so we switch that.

!

*foreground: maroon

*background: orange


! End of file XTerm (note capitalization).
```

Listing 7-2: THE XCLOCK FILE

```
! We'll change xclock to

! show a red background.

*background: bisque2


! The foreground just colors the tic marks.

*foreground: navyblue

*hands: maroon


! A value of 30 seconds or less will

! cause xclock to display a seconds

! hand. If you don't set it to 1,

! it won't move every second.

*update: 1
```

FIND IT ONLINE

For programs to edit resources, see **http://www. motifzone.com/tmd/articles/Editres2/Editres2.html**.

Window Managers

Windowing systems, such as Microsoft Windows, Mac OS, or Be OS, integrate the window manager as part of the system. X does not, which leads to a lot of confusion. X enables you to choose among window managers, so if you don't like what you see, you can always find something else to try.

In X, the window manger is simply another X client application. Windows managers are special in that you can run only one and they have certain rights over the desktop. The window manager:

- ▶ Controls how windows get placed on the screen.
- ▶ Provides the means to move and resize windows.
- ▶ Totally controls the title bar area and window frame on each top-level window.
- ▶ May enable you to minimize or iconify windows.
- ▶ May provide for multiple workspaces.

Window managers provide a distinctive look, but only for the title bars and borders of windows. This makes window managers more confusing to some. Some window managers, notably WindowMaker, provide a look and feel similar to that of the NeXTStep interface common on older NeXT computers. If the window manager provides a NeXTStep look and feel, do applications share that same look? No, each application provides its own look and feel, which often leads to inconsistencies between applications and the window manager, as well as between applications. Usually, these inconsistencies are relatively minor. That's the price of freedom.

Under the Windows, MacOS, and BeOS windowing systems, the look of the window manager is generally set. Although you have some control, the system always operates in a predefined manner. Under the X Window

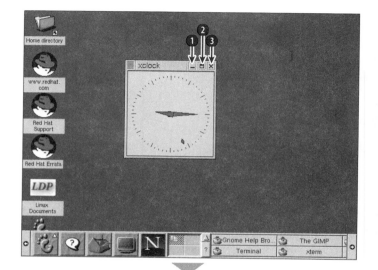

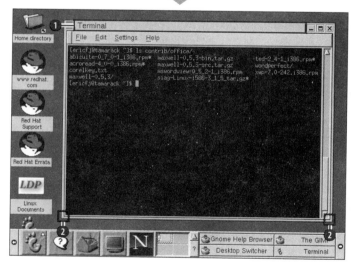

❶ Click the minimize button to shrink the window into the taskbar.

❷ Click the maximize button to expand the window to full size.

❸ Click the close button to send the window away — often quitting the application.

❶ From the title bar, you can drag the window to a new position by holding down the leftmost mouse button.

❷ From the bottom corners or sides, you can resize the window.

CROSS-REFERENCE

The task, "Configuring the Red Hat Desktop," earlier in this chapter, covers more on virtual screens.

150

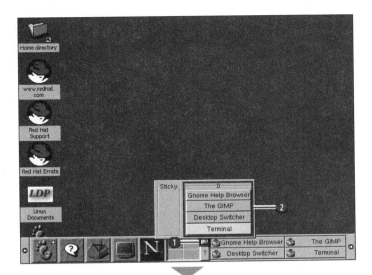

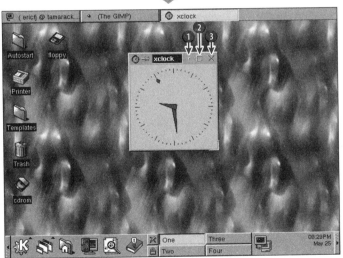

System, the window manager creates the title bar and other decorations, such as the iconify and maximize buttons. These doodads — to use the technical term — appear differently under different window managers. Some window managers, like the default Enlightenment window manager, provide for Windows 95-like close buttons on the title bar. This window manager is the default with Red Hat Linux, so as to make Windows users feel more at home. Fvwm95 also provides for a taskbar along the bottom of the screen, again like Windows 95.

The KDE window manager provides most of the same controls, but a different look, as shown on the facing page.

You can minimize or iconify most windows. Under the Enlightenment window manager, minimized windows appear in the taskbar at the bottom of the screen. KDE's window manager shows minimized windows on a bar across the top of the screen.

Continued

① *To get a list of the windows, click the arrow icon.*

② *Select a window to restore the window to the top.*

▶ *KDE window manager controls.*

① *Click the minimize button to shrink the window into the taskbar.*

② *Click the maximize button to expand the window to full size.*

③ *Click the close button to send the window away — often quitting the application.*

TAKE NOTE

▶ WINDOW MANAGER REQUIREMENTS

KDE is bundled with its own window manager, kwm, and works best with that desktop. GNOME defines a set of window manager extensions for window managers to work with GNOME. By default, GNOME runs the Enlightenment window manager, but you can change to the WindowMaker window manager from the GNOME Settings menu. In the future, other window managers should support the GNOME extensions, providing even more choices.

FIND IT ONLINE

A list of virtually all X window managers is available at http://www.PLiG.org/xwinman.

Window Managers
Continued

With the GNOME desktop, the default window manager is called Enlightenment, a window manager you can run outside of GNOME. The default Enlightenment look appears vaguely like that of Windows 95. Prior to Red Hat 6.0, the default window manager was fvwm95, which also provides a look similar to that of Windows 95. You should see a trend here. The purpose is obviously to make Windows users feel more at home on Linux, easing their transition.

Enlightenment provides an extensive set of customization screens, but they are hard to find (we originally found these by accident). Because GNOME allows for any window manager, window managers aren't as tightly integrated in GNOME as with KDE, which includes its own window manager. You can find the Enlightenment configuration screens by first calling up the GNOME configuration tool from the taskbar, then selecting the Window Manager item. From the window that appears, click Run Configuration Tool for Enlightenment.

Once you have the Enlightenment configuration tool window up, you can configure quite a lot about the window manager. Famous for using lots of colors and providing special graphics effects (abbreviated FX), you can configure how windows get moved, and even set themes for the window title bars. These themes provide radically different title bars. In general, we found the CleanBig theme — the default — works best with GNOME. On smaller screens, try the Clean theme, which uses less screen space for the title bars.

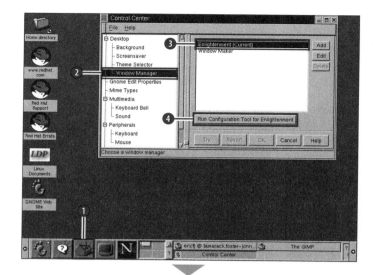

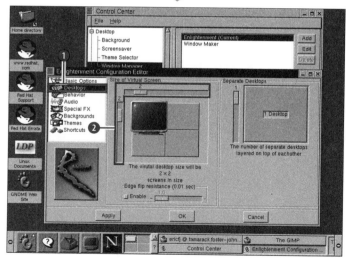

❶ *To configure Enlightenment, select the GNOME configuration tool icon.*

❷ *In the Control Center, select Desktop ⇨ Window Manager.*

❸ *Select Enlightenment.*

❹ *Click Run Configuration Tool for Enlightenment.*

❶ *To control the number of virtual desktops, select Desktops from the Enlightenment Configuration Editor.*

❷ *Adjust the sliders to change the size of the virtual screen from the default two-by-two screens.*

CROSS-REFERENCE

Chapter 4 covers online help on Linux commands — including desktop commands.

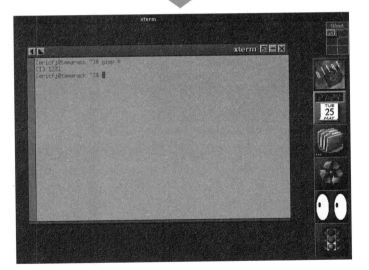

① Select Themes to change Enlightenment's themes. These themes are likely to conflict with GNOME.

② The Brushed Metal-Tigert theme provides a different-looking title bar for windows.

Other desktops

Many aspects of Red Hat's older desktop setup can be hard to fathom. We found it best to use the desktop switching tool to switch to the AnotherLevel desktop and then work from there to switch to other window managers or configure things. That's mostly because the AnotherLevel desktop isn't really a desktop. Instead, it's a window manager, fvwm95 with a taskbar and a set of menus.

Once you're in the older default desktop, you can use the fvwm95 menus to switch to other window managers. In this desktop, a file named .wm_style in your home directory names which window manager to run. By default, this will hold Fvwm95. You can edit the file to change to other window managers, including AfterStep for another NeXTStep-like window manager. You can test both AfterStep and LessTifMWM, a window manager similar to the Motif window manager (mwm), from the fvwm95 menus. Hold down the leftmost mouse button and select Exit Fvwm. From that submenu, select Switch To and then pick the window manager you want to try. This is a great way to explore other window managers.

TROUBLESHOOTING

WORKING WITH WINDOWMAKER

WindowMaker, the second window manager provided for the GNOME desktop, presents a clean look that is close to the look of NeXTStep. We especially liked the default setting for resizing windows. When you resize windows, you see small lines similar to technical drawings.

FIND IT ONLINE

The Enlightenment home page is **http://www.enlightenment.org.**

Screen Savers and Backgrounds

No graphical user interface would be complete without some really nifty screen savers. The default screen saver simply turns the entire screen black, but there are screen savers that will show bouncing images or statements attesting to your high status.

With the GNOME desktop, the default screen saver will lock your display, forcing you to reenter your password to gain access to your screen. You can turn off the lock by unsetting the Require Password toggle in the GNOME Control Center.

From the GNOME Control Center, you can also select other screen savers. A neat feature, shown on the facing page, is that you can preview screen savers to see how they act before selecting one.

You can turn off the screen saver with the following command:

```
$ xset s off
```

To turn it back on, use:

```
$ xset s on
If your monitor supports low-power energy
saving modes, you can enable them using$
xset dpms [standby] [suspend] [off]
```

where [standby] [suspend] and [off] are the number of seconds of inactivity X waits for until it enters that mode. 300, 900, and 1800 (5 minutes, 10 minutes, and 30 minutes) work well.

Setting the background

From the GNOME Control Center, you can change the screen background color, or select an image to display. You can tile the image across the background, or just show one copy of the image. You can also set an image into the screen background from the **ee**, or Electric Eyes, image-viewing program. (Hold down the rightmost mouse button to get the **ee** menus.)

The **xsetroot** command can set the screen background to a solid color, or to a monochrome bitmap image tiled over the display.

To get a listing of the standard X color names, use the **showrgb** command. In addition to these color names, you can form colors from their red, green, and blue components using the following syntax:

#RRRGGGBBB

Replace the RRR, GGG, and BBB with the red, green, and blue numeric components (in hexadecimal) for the desired color. Red, for example, is #FFF000000. The color bisque2 works well in many offices.

The **xloadimage** command, covered in Table 7-3, also display images on the root window.

TAKE NOTE

VIRTUAL ROOTS AND CONFLICTING BACKGROUNDS

When you mix virtual screens and desktops, you may get conflicting backgrounds, where the window manager or desktop manager impose their background on top of the one you want. The image you set is likely still there, it's just that you cannot see it, because it is covered by a full-sized window placed on the screen.

To deal with this, you need to configure Enlightenment to display no background. Then you can configure a background image from GNOME.

CROSS-REFERENCE

The task on window managers shows how to configure Enlightenment.

FIND IT ONLINE

The sources to another image viewer, xv, are available at **ftp.cis.upenn.edu/pub/xv/**.

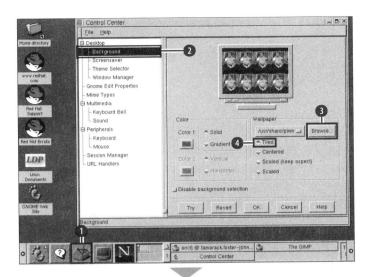

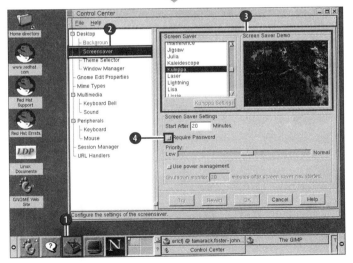

❶ Click the GNOME configuration tool icon.

❷ Select Background.

❸ Click Browse to select an image.

❹ Click the Tiled toggle to tile a small image across the screen.

❶ Click the GNOME configuration tool icon.

❷ Select Screensaver.

❸ Preview screen savers before selecting one.

❹ The Require Password field toggles whether or not to force you to reenter your password to get back in.

Listing 7-3: THE SHOWRGB COMMAND

```
$ showrgb | more
220 220 220    gainsboro
255 250 240    floral white
253 245 230    OldLace
250 240 230    linen
255 240 245    LavenderBlush
106  90 205    SlateBlue
 72 209 204    MediumTurquoise
124 252   0    LawnGreen
255 160 122    light salmon
218 112 214    orchid
238 213 183    bisque2
—More—
```

▶ X supports a huge number of color names, a small sample of which appear here.

Table 7-3: COMMANDS TO CHANGE THE SCREEN

Command	Action
xloadimage –onroot *filename.jpg*	Tiles screen background with *filename.jpg*.
xloadimage –onroot –fullscreen *filename.jpg*	Does the same, and expands image to edge of screen.
xloadimage –supported	Lists file types supported, such as JPEG, but not GIF.
xset s off	Turns off screen saver.
xset s on	Turns on screen saver.
xset s *start_timeout change_timeout*	Set the screen saver to start after *start_timeout* seconds, and change its pattern (if there is a pattern) after *change_timeout* seconds.
xsetroot –solid color	Sets screen background to solid *color*.
xsetroot –bitmap *bitmap*	Sets screen background to monochrome X bitmap file.

Setting Up an X Login

The normal way to start X is to log in to a text console and then run the **startx** command. This launches the X server software as well as the default set of X applications that you have configured. You can extend this, though, to always run X and log in through a graphical login window.

In this mode, you boot Linux and see a login window rather than a text-mode login prompt. This login window is provided by a program called gdm, short for the GNOME Display Manager. Red Hat also comes with the standard X login program called xdm and a KDE version called kdm. The symbolic link /etc/X11/prefdm points to the display manager program that you want to use.

To provide the X login window from the beginning, xdm, gdm, or kdm needs to start when Linux boots. To do this, you need to choose Log in to X at installation time, or later edit the /etc/inittab file, which defines various run-levels for Linux and what happens at each run-level. For example, Linux defines a single-user run-level, used mostly for administration purposes (and *not* if you are the only user to log in to your Linux box).

Other run-levels start up networking, and shut down the system. If you didn't choose Log in to X during the installation, the default Red Hat run-level is 3, which supports multiple users, networking, and the basic operations described in this book. In the file /etc/inittab, the default run-level gets set by the following line:

```
id:3:initdefault:
```

For Red Hat Linux, the default run-level for gdm or xdm is 5. So, you merely need to change the default run-level line to:

```
id:5:initdefault:
```

Before making a change, test that everything works. You can switch run-levels with the **init** command, run as root:

```
# init 5
```

Don't do this from an X Window display. Instead, quit X if it is running. When run-level 5 gets started, you should see a graphics display — provided by X as you'd expect — and a login window, which is shown on the facing page.

By default, Red Hat Linux runs gdm, the GNOME login display manager. This really has no effect on which desktop is run. You can still run your KDE desktop after logging in via **gdm**.

From the login window, you can halt or reboot the machine, which is quite handy, but may be a security issue for multiuser sites.

CROSS-REFERENCE

See Appendix B for where to look for more information on **xdm**.

FIND IT ONLINE

For more on the Common Desktop Environment, see http://www.opengroup.org.

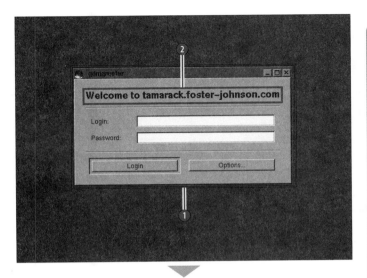

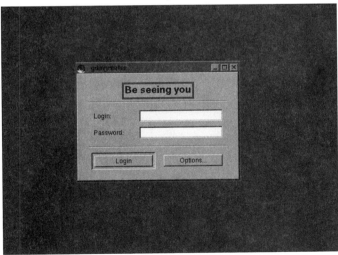

① Log in through the gdm login window.

② Look at the current message.

▶ After changing the login message in /etc/X11/gdm/gdm.conf, the new message appears in the login window.

Configuring the display manager

If you run the default gdm display manager, look to /etc/X11/gdm for the configuration files. The main configuration file, gdm.conf, controls things such as the message shown in the login window (one thing that you are likely to want to change). To find the message, look for the following lines in the gdm.conf file:

```
[messages]
Welcome=Welcome to %h
```

Gdm replaces the %h with your system's host-name. To change this message, put in something else, such as:

```
Welcome=Be seeing you
```

The new login window is shown in the second image. For more on gdm, see the files in /usr/doc/gdm-1.0.0. Most of the file locations listed in these documents are not where Red Hat has chosen to place the configuration files. Look in /etc/X11/gdm instead.

Table 7-4: RED HAT LINUX RUN-LEVELS IN /ETC/INITTAB

Level	Usage
0	Halt (never set initdefault to this value)
1	Single-user mode
2	Multiuser without the network file system (NFS)
3	Multiuser with NFS
4	Not used
5	XDM
6	Reboot Linux (never set initdefault to this value)

Personal workbook

Q&A

1. What does GNOME stand for?

2. Name two different window managers.

3. Can different window managers be run under the GNOME desktop?

4. Can you set up a screen saver?

5. What can you use to get a graphical login screen?

6. What is the default run-level for Red Hat Linux?

7. How do you set the screen background?

8. If you set the screen background and cannot see it, what is the likely cause?

ANSWERS: PAGE 337

EXTRA PRACTICE

1. Look for updates to GNOME at **http://www.gnome.org** on the Internet.

2. Run the **xprop** command and click on a window. Look at all the window information — called properties — **xprop** prints out to your shell window. Try this with a few more windows. Compare the information printed out with things such as the window's title bar. You can find out a lot of information this way about how the underlying window system works.

3. Switch from the default GNOME desktop to KDE. Try it for a week or so to see which desktop you prefer. (We actually prefer some KDE applications, but run GNOME because it provides the GNOME, KDE, and AnotherLevel menus right out of the box.)

REAL-WORLD APPLICATIONS

✔ People at your site are sticklers for product licenses. While Linux is free, each software package comes with its own license. You've heard worries about the KDE and Qt licenses. (KDE is based on a set of programming libraries called Qt.) Look these up at **http://www.kde.org** and **http://www.troll.no/qpl** to decide for yourself.

✔ Look for System Info on the GNOME Utilities menu. Use this to get a listing of your system's disk usage, processor type, and total memory.

✔ Your colleagues complain that logging into Linux seems so primitive compared to Windows NT. Logging into Linux in text mode and then running the **startx** command to launch the X Window System is too much for them. Set up a graphical login using **gdm**.

VISUAL QUIZ

What window manager is running in this picture?

_____

_____

_____

_____

_____

_____

159

CHAPTER 8

MASTER THESE SKILLS

- ▶ Managing Files
- ▶ Word Processing
- ▶ Managing Your Schedule
- ▶ Crunching Numbers
- ▶ Sending Faxes
- ▶ Multimedia Tools

Desktop Applications

The default GNOME and optional KDE desktops, discussed in Chapter 7, provide the basic interface to Linux from a graphics screen. Starting with that interface, the next step is to run some applications—the real reason people use computers. One of the reasons Microsoft Windows is so popular is not because of Windows itself but because of the rich array of applications available for that operating system. While still lagging in some areas, Linux has made great strides toward providing useful applications, as you'll see as we introduce just the tip of the iceberg in this chapter. This chapter delves into desktop productivity applications for Linux.

Choice is the hallmark of Linux, which has both good and bad aspects. Instead of selecting one dominant suite of office applications, Linux provides a choice of many applications and enabling you to pick the best of breed for a particular class of programs. Many of the applications we discuss here are tied to either the KDE or GNOME desktops, introduced in Chapter 7. Although KDE applications can run under GNOME, and vice versa, these applications work best in their own environment.

Other applications, such as the ical calendar and tkdesk file manager, are not tied to a particular environment. These applications are especially handy for those who don't have the RAM or processing power to run the larger KDE or GNOME desktops.

Commercial applications, while not as prevalent as on Windows, are starting to abound on Linux. We find it odd that in many comparisons between Windows and Linux, reviewers compare Linux freeware against add-on commercial applications for Windows. You can get a variety of office productivity suites, although Microsoft Office is not available as of this writing. Unless mentioned otherwise, the applications we cover here are free and come with Red Hat Linux.

Many of the applications we describe are in very early stages of development. In the last few years, Linux development has really taken off. No longer are device drivers to support various hardware options the main focus of development. Now, the focus has turned to applications. So don't be put off by the lack of features that some of these programs offer. Simply check the application's home page on the Web for newer versions. This is a great thing, as Linux programs are constantly improving.

Managing Files

So much of Linux deals with files that a file manager provides a very handy way to operate with your system. Although you can manage your files with the commands introduced in Chapter 3, such as **ls**, **cp**, and **rm**, a file manager really helps when you want to browse file systems, such as the Red Hat Linux CD-ROMs that accompany this book. File managers also help those more familiar with Windows make the transition to Linux.

The GNOME file manager, gmc or GNU Midnight Commander, appears in the first image on the facing page. From it you can create directories, copy, rename, and delete files, and so on. You can also double-click a file and GNOME will call up the application associated with the type of file. For example, double-clicking a JPEG image file will launch the Electric Eyes image viewer so that you can view the image. You can configure gmc to associate applications with various file types, too. Just double-click a file and gmc prompts you if it doesn't know what application to run to show the file.

Because so many Linux files are text files, you'll launch a text editormore often than not. Unfortunately, we found the default emacs configuration didn't work (even though emacs worked just fine). To change the editor, call up the GNOME control panel from the taskbar. Then, select Gnome Edit Properties. You can then select an editor from the list. Ignore the seemingly handy Test button. To test the editor, select OK and try to double-click a file ending in .txt from the file manager, or run the command **gnome-edit** from a shell window. We found gEdit worked fine.

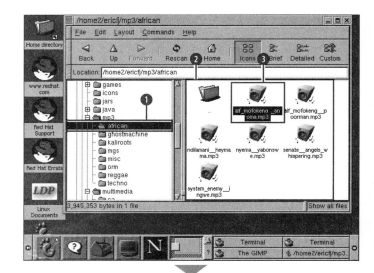

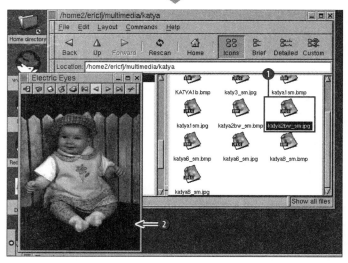

❶ Select a directory from the list in the GNOME file manager.

❷ The content of the directory appears in the right-side window.

❸ Special icons indicate file types.

❶ Double-click an image file.

❷ The file manager launches the ee (Electric Eyes) image viewer.

CROSS-REFERENCE

Chapter 3 covers file and directory commands.

162

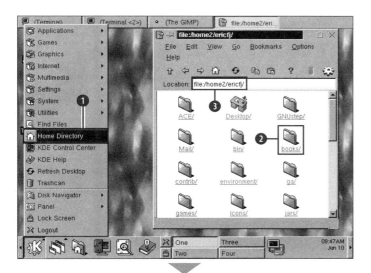

The KDE file manager, part of the optional KDE desktop, acts much the same as the GNOME manager. One big difference is that the KDE file manager also acts as a Web browser. A single click goes down to a subdirectory. In addition, the KDE file manager looks for files named index.html and will present those instead of a directory, much like Web browsers do.

The KDE taskbar menus also provide a handy disk navigator that is available from the taskbar menus, if KDE is your desktop.

TAKE NOTE

▶ TKDESK

Another very fine file manager that is not associated with any desktop is tkdesk. Written partially in the Tcl/Tk scripting language — hence the tk in the name — tkdesk includes a desktop launcher bar, a built-in text editor, and lots of other features. Ironically, these features make tkdesk overlap with desktop environments such as KDE and GNOME, so it is most often used where no major desktop is running.

▶ WEB LINKS

The GNOME file manager will call up **Netscape** to view files ending in .html. The KDE file manager goes further and displays Web pages from URLs. Just type in a URL, such as **http://www.idgbooks. com/**, and you'll see the Web page inside the **kfm** window.

① Call up the KDE file manager using the Home Directory choice on the main KDE menu.

② Click a folder icon once to see the contents of that directory in the KDE file manager.

③ Enter a URL to a local file or a Web document in the Location area.

① View files and directories from the **tkdesk** listing window.

② Quickly launch common applications from the launcher bar.

FIND IT ONLINE

The tkdesk home page is **http://www.people.mainz. netsurf.de/~bolik/tkdesk/**.

Word Processing

Word processors are the most commonly used office applications. Coming from its UNIX roots, Linux supports the groff text-formatting package, by which you enter special codes — called *dot codes* — into a plain text file to control formatting. You then run the document through groff (troff on UNIX) and output a file in PostScript or some other output format. A similar package called TeX, and pronounced *tech,* also uses codes that you embed in text files. TeX goes so far as to enable you to format text with greater control than just about any package. (In fact, to make life difficult, only TeX can properly typeset the name TeX.) Neither TeX nor groff are WYSIWYG, or What You See Is What You Get, word processors. You edit text files, insert codes, and then run a separate program to format the text.

For the rest of us, Linux supports a number of word processors that do provide WYSIWYG capability. These word processors go from the simple free programs to full-blown commercial packages.

One of the best freeware word processors is Maxwell, which supports its own format as well as RTF, or Rich Text Format, files. Most word processors support RTF, giving you a somewhat easy way to exchange files between Linux and Windows systems. AbiWord, from AbiSoft, can load many Microsoft Word files, but saves only to its format, text, or HTML. See Table 8-1 for URLs to these word processors.

GNOME provides a number of extensible text editors that allow you to perform more tasks than you'd expect of a text editor. The gnotepad+ editor includes extensive support for creating HTML files — Web documents — including headlines, bold, italic, and other text attributes, along with left, right, and center justification of text. All together, gnotepad+ is a somewhat primitive word processor.

Continued

TAKE NOTE

▶ VIEWING MS WORD FILES

mswordview converts Microsoft Word files into HTML, so that you can view the files with a Web browser. While not as convenient as two-way file transfer from programs such as WordPerfect, mswordview is free and helps out in a pinch if you have some MS Word documents that you need to view. We found that mswordview did a much better job converting Word 97 files than did WordPerfect 8. The basic syntax is:

`$ mswordview filename.doc`

Replace filename.doc with the name of your Word file. mswordview will then output filename.doc.html.

Download mswordview from **http://rufus. w3.org/linux/RPM/contrib/libc6/i386/ mswordview-0.5.2-1.i386.html**.

▶ ADOBE ACROBAT PDF FILES

To make online documents appear exactly like their printed counterparts, many organizations use the Adobe Acrobat or PDF format. You'll find PDF manuals with many software packages, as well as PDF marketing literature on the Web. On Linux, you can use the program xpdf to view these files. The xpdf RPM file comes on the CD-ROMs that accompany this book.

There are some files that xpdf cannot handle, though. For these, you need software from Adobe, inventors of the PDF format. You can download the Adobe program acroread from **http://www. rpmfind.net/linux/RPM/contrib/libc6/i386/ X11_Applications.html** or any site that includes Red Hat contributed packages.

Downloading KOffice

The KDE team plans an entire integrated suite called KOffice, which is in its initial stages of development. Red Hat Linux does not provide the KDE office suite, called KOffice. There's just so much that will fit on a CD-ROM. So, if you want to run KOffice, which includes a spreadsheet, a presentation package, a word processor, and much more, you need to download KOffice from the Internet.

While you can download prebuilt binary RPMs of the KOffice packages, these are clearly marked as not working on Red Hat Linux. This means you need to build KOffice from the source code. For most Linux packages, this isn't that hard, but KOffice appears to be much more involved.

As of this writing, KOffice requires a bit of work to download and get going. You first must have installed KDE and the KDE development RPM packages. You then need to download the sources to KOffice, along with special versions of the Qt library, the Python scripting language, and the MICO CORBA object request broker. You need particular versions, such as MICO 2.2.3, and not any more recent version. All of this is described at **http://koffice.kde.org/install-source.html**. Because of this hassle, you probably want to wait on KOffice until you can download binary RPM files that work with Red Hat Linux or until the Red Hat Linux release includes this package.

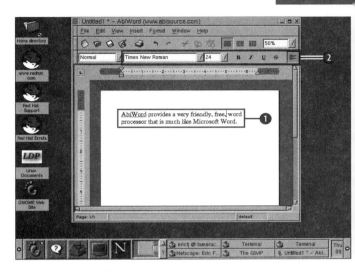

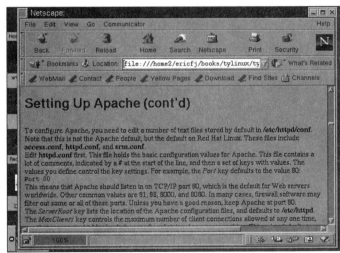

➊ Enter text in the main abiword window.

➋ Select fonts and styles from the toolbar.

▶ View Microsoft Word files as HTML after converting with mswordview in Netscape.

CROSS-REFERENCE

Chapter 5 covers text editors.

FIND IT ONLINE

The KOffice home page is **http://www.koffice.kde.org**.

Word Processing
Continued

Commercial applications and suites

In addition to the freeware applications discussed so far, you can purchase word processors and full-blown office suites from a number of vendors. One of the neat things about the free nature of Linux is that it tends to hold down prices for commercial applications. Thus, you can purchase Corel WordPerfect for between $50 and $70, depending on the vendor. That is, if you need to purchase it. You can get a free license for WordPerfect for personal noncommercial use. (See their Web pages for more on this.) In either case, you get a free 90-day evaluation.

WordPerfect requires a bit of work to download and install. First off, the download is almost 24MB, which takes a long time for dial-up Internet users. What you get is a gzipped tar archive. Uncompress the file with **gunzip** and then extract it, using **tar**, to an empty directory.

```
$ gunzip guilg00.gz
$ tar xvof guilg00
```

Then, run the script Runme with the sh shell to perform the full installation:

```
$ sh Runme
```

The full installation requires between 61 and 70MB of disk space. You also need write permission to the directory in which you install WordPerfect, such as under /usr/local. There are a few other quirks. You must run the WordPerfect executable, xwp, the same day you install it and you must have write permissions to the installation directory. This starts a 90-day clock during which time you need to register at **http://www.linux.corel.com**. (Registration is free.) After registering, you

get a license key, a series of letters and numbers purposely mixed up. In our tests, though, Word Perfect 8 could not properly load most Microsoft Word 97 files. In a number of cases, even simple Word files caused WordPerfect to hang while converting.

If you have a UNIX background, check out Applixware from Applix. Developed originally on UNIX, you can buy Applixware for a variety of UNIX platforms — along with Linux, of course.

If, instead, you or the users at your site have more of a Windows background, Corel's WordPerfect or StarDivision's StarOffice is a good choice. StarOffice provides a Windows version, along with OS/2, Macintosh, Solaris, and Linux versions. And, StarOffice provides good conversions to and from MS Word and other Microsoft applications. This makes StarOffice a great choice for sites with Linux and Windows systems, and where you want to standardize on one office productivity suite.

Corel's WordPerfect Office suite, when fully ported to Linux, should provide similar capability.

CROSS-REFERENCE

Chapter 16 covers Web servers.

166

Table 8-1: OFFICE SUITES AND APPLICATIONS FOR LINUX

Suite	Notes
WordPerfect	Free for personal use. A commercial version is also available. Corel plans to port its entire office suite to Linux. Has Windows version. See **http://www. linux.corel.com**.
StarOffice	Full suite. Free for personal use. Has free personal version and nonfree commercial version. Has Windows version. See **http://www. stardivision.com**.
Applixware	Full suite. Originated on UNIX. See **http://www.applix.com**.
AbiWord	Free word processor and future suite of office applications. See **http://www. abisoft.com**.
KOffice	Free KDE office suite under development. See **http://www.koffice. kde.org**.
Siag Office	See **http://www.edu.stockholm. se/siag** or **http://www.siag.nu.**
OffiX	Freeware suite located at **http:// www.leb.net/~offix/index.html**, still in alpha release.
GWP	GNOME word processor. Still in very early stages of development. See **http://www.hungry.com/ products/gwp**.
LyX	A front end for creating LaTeX files. See **http://www.lyx.org**.
Maxwell	Another free word processor; see **http://www.eeyore-mule.demon. co.uk**. Download a binary version from **http://www.linux.davecentral. com/3373_officeword.html**.
List of programs	See **http://www.hex.net/ ~cbbrowne/wp.html** for a good list of word processors.
List of word processors	Part of the Scientific Applications List, at **http://www.SAL.KachinaTech. COM/G/3/index.shtml**.
List of word processors	Another list resides at **http://www. linux-center.org/en/applications/ publishing/**.
Download site	See **http://www.linux.davecentral. com** for many freeware packages.

▶ *Running the WordPerfect word processor.*

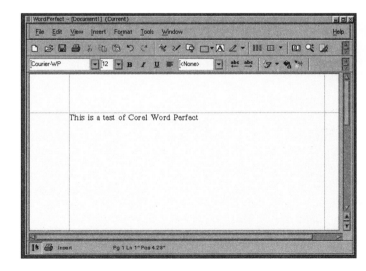

FIND IT ONLINE

See **http://www.hex.net/~cbbrowne/wp.html** for a list of most Linux word processors.

167

Managing Your Schedule

If you're like us, you face a daunting schedule and far too little free time. Linux has a number of tools to help manage your busy schedule. Most scheduling programs act similarly. A calendar is displayed and you can place your appointments, meetings, and deadlines on the days they happen. Some programs, including the GNOME and KDE calendars, provide separate views of the current day, week, and month.

If you're running the GNOME desktop, try gnomecal, shown in the first image on the facing page. Under KDE, try korganizer, shown in the second image. If you don't run one of these major desktops, try ical, shown in the third image on the facing page. Inside any of these programs, you can enter your appointments, glance at your busy schedule, and moan with despair.

Under GNOME, the first thing to do with gnomecal is to change the settings from 24-hour time, which is more common outside North America, to 12-hour time. Use the Preferences choice on the Settings menu to change this.

To enter an appointment for the current day, select the time, hold down the rightmost mouse button, and select New appointment from the pop-up menu. From the dialog that pops up, you can fill in all the necessary details. For most appointments, simply entering what it is and the time usually suffices.

You can type directly in the daily planner window, but you must first press Enter, then type in an appointment, and then don't press Enter. (If you do press Enter, the one-line appointment will be scrolled up, so that you will see an empty text-entry field. This is not very intuitive.)

Continued

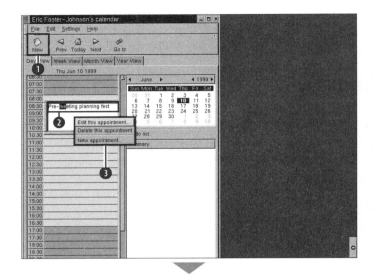

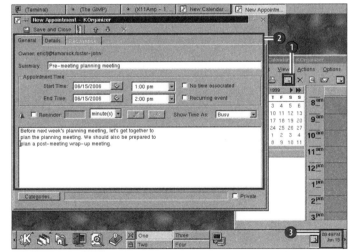

❶ Click the New icon to create a new appointment in the GNOME calendar.

❷ Or select a time period, press Enter, and start typing.

❸ Hold down the rightmost mouse button to pop up a menu for editing the appointment information.

❶ Click New Appointment to create an appointment in the KDE organizer.

❷ Enter in the event in the New Appointment window.

❸ Note the current time and date in the KDE taskbar.

CROSS-REFERENCE

Chapter 13 introduces Netscape, which can run many emerging Web calendar tools.

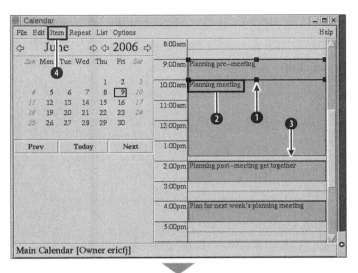

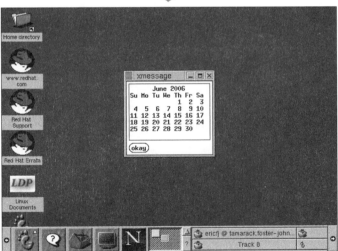

1. *Select the time for the appointment in the **ical** calendar.*

2. *Enter the text that is to appear in your calendar.*

3. *Stretch the block to the time required.*

4. *Modify the appointment from the Item menu.*

▶ *Show a simple calendar by running the **cal** and **xmessage** commands.*

TAKE NOTE

▶ CREATING A PRIMITIVE CALENDAR

If you just want to see a listing of the days of the month, run the following command:

```
$ cal | xmessage -file - &
```

This command pipes the output of the **cal** command, which prints the calendar for the current month, to the xmessage program, which displays the text in a window. The **–file** option tells xmessage to read its data from a file; the lone "–" acts as a shorthand for standard input, which in our case comes from the piped output of the **cal** command. Many Linux commands use a dash as a shortcut for standard input or output.

▶ SYNCING YOUR ICAL CALENDAR WITH A PALM PILOT

A package called syncal syncs the ical database with the Palm Pilot Datebook. See **http://rpmfind.net/ linux/RPM/contrib/libc6/i386/Applications_ Productivity.html**.

▶ EMERGING WEB CALENDARS

The most recent developments in scheduling lie in Web-based applications that use Web protocols, HTML, Java, and JavaScript to handle your schedule. Because Netscape supports all these tools, you're in business should you want to use a Web calendar. The only problems you'll face are poorly designed systems that require a certain browser, such as Internet Explorer, or Windows ActiveX controls. In this case, you're pretty much out of luck. If vendors refuse to follow Internet standards, though, you should call them on that.

FIND IT ONLINE

You can find more on ical on its homepage, **http:// www.research.digital.com/SRC/personal/Sanjay_ Ghemawat/ical/home.html**.

Managing Your Schedule
Continued

Keeping contact

Closely tied to schedulers are address books, which you can use to store contact information about the people you deal with. There's not a lot to these programs, beyond a small database that stores information on people. You typically want to store, at a minimum, phone numbers, postal addresses, and e-mail addresses.

The GNOME address book, gnomecard, supports the vCard format, common among Internet tools. KDE desktop users can run kab, the KDE address book. In each, you have an entry, also called a card, for each person you want to record. You can then search through your list of contacts, look up phone numbers, and so on.

Netscape Communicator, included with Red Hat Linux, comes with a built-in address book. If you use Netscape for e-mail, you may want to use Netscape's address book as well, because of the tighter integration with its e-mail package. You can, for example, add the sender of an e-mail message directly to your address book, without reentering all the data in the message header, such as the sender's e-mail address. This speeds things and avoids tedious data entry.

TAKE NOTE

SYNCHRONIZING WITH THE PALM PILOT ADDRESS BOOK

The pi-address program provides a friendly frontend to Palm Pilot address books. Pi-address enables you to enter addresses, look up contacts, and so on from your Linux system. You can then run programs from pilot-link, which is a separate package, to transfer the address book to a Pam

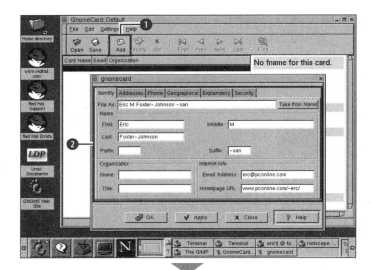

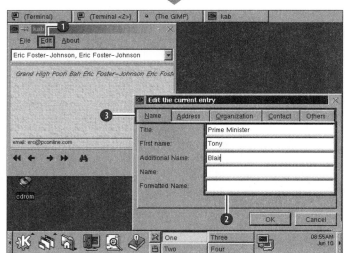

① *Click Add in the gnomecard application to add a new person to your address book.*

② *Fill in the person's data in the dialog.*

① *Select Add Entry in the Edit menu to add a new person to the KDE address book.*

② *Enter the person's data into the dialog.*

③ *Select the tabs to enter data such as the postal address and contact information.*

CROSS-REFERENCE
Chapter 7 covers more on the GNOME and KDE desktops.

170

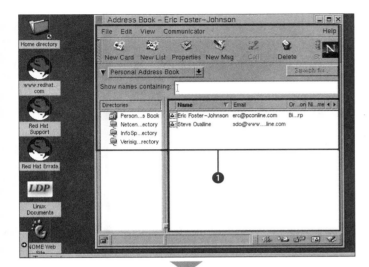

Pilot handheld. **See http://www.in-berlin.de/User/ miwie/pia** for more on pi-address. The pilot-link package that comes with Red Hat 6.0 includes utilities to convert the PalmPilot calendar into the format used by ical. The pilot-xfer program enables you to transfer files to and from a PalmPilot.

▶ TRACKING TIME

The GtimeTracker, or gtt, tracks the time you spend on various projects — very useful for figuring out how much time you're wasting, or for those who must report the hours they spent on a given project. You first enter the projects that you are working on, and then turn on the timer. Turn off the timer when you stop working on that project. On the KDE desktop, you can run karm, available from the Utilities desktop menu, to track the time you spend on projects.

▶ TELLING TIME

Both the KDE and GNOME desktops display the current time in the taskbar. You can also run a number of different clock programs if you prefer a different way to display the time. The traditional X Window clock program is called xclock. (Red Hat Linux does not include the rounded-clock program oclock.) A fancier clock is xdaliclock, inspired by artist Salvador Dalí, which shows numbers merging together on a digital clock. You can see these clock windows in the last image on the facing page.

① *Enter your contacts into the Netscape address book if you use Netscape for e-mail.*

① *Track the time you spend on projects with **gtt**, the GNOME desktop time tracker.*

② *Tell time with the lowly **xclock**.*

③ *Tell time with the fancier **xdaliclock**.*

FIND IT ONLINE

For more on Salvador Dalí, see **http://www. salvadordali.com.**

Crunching Numbers

After planning your busy schedule, it's time to get down to business. The GNOME desktop includes a spreadsheet program called gnumeric. You can use this for financial planning, what-if budget scenarios, calculating your taxes, and reporting on your work, just as you can with any spreadsheet.

As shown on the facing page, gnumeric presents a traditional spreadsheet interface full of cells waiting for data. If you're familiar with Microsoft Excel or Lotus 1-2-3, you should feel at home with gnumeric.

gnumeric labels columns A, B, C, and so on, just like Excel and Lotus 1-2-3. Rows are numbered 1, 2, 3, and so on. Many actions in a spreadsheet require you to identify particular cells. To do that in gnumeric, you use the column letter first, then the row number, such as B3 for cell in the second column (B) and third row (3). A colon (:) is used to separate a range of cells, such as B1:B3 for the cells B1, B2, and B3. These ranges are important in formulas, where computations are generated based on the contents of the cells — in other words, the main reason you use a spreadsheet in the first place.

Like Excel, gnumeric supports the *=function* notation, such as =sum to generate the sum of a range of cells. Also, like Excel, the following formula calculates the sum of the values stored in the cells in the range of B1 to B3, in other words, the cells B1, B2, and B3:

`=sum(B1:B3)`

The sum formula is the most commonly used formula, and this syntax works in both Excel and gnumeric. To help you get going, gnumeric provides extensive online documentation, including a listing of all the built-in functions. There are two main choices

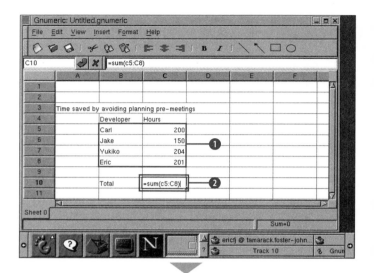

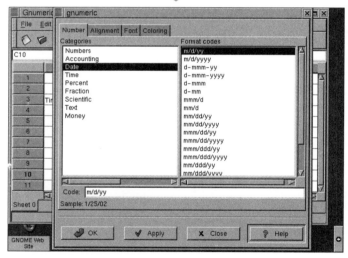

1 *Enter text and values into cells in the gnumeric spreadsheet.*

2 *Enter formulas to perform calculations.*

▶ *Choose Cells from the Format menu in gnumeric.*

▶ *Control data formats, such as how to display dates.*

CROSS-REFERENCE

The task on word processors discusses how to download KOfiice.

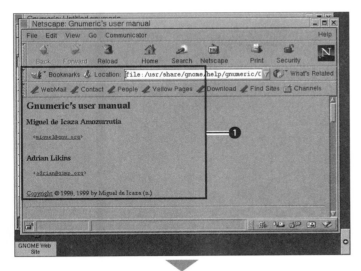

on the Help menu, a general-purpose gnumeric manual, and a separate function reference. Use the manual to get going with gnumeric and the function reference to learn the exact commands you can use.

The optional KDE desktop also has a spreadsheet, kspread, which is part of KOffice and does not come with Red Hat Linux.

TAKE NOTE

▶ CALCULATORS

If you just want to whip up some calculations, you don't need a spreadsheet; a simple calculator will do. There are quite a few X Window calculators to choose from. The GNOME and KDE desktops both offer calculator programs and you can always run the very simple xcalc program.

▶ COMMERCIAL SPREADSHEETS

A number of office suites, such as the aforementioned Applixware, StarOffice, and the free Siag Office, include spreadsheet programs. In addition, WingZ and NExS are two commercial spreadsheets that you can purchase for Linux. See **http://www.wingz.com** and **http://www.xess.com** for more information.

▶ BALANCING YOUR CHECKBOOK

One of the most popular software packages for personal finance is called cbb, short for check book balancer. Available from **http://www.menet.umn.edu/~curt/cbb/**, cbb isn't tied to any particular desktop. cbb is partially written using Tcl/Tk and Perl, popular scripting languages. This makes it relatively easy to customize **cbb**.

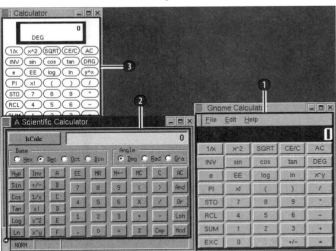

❶ Call up extensive online help from **gnumeric**.

❶ Perform calculations with the GNOME calculator.

❷ Run scientific functions from the optional KDE **kcalc**.

❸ Run **xcalc** if you have not installed a desktop environment.

FIND IT ONLINE

The Linux applications page lists a number of spreadsheets at **http://www.linuxapps.com**.

Sending Faxes

Most modern modems support both data and fax protocols, which means that your Linux system probably has all the hardware necessary to send and receive faxes, if you merely have a modem.

With Linux, you have a variety of fax packages to choose from. One of the easiest to get going is called efax. efax enables you to send and receive faxes.

To make life easier, the **efax** command comes with a handy script called fax. This script automates most of the **efax** options and — if everything works out — can make life a lot easier. Using the fax script, and facing a few setup problems, we were faxing within six minutes from starting out.

To send a fax, follow these steps:

▶ Set up your fax device
▶ Verify the fax device
▶ Test your fax setup
▶ Convert a text file into the fax format
▶ Try to send your file as a fax

The fax script assumes that you have a modem set up with the device file /dev/modem. Unless you set up a modem when installing Linux, you won't have this file. Don't worry, you can create /dev/modem as a symbolic link from the device file representing the serial port your modem is attached to. For example, /dev/ttyS0 is the first serial port (COM1: to DOS), /dev/ttyS1 is the second (COM2: to DOS), and so on. If your modem is attached to the first serial port, you can run the following command as root:

```
# ln -s /dev/tyS0 /dev/modem
```

Now, verify that your modem is connected to the proper port. Turn on your modem (if you need to,

internal modems should already be on). If your modem has status lights, you can run the following command:

```
$ echo "AT" > /dev/modem
```

The lights on the modem should briefly light up. If not, you can use a command such as **minicom**, a serial communications package, to test the modem. Set up **minicom** and then type in the command **AT**. Press **Enter**. You should get a response such as OK. If you don't, chances are you have plugged your modem in a different port than you set up.

Next, edit the fax script, /usr/bin/fax. You'll want to change the settings for FROM (put in your return fax number) and NAME (put in your organization's name) at the very minimum.

TAKE NOTE

▶ **SOLVING FAX PROBLEMS**

If the simple fax script doesn't work for you, start with the efax program. Check the online manual information with the **man efax** command. You can control many aspects of the fax output and dialing, as well as set special modem initialization settings.

▶ **SENDING POLITE FAXES**

Your fax files should clearly state who should get the fax (the recipient), as well as your name and phone number and the total number of pages.

▶ **OTHER FORMATS**

The fax script and efax programs convert text files into fax format. The GhostScript package's **gs** command can convert PostScript files to fax format. Many Linux word processors can output PostScript. xv, which you can download from the Internet, can convert image files to fax format.

CROSS-REFERENCE

Chapter 13 covers the minicom program and serial communication.

▶ *View a fax file with the* **viewfax** *command.*

▶ *Press and hold the middle mouse button while adjusting the image in the window.*

▶ *Click on the leftmost mouse button to zoom in, the rightmost to zoom out.*

❶ *With the KDE* **kfax** *program, call up fax files from the File menu.*

❷ *Click the icon to zoom in.*

❸ *Click the icon to zoom out.*

Faxing

Once you verify that your modem is set up, you can test the fax script with the **fax test** command:

```
# fax test
```

You may have to run this command as root, because the fax script needs to create lock files in /var/lock. The fax test script won't tell you a lot about whether it worked or not, as the output is nearly similar. If it works, you should hear noises from the modem speaker. If not, the modem will remain silent. (This isn't a great test, but it helps.)

Now, you're ready to send a fax. Create your message in a text file. Convert that file to the fax format with **fax make**:

```
$ fax make filename.txt
```

fax make creates a file for each page, ending in .001 for the first page, .002 for the second page, and so on.

To send this file (or files), use **fax send**. Again, you are likely to need root permissions to do so:

```
# fax send -v 6125551111 filename.txt.001
```

You should hear the modem dial and send the fax. The **–v** option requests lots of output. On a successful fax attempt, you should see the last line of output such as the following:

```
efax: 07:48 done, returning 0
```

On errors, you see a message similar to this:

```
There were errors (see 0522120636.log).
```

You can view the log file to see the errors. The most common error we saw was lack of permission to access the lock files in /var/lock.

ON THE CD-ROM

Another Linux fax package is **mgetty-sendfax**.

Multimedia Tools

The premiere graphic application on Linux is called The GIMP, short for The GNU Image Manipulation Program. Working sort of like Adobe Photoshop, The GIMP enables you to create images and perform quite a lot of manipulations on images. It's so extensive in fact, that there's a book on just The GIMP.

The GIMP's influence goes far. Quite a few Web pages sport The GIMP logo, crediting the application as helping with the site's graphics. The GIMP influences more than just Web pages. The developers of The GIMP needed a graphic toolkit to create the application in the first place. Unsatisfied with what was then available, they developed a toolkit called GTK, short for GIMP Toolkit. GTK, in turn, provides the underlying toolkit used by the GNOME desktop applications, described in this chapter and others.

The first time the **gimp** command runs, it creates a .gimp subdirectory inside your home directory (note the leading period, making it a normally hidden directory). The GIMP uses this subdirectory to store customizations particular to your account. Whenever you run The GIMP thereafter, you'll see windows like those shown on the facing page.

Continued

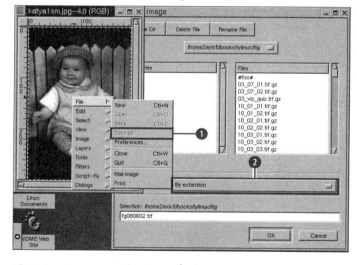

TAKE NOTE

HOLD DOWN THE RIGHTMOST MOUSE BUTTON

Most of the GIMP's features are available for a set of cascading menus that appear when you hold the rightmost mouse button down over an image. To save a file, you need to do this.

① Select the zoom tool in The GIMP to zoom in on an area in the image.

② Select the area to zoom in on with the mouse.

① Choose Save as from the File menu to save a file under a different format.

② Choose a format, or leave it at By extension to take the format from the filename extension you choose, such as .tif for TIFF images.

CROSS-REFERENCE

For information on the Artist's Guide to The GIMP, see Appendix B.

176

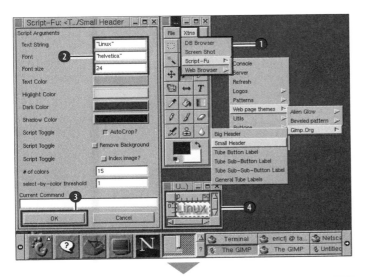

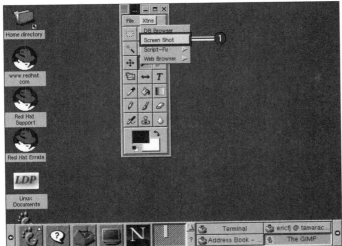

① *From the Xtns menu select Script-Fu, and then pick a script to run.*

② *Enter the text to display, and modify any settings.*

③ *Click OK to create the image.*

④ *The GIMP creates the image in a separate window. You need to save this image.*

① *Select Screen Shot from the Xtns menu to make a screen image.*

GIMP PLUGINS

GIMP was designed to allow developers to extend its basic functionality in new and interesting ways by writing plugins, add-ons that GIMP can run to provide new functionality. Similar to modules for the Apache Web server covered in Chapter 16, you can write small programs that follow the GIMP programming API and extend the application. You can write scripts in the GIMP Script-Fu language if you'd rather not go to the trouble to write programs. Look on the Xtns, or extensions, menu in the main GIMP window. Under the Script-Fu submenu, you'll see a large number of utilities, run as GIMP scripts, that can create things such as screen backgrounds, beveled buttons for Web pages, and so on.

SAVING TO DIFFERENT FORMATS

When you choose Save As from the File submenu, the GIMP offers a neat feature. You can select By extension for the Determine file type entry in the Save as dialog and simply type in the file name you want. The GIMP determines the file format from the file name extension. For example, enter .jpg for a JPEG image or .tif for a TIFF image.

SCREEN SHOTS

The GIMP provides an excellent utility to capture screen images. We found it was able to capture more images, especially of menus, than **xv**, our previous favorite tool. To capture a screen shot, select Screen Shot from the Xtns (extensions) menu. In the dialog that appears, choose whether to capture a window or the full screen, and away you go.

FIND IT ONLINE

The GIMP home page is **http://www.gimp.org**.

Multimedia Tools

Continued

Viewing images and movies

With The GIMP, you get a full-featured application for editing images. In many cases, though, The GIMP is overkill for your needs, leading you to other programs. If you want to display images but see only small thumbnail versions of the pictures, you can run **ee**, short for Electric Eyes, the GNOME image viewer. **ee** comes with the GNOME desktop. In **ee**, hold down the rightmost mouse button to get the **ee** menus. From the View submenu, you can call up the list window. This window can show thumbnail versions of the images within a directory. From the File submenu, you can make any image you're viewing appear on the screen background. The optional KDE desktop provides the kview image viewer.

If you want to go further than still images, Linux includes a number of tools to play movie files, especially MPEG, QuickTime, and Windows AVI movies.

xanim can play MPEG, MOV, and AVI movies, but does not support many modern *codecs*, the algorithms used to encode the video image. You'll find this problem especially acute with AVI movies made on Microsoft Windows. You'll see errors like the following:

```
AVI Video Codec: Radius Cinepak is
unsupported by this executable.
```

You can download extra codecs from the xanim home page, though. Many of these are proprietary and so cannot be distributed with Linux. Other programs that display movies include xmpeg and aktion.

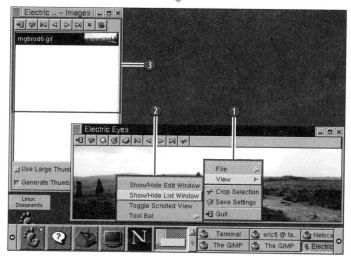

▶ *Viewing an image with ee.*

❶ *From ee, hold down the rightmost mouse button to see the menus.*

❷ *From the View menu, select Show/Hide List Window.*

❸ *You will see the list window, which presents thumbnail images.*

TAKE NOTE

LIGHTS, CAMERA, AKTION!

The aktion program, which is part of the optional KDE desktop, plays movie files quite well. We found it worked better than the old mainstay, xanim.

178

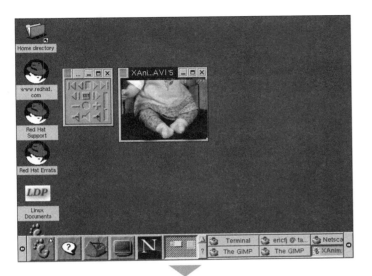

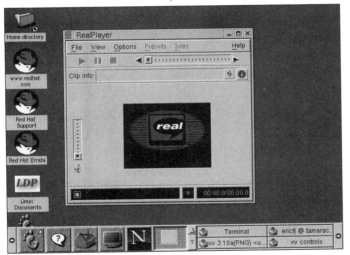

▶ Playing an AVI movie with **xanim**.

▶ Download RealPlayer for streaming audio and video.

aktion supports more of the formats used with Windows, which is a large source of movie files, making this another reason to install KDE when you install Linux.

aktion has the annoying feature, though, of clearing the final image when the movie file ends, leaving a gray window. Most other movie players leave the last image on the screen when the movie ends. aktion has the unsettling effect of playing a short movie file and then instantly clearing it off the window, often before you are even aware the file was fully played.

▶ ### REAL PLAYERS

Real Networks has captured a lot of the Internet market for streaming video and audio, often as a preview for buying music online. You can download Linux RealPlayer software called realplay from **http://www.real.com**.

▶ ### MOUNTING CD-ROMS

Many media files tend toward hugeness, so you'll often get them on CD-ROMs. To mount a CD-ROM, use the following command as root:

```
# mount -t iso9660 -r \
    /dev/cdrom /mnt/cdrom
```

This command mounts an ISO-9660 CD-ROM, the least common denominator format among CD-ROMs. Each platform has its own conflicting CD-ROM standard. There is a Macintosh-specific format, a UNIX format called Rock Ridge, and a number of Windows formats. For a Windows Joliet CD-ROM, skip the –t (type) iso9660 and just use the following command:

```
# mount  -r /dev/cdrom /mnt/cdrom
```

CROSS-REFERENCE

Chapter 10 covers applications that play sounds and music.

FIND IT ONLINE

The xanim home page is **http://www.xanim.va. pubnix.com/home.html**.

Personal Workbook

Q&A

1 Critics attack the lack of applications on Linux. Does Microsoft Office run on Linux?

2 Can you get any office suites that are written for Linux?

3 Name two free Linux word processors.

4 Can Linux send faxes?

5 Which programs can you use to create budgets, crunch numbers, and otherwise perform calculations on Linux?

6 Can you play Microsoft Windows AVI files on Linux?

7 How can you get the ee image-viewing program to display a set of thumbnail images?

8 Can you display Adobe Acrobat PDF files on Linux?

ANSWERS: PAGE 337

180

EXTRA PRACTICE

1 Take the gnumeric spreadsheet for a test drive. Try it to see how you like its feel. Determine whether it could work for you in place of Microsoft Excel.

2 Try to break one of the calculator programs by entering in strange calculations to try to find flaws.

3 Look up the online manual information on efax. You'll see quite a lot of options along with some good examples.

REAL-WORLD APPLICATIONS

✓ Your boss is willing to allow Linux in the workplace but demands that you come up with a way for Windows and Linux users to share the same word processing, spreadsheet, and presentation files. You know of at least one suite that supports Windows and Linux: StarOffice from StarDivision. Check out pricing and compatibility information at StarDivision's Web page, **http://www. stardivision. com**.

✓ When you double-click a text file in the GNOME file manager, you aren't likely to see the file, due to configuration issues with GNOME. Change the editor defined with GNOME to fix this, as described in the task on managing files.

VISUAL QUIZ

What can you use to convert Microsoft Word files to HTML?

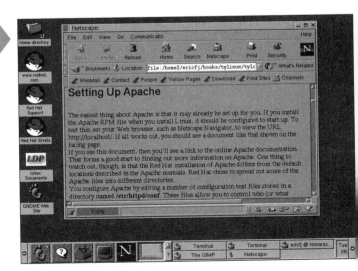

CHAPTER 9

MASTER
THESE
SKILLS

► Shell Windows
► Controlling Fonts and Setting the Window Size
► Copy and Paste

Command Windows

We've tried to break through the great myth that Linux is hard to learn and users are forced to memorize zillions of arcane commands. While Linux does include numerous commands, this just emphasizes the richness of the operating system. What you have to pay money for on other systems comes free on Linux.

We've highlighted the applications that can be launched from the desktop taskbars and shown how you can get most of your work done without ever touching a command line. Even so, there comes a time when you need to enter a Linux command. If you're using X, the easiest way to do this is to call up a shell window, which provides a shell (discussed in Chapter 3) inside a handy window. You can move and resize these windows just like any other windows on the desktop.

With names like **xterm**, **nxterm**, **gnome-terminal**, or **rxvt**, these windows provide a command line — a shell — inside an X window. Similar to the MS-DOS prompt window in Windows or the Terminal application in BeOS, these terminal windows generally provide a number of features, including:

▶ Your default shell inside a window
▶ Control over font size and face
▶ Control over the number of lines and columns displayed
▶ Ability to scroll back to earlier commands with an optional scroll bar
▶ Ability to select text and paste the text in other windows
▶ Control over colors, either through a menu-based interface or through X resource files

And, because both Windows and Be OS include shell windows of some sort, no one can claim that Linux is too hard to learn just because it includes shell windows!

Because Linux was designed to run over networks, you can use shell windows to log in to other systems using the telnet or rlogin programs. This provides a very handy way to bring other systems to you, instead of your having to go to the other systems.

With all these features, it's hard to go back to text-based consoles.

Shell Windows

The main shell window under the X Window System is called xterm. This was a very unfortunate name to choose, because an X terminal — a hardware device for displaying X applications — has nothing at all to do with an xterm — a shell window where you enter commands. This can be quite confusing.

xterm provides a basic window with a shell prompt. By default, xterm displays your default shell (normally bash). Through X resource files (*scrollBar: true) or a command-line option (**–sb**) you can turn on scroll bars for xterm that enable you to scroll back over previous commands and their output. This is very handy because many Linux commands are similar to previous commands that you've run.

Prior to adopting the GNOME desktop, RedHat Linux provided nxterm as the default shell window. nxterm is pretty much the same as xterm, but it includes color control and a slightly nicer look, as shown in the second image on the facing page. If you don't install GNOME or KDE, nxterm acts as your default terminal window.

The GNOME desktop provides a shell window, too, called gnome-terminal, which is shown in the third image on the facing page. This program includes menus for configuration and an online manual that helps you work with the program. One of the features of the gnome-terminal is that you can place a bitmap in its background. You don't want to do this on systems without a lot of RAM, though, as it eats memory.

As you'd expect, the KDE desktop also provides a terminal window, which is called kvt.

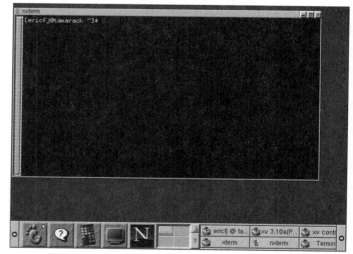

▶ The bare bones X Window shell program is xterm. The gray bar on the left is the scroll bar.

▶ With the older AnotherLevel desktop, nxterm forms the mainstay shell window. **nxterm** offers a scroll bar that is easier to work with.

CROSS-REFERENCE

Chapter 14 covers rlogin. Chapter 3 covers shells.

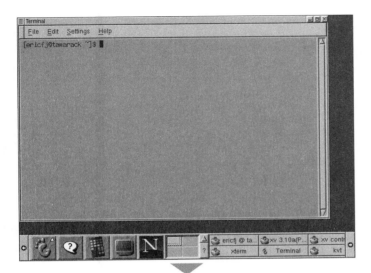

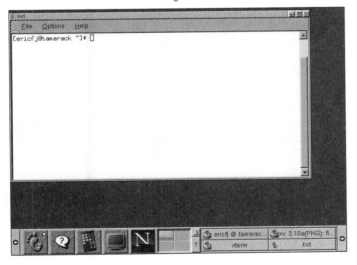

▶ GNOME provides gnome-terminal, an enhanced shell window. Note the bitmap background and the menu bar, from which you can call up new windows or set options.

▶ KDE also provides an enhanced shell window, kvt, which also provides a menu bar for setting options.

TAKE NOTE

▶ **CDE DTTERM**

If you purchase the Common Desktop Environment, or CDE, you have another shell window that you can choose: dtterm, the desktop terminal window. Dtterm is the default shell window on CDE systems.

▶ **LAUNCHNG OTHER PROGRAMS**

By default, shell windows, such as xterm, run your shell inside the window. You can change this by using the **-e** (execute) option to **xterm** or **nxterm**. For example:

$ nxterm -e rlogin nicollet

This command tells nxterm to execute the **rlogin** command instead of your default shell. All parameters after the **-e** option are considered part of the command to run. In this case, that means nxterm will try to run the command **rlogin nicollet**, to remotely log into a system named nicollet.

▶ **KTERM IS NOT THE KDE TERMINAL WINDOW**

Don't be fooled by the *k*; the program called kterm predates the KDE desktop's use of the k prefix. kterm is short for Kanji terminal and supports multiple languages, especially Asian ones. The KDE terminal program is called kvt.

FIND IT ONLINE

GNOME is available at **http://www.gnome.org**.

Controlling Fonts and Setting the Window Size

Even if you prefer to use the shell for everything, by setting the fonts, you can read the screen better and control how many shell windows fit on the display. For example, by properly selecting font sizes, you can ensure that two shell windows can fit side by side on the screen without overlap. If you have a hard time reading the screen, due to lighting conditions or visual acuity, you can select larger, easier-to-read fonts. And, you can also select the fonts that you like.

How you select fonts depends on which shell window you run. If you're running the GNOME or KDE terminal windows, you can select fonts from the window's menus, as shown on the facing page. This makes things a lot easier. If you're running nxterm or xterm, hold down Ctrl and the rightmost mouse button. From the menu that appears, you can select from a number of different-sized fonts. If these fonts meet your needs, you don't have to go any further.

If you want to take a look at the fonts available for your system instead of limiting yourself to the choices provided so far, you can run a number of font-selecting tools, including the GNOME font selector, the KDE font manager, or the X Window program xfontsel. All of these programs provide a preview area so that you can preview the selected font. X Window font names are quite long. The elements in the names are described on the facing page.

You can use the font in the X resource files. For example, to set the default font for nxterm windows, place the following line inside a file named NXTerm in your home directory:

```
*font: -*-courier-*-r-*--12-*-*-*-m-*-*
```

Note the use of wild cards for parts of the long X Window font names. See Table 9-1 for an explanation of all the fields in these long names.

You can list the available fonts within a shell window with the xlsfonts program, short for X list fonts. This program pumps out lots of data, so pipe the results to **more** or **less**.

TAKE NOTE

▶ **DON'T USE PROPORTIONAL FONTS IN SHELL WINDOWS**

All shell windows are intended to work with mono-spaced (fixed-width) or character-cell fonts. If you accidentally choose a proportional font, the characters get spaced inside of fixed-width areas, making the screen hard to read because you cannot always tell where one word ends and another begins.

▶ **SETTING THE WINDOW SIZE**

You can set the starting size for xterm and nxterm windows using the **–geometry** option discussed in Chapter 7. The main difference for shell windows is that these programs take the width and height in terms of characters — most other applications assume the width and height are in pixels. Thus, to create an nxterm window with 80 columns and 42 lines, use the following command:

```
$ nxterm –geometry 80x42 &
```

This does not create a tiny 80-by-42-pixel window, as you might expect.

CROSS-REFERENCE

Chapter 7 discusses command-line parameters and X resource files.

FIND IT ONLINE

For more on X font names, see
http://www.pconline.com/~erc/xfonts.htm.

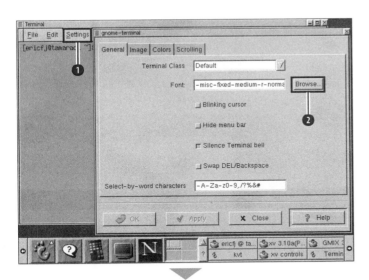

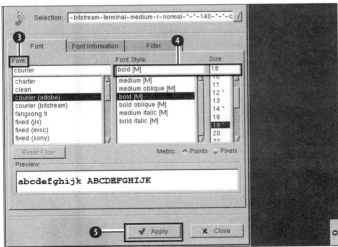

❶ *Call up the gnome-terminal preferences window from the Settings menu.*

❷ *Select a font.*

❸ *Select the font family.*

❹ *Pick the style and size.*

❺ *Click Apply to select the font. You can paste the font name into other windows.*

Table 9-1: PARTS OF A LONG FONT NAME, IN ORDER

Part	Example	Holds
Foundry	adobe, b&h	Font creator
Font family	times, lucidasans	Basic font family name
Weight	bold, medium	Letter thickness
Slant	r	Italic (i), roman (r), oblique (o), reverse italic (ri), reverse oblique (ro), other (ot), or a number for a scaled font
Set-width name	normal, condensed	Width of characters
Additional style	sans	Extra information to describe the font
Pixel size	26	Character height (pixels)
Point size	190	Ten times the character height in points
Dots-per-inch	100–100	Dots per inch in both X and Y directions, usually 100 or 75
Spacing	m	Character cell (c), monospaced (m), proportional (p), or a number for a scaled font
Average width	94	Ten times the average width in pixels
Character set registry	iso8859-1	Character set used for encoding the font, including iso8859-1 (Western European), jisx0208.1983-0 (Japanese), and ksc5601.1987-0 (Korean)

Copy and Paste

One thing that makes shell windows so productive is that you can copy and paste text between shell windows and other windows on your display. All of a sudden, your command line is so much more efficient.

In most windowing systems, such as Windows and the Mac OS, you select text, then copy the text to a clipboard. The clipboard forms a sort of passive data repository. When you paste, you then get the text stored in the clipboard. The X Window System, on the other hand, eliminates the need for the intermediary clipboard, providing a more active form of copy and paste.

You select text within an application. When it comes time to paste — usually by pressing the middle mouse button — your current window queries the window owning the selected text and gets that text directly. There's no intermediary clipboard, so you don't have to stop and copy the text into a clipboard. Instead, you simply select and then paste.

In most applications, particularly command windows, you select text by pressing the leftmost mouse button, holding the button down, and dragging the mouse over the text you want to select. As you drag the mouse, the text should be highlighted.

To paste, activate the window you want to paste in, and then click the middle mouse button. As usual, X expects a three-button mouse. And, as with most things to do with X, you can customize these settings on a per-application basis.

In most applications, double-clicking the leftmost mouse button selects the entire word under the cursor; triple-clicking selects the entire line. This is not supported in all applications, though.

GNOME adds a subtle quirk to this mix. From the Settings menu, you can enter the characters used to control what makes up a word for double-click selecting. By default, a – is treated as part of a word in the GNOME terminal, but not in nxterm or xterm, which may result in selecting more than you expected. Luckily, you can control this behavior in the gnome-terminal application.

TAKE NOTE

PASTED-TEXT SURPRISES

The shell doesn't really know about copying and pasting — that's a function of the shell window wrapped around the shell. Because of this, pasting is treated as simply fast typing. Thus, if you paste into a shell window running the vi text editor, or some other program that requires modes, you might not get what you expect. If you paste into vi, in particular, make sure that the editor is in insert mode before pasting. Otherwise, your text will be interpreted as vi commands, most likely with unpleasant results. The emacs editor knows more about the mouse and should handle pasting correctly. You can also enable mouse support in vim, the enhanced vi, to handle pasting better.

CLIPBOARDS

While X doesn't need a clipboard, you can run **xclipboard** or the KDE **klipper** programs to store multiple selections in a form of clipboard. You can then select the text in part of the clipboard to paste that into another application.

CROSS-REFERENCE

Chapter 5 discusses the vi text editor. Chapter 7 covers the mouse.

FIND IT ONLINE

The KDE home page is **http://www.kde.org**.

Table 9-2: COPY AND PASTE ACTIONS

Action	Results
Drag mouse holding down left button	Selects text
Press middle mouse button	Pastes text
Double-click left button	Selects word under mouse cursor
Triple-click left button	Selects entire line under cursor

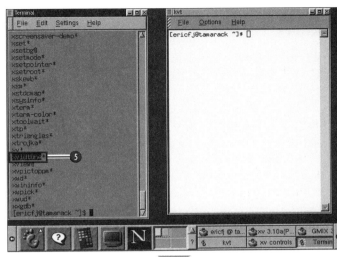

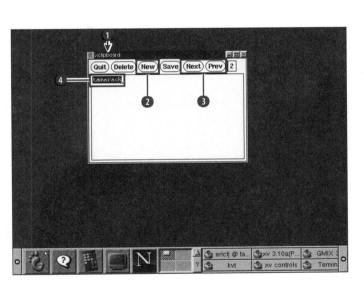

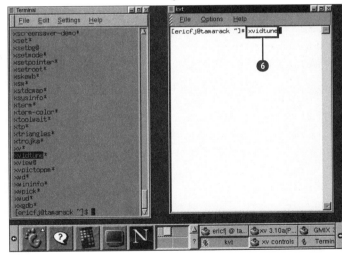

1 *You can store text you select in xclipboard.*

2 *When you want a new area for storage, click New.*

3 *To navigate, click Next or Prev.*

4 *Select the text to be pasted in other applications.*

5 *Select text with the leftmost mouse button.*

6 *Paste with the middle mouse button.*

189

Personal Workbook

Q&A

1. When you run a graphical desktop, can you get access to a Linux shell?

2. Name three different shell window programs.

3. Which mouse button do you normally use to select text?

4. Does text need to be copied to a clipboard before it can be pasted?

5. Which mouse button is normally used for pasting text?

6. How much text does a triple-click select?

7. Can you run a clipboard program on Linux?

8. How can you make nxterm run a program other than your shell?

ANSWERS: PAGE 338

190

EXTRA PRACTICE

1. Paste text into a shell window running the **vi** text editor. If the initial letters are not *a, A, i, l, o,* or *O,* then it is likely that you will run a number of vi commands. Test this with a scratch file that is not essential to your work. Always be careful when pasting into vi windows.

2. Select text in a shell window and paste it in an emacs window. (Chapter 5 covers emacs if you are unfamiliar with this editor.) Open a scratch file and click in the middle of the window to paste, and watch what happens. Notice how this is different from pasting in vi.

3. Run the xclipboard application and paste a number of text messages into the window. Now, select some of these messages and paste them in a text editor window.

REAL-WORLD APPLICATIONS

✔ You or some of your colleagues are software developers who want to display two shell windows side by side. Figure out the right font settings to enable this for your display.

✔ Other colleagues want to run the KDE terminal program **kvt** from the GNOME desktop, but have been told that this is not possible. Prove to them that they can run it by launching **kvt**. Then show the KDE menus under the main GNOME menus from the taskbar.

✔ Users are arguing about shell window programs and efficiency. Run **nxterm**, **kvt**, and **gnome-terminal**. Use the **top** program to determine which uses the least amount of memory.

Visual Quiz

How would you change fonts from this **nxterm** window?

_____

_____

_____

_____

_____

_____

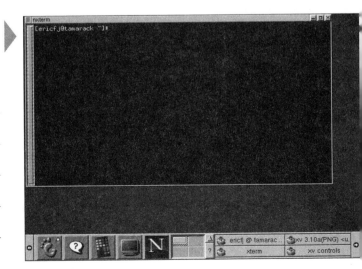

CHAPTER 10

MASTER
THESE
SKILLS

▶ **Setting Up Your Sound Card**

▶ **Playing Sounds**

▶ **Playing Audio CDs**

Playing Sounds and Music on Your PC

Basic PCs cannot do a lot with sound. The built-in speaker allows for simple beeps and that's about it. To provide better output, you need some form of sound adapter card. With such an add-on card, you can play sounds, record sounds, and impress your neighbors. You can also share a sound card amongst a number of applications. Fortunately, Linux includes a wide variety of sound software. This chapter discusses setting up and using your sound card under Linux.

Until recently, quality sound output cost enough money that many people skipped sound cards entirely. Owners of business PCs especially avoided the extra money that it cost to add sound support. Home users stuck to low-cost systems, too. So, for most of its history, Linux's emphasis has not been on support for audio output. Instead, Linux has focused on server applications, graphics, networking, and supporting hard disks and backup media. In recent years, though, that's changed.

As costs have dropped, sound cards are now common in just about every PC. As of this writing, you can get high-quality sound cards for under $40, and many motherboards come with built-in "sound cards." In fact, you can even buy subwoofers and other high-end speakers for your PC, just like your real stereo. So, the next logical step is to take advantage of your hardware to play music, add sound to user interfaces, or have a lot more fun playing games.

Today, Linux supports a large number of sound cards. Red Hat Linux includes a handy **sndconfig** utility, which you can use to configure your sound card. And, unlike Windows, you don't have to reboot after setting up your sound card.

Red Hat Linux comes with a good assortment of tools for playing and working with sounds. Even so, because of the fast-paced nature of multimedia on PCs, it is likely that you will need to download new tools and updates to existing tools to handle all the advances in sound-playing technology.

Many of the tools available to play sound on your PC also require an X Window desktop. Just like Windows, many of the sound tools display from the desktop and present a graphical interface using a stereo equipment metaphor, such as play, stop, and pause buttons. If you haven't yet set up X, now is the time to do so. There are, however, text-only tools that allow you to accomplish everything on the console that you can under X.

Setting Up Your Sound Card

You must first verify that you have a compatible sound card. Table 10-1 lists the current choices. Many sound cards are compatible with the main SoundBlaster formats, so even if your card isn't on this list, Linux may still see the card as a SoundBlaster.

Before you can play any sounds from your speakers, you need to set up your sound card. To set up your sound card, run the **sndconfig** program, stored in /usr/sbin (not in your default path):

```
# /usr/sbin/sndconfig
```

You should run this program as the root user, hence the # prompt, which indicates you're logged in as the special root user.

The first screen you see, shown in the upper-left corner of the facing page, tells you it will probe for your sound card. In general, if you have a SoundBlaster or compatible card, **sndconfig** should find it.

After probing, **sndconfig** writes the proper kernel module configuration files to add your sound card. Then, you hear Linus Torvalds, the creator of Linux, explain how he pronounces Linux (as something like LEE-nooks). This test sound proves that **sndconfig** set things up correctly.

If you don't hear Linus talk, then you need to troubleshoot your setup. Unfortunately, troubleshooting sound problems is not easy, especially if you have a Plug-and-Play sound card (most cards made within the last four years are Plug-and-Play). The best places to go for help are the Sound HOWTO and the Plug-and-Play HOWTO. The procedures in these documents will work for 90 percent of the soundcards available today. If you know the card is supported, that means someone has gotten it to work. If you have access to the World Wide Web, search for someone who has gotten it to work, and ask how they did it.

If you've gotten the card to work, you can get information on the card from the special sound device information file /dev/sndstat:

```
$ cat /dev/sndstat
OSS/Free:3.8s2++-971130
Load type: Driver loaded as a module

Kernel: Linux tamarack.foster-johnson.com
2.0.36 #1 Tue Oct 13 22:17:11 EDT 1998
i686
Config options: 0

Installed drivers:

Card config:

Audio devices:
0: Sound Blaster 16 (4.16)

Synth devices:
0: AWE32-0.4.2c (RAM512k)

Midi devices:
0: Sound Blaster 16

Timers:
0: System clock

Mixers:
0: Sound Blaster
1: AWE32 Equalizer
```

If you see output similar to this, then your sound card is set up and running. If not, start digging into the HOWTO documents for the make and model of your card.

CROSS-REFERENCE
Chapter 6 covers kernel modules.

ON THE CD-ROM
Look up Sound-HOWTO and Sound-Playing-HOWTO in /usr/doc/HOWTO.

Playing Sounds and Music on Your PC

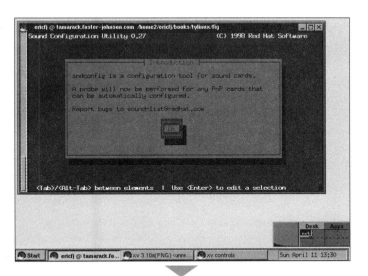

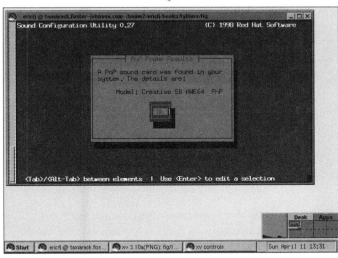

## CHAPTER 10

▶ Click OK to tell **sndconfig** to probe for your sound card.

▶ After probing, **sndconfig** found a SoundBlaster AWE sound card or close compatible. Click OK to update the Linux configuration files for your sound card.

Table 10-1: COMPATIBLE SOUND CARDS

Card	Notes
Ensoniq SoundScape	Reveal and Spea compatibles
Gravis Ultrasound	
Gravis Ultrasound ACE	
Gravis Ultrasound Max	
Gravis Ultrasound	Version with 16-bit sampling
Logitech SoundMan	SoundMan 16, Games, and Wave
MAD16 Pro	Only the OPTi 82C928, 82C929, 82C930, 82C924 chipsets
Media Vision Jazz16	
MediaTriX AudioTriX Pro	
Microsoft Windows Sound System	Also called MSS or WSS
Mozart	OAK OTI-601
Personal Sound System	Also called PSS
Pro Audio Spectrum 16	Pro Audio Studio 16
Pro Sonic 16	
Roland MPU-401 MIDI interface	
SoundBlaster 1.0	
SoundBlaster 16	
SoundBlaster 16ASP	
SoundBlaster 2.0	
SoundBlaster AWE32	
SoundBlaster Pro	
TI TM4000M notebook	
ThunderBoard	
Turtle Beach Tropez	Classic model but not Plus
Turtle Beach Maui	
Yamaha FM synthesizers	OPL2, OPL3, and OPL4 models
6850 UART MIDI Interface	

Playing Sounds

Once your sound card is set to go, you'll likely want to play sounds. Linux includes a number of sound utilities, and you can download more from the Internet.

One of the big problems with sound files lies in the proliferation of incompatible formats. You'll find sound files with .au, .aiff, .wav, and a host of other extensions — each indicating a different file format. Some of these formats come from particular vendors of UNIX systems, such as Sun Microsystems and Silicon Graphics.

The main Windows sound format is WAV, promoted by Microsoft. An up-and-coming format is MP3, which is short for MPEG 2 Level 3, a major format used for digital music.

You can use the Linux **play** command for all formats except MP3:

```
play filename
```

For example:

```
$ play incomingmessage.wav
```

In addition to the .wav format, **play** supports a host of other formats, including .au. For example:

```
$ play exterminate.au
```

To deal with the plethora of sound file formats, you can use the **sox** (sound exchange) utility, which is part of the **play** package. **sox** enables you to convert sound files from one format to another. Table 10-2 list the supported formats.

The online manual page for **sox** lists a zillion options, but for most usage you can simply pass the name of the input file and then the name of the output file, as shown here:

```
$ sox filename.au filename.wav
```

CROSS-REFERENCE

Chapter 8 covers MPEG video.

In this example, the file name extensions tell **sox** which formats to use. The .au extension tells **sox** that the input file is a Sun audio format file; the .wav extension tells **sox** that the desired output is a Windows .wav sound file.

The main area left unsupported by **sox** and **play** commands is the rapidly expanding arena of MP3 files. These files are used to store almost CD-quality music in a greatly compressed form. MP3 is often claimed as the bane of recording industry distributors, because files can be freely exchanged over the Internet. To play MP3 files, you need to use either the **mpg123** command-line program or **x11amp**, which runs under the X Window System. You can also download programs such as freeamp from the Internet. Table 10-3 lists a number of sites for these applications.

TAKE NOTE

INSTALLATION PROBLEMS WITH FREEAMP

The FreeAmp installation notes don't clearly indicate where you need to install the freeamp plugins. The installation notes tell you to copy the plugins directory to /usr/local/lib/freeamp. What this really means is copy all files in the FreeAmp plugins directory to /usr/local/lib/freeamp/plugins. If you get an error that FreeAmp cannot find a plugin, it is because the plugin files were not installed in /usr/local/lib/freeamp/plugins.

SOUNDBLASTER AWE UTILITIES

The awesfx package contains a number of utilities specifically for the SoundBlaster AWE series of sound cards. If you have one of these cards, this package is for you.

XAUDIO IS SHAREWARE

If you download and use it, you should pay the licensing fee.

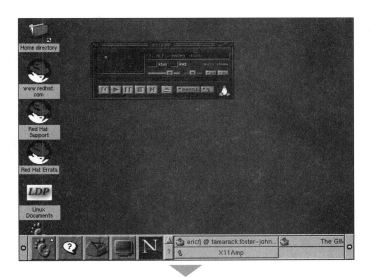

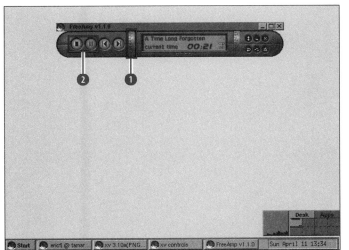

▶ *Click the x11amp play button to play MP3 music files. The x11amp interface closely mirrors that of the Windows winamp program.*

❶ *Adjust the music volume in the FreeAmp player.*

❷ *Pause or stop the music when your boss comes by.*

Table 10-2: SOUND FORMATS SUPPORTED BY THE PLAY AND SOX COMMANDS

Extension	Format
.8svx	Amiga 8SVX format for musical instrument descriptions
.aiff	Apple/Silicon Graphics sound format
au	Sun Microsystems sound format
.cdr	Raw CD-R stereo audio samples
.dat	Special textual format
.hcom	Macintosh HCOM sound format
.maud	Another Amiga IFF sound format
.raw	Special raw sound format
.sf	IRCAM sound format
.smp	Turtle Beach SampleVision format
.voc	SoundBlaster VOC format
.wav	Windows sound format
.wve	Psion handheld sound format

Table 10-3: MP3 SOFTWARE FOR LINUX

URL	Holds
http://www.freeamp.org	FreeAmp
http://www.x11amp.org	X11Amp
http://www.xaudio.com	XAudio shareware player
http://replay.linuxpower.com	Replay
http://www.xmms.org	XMMS is the new name for x11amp

FIND IT ONLINE

You can download many MP3 songs from Web sites such as **http://www.mp3.com**.

Playing Audio CDs

Linux also supports playing audio CDs, and you don't need a sound card to do so if your CD drive has a headphone jack. With its superb multitasking capability, you can turn your computer into a stereo system as well as continue with your computing work.

GNOME and KDE come with their own CD players, called **gtcd** and **kscd**, respectively, or you can use the **xplaycd** program. When **gtcd** starts, a window similar to that shown in the first image on the facing page displays, with buttons that match the traditional controls on a CD player. From this window you can start, stop, and skip tracks. You can also control the output volume (which only works if you're playing through a sound card).

If you click the open track editor icon, you can call up the Track Editor window to enter in the CD's title and the title of each song. If you do this, then every time the CD plays, you'll see the name of each song as it plays. **gtcd** keeps a local database of all the CDs for which you've entered information. **gtcd** can also connect to the global CDDB — Compact Disc Database — maintained by cddb.com on the Internet. Select the Preferences icon to configure the location of the CDDB site. After you are finished entering the CD and song names, click OK to apply your changes. Also, use the right mouse button to call up the menu and select Save to ensure that your new entry is saved.

Another handy program is called **gmix**. This program enables you to mix audio sources together for output to the speakers. The last image on the facing page shows **gmix**. If you don't run the GNOME desktop, you can also run **xmixer**.

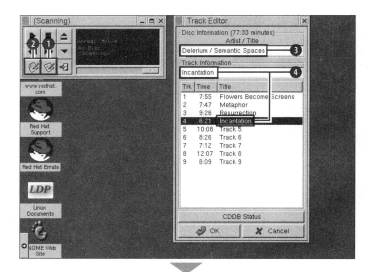

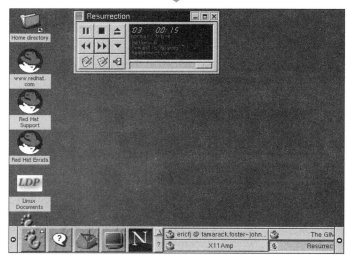

❶ Click the Preferences icon in **gtcd** to configure the CDDB settings.

❷ Click the open track editor icon to get the Track Editor window.

❸ Enter the name of the CD.

❹ Select a track and enter in the song title.

▶ The artist name, CD name, and song title appear in the **gtcd** window after editing the track information.

CROSS-REFERENCE

Chapter 3 covers the **chmod** command.

198

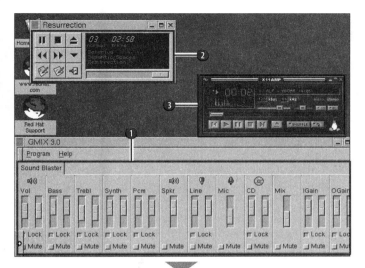

❶ The **gmix** application lets you mix sounds from various sources and control the volume.

❷ **gtcd** plays CDs.

❸ **x11amp** plays MP3 files.

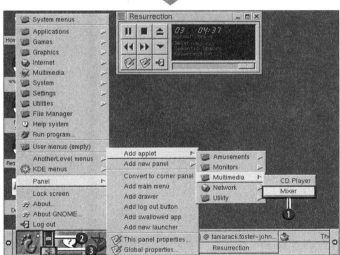

❶ From the GNOME Panel menu select Add applet. Choose the Mixer applet to add volume control to the desktop. You can also add a CD player.

❷ Once added, adjust the volume from the GNOME taskbar.

❸ Mute the sound by clicking the mute button.

TROUBLESHOOTING

▶ ERRORS WHEN PLAYING CDS

If you run **xplaycd** and cannot get your CD to play, look for the following error on the shell window you used to launch **xplaycd**:

As root, please run

chmod 666 /dev/cdrom

to give yourself permission to access the CD-ROM device.

If you see this error, then you need to run the following command as root:

chmod 666 /dev/cdrom

You should now be able to play audio CDs. **gtcd** or **kscd** may give you a similar error.

▶ ERROR EDITING TRACK INFO

When you click the right mouse button in **xplaycd** and try to edit the track info for a CD, you may see an error dialog that /usr/local/lib/cddb doesn't exist or that you have no permissions to write to it. You need this directory to store the CD track information. The following commands, when executed by the root user, solve the problem:

mkdir /usr/local/lib/cddb
chmod a+rwx /usr/local/lib/cddb

▶ GTCD KEEPS ON PLAYING

If you exit **gtcd** without stopping the CD, it continues to play.

FIND IT ONLINE

Another CD player is called **XFreeCD**. See
http://www.tatoosh.com/nexus/xfreecd.shtml.

199

Personal Workbook

Q&A

1 Can Linux systems play sounds or do you have to run Windows?

_____

_____

_____

2 What command do you use to play Windows .wav sound files?

_____

_____

_____

3 What command do you use to play Sun .au sound files?

_____

_____

_____

4 Can you play audio CDs in Linux?

_____

_____

_____

5 Does Red Hat Linux come with utilities to play MP3 files?

_____

_____

_____

6 What does MP3 stand for, anyway?

_____

_____

_____

7 How can you convert a sound file from one format to another?

_____

_____

_____

8 Which command do you use to mix audio sources together?

_____

_____

_____

ANSWERS: PAGE 339

EXTRA PRACTICE

1. Check the permissions of the CD-ROM device, /dev/cdrom, to see whether you can access it.

2. Verify that your sound card is compatible with Linux.

3. Download an MP3 player such as FreeAmp (from **http://www.freeamp.org**).

4. Download another MP3 package. Use the one you like better.

5. Download some MP3 songs from a legal site such as **http://www.mp3.com**.

6. Play music from a CD as well as from another source, such as an MP3 file and use the **xmixer** or **gmix** programs to adjust the sounds to something you find coherent.

REAL-WORLD APPLICATIONS

✔ Your sound card doesn't appear to work. Reboot the machine and review the section "Setting Up Your Sound Card" in this chapter to try to determine the problem.

✔ A number of examples in this chapter discussed opening various device files, such as /dev/cdrom, to allow any user access. Consider whether, from a security point of view, this is a good idea for your site.

✔ MP3 files are often used to bootleg music illegally. They are also used legitimately by thousands of bands, many of which do not have big-label recording contracts. You don't want to get the recording industry associations after you, but you want to listen to great music. Besides, where else can you get Swedish reggae music? Discuss what you should do with your colleagues.

Visual Quiz

How could you increase the treble volume using the program shown here?

_____

_____

_____

_____

_____

_____

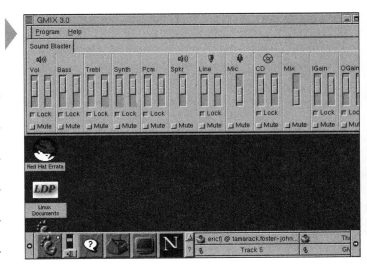

CHAPTER 11

MASTER
THESE
SKILLS

- ▶ Accessing Windows Floppy Disks
- ▶ Accessing Windows File Systems
- ▶ Running Windows Applications

Working with Microsoft Windows

Microsoft Windows exists. So there! Much as some would like it to happen, Windows isn't going to disappear anytime soon. In fact, the PC you're running Linux on probably originally ran Windows. You may still have a dual-boot system or you may be running Linux only on your system. In any case, it is likely that you will need to exchange data with Windows systems.

And that's not too bad. One of Linux's hallmarks is its support for standards such as Internet protocols for networking. It's Windows that likely wants to live in its own world. So, you need to set up your Linux box to talk the way Windows wants in order to get much done.

One of the most comon tasks Windows users perform is working with office software such as Microsoft Word and Excel. (Microsoft clearly dominates that market.) There are a number of Linux alternatives that support a reasonable file conversion capability with MS Word. Typically, these programs won't support all the features of Microsoft Word or the latest file formats, but, in general, you can save your data in Word format and then transfer the files to your Windows systems.

Software such as WordPerfect from Corel, ApplixWare from Applix, or StarOffice from Star Division maintain a reasonable conversion to and from Microsoft Office formats. All are discussed in Chapter 8. And both WordPerfect and StarOffice sell Windows versions of their software as well, so you could standardize on an office suite that runs on multiple operating systems, including Linux. To convert your files, though, you need to transfer the files between the Linux and Windows systems. Here, a number of Linux commands can help.

You can access Windows hard disks and floppies from Linux. You can mount Windows hard drives as Linux file systems under the root, and you can copy files to and from DOS-formatted floppies. Using special mtools commands, you don't even have to mount Windows floppies; you can access them directly. Furthermore, you can run some DOS and Windows applications from special emulators that run on Linux.

This chapter covers a number of specific ways in which you can work with Windows systems from Linux, be it transferring files via floppy disks or over a network.

Accessing Windows Floppy Disks

In the PC realm, virtually all PCs still ship with floppy disk drives. This makes floppies a great medium for exchanging files between Linux and Windows systems.

A suite of utilities called mtools provides the capability to read and write DOS floppy disks. In this suite, most of the programs are named for the corresponding DOS tools, with an m in front. For example, the program to copy files to and from a floppy disk is **mcopy**, and it acts like the DOS copy program. To copy a Linux file to a DOS-formatted floppy disk in drive A:, use the following command:

```
$ mcopy report.txt "a:"
```

The mtools programs understand the name A: to mean the first floppy. Under the hood, Table 11-1 lists the Linux device files for the A: and B: floppy drives. The file **/etc/mtools.conf** tells the mtools which Linux devices to use for the A: and B: drives.

To copy files from a DOS floppy to your Linux hard disk, use the following format:

```
$ mcopy "a:*.txt" .
```

This command passes the a:*.txt to **mcopy** in double quotes because you don't want the Linux shell expanding the wildcard *.txt. The final . on the comand tells **mcopy** to place the files in the current directory.

To see what files are on a DOS floppy, use the **mdir** command:

```
$ mdir "a:"
```

As Listing 11-3 shows, mtools support long filenames on the floppy. This is very handy because Linux files seldom have short DOS-compatible file names.

To delete a file on a floppy, use **mdel**.

TAKE NOTE

▶ **PERMISSION ERRORS ON FLOPPIES**

You may see the following error when you first try to access a floppy disk using one of the mtools utilities:

```
$ mcopy chap10.txt a:
Can't open /dev/fd0: Permission
denied
Cannot initialize 'A:'
Bad target a:
```

In this case, the permissions on the floppy disk device, /dev/fd0, do not allow you access. This was done purposely to shore up a security hole and prevent users from accessing the floppy drives. If you're the only user of your Linux system, chances are this isn't an issue. In any case, you can run the following command as root to enable all users to have access to the A: drive:

```
# chmod 666 /dev/fd0*
```

You can do the same for /dev/fd1, the B: drive.

▶ **TEXT FILE TRANSLATIONS**

The –t option to **mcopy** tells the command to translate text files to and from the Linux format (one newline character ends a line) and Windows format (a carriage return and a newline character end each line).

▶ **CHECK WHETHER INSTALLED**

Use the following command to verify that mtools is installed:

```
$ rpm –q mtools
mtools-3.9.1-5
```

CROSS-REFERENCE

The task "Accessing Windows File Systems" covers mounting a floppy disk.

204

Table 11-1: FLOPPY DEVICE FILES

Drive	Device
A:	/dev/fd0
B:	/dev/fd1

Listing 11-1: COPYING FILES TO A FLOPPY

```
$ mcopy *.java "a:"
```
▶ The **mcopy** command works similarly to the **cp** command.

Listing 11-2: READING FILES FROM A FLOPPY

```
$ mcopy -v "a:*.java" .
Copying A:/ConUI.java
File "./ConUI.java" exists,
  overwrite (y/n) ? y
Copying A:/Hello.java
Copying A:/UI.java
```
▶ When copying files from a floppy to your hard disk, if the file already exists on your hard drive, you get a prompt asking whether to overwrite the file. Use the **–v** option for verbose output from **mcopy** that lists all the files copied.

Listing 11-3: LISTING THE FILES ON THE FLOPPY

```
$ mdir "a:"
 Volume in drive A has no label
 Volume Serial Number is 7694-1B87
Directory for A:/

CONUI    JAV 806 04-27-1999 20:34 ConUI.java
HELLO~1  JAV 105 04-27-1999 20:34 Hello.java
UI~1     JAV 184 04-27-1999 20:34 UI.java
         3 files            5 788 bytes
                      1 450 496 bytes free
```
▶ The **mdir** command lists the files on a floppy disk.

Listing 11-4: DELETING FILES

```
$ mdel "a:chap15d.txt"
```
▶ The **mdel** command deletes files on floppy disks.

Listing 11-5: DELETING ALL FILES ON A FLOPPY

```
$ mdel "a:*.*"
```
▶ When using wildcards for files on the floppy, enclose the pattern in quotes so that your Linux shell doesn't try to expand the asterisk. Do this because your shell doesn't know about the a: and b: that **mtools** support.

Listing 11-6: CREATING DIRECTORIES

```
$ mmd "a:tmp"
$ mdir "a:"
 Volume in drive A has no label
 Volume Serial Number is 7694-1B87
Directory for A:/

tmp    <DIR>    05-30-1999  11:04  tmp
       1 file            0 bytes
                 1 457 152 bytes free
```
▶ The **mmd** command creates directories on DOS floppies.

Listing 11-7: CHANGING DIRECTORIES

```
$ mcd "a:/tmp"
$ mcd
A:/tmp
```
▶ If the floppy has subdirectories, you can change directories with the **mcd** command. Typing in the command alone prints out the current directory on the floppy.

SHORTCUT
The KDE disk navigator menu enables you to access floppies from the desktop.

Accessing Windows File Systems

You can access Microsoft Windows file systems from Linux just as you can Linux file systems. And, just like Linux file systems, you must first mount an MS-DOS file system somewhere under the Linux root directory. This may seem odd if you're more used to the Windows notion that each disk has its own root directory, such as C:\ and D:\. On Linux, all file systems from all disks appear underneath the one root file system. The Linux method makes it easier to navigate.

To mount an MS-DOS file system under a directory named **/dosc** (short for DOS C drive), use the following command as root:

```
# mount -t vfat /dev/hda1 /dosc
```

This command mounts the first partition on the first IDE hard drive (/dev/hda1) under a directory named **/dosc** with a file system type of vfat, which supports the long filenames allowed by Microsoft Windows 95 and NT. (If this directory does not already exist, you need to create it first with the **mkdir** command.) A Windows system typically has Windows loaded on C:\, which, in most cases, is the first partition of the first IDE hard drive. If not, change /dev/hda1 in the previous example to the appropriate device name as discussed in Chapter 1.

Now, you may have taken care of all this if you ran Disk Druid when you installed Linux. Disk Druid should have automatically detected your Windows partitions and offered to mount them for you. You can check this by looking in the file /etc/fstab and searching for the term msdos. Use the **grep** command as root:

```
# grep msdos /etc/fstab
/dev/hda1 /msdos msdos defaults 0 0
```

You should see something similar to the /dev/hda1 output shown here. By default, Disk Druid sets the file system type to msdos, which does not support long filenames. If you want long filename support (and most people do), change the third column in fstab from msdos to vfat.

TAKE NOTE

▶ DEALING WITH SPACES

Microsoft Windows supports spaces in filenames. You especially see these with CD-ROMs that were formatted using Microsoft's proprietary Joliet extensions. Spaces are a bad thing for Linux, because spaces separate parameters to commands. This means that if you copy, delete, or otherwise act on a file, the commands will likely fail. To get around this, enclose the file name with double quotes. For example:

```
$ rm "8598-9 fg110101.tif"
```

▶ MOUNTING FLOPPIES

mtools enables you to access DOS-formatted floppies without running the **mount** command. If you prefer, though, you can also mount a floppy disk and then access its files. Typically, the mount point for floppies is /mnt/floppy. The basic command to mount the floppy follows:

```
# mount -t vfat /dev/fd0 /mnt/floppy
```

After you do this, you can see the files on the floppy disk using normal Linux commands such as ls:

```
$ ls /mnt/floppy
03_07_01.tif.gz*    03_vizq.tif.gz*
16_01_02.tif.gz*
03_07_02.tif.gz*    16_01_01.tif.gz*
```

Before you can mount a floppy disk, it must be formatted. The example shown here assumes the disk is formatted with an MS-DOS file system. You can also format floppy disks with a Linux file system.

CROSS-REFERENCE

Samba, covered in Chapter 15, provides for Windows and Linux systems to share files over a network link.

Formatting floppy disks

From Linux, you can format floppy disks with either an MS-DOS file system or a Linux file system. To do this, you need to run two commands. First, you run the **fdformat** command to perform a low-level format. You need to do this no matter which file system you want to use on the floppy — MS-DOS or Linux.

Then, you run a second command, which differs for MS-DOS and Linux, based on which type of file system you want to place on the floppy. To format an MS-DOS floppy, use the **mformat** command, or, if you have the mkdosfs-ygg package installed, you can run mkdosfs which formats the disk a lot faster. If you instead want to format a Linux file system on the floppy, use **mke2fs**.

To run **fdformat**, you need to determine the raw device file name for your floppy disk. The basic format is:

```
/dev/fdNLsz
```

Replace N with the number of the drive, 0 for A:, 1 for B:. Replace the letter L with the code for the type of drive: d for a low-density 5.25-inch drive; D for a low-density 3.5-inch drive; h for a high-density 5.25-inch drive; or H for a high-density 3.5-inch drive. Replace sz with the size of the drive: 360, 720, 1200 (5.25-inch), or 1440 (3.5-inch). The vast majority of A: drives now are high-density 3.5-inch floppy drives with a name of /dev/fd0H1440. So, your command to perform a low-level format will be:

```
# fdformat /dev/fd0H1440
```

After running **fdformat**, you need to place a file system on the drive. Use **mformat** to place an MS-DOS file system on the disk. For a 3.5-inch standard A: drive use the following command:

```
# mformat -h 2 -s 18 -t 80 a:
```

or

```
# mkdosfs /dev/fd0
```

This is for a 3.5-inch 1.44MB standard floppy. The mtools documentation, available with the **info** command, lists the complete options for the disk geometry.

If, instead, you want a Linux file system on the floppy, use the **/sbin/mke2fs** command to make an e2fs file system on the floppy. For example:

```
# /sbin/mke2fs -m 0 /dev/fd0H1440
```

The **-m** option tells **mke2fs** to reserve zero blocks, instead of the default five percent, for the superuser. With floppies, you really don't need to reserve these blocks.

Running Kfloppy on the desktop

If you installed the KDE desktop, you can run the program **kfloppy**, which provides a graphical interface on top of the floppy disk formatting commands. **Kfloppy** formats DOS or Linux (ext2fs) file systems on floppy disks. To do this, you need to tell **kfloppy** which drive, A:, or B:, the floppy is in, along with its size (3.5-inch or 5.25-inch). You need to select whether the disk is high density (HD) or double density (DD). Finally, you need to pick whether to format a DOS file system or the Linux ext2fs file system. **Kfloppy** defaults to the most common case: a 3.5-inch DOS HD disk in drive A:.

When you're ready, click Format.

Kfloppy presents a nice progress bar as it formats the disk. You also see numeric output of the sectors formatted.

After you format a floppy with the Linux ext2fs system, you'll see the lost+found directory that all ext2fs file systems require as a location for storing files that become somehow lost in the file system.

FIND IT ONLINE

The KDE home page, where you can find **kfloppy**, is **http://www.kde.org**.

Running Windows Applications

Wine, a Windows emulator, provides an environment from which you can run Windows applications. The basic concepts behind Wine are fairly simple. Because Linux runs on the same x86 processors as Windows, code compiled to the binary x86 instruction set for Windows is pretty similar to the code compiled for Linux. Only when a program needs to access the operating system — for disks, graphics, keyboard input, files, and so on — is there a difference. Luckily, most Windows applications use shared libraries — called DLLs or *Dynamic Link Libraries* on Windows. So, the Wine developers wrote the Linux equivalent of many of the core DLLs, and therefore Linux can run a number of Windows applications.

You won't get Wine with Red Hat Linux. Instead, you need to download Wine — you can get a .rpm file for WINE from the Red Hat site at **ftp://contrib.redhat.com/libc6/i386/** or from the Wine home page, **http://www.winehq.com**. The package name will be something like **wine-990328-1.i386.rpm**.

To install Wine, download the .rpm file and then issue the following command as root:

```
# rpm -ivh wine*
```

Then, there are a few other things you must do. Check the main Wine configuration file, located in either /etc/wine.conf or /usr/local/etc/wine.conf. This file contains entries for mapping the various MS-DOS disks, such as the A: drive to the Linux device file for the floppy /dev/fd0. The wine.conf file appears as an old-fashioned Windows INI (initialization) file with sections such as [Drive A] to configure the A: drive. The most important entry to edit is the [Drive C] section, as shown here:

```
[Drive C]
Path=/home/msdos
Type=hd
Label=MS-DOS
Filesystem=msdos
```

By default, Wine expects a home of /home/msdos for the top-level directory of what it considers to be the C: drive. Now, if you have mounted a Windows file system, you can use that. Otherwise, you can create a Linux directory of /home/msdos, and then at least two subdirectories: windows and windows/system. These directories are expected to match the C:\WINDOWS and C:\WINDOWS\SYSTEM directory under Windows.

Whichever approach you take — mounting an MS-DOS partition or creating directories on your Linux partition — you need to ensure that the DLLs needed for an application reside in the proper place, typically /home/msdos/windows/system for most system DLLs.

To run the Freecell game, for example, you need two files: freecell.exe (usually in C:\WINDOWS) and cards.dll (usually in C:\WINDOWS\SYSTEM). Copy these files to their respective locations under /home/msdos (or mount an MS-DOS file system). You can then run the freecell game with the following command:

```
$ wine /home/msdos/windows/freecell.exe
```

The basic format of the **wine** command is:

```
$ wine program_name
```

When you run a program, you may get an error similar to the following:

```
$ wine windows/freecell.exe
Could not load 'C:\WINDOWS\CARDS.dll'
required by 'FREECELL', error=2
wine: can't exec 'windows/freecell.exe':
file not found
```

FIND IT ONLINE

Another means to run Windows itself under Linux is available from **http://www.vmware.com**.

This error tells us that Freecell required a particular DLL. You then need to get the proper DLL file and install it in /home/msdos/windows/system, or the same directory as the program.

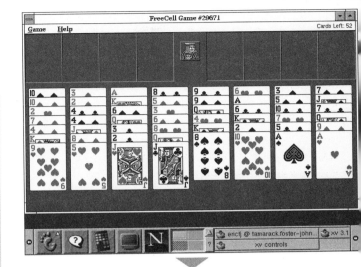

TAKE NOTE

▶ BE LEGAL

You should have a legal copy of Windows if you use any of the Windows shared libraries (DLLs).

▶ WINE IS NOT FOR ALL USERS

Wine is still under active development. Some major applications, such as Microsoft Word and Excel, do not work well — if at all — under Wine, but others work just fine. Your mileage may vary, as they say. Don't be surprised if Wine does not work at all.

For us, the Wine consistently dumped **core** (indicating a program crash) when we quit the simple Freecell application. Luckily, this only happened when we quit the application.

There's an online database listing which programs work with Wine at **http://www.winehq.com/Apps/query.cgi**. Applications such as Microsoft's Word and Excel are not rated as working very well in this list. Check the Wine home page (**http://www.winehq.com**) frequently to download updates.

▶ DOSEMU

A package similar to Wine is called DOSEMU, short for DOS emulator. DOSEMU runs DOS programs in virtual-86 mode. To install DOSEMU, install all rpm files from the Red Hat FTP site (see Appendix B) that start with dos. Then test DOSEMU. First, edit the /etc/dosemu.users file as root and make an entry for yourself (you can copy the root entry and replace root with your user name for full access, which does form a security hole). Then, type the **dos** command.

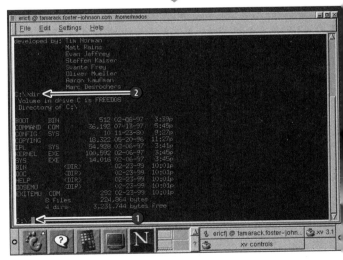

▶ *The freecell game under Wine.*

❶ *Run the **dos** command to see something akin to DOS.*

❷ *Enter DOS commands such as **DIR** to see a directory listing.*

Personal Workbook

Q&A

1 What program can you use to copy files to a floppy disk?

_____

_____

_____

2 What program can you use to copy files from a floppy disk to your Linux hard disk?

_____

_____

_____

3 What is the Linux device filename that corresponds to the A: drive?

_____

_____

_____

4 What do you need to know to format a floppy drive?

_____

_____

_____

5 Can Linux support long format Windows filenames on floppy disks?

_____

_____

_____

6 Where is the typical location for mounting floppy disks?

_____

_____

_____

7 What does **DOSEMU** do?

_____

_____

_____

8 What can you use to run Windows applications under Linux?

_____

_____

_____

ANSWERS: PAGE 339

EXTRA PRACTICE

1. Look up the online manual information on the mtools programs. There's an online manual page (**man mtools**) as well as information available from the **info** command (**info mtools**).

2. Format a floppy disk using the **fdformat** command. After the low-level format completes, format for a DOS file system with **mformat**.

3. Now, format a floppy disk again with **fdformat**, and then place a Linux ext2fs file system on the disk with **mke2fs**.

4. If you've loaded the KDE desktop, try out **kfloppy**, which makes the task of formatting floppy disks a lot easier.

5. Check the Wine home page for updated software.

REAL-WORLD APPLICATIONS

✔ Your organization uses Microsoft Word and Excel as a corporate standard. You want to run these applications from Linux. Check the Wine Web compatibility lists at **http://www.winehq.com/Apps/query.cgi** to see what other users have reported about running Excel or Word under Wine.

✔ Now try Wine for yourself. See if you can get a Microsoft Windows application to run under Wine.

✔ Because most floppy disks come preformatted for DOS, try exchanging files from a Microsoft Windows system to a Linux system. In general, it's a good idea to avoid file names with spaces in them when exchanging files with Linux.

Visual Quiz

What type of commands could you enter at this prompt?

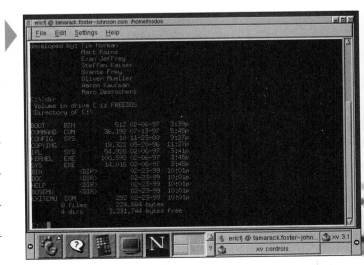

CHAPTER 12

MASTER THESE SKILLS

- ▶ Shoot 'Em Up
- ▶ Quiet Contemplation

Games

While Linux supports quite a few serious business applications, your life with Linux doesn't have to be all serious. Linux also runs quite a few games, including big-time shoot-'em-ups such as Quake, Doom, and Heretic.

Major gaming companies have awakened to the Linux phenomenon, including id Software, makers of the aforementioned games, and Loki Entertainment Software, which ported Civilization: Call to Power to Linux. Linux is nowhere near as popular as Windows for gaming software, but in the next year or so, we expect to see a lot more games available for Linux. Home hobbyists make up a large portion of the Linux installed base, as well as a large portion of game buyers. Many of these Linux users run dual-boot machines just to run certain games that do not yet have Linux counterparts.

Furthermore, many games already exist on Linux, especially in the form of freeware clones of commercial games. For example, Freeciv is a freeware clone of the popular game Civilization. You can also purchase the commercial version.

One of the most popular applications that ships with Windows is the card game Solitaire, with a variant called Freecell close behind. You'll find clones of these games on Linux. In fact, there's about four or five versions of Freecell to pick from, in addition to a plethora of other games.

No matter which X Window desktop environment you run, be it Red Hat's AnotherLevel, GNOME, or KDE, there is a Games menu on the taskbar at the bottom of the screen. Most of these games are rather simple affairs, such as variants of the Solitaire card game and a version of Minesweeper.

To run more complex games, such as Doom or Quake, you need to install extra packages. Sometimes these come in Red Hat package manager, or RPM, format, but most often they do not. We also found that many games require a fairly complex set up and configuration process, so be patient if you want to run the big-time games.

To help set these games up, you'll appreciate the information available at **http://www.linuxgames. com**, a major Linux gaming site. And, true to the tradition of Linux, look for HOWTO documents to help you get going with various games. For example, the Quake HOWTO proved very helpful, and there's even a HOWTO to getting Blizzard Entertainment's StarCraft — a Microsoft Windows game — to run under Linux using Wine, a Windows emulator that is discussed in Chapter 11.

Shoot 'Em Up

One of the most popular genres of games is the classic travel-around-the-universe-meet-strange creatures-and-kill-them game. The premiere games in this genre at various times have been Doom, Heretic, and the various versions of Quake, all of which are first-person shooter games, in which your weapon points forward in a three-dimensional environment and you get to kill enemies.

When we first saw the various Quake, Doom, and Heretic packages, we thought these would be way cool to run on Linux. After spending far too much time trying to get them to work and downloading alternative packages, we fully appreciated the fragility of these games, originally designed for the DOS platform.

You can get these games from the Web sites listed in Table 12-1. We were able to find RPM packages for Doom and Heretic. Heretic ran, but Doom did not. Quake came in a number of different formats, including a plain Linux executable with no documentation.

All of the games require special files — called WAD files — that hold information about the levels of play (the areas you explore) and all those nasty monsters. To get the WAD files, you typically need to install the DOS version of the game on a system running DOS. Then, you can transfer the very large WAD files to your Linux system. You can also run a number of utilities designed to extract the DOS files from the specially compressed DOS game packages. Heretic includes a runnable WAD file in /usr/lib/games/heretic when you install the RPM package listed in Table 12-1. If you change to this directory and run heretic, everything goes fine. With the version of Doom from the RPM file, the music server, or **musserver**, failed, bringing down the whole game engine. We even tried WAD files from the commercial

version of Doom II, to no avail. (The game engines are surprisingly fragile.)

We were able to get another version of Doom, called LxDoom, to run, after downloading it from **http://lxdoom.linuxgames.com**. This version requires a commercial WAD file and will not run the shareware WAD files that you can download from the Internet.

All of these games appear somewhat small on the Linux display. For performance reasons under DOS, these games appear in a 320-by-240-pixel window, which appears incredibly small on modern X Window displays.

TAKE NOTE

▶ BE LEGAL

Game vendors such as id Software release Linux versions of their game players, but you should either register the shareware version or purchase a commercial version to get the WAD files, the files that describe the actual levels of the game. If game vendors see that Linux has no revenue potential, they will avoid our favorite operating system and stick to Windows. We'd like more vendors to wake up and port their wares to Linux. You can also purchase a commercial version of Quake for Linux.

▶ QUAKE 3 ARENA

Quake 3 Arena morphs the popular Quake game away from its first-person shooter style to full-blown arena combat. You can get Linux versions from **http://www.quake3arena.com**.

CROSS-REFERENCE
Chapter 14 covers the **tar** and **gzip** commands needed to unpack LxDoom.

FIND IT ONLINE
Check out the Linux-Quake HOWTO at **http://www.linuxgames.com/quake/**.

Table 12-1: GAME-RELATED WEB SITES

URL	Contains
http://lxdoom.linuxgames.com	LxDoom
http://www.idsoftware.com	Home site for id Software, makers of Quake, Doom, and Heretic
http://rufus.w3.org/linux/RPM/contrib/libc6/i386/Games.html	RPMs for Doom and Heretic, amongst other games
http://www.handeye.com	Sells Linux games
http://www.linuxgames.com/	Linux Games site
http://www.linuxgames.com/quake/	Quake HOWTO
http://www.happypenguin.org/news	Linux Game Tome News
http://www.freeciv.org	Home for the freeciv Civilization clone
http://www.quake3arena.com	Home of id Software's newest version of Quake

Listing 12-1: UNPACKING AND RUNNING LXDOOM

```
$ gunzip lxdoom-v1_3_7_i386_tar.gz
$ tar xvof lxdoom-v1_3_7_i386_tar
$ cd lxdoom
$ lxdoom -iwad doom2.wad
```

▶ You can run **lxdoom** but you need a commercial Doom WAD file. Here we use the file from Doom II.

▶ LxDoom appears in a very small window.

▶ Run /usr/games/heretic from /usr/lib/games/heretic.

Quiet Contemplation

If you don't like the high-octane violence-prone games discussed so far, or maybe just want to play something that doesn't alert your officemates with lots of noise, which you get running a game like Doom, Linux offers a number of quieter games as well.

Both the KDE and GNOME desktops offer virtually identical Freecell clones, a form of solitaire card game popular on Microsoft Windows.

Both the GNOME and KDE desktops include a number of other games, including versions of mahjongg, an Asian game where you remove tiles in pairs. KDE includes Shisen-Sho, a game similar to mahjongg that proves especially addicting when you should be working. Other games include AisleRiot, a Klondike version of solitaire, as well as numerous Tetris and Minesweeper clones. Launch these games from the taskbar's Games menu. Also look to the KDE and AnotherLevel Games menus.

Based on the popular Civilization game, Freeciv is a freeware clone of the game in which you build cities, industry, and armed forces in an attempt to dominate the world. In Civilization, you act as the ruler or deity over a group of people from 2000 B.C. to beyond A.D. 2500. You get to pick from a number of ancient civilizations such as the Romans, Greeks, and Egyptians, as the base for your cities and forces.

And, if you get tired of playing alone, Freeciv is designed for multiuser play. The main part of the game is run by the freeciv server, civserver. Each player then runs the Freeciv client program, civclient. From civclient, you can specify the location of the Freeciv server as any machine on the network, allowing for network play between a number of users.

To run Freeciv, you need to first start the server, civserver, on a Linux machine on your network. Then, start the client program, civclient. Start one copy of civclient for each player. When you start civclient you need to tell it the location of the machine running the civserver program, if the server is running on a different system. Listing 12-3 shows this. Then, when all the players have logged in, go to the civserver prompt and type **s**, start the game.

You can also start the Freeciv client and server from separate choices on the taskbar menus. Call up the AnotherLevel menu and look for the Games menu.

TAKE NOTE

GETTING THE REAL CIVILIZATION GAME
You can purchase the commercial version of Civilization: Call to Power for Linux from **http://www.handeye.com**.

PERCY, THE TALKING PENGUIN
While not so quiet, **percy**, by Malcolm Kavalsky, creates a talking Linux penguin on your display. You can get **percy** from **http://members.xoom.com/kavalsky/percy.htm**.

EARTHRISE OVER LINUX
xglobe and **xplanet** both enable you to place images of planets in the background of your screen. With **xplanet**, you can even move the position of the earth to see different hemispheres. See **http://wwwrzstud.rz.uni-karlsruhe.de/~uddn/xglobe/** and **alumnus.caltech.edu/~hari/xplanet**.

CROSS-REFERENCE
Chapter 11 shows how to run the Windows Freecell game via Wine, a Windows emulator.

FIND IT ONLINE
The Freeciv home page is **http://www.freeciv.org**.

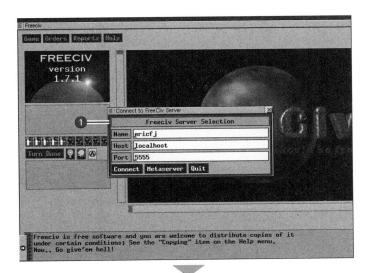

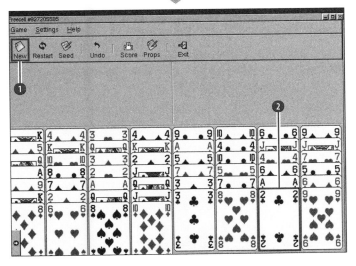

① Click New to start a game.

② Use the mouse to move cards.

Listing 12-2: LAUNCHING THE FREECIV SERVER

```
$ civserver
Freeciv version 1.7.1 server
> 1: Sending info to metaserver
    [platinum.daimi.aau.dk 12245]
Metaserver: address error:
    Message too long
Not reporting to the metaserver
    in this game
Use option —nometa to always enforce this
> 1: Now accepting new client connections
1: Connection from ericfj with
    client version 1.7.1
1: ericfj[localhost] has joined the game.
>1: ericfj is the Mongol ruler Genghis
1: The map has 1 starting positions
    on 1 isles.

> s
starting game
```

▶ Launch the **civserver** command and then wait for all the clients to connect. Once all the clients have connected, type **s** to start the game. Type **q** to quit.

Listing 12-3: RUNNING THE FREECIV CLIENT PROGRAM

```
$ civclient -server tamarack
```

▶ This runs the freeciv client program, telling the program that the freeciv server is running on a machine named tamarack. Replace tamarack with the name of your server system.

▶ From the freeciv client program, connect to a server.

Personal Workbook

Q&A

1 Linux comes from boring UNIX with zillions of cryptic commands. Can you run any games or have any fun on Linux?

_____

_____

_____

2 If you feel like killing and maiming, can you run games such as Doom and Heretic on Linux?

_____

_____

_____

3 Are these games easy to set up?

_____

_____

_____

4 Can you start the Freeciv program from the GNOME desktop taskbar menus?

_____

_____

_____

5 Freeciv requires at least two programs to run. Name them.

_____

_____

_____

6 Can you play Freeciv with your friends?

_____

_____

_____

7 Is there a commercial version of the game Civilization that you can purchase for Linux?

_____

_____

_____

8 What other games are there for Linux? Are some available from the GNOME taskbar?

_____

_____

_____

ANSWERS: PAGE 340

EXTRA PRACTICE

1. Check out the id Software site at **http://www.idsoftware.com** for the latest versions of Quake and Quake II.

2. Check out the id Software site for Quake 3 Arena.

3. If you have the hardware to run it, download all the required software for Quake 3 Arena and play it.

4. Read the online documentation for Heretic.

5. Do a Web search to see how many games are available for Linux.

6. Now, narrow your search to just commercial games.

REAL-WORLD APPLICATIONS

✔ You've bought Quake for Windows. Look on the Quake CD-ROM for the WAD files that you need to run Quake on Linux.

✔ Use the GNOME time-tracking program **gtt** to track the amount of time you spend playing games on Linux. Now find a way to justify this time for your boss.

✔ When your boss stops by, it isn't a good idea to have games on your screen. Practice switching to a different virtual desktop — quickly — to hide your illicit activity. Look at the desktop switcher on the taskbar at the bottom of the screen.

Visual Quiz

OK, you see a creature in the Doom window. What do you do?

_____

_____

_____

_____

_____

_____

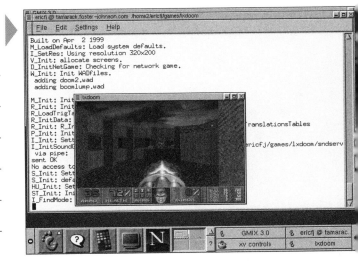

PART III

Connecting to the World

Linux isn't an island. It works well connected to the Internet or local networks that you may have. In fact, if it weren't for the Internet, we wouldn't have Linux today. Developers spread all over the world complete most of the work on Linux. Chapter 13 introduces you to this unique relationship.

Linux supports most of the standard networking protocols, especially those that make up the Internet. You can place a Linux system as an Internet server, as do many Internet Service Providers. You can also create your own local area network using standard protocols for your office or home.

In addition to basic networking, Linux supports a huge number of network-aware tools, from e-mail readers to Web browsers (including the ubiquitous Netscape) to newsreaders to chat programs and beyond. Chapters 14 and 15 discuss tools and networking.

Linux includes the Web server that runs more Web sites than any other server — Apache, which is discussed in Chapter 16. Linux also includes support for the Windows proprietary SMB or LanManager protocols, enabling your Linux system to act as a Windows file and print server, with the potential to save lots of money in licensing costs.

In the final chapter, we discuss advanced kernel configuration. Some networking options require you to create a new Linux kernel — a task that appears daunting but really isn't that hard — as discussed in Chapter 17.

CHAPTER 13

MASTER THESE SKILLS

- ▶ Connecting to the Internet
- ▶ Setting Up a PPP Connection
- ▶ Trying Out Your PPP Connection
- ▶ Configuring Netscape
- ▶ Setting Up a Cable Modem
- ▶ Cable Modems and Local Networks
- ▶ Setting Up a Masquerading Clients and Security

The Internet and Linux

Linux was made for the Internet. Networking is built in to the operating system and comes with a very rich set of tools that let you tune and configure it for maximum Internet effectiveness. For example, a common way to connect to the Internet is through a modem. Linux contains tools that will automatically dial up your Internet Service Provider (ISP) using either the SLIP or PPP protocol. Linux also works well if you have a direct connection to the Internet. Whether you have a T1 line, a cable modem, DSL, or an ISDN line, Linux can handle it.

Once you get connected, Linux contains more Internet tools than you'll ever need to use. Of course, you get the usual Netscape Navigator, but you also get several FTP programs for transferring files, **telnet** for logging in to remote computers, and myriad other programs.

Aside from Web surfing, the other major use for the Internet is to exchange e-mail. Linux comes with lots of different mail readers, such as **mail**, **pine**, **elm**, and **mutt**, or you can just use Netscape Mail. Linux also can fetch your mail from your ISP using standard POP or IMAP protocols and the **fetchmail** tool. No matter how your mail is sent to you, Linux can handle it.

Another area of networking that Linux handles very well is security. Linux provides a wide range of security tools — everything from advanced firewalls to threat detectors — to help keep your system safe. It should be noted that because Linux is an open-source system, fixes for security problems get promptly published. With most commercial software, if someone finds a security hole and reports the bug, the company does not always respond promptly, if at all. Security holes in commercial software are publicized and fixed only if they are large and severe. In Linux, security bugs are publicized and fixed even if they involve changing only a single line of code.

The programmers attached to Open Source projects have an interest in fixing problems, not just in earning a salary. With the source code they can do just that, and then as a service to the community they publish their fix.

But whatever your Internet concerns, be they security, connectivity, flexibility, or performance, Linux provides low-cost, high-quality Internet service.

Connecting to the Internet

Linux is a good match for the Internet. Not only do you get all the networking utilities that come standard with UNIX, but also you get all the practical user tools that come with Open Source software.

There are three common ways of connecting to the Internet: direct network connection, modem connection, and cable modems or DSL links.

Direct connections

Direct network connections are commonly found in the business environment or at universities. After all, it costs a lot of money to provide a dedicated high-speed route to the Internet.

The instructions for configuring your system for a direct connection are fairly simple: ask your network administrator for instructions and do what he or she says. Each small network has it's own unique features and you should configure your system to work with them.

Modem connections

The modem provides cheap Internet access, and thus is the most popular method for connecting. Linux uses a protocol called PPP to communicate with your Internet Service Provider (ISP). This turns your serial port into a network connection.

Setting up a PPP connection requires a little work. See the next task for details.

Cable modems and DSL links

High-speed cable and DSL (Digital Subscriber Line) modems are the future of Internet access. They run at speeds dozens of times faster than standard modems and cost only slightly more, and are offered by a rapidly growing number of cable and phone companies. Most cable service providers, such as Cox@home, and phone

companies use standard network protocols for their connections. Although they don't officially support Linux, they provide the information you need to connect your system.

Other services, such as RoadRunner (offered by Time Warner), are not entirely Linux friendly. They use custom programs to connect to their network. Fortunately, in the case of Roadrunner, some hackers (in the "gifted programmer" sense) have figured out how to write their own connection program. In the section "Setting Up a Cable Modem" we discuss in detail the procedures for setting up your own cable modem. Although we won't cover DSL modems specifically, the procedure is basically the same no matter which technology you use.

Key information from your ISP

Before you can set any Internet connection, you need the information listed in the form on the facing page. Your Internet service provider should provide all of this information.

For example, our ISP gave us an Account Configuration Sheet with a section called System Information.

Name Server (DNS) configuration

DNS is the Internet service that turns domain names such as **www.idgbooks.com** into IP addresses such as 38.170.216.15. There are several ways it does this, but the primary method is to query the nameserver on your Internet service provider.

You need to tell Linux about your ISP's nameserver. To do this, start **linuxconf** and select Config ⇨ Networking ⇨ Client Tasks ⇨ Name server specification. Check DNS is required for normal operation and fill in the domain name of your ISP as the default domain. Enter the address of the primary nameserver and any other nameservers your ISP uses.

Listing 13-1: ISP INFORMATION SHEET

```
Domain Name
Server Address:          207.110.0.60
Secondary Domain
Name Server:             207.110.0.128
Time Server Address:     207.110.0.60
News Server name:        news.genericisp.com
Pop Server:              pop3.genericisp.com
SMTP Server:             smtp.genericisp.com
```

Connection via modem

Computer / Modem

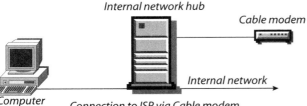

Connection via cable modem

Computer network card / Cable modem

Internal network hub

Connection to ISP via Cable modem and an internal network using IP Aliases.

Computer network card / Cable modem / Internal network

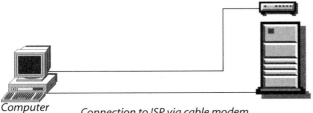

Connection to ISP via cable modem and an internal network using two network cards. Internet connections on the internal network can be provided through use of IP masquerading.

Computer

Table 13-1: INTERNET INFORMATION FORM

Domain Name _____

The address of the nameserver _____

Address of secondary name server (if any) _____

The name of the news server _____

Incoming mail service: (Pop or IMAP) _____

The name of your POP or IMAP mail server _____

The name of your SMTP (outgoing) mail server _____

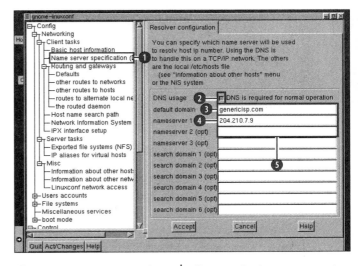

❶ Select the category Config ⇨ Networking ⇨ Client tasks ⇨ Name server specification.

❷ Enable DNS is required for normal operation.

❸ Enter the domain name of your ISP.

❹ Enter the IP address of your primary nameserver.

❺ Enter any secondary or tertiary nameservers.

Setting Up a PPP Connection

PPP (Point-to-Point Protocol) is a protocol for doing network communications over a serial link. It replaces an earlier serial protocol named SLIP (Serial Line Protocol). This protocol had many limitations that PPP removed. To connect to the Internet using PPP, you first need to get your computer to make a phone call to your Internet service provider and login. After this is accomplished, the program **pppd** will take over and handle the connection from there.

Now the only thing needed to get on the Internet is the login details. This can easily be determined by a little experimentation.

The program **minicom** is a terminal emulation program that can be used to contact your ISP. You won't be able to do anything after you get connected because **minicom** doesn't understand PPP, but you can turn on logging to record everything you need to do to get onto the system. You can then create a login script for your PPP connection.

Start **minicom** with the command **$ minicom.**

Check to see if you're connected to the modem by typing AT. The modem should respond OK. If you get nothing, check your /dev/modem link and your serial line. You may need to change your communication settings.

Turn on logging by typing **Ctrl+A** and then **L.** Type **ATZ** to reset the modem. Things will be easier if we start with the modem in a known state.

Dial the phone number by typing **ATDT** *number.* (We are not using **minicom**'s built-in dialer because PPP doesn't have a built-in dialer.) For example, if your ISP's number is 123-4567, type **ATDT1234567.**

After a few seconds you should be connected to the remote machine. Log in; this will probably involve typing in a user name and password at a prompt. When the machine says "PPP session beginning," or something similar, and starts to output garbage, you're in.

Tell **minicom** to hang up the phone by pressing Ctrl+A, then H. Exit **minicom** by pressing Ctrl+A, then X.

Print the file minicom.cap. This file will be used to configure the chat program so that we can automatically log in.

Listing 13-2 is a sample minicom.cap.

The next step is to configure your PPP interface. Start by running **linuxconf** and selecting Config ⇨ Networking ⇨ PPP/SLIP/PLIP. Click Add to add a new PPP configuration. Select PPP as the type of interface to use.

The next dialog enables you to enter the phone number for your ISP. If your system uses PAP (Password Authentication Protocol) authentication, enter your login name and password. (PAP is an advanced method for authenticating your PPP session.)

Click the newly defined interface (ppp0) to bring up the interface configuration dialog. Click Communication to bring up the **chat** configuration dialog. The **chat** program is automatically started by the PPP script and is designed to initiate the connection between your computer and your ISP.

Input to the **chat** program is a series of Expect/Send strings. The **chat** program examines the data coming back from the modem and looks for an Expect string. When it sees it, it responds with the Send string. Each pair is processed in order.

In this example, when the ISP sends Login:, the response should be the user name (a_user). The expect string is set to ogin, in case the connection accidentally drops a character, and the Send string is a_user. The password is handled similarly.

If you select Debug connection, **chat** will write a complete log of everything that comes in and goes out in the message log /var/log/messages. If you have problems getting connected, turn on debugging and examine this file.

Listing 13-2: SAMPLE MINICOM SESSION

```
ATZ
OK


ATDT555-1212
CARRIER
PROTOCOL:LAP-M
COMPRESSION:V.42BIS
CONNECT38400/ARQ


Welcome to Generic ISP
login: a_user
Password:


Entering PPP Mode.
IP address is 204.252.1.154
!#$!@#$#@!#%!@%^^^&
```

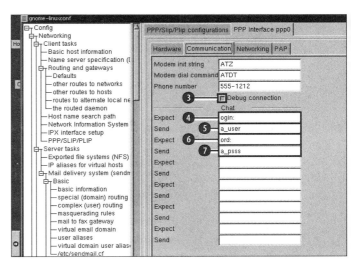

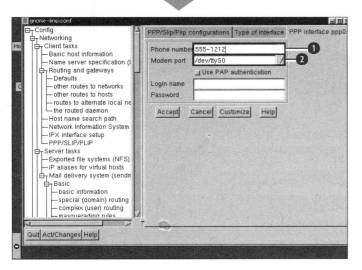

▶ *The minicom welcome screen.*

❶ *Enter the phone number.*

❷ *Select the device containing the modem.*

❸ *Set this to cause debug messages to be placed in /var/log/messages.*

❹ *Expect Login to be sent by the ISP. (Truncated to ogin in case a character gets dropped.)*

❺ *When ogin is seen, send a_user.*

❻ *Password should follow. (But we only look for the tail end: ord:).*

❼ *Send a_pass when the password comes in.*

Trying Your PPP Connection

If all goes well, you can now establish a PPP link by becoming root and executing the command **/sbin/ifup ppp0**. If you are connected, great!

If your modem fails to connect, or dials and then hangs up, examine /var/log/messages to see what happened. This file contains the debug output of the chat script. A typical log is shown in Listing 13-3.

Terminating the connect

To terminate the connection, execute /sbin/ifdown ppp0.

One common problem occurs when the PPP daemon can't establish a default route even though you included the **defaultroute** option on the command line. Although you connect to the remote computer, you can't do much of anything. In the file /var/log/messages, is the error message:

```
Mar 4 18:59:52 pc pppd[2402]: Can't
establish default route.
```

Examine your routine tables. These are the internal Linux tables that tell Linux where to send packets. A typical session looks similar to this:

```
$ /sbin/route -n
Kernel IP routing table
Destination  Gateway        Genmask
192.9.200.0  0.0.0.0        255.255.255.0
127.0.0.0    0.0.0.0        255.0.0.0
0.0.0.0      192.9.200.120  0.0.0.0

Flags   Metric   Ref   Use   Iface
U       0        0     9     eth0
U       0        0     1     lo
UG      0        0     2     eth0
```

The last entry is the one that troubles us. The destination of 0.0.0.0 indicates a default route. The reason that we can't set a default route is that one is already set.

But why is it set. As root, start the control panel program. Start the Network Configuration module and click Routing. The Default Gateway and Default Gateway Device: should be blank. If they aren't, clear them, exit, and reboot your system.

When it comes up again, use the **route** command to check for a default route. There should be none and our PPP connection should now work.

Listing 13-3: /VAR/LOG/MESSAGE FILE SHOWING A GOOD PPP CONNECTION SESSION

```
Mar 4 18:59:59 my_sys pppd[2461]:pppd 2.2.0 started by root, uid 0
Mar 4 19:00:01 my_sys chat[2465]: send(ATZ^M)
Mar 4 19:00:01 my_sys chat[2465]: expect(OK)
Mar 4 19:00:02 my_sys chat[2465]: ATZ^M^M
Mar 4 19:00:02 my_sys chat[2465]: OK — gotit
Mar 4 19:00:02 my_sys chat[2465]: send(ATDT555-1212^M)
Mar 4 19:00:02 my_sys chat[2465]: expect(CONNECT)
Mar 4 19:00:02 my_sys chat[2465]: ^M
Mar 4 19:00:21 my_sys chat[2465]: ATDT555-1212^M^M
Mar 4 19:00:21 my_sys chat[2465]: CARRIER 26400^M
Mar 4 19:00:21 my_sys chat[2465]: ^M
Mar 4 19:00:21 my_sys chat[2465]: COMPRESSION:V.42BIS^M
Mar 4 19:00:21 my_sys chat[2465]: ^M
Mar 4 19:00:21 my_sys chat[2465]: CONNECT — gotit
Mar 4 19:00:21 my_sys chat[2465]: send(^M)
Mar 4 19:00:21 my_sys chat[2465]: expect(ogin:)
Mar 4 19:00:21 my_sys chat[2465]: 38400/ARQ^M
Mar 4 19:00:27 my_sys chat[2465]: ^M
Mar 4 19:00:27 my_sys chat[2465]:
Mar 4 19:00:27 my_sys last message repeated 23 times
Mar 4 19:00:27 my_sys chat[2465]: Welcome to Generic ISP^
Mar 4 19:00:27 my_sys chat[2465]: ^M
Mar 4 19:00:27 my_sys chat[2465]: ^M
Mar 4 19:00:27 my_sys chat[2465]: login: — gotit
Mar 4 19:00:27 my_sys chat[2465]: send(a_user^M)
Mar 4 19:00:27 my_sys chat[2465]: expect(ssword:)
Mar 4 19:00:27 my_sys chat[2465]: a_user^M
Mar 4 19:00:27 my_sys chat[2465]: Password: — gotit
Mar 4 19:00:27 my_sys chat[2465]: send(the_pass^M)
Mar 4 19:00:27 my_sys pppd[2461]: Serial connection established.
Mar 4 19:00:28 my_sys pppd[2461]: Using interface ppp0
Mar 4 19:00:28 my_sys pppd[2461]: Connect: ppp0 <—> /dev/modem
Mar 4 19:00:29 my_sys pppd[2461]: local IP address 204.252.1.123
Mar 4 19:00:29 my_sys pppd[2461]: remote IP address 207.110.0.120
```

▶ *This log shows a healthy connection. Bad chat scripts generally leave a trail in this file.*

Configuring Netscape

Netscape needs no configuration if you just plan to surf the Web. However, if you want to use e-mail or read Internet news, you need to do some configuration. This process is detailed on the opposite page.

Internet mail

The easiest way of reading mail is through Netscape. It has a nice interface and does a good job. Just to make sure you've entered everything correctly, it's a good idea to send yourself mail and see if you receive it.

There are other mail readers around, most of which understand the POP protocol used by most Internet service providers. One that is distributed with Netscape is called **movemail**. A full discussion of the many mailers and ways of sending mail is, unfortunately, beyond the scope of this book.

The **fetchmail** program is designed to go out to a mail server and get your mail. This program understands a lot of different protocols. No matter how your ISP stores your mail, **fetchmail** can probably get it.

To configure this program, use the command **fetchmailconf**. This is an X Window program that lets you set up all the **fetchmail** options you'll ever need.

News

Most Internet service providers make Usenet news available through the use of an NNTP server. Linux has several readers that get their news from a remote server.

Before you start, you must set the environment variable NNTPSERVER to the name of your server.

```
$ NNTPSERVER=news.genericisp.com
$ export NNTPSERVER
```

This should probably be put in your **.profile** initialization file.

After that, you can run your favorite newsreader. The popular programs for Linux are **trn**, **tin**, and **slrn**. Each has its advantages, disadvantages, and loyal followers.

230

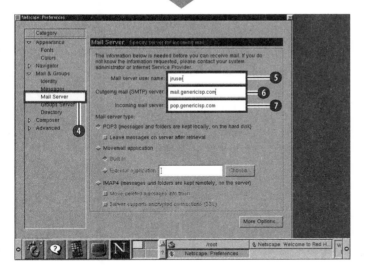

TAKE NOTE

WHY SO MANY MAIL SERVICES

In the beginning, before the invention of the PC, only mainframes were connected to the Internet. Because these machines were always on, they could send and receive mail at any time, and store all their mail locally. The protocol used was SMTP (Simple Mail Transfer Protocol). When the PC came along, a new protocol was needed. The first version was called POP (Post Office Protocol). POP is being replaced by a more advanced protocol: IMAP (Internet Message Access Protocol).

The reason that you still use SMTP to send messages is that the machine receiving the mail (your ISP) is always on. For machines that connect and disconnect from the Internet (your computer), you need POP or IMAP.

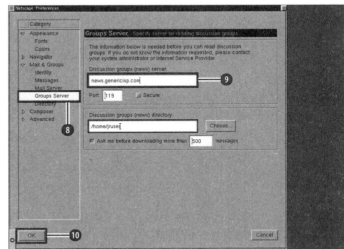

▶ Start **Netscape** and select Edit ⇨ Preferences.

❶ Click Mail & Groups ⇨ Identity.

❷ Fill in the blanks. Leave the Reply-to-address blank.

❸ The signature file (.signature in your home directory) is automatically appended to each sent message. Leave this blank alone.

❹ Click Mail Server.

❺ Enter your account name.

❻ Your ISP should provide an SMTP server name. Enter it here.

❼ Fill the Incoming mail server blank with the name of your POP or IMAP server. (Again, this supplied by your ISP.)

❽ Click the Groups Server category.

❾ Fill in the name of your news server in the Discussion groups (news) server blank.

❿ Click OK to confirm your changes.

231

Setting Up a Cable Modem

Cable modems provide high-speed Internet access through the same wire that provides cable television to your house. Almost every cable company supports Microsoft Windows 95 and Microsoft Windows 98. Many support Macintosh and Microsoft Windows NT.

The bad news is that practically no one supports Linux. The good news is that they don't have to. Almost all cable systems use standard network tools. All you have to do is set them up right and you can connect to the Internet.

A few, such as Roadrunner, use custom protocols to log in to your cable connection. Fortunately, the Linux community contains a number of hackers with a craving for high-speed access, so unofficial Linux software exists to get you connected to these systems.

Connecting your modem

In most cases, your cable modem connects to a network card in your computer just like any other network card, or it may even be a card itself, that goes inside the system. The modem uses a protocol called DHCP (Dynamic Host Configuration Protocol) to give your computer an IP address. This is a protocol that "leases" an IP address from a central authority (that is, your cable company).

To set up your network card, start **linuxconf** with Foot ⇨ Red hat menus ⇨ Administrator ⇨ linuxconf. Select the Config ⇨ Networking ⇨ Client Tasks ⇨ Basic host information category. Select the Adaptor 1 tab.

For Config mode select Dhcp. Enter the name of the Ethernet device (eth0) in the Net device blank and leave all the other fields empty.

Click Accept, and then Act/Changes to confirm the changes.

Notes on specific cable service providers

In this section, we discuss some of the issues concerning various cable companies. Please note that cable companies are changing technologies and rules all the time, so the information here may not be current. This is merely the best information available at the time of this writing.

COX@Home

The COX@Home service uses standard DHCP to provide its customers with an IP address, which makes running Linux simple and easy — just use the standard DHCP client that comes with Linux.

COX's service is also Linux-friendly. Although it doesn't officially support Linux, it does understand Linux and sometimes will give you unofficial advice about using it. There are also hundreds of other COX@Home Linux users who will be willing to help you.

Roadrunner (Time Warner)

Like COX@Home, the Roadrunner system uses DHCP to distribute IP addresses. There's one problem, however, and it's a big one. Before you can connect to a machine outside of Roadrunner, you must use a special login program to identify yourself to the network.

Roadrunner will supply you with a Microsoft Windows or Macintosh version of the login program, but that's it. Linux is officially unsupported and the people at Roadrunner will tell you that connecting a Linux box to Roadrunner is impossible.

They underestimated the power of the Linux community. People have reverse-engineered the Roadrunner login program and found out how to write one for Linux. You can obtain a copy of it from **http://www.qualcomm.com/~karn/rr/index.html**.

Listing 13-4: OUTPUT OF /SBIN/IFCONFIG

```
lo Link encap:Local Loopback
 inet addr:127.0.0.1 Bcast:127.255.255.255 Mask:255.0.0.0
 UP BROADCAST LOOPBACK RUNNING MTU:3584 Metric:1
 RX packets:76111 errors:0 dropped:0 overruns:0
 TX packets:76111 errors:0 dropped:0 overruns:0

eth0 Link encap:Ethernet HWaddr 00:A0:24:18:8D:A1
 inet addr:192.168.0.2 Bcast:192.168.0.255 Mask:255.255.255.0
 UP BROADCAST RUNNING PROMISC MULTICAST MTU:1500 Metric:1
 RX packets:2492305 errors:862 dropped:0 overruns:1119
 TX packets:863247 errors:0 dropped:0 overruns:0
 Interrupt:7 Base address:0x300

eth1 Link encap:Ethernet HWaddr 00:10:4B:D5:31:B7
 inet addr:24.30.135.69 Bcast:24.30.135.255 Mask:255.255.255.0
 UP BROADCAST NOTRAILERS RUNNING MULTICAST MTU:1500 Metric:1
 RX packets:997385 errors:42899 dropped:0 overruns:1
 TX packets:108677 errors:0 dropped:0 overruns:0
 Interrupt:10 Base address:0xac00
```

▶ *This listing shows the "loopback" device (always present) and two Ethernet cards (eth0 and eth1). The first is configured for a local network and the second for a cable modem. (The inet addr fields are the important ones in this listing.)*

TAKE NOTE

▶ **WHAT IS DHCP?**

DHCP (Dynamic Host Configuration Protocol) is a method of assigning IP numbers to hosts. DHCP was invented to make the distribution of IP addresses easier. Using DHCP, a host can send a message to a central server and say, "I just booted, give me an IP address. Here's my Ethernet hardware address." The host responds, "Here's your IP address."

The client gets an IP address that the client leases for a certain period of time. If the client does not renew the lease in that time, the central server assumes that the client's down and may reassign the IP address.

DHCP makes it easy to administer a constantly changing network from a central authority. For ISPs and other large network providers, it provides a simple way to handle IP configuration.

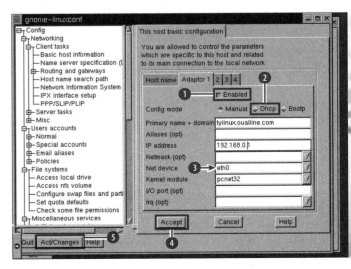

❶ *Enable the adapter.*
❷ *Select Dhcp configuration.*
❸ *Select the Net device.*
❹ *Click Accept.*
❺ *Click Act/Changes.*

233

Cable Modems and Local Networks

Suppose you have more than one computer at home (or work) and you want them all connected to the Internet by the cable modem. How do you do it? You could get separate IP addresses from your cable company, but most charge you a lot to connect more than one machine.

A better solution is to connect your cable modem to your Linux box, connect your Linux box to your internal network, and let Linux do the routing. One way to do this is to have two network cards. One is connected to the cable modem, the other to the internal network. Linux can then be configured to pass messages between the two. For example, your first Ethernet card (eth0) can connect to the internal network and the second Ethernet card (eth1) can connect to the cable modem.

But what if you don't want to use two network cards? Linux can do IP aliasing. This is where a single network card pretends it has two cards. The card responds to two network addresses. Thus, you can reserve the main interface (eth0) for the internal network and the other (eth0:1) for the cable modem. Using this system, the cable modem is physically connected to your internal hub, but logically connected to its own interface (eth0:1). (DHCP only works on the main interface. It cannot be used for aliases.)

This second system has the advantage of using only one network card. The disadvantage is that your internal network is exposed to the cable system (a big security concern). Also, this system adds some load to your internal system because packets coming in from the cable modem first go to your Linux box for retransmission to your local machines.

IP masquerading

IP masquerading (also known as NAT or Network Address Translation) is a technique that Linux can use to hide the existence of a local network from the outside world. Start by connecting your Linux system to two networks (through two network cards, or by using IP aliasing.)

Next, you configure your system to use IP masquerading. All systems on your internal network are told to connect to the Internet through your Linux box.

The Linux box then takes packets from your internal network and rewrites the address to make it appear as if they came from your Linux system. Any response packets are rewritten and forwarded back to the original machine.

Setting up Linux for masquerading

To setup a Linux system for masquerading, you must first create a kernel with the Networking options named Network Firewalls, IP: Firewalling, IP: Always defragment, and IP: Masquerading enabled. If you're planning to go the IP aliasing route, you have to enable IP: Aliasing as well.

There are some problems associated with IP masquerading. It's easy for the masquerading software to rewrite outgoing requests to use the Linux IP address, but some programs (such as **ftp**) open sockets back to the original computer. The masquerading software, sitting in the middle, doesn't normally connect outside requests to an inside machine.

However, to get programs such as **ftp** to work a handful of kernel modules have been created to help masquerading. The one for **ftp** is called ip_masq_ftp. Load this module if you plan to use **ftp** from machines behind your Linux network.

There are lots of other modules for services such as IRC, RealAudio, CuSeeMe, and many others. (For a complete list check out the Linux IP Masquerade Resource page at **http:// ipmasq.cjb.net/.**)

You need to load the modules before turning on masquerading. This is done through the use of the **ipchains** command. Listing 13-5 has a complete set of commands to turn on masquerading.

Listing 13-5: TURN ON MASQUERADING (/ETC/RC.D/RC.MASQ)

```
# Load all required IP MASQ modules
#
# NOTE: Only load the IP MASQ modules you
need.

/sbin/modprobe ip_masq_ftp
#/sbin/modprobe ip_masq_raudio
#/sbin/modprobe ip_masq_irc
#/sbin/modprobe ip_masq_quake
#/sbin/modprobe ports=ip_masq_quake
26000,27000,27910
#/sbin/modprobe ip_masq_cuseeme
#/sbin/modprobe ip_masq_vdolive

# Flush all current policies and set the
default rules
ipchains -F
ipchains -P input ACCEPT
ipchains -P output ACCEPT
ipchains -P forward DENY

# MASQ timeouts
#
# 2 hrs timeout for TCP session timeouts
# 10 sec timeout for traffic after the
TCP/IP "FIN" packet is received
# 60 sec timeout for UDP traffic (MASQ'ed
ICQ users must
# enable a 30sec firewall timeout in ICQ
itself)
#
ipchains -M -S 7200 10 60
```

```
# Enable simple IP forwarding and
Masquerading
#
# NOTE: The following is an example for an
internal
# LAN address in the 192.168.0.x
# network with a 255.255.255.0 or a "24"
bit subnet mask.
#
# Please change this network number and
# subnet mask to match your internal LAN
setup
#

ipchains -A forward -s 192.168.0.0/24 -j
MASQ

# Change "ppp0" in the following lines to
match your external
# interface (ppp0, eth0, eth1, eth0:1,
etc), and NOT the one
# that is for your internal network

ipchains -A input -s 10.0.0.0/8 -i ppp0 -j
DENY
ipchains -A input -s 172.16.0.0/12 -i ppp0
-j DENY
ipchains -A input -s 192.168.0.0/16 -i ppp0
-j DENY
```

▶ Note: You need to edit the file /etc/sysconfig/network and change FORWARD_IPV4=false: to **FORWARD_IPV4=true:**.

▶ After this add the line **. /etc/rc.d/rc.masq** at the end of the file /etc/rc.d/rc.local to automatically run this script.

Setting Up Masquerading Clients and Security

After you get your Linux system setup, you'll want to setup your local clients. You'll also want to do a security audit of your system and make sure that things are locked down so that hackers can't get in.

Setting up a Linux client

You can configure Linux clients to send all messages. First you need to point your system at the cable company's name server. Use the steps at the right to enter the resolver configuration.

You also need to setup a default route to the machine connected to the cable modem. A default route tells the client system where to send packets for machines that don't have a direct connection.

Once these two configuration steps are performed, you can access the Internet from your system and it will look just like you have a direct connection.

Setting up a Microsoft Windows client

To setup a Microsoft Windows client, go to the Control Panel and select Networking.

Select the TCP/IP Protocol and click Properties.

Under the Gateway tab, enter the IP address of your Linux machine. Click Add to add the address.

Under the DNS Configuration tab, fill in the name of your system under Host. Under Domain, enter your ISP's domain name. Enter the IP addresses of the first nameserver and click Add. Repeat this process if any other nameservers are defined.

Click OK to close the window and OK on the network window to finish the configuration. Your Windows box will restart and you can now surf the Internet.

Internet security

Connecting to the Internet attracts hackers. There are lots of novice hackers who have downloaded one of the many hacker toolkits and who will try to break into your system. Steve Oualline's server **http://www.oualline.com** gets two or three break-in attempts per *day*.

There are several things you should do to secure your system. First, turn off all services to the outside world. You can do this by editing the file **/etc/hosts.deny** so that it looks like Listing 13-6.

If there are machines that you trust and that you want to give access, let them in by listing them in the /etc/hosts.allow file (see Listing 13-7). (Be aware, however, that your security is only as good as the weakest system on your net.)

Check the Red Hat Web site for security updates (**http://www.redhat.com**). Hackers check this site looking for security fixes as well. They want to see what was fixed so that they can exploit unpatched systems, so you must stay current.

When someone tries to connect to your system or use a service illegally, an entry is added to the file /var/log/secure. Check this file regularly and report anyone who tries to break in to that person's ISP.

There are a number of security software packages out there. One of the oldest and most notorious is called SATAN, which can be found at **http://rpmfind. net/linux/RPM/contrib/libc5/i386/satan-1.1.1.linux-3. i386.html**. This package scans your system looking for security holes and reports any that it finds. Another is Nessus, which can be found at **http://www.nessus.org**.

There are also password-cracking programs such as **crack**. If a hacker is able to break into your system and steal the password file, the hacker can use this type of program to guess passwords. Fortunately, Linux uses shadow passwords, so getting the passwords is a little harder.

Listing 13-6: /ETC/HOSTS.DENY

```
#
# hosts.deny This file describes the names
of the hosts which are
# *not* allowed to use the local INET
services, as decided
# by the '/usr/sbin/tcpd' server.
#
# The portmap line is redundant, but it is
left to remind you that
# the new secure portmap uses hosts.deny
and hosts.allow. In particular
# you should know that NFS uses portmap!

ALL: ALL
```

▶ Note: By disallowing everything, we prevent people from getting in that shouldn't. We probably want to allow access to a few, but these will be explicitly listed in /etc/hosts.allow.

Listing 13-7: /ETC/HOSTS.ALLOW

```
#
# hosts.allow This file describes the names
of the hosts which are
# allowed to use the local INET services,
as decided
# by the '/usr/sbin/tcpd' server.
#
ALL: wifes_machine.mynet.com
http: ALL
```

My wife's machine is allows access to all services.
Everyone is allowed to access the web services.

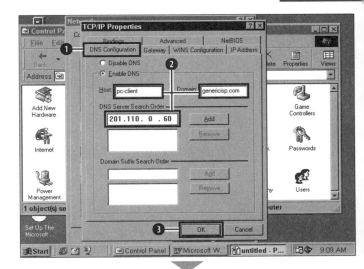

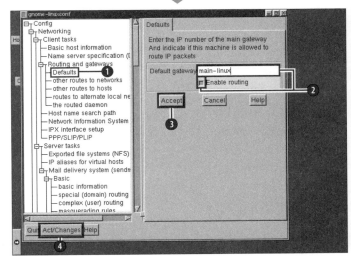

▶ Select Start ⇨ Control Panel ⇨ Network. Select the TCP/IP item. Click Properties.

❶ Select DNS Configuration.

❷ Fill in the blanks with your system, your domain name, and the address of your IPS's nameserver.

❸ Click Add to select the nameserver.

❶ Select Config ⇨ Networking ⇨ Client Tasks ⇨ Routing and gateways ⇨ Defaults.

❷ Fill in the blanks. Enter the name or IP address of the Linux system connected to the cable modem. Enable routing.

❸ Click Accept.

❹ Click Act/Changes to enable the changes.

Personal Workbook

Q&A

1 What protocol is used for connecting to the Internet using a modem?

_____

_____

_____

2 Why do most Internet service providers (ISPs) use two different protocols for mail: one for sending, and one for receiving?

_____

_____

_____

3 Define *IP Aliasing*.

_____

_____

_____

4 Define *IP Masquerading*.

_____

_____

_____

5 Define *chat script*. Where does linuxlonf put chat scripts?

_____

_____

_____

6 Describe *DHCP*.

_____

_____

_____

7 Define *routing*. How can you view the current routing tables?

_____

_____

_____

8 What is a *default route*?

_____

_____

_____

ANSWERS: PAGE 340

238

EXTRA PRACTICE

1. Connect to the Internet and use Netscape Navigator to verify the connection.

2. Send yourself a mail message from a remote machine to make sure that the mail gets through.

3. Reply to the message you sent yourself to make sure that outgoing mail works.

4. Check out **http://www.redhat.com** for any security updates for Linux.

5. Set up a home network using a cable modem and IP masquerading.

6. Edit the files /etc/hosts.allow, /etc/inetd.conf, and /etc/hosts.deny to make your system more secure. Check out the file /var/log/secure and to determine whether anyone has tried to get in recently.

REAL-WORLD APPLICATIONS

✔ Use Linux for your personal machine, which connects to the Internet occasionally using a modem.

✔ A small business can use Linux for an Internet router/firewall connected to the Internet by an ISDN line.

✔ Linux makes a cheap and robust WWW server connected by a cable modem to the Internet.

✔ An Internet server connected by a cable modem which also serves a local network using IP Masquerading.

Visual Quiz

How would you configure the Ethernet device named eth0 for an internal, private network system named Linus, with a fixed IP address?

Fill in the following: Primary name + domain, Alias, Blank, IP address, Netmask, and Net device. Leave the rest blank (select defaults.)

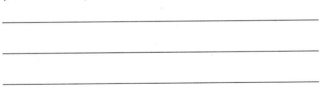

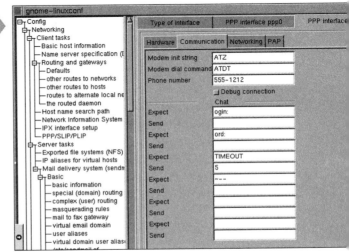

CHAPTER 14

MASTER
THESE
SKILLS

- ▶ **Configuring Netscape**
- ▶ **Viewing Web Pages with Netscape**
- ▶ **Understanding E-mail Protocols: POP, IMAP, and SMTP**
- ▶ **Mailers and Mail Checking Programs**
- ▶ **Transferring Files with FTP**
- ▶ **Downloading Linux Software**
- ▶ **Internet Relay Chat**
- ▶ **Logging on to Remote Systems**
- ▶ **Reading the News**
- ▶ **Posting Messages to Newsgroups**

Internet Tools

In the last chapter, we discussed how to get on the Internet through dial-up or cable-modem connections, as well as the initial setup tasks that you need to go through. This chapter extends the discussion to the tools that you can use to make the most of your network connection. Most of these tools require some setup. Usually you need to tell the tools which machines provide the services on your network. In most cases, though, that's it. You should be up and running quickly.

Because the Internet is really a collection of networks, and because Linux supports networking standards, you can use these same tools on local area networks (LANs) (the subject of Chapter 15), or on an Internet connection (discussed in Chapter 13), or through any networking scheme in use at your location. So, for example, a local Web server presents Web pages the same way that remote Web servers do.

The main network services available both locally and on the Internet include transferring files, exchanging messages such as e-mail, viewing documents, and logging in to remote systems. Many of these services are known by the protocols used for access, and you'll unfortunately see a lot of acronyms to wade through. (A protocol is simply an agreed upon means of communication. Both sides to a network link have to agree on a way to get messages across.) Furthermore, the Internet did not all appear at once. Instead, the Internet, its services, and its protocols have all changed over time. Because of this, there are a number of alternate protocols, such as IMAP or POP, for e-mail, as well as version numbers, such as IMAP4 and POP3. See the task, "Understanding E-mail Protocols: POP, IMAP, and SMTP," for more on these protocols in particular.

Linux provides a whole range of tools for accessing these network services. True to its UNIX roots, Linux includes a number of command-line programs that you launch from the shell and access in text mode. Linux also includes a number of graphical tools that can make accessing network services a lot easier. We cover the major tools in each area and mention a number of alternatives.

The prime tool of the graphical sort is Netscape, which includes a Web browser, an e-mail program, and a newsreader. Netscape even goes so far as to include an address book to store contact information for the people you frequently communicate with. Netscape supports Web protocols for viewing documents, as well as the file transfer protocol (FTP) for downloading.

The GNOME and KDE desktops are also adding more and more networking tools. For transferring files, we really like the GNOME's **gftp**, discussed in the task, "Transferring Files with FTP."

Configuring Netscape

Netscape provides a sort of all-in-one Internet tool. Technically, it's a commercial application that's available for free. Just about every Linux distribution, including the Red Hat version that accompanies this book, includes the full Netscape Communicator package. Communicator includes a Web browser for viewing Web documents, a Web page editor for creating these documents, an e-mail client for reading and sending e-mail messages, a newsreading client for reading and sending Usenet news messages, and an address book for storing information on how to contact your friends and associates.

In addition to displaying Web documents, Netscape supports a number of other protocols including file transfers, and an older protocol called Gopher (which provided a sort of precursor to the World Wide Web). Netscape can view text files and it can run applications written in Java or JavaScript. This latter capability enables you to access Web-based applications from Linux.

Because it is so versatile, and because it is fairly robust as a commercial application, Netscape has superseded a number of freeware Web and e-mail alternatives. While there are still many other programs still available, we recommend starting with Netscape and moving on to others in various areas such as Web browsing or e-mail should you find problems with Netscape. Netscape does so much and it's relatively easy to learn, so start with it.

You can call up Netscape from the icon on the GNOME taskbar. You can also enter the following command in any shell window:

```
$ netscape &
```

Netscape is a graphical application, so you must be running the X Window System.

When you first call up Netscape, you see a Red Hat Linux start page as shown on the facing page. This page is a local file installed on your system in /usr/doc and set up as the default start page for Netscape. It's a good starting page, as it contains links to online documentation about your Linux system. What could be better?

If your Linux system is connected to a network, you can type in the URL, or Uniform Resource Locator, into the box near the top of the Netscape window. Netscape will try to display the page. (Anyone who's worked with the Internet for a while knows that you don't always succeed.) That's all you really need to configure if you only want to use Netscape to browse Web pages.

If you want to do more, though, such as send e-mail responses, you need to configure a few settings. Select the Preferences from the Edit menu to call up the main Netscape configuration dialog.

The dialog window that appears has a number of categories, which are shown in a list at the left of the window. Select a category, such as Mail and Newsgroups, to configure individual settings. These categories present a hierarchical list, so selecting a top-level category also expands a list of the subcategories. Take a moment to go through the different choices.

Continued

CROSS-REFERENCE

Chapter 7 covers the X Window System.

TAKE NOTE

COOKIES

A *cookie* is a piece of information from a Web server that Netscape stores. In most cases, cookies track your access to a Web site. In many cases, this is a good thing, as it helps make for Web pages that can track the items you've selected and so on. In other cases, cookies are used to keep track of you so that others can profit. From the Advanced category in the Preferences dialog, you can control whether Netscape allows or disallows cookies.

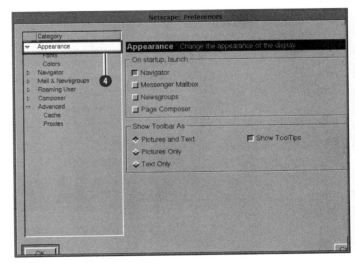

▶ */usr/doc/HTML/index.html* is the starting page you first get with Netscape.

① *Launch Netscape from the GNOME taskbar icon.*

② *The first Web page that you see in Netscape includes this Red Hat start page.*

③ *Enter the URL for a Web page to ask Netscape to try to display the page.*

④ *From the Preferences dialog, select a category at the left.*

FIND IT ONLINE

To upgrade to newer versions of Netscape software, see **http://home.netscape.com**.

Configuring Netscape
Continued

One of the first things to do with Netscape is to set up your own *start page*, which is the first page that you see when you launch Netscape. You may want to start at your own personal home page, or some other page that you're likely to need right away. We typically start at a page that has the links that we use most often. For example, at work, you may want to start with a page that links to important work information.

At home, you may want a different start page. If your system is not always connected to the Internet, you may want to set up the start page as a local document on your hard disk, using a file:// URL. This means that Netscape will start faster and won't present an error if you're not yet connected to the Internet.

Bookmarking interesting sites

The Internet contains a huge number of Web sites. To help make sense of this giant mess, you can bookmark the sites that you find interesting to have a fighting chance of finding the site again. To bookmark the current page you're viewing, call up the Bookmarks menu as shown on the facing page. Select Add Bookmark and the current page is added to your bookmarks. The page's title becomes the entry you see in your bookmark list.

We find, though, that the page's title often doesn't explain why we bookmarked the page in the first place. For example, you may have bookmarked a page that contains lots of images of Angelina Jolie but the title may be something like Fred's Home Page or the dreaded Under Construction. And many Web pages don't even have titles. One way around this is to edit the entry in your bookmarks.

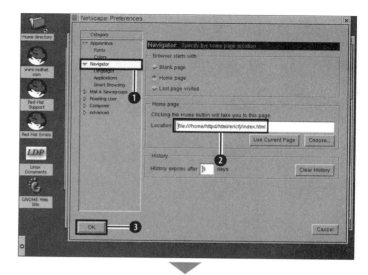

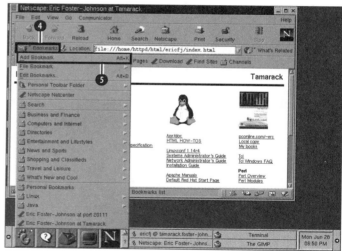

❶ Select the Navigator category in the Netscape Preferences dialog box.

❷ Enter the URL of your desired start page.

❸ Click OK to lock in your new start page.

❹ Press and hold the left mouse button over the Bookmarks menu in Netscape.

❺ Select Add Bookmark to add the current page to your bookmarks.

CROSS-REFERENCE

Appendix B lists a number of sites that present information on Linux.

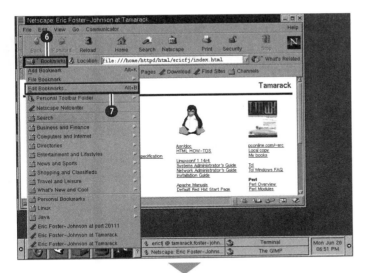

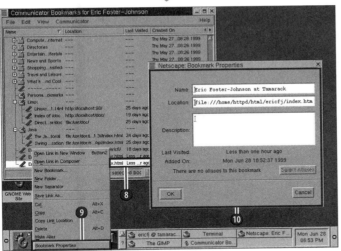

To do this, call up the Bookmarks menu again and select Edit Bookmarks. You'll see a window like that shown on the facing page. From this window, you can move bookmarks around, and create subfolders (really submenus) to organize your bookmarks.

TAKE NOTE

CHANGING FONTS

You can select the default fonts Netscape should use to display Web pages from the Preferences dialog's Fonts category, which is under Appearance. For example, you can choose larger fonts if most Web pages seem too small. Or, on a low-resolution screen, you may want to choose a smaller sized font to be able to see more text on a page. In either case, you're setting the default fonts for Web pages that don't specify fonts.

WHAT IS ARIAL?

Arial is a commonly used font on Web pages created with proprietary tools. This font is really a version of Helvetica, a font available on just about every platform but called Arial for some reason on Microsoft Windows. Many Web pages set up absolute font names to Windows-specific fonts. If that's the case, you'll likely see an ugly replacement font on Linux. Bug the people behind the Web page to specify both Arial and Helvetica for their fonts and all should be fine.

⑥ *Press and hold the leftmost mouse button over the Bookmarks menu in Netscape.*

⑦ *Select Edit Bookmarks to see the bookmarks window.*

⑧ *In the bookmarks window, select a bookmark.*

⑨ *Hold down the rightmost mouse button and select Bookmark Properties.*

⑩ *Edit the bookmark in the Properties window.*

FIND IT ONLINE

A good start page when starting Netscape is
http://www.slashdot.org.

245

Viewing Web Pages with Netscape

As you may already know, it's relatively easy to get Netscape to display a Web page. Simply type in the URL of the Web page in the Location entry near the top of the Netscape window and press Enter, and the Web browser starts trying to call up the given document.

You can pass a URL to Netscape on the command line to tell Netscape to start with a different page. For example:

```
$ netscape http://www.redhat.com &
```

This command tells Netscape that the first document to display is the Red Hat home page at **http://www.redhat.com**.

You can also select a Web page from your bookmarks or by clicking on a link within a Web page. We find these methods the most convenient. You don't have to type in a long URL, and chances are that you won't get a typing error. (This is not always the case. Web page creators can make typos in the links they specify, too.)

With Netscape, there's no real difference between browsing locally and remotely. In each case, Netscape connects to a Web server (local or remote) and requests a Web page. Most URLs start with http://, which tells the Web browser (Netscape) to connect to the server using the Hypertext Transport Protocol, or HTTP. Other types of URLs tell Netscape to connect using the File Transfer Protocol, FTP, with ftp://, or with the older Gopher protocol with gopher:// (See Table 14-1.)

URLs that end in a slash (/) either list the files within a directory or display a special file, typically named index.html.

The file:// URL tells Netscape to call up a local file. And, because Linux includes a huge number of online documents, you can browse program documentation using Netscape, too. Just call up the appropriate file links, starting with file:///usr/doc/ to get a listing of the /usr/doc directory. Netscape can call up text files or files in HTML, or Hypertext Markup Language, format. Most Web documents are in HTML. In this case, Netscape reads the file directly and doesn't go through a Web server.

TAKE NOTE

USE THREE SLASHES WITH FILE LINKS

With file:// URLs, you need to give the name of a file, which starts with a leading slash. This makes for three slashes. For example:

```
file:///home/ericfj/startpage.html
```

Note the three slashes after *file:*.

BROWSING THE WEB FROM A TERMINAL SCREEN

Linux includes a text-only browser called **lynx**. Although **lynx** is unlikely to be your preferred Web browser, it can help out in a pinch if you're not running the X Window System, or just have a **telnet** connection to a site from which you browse the Web. Furthermore, **lynx** has a great feature in that it can dump the contents of a Web page formatted as text with the **–dump** option. For example:

```
$ lynx -dump http://localhost/  >
localhost.txt
```

With this command, the output gets stored in a file named **localhost.txt**.

CROSS-REFERENCE
Chapter 16 discusses Web browsers and helps make the connection between URLs and files.

FIND IT ONLINE
The KDE home page is **http://www.kde.org**.

Table 14-1: URL TYPES AND EXAMPLES

Type	Example	Meaning
http://hostname/directory/filename	http://www.linux.com/howto/Mail-HOWTO.html	Call up directory/filename on system hostname as a Web page.
http://hostname/directory/	http://www.linux.com/howto/	Call up directory on system hostname as a Web page.
http://hostname/~username/	http://www.pconline.com/~erc/	Call up a user's home page.
http://hostname/	http://www.idgbooks.com	Call up a host's top-level home page.
ftp://hostname/directory/	ftp://contrib.redhat.com/libc6/i386/	View the given directory from hostname using FTP.
ftp://hostname/directory/filename	ftp://contrib.redhat.com/libc6/i386/xchat-0.9.6-1.i386.rpm	Download the given directory/filename from hostname using FTP.
mailto:user@domain.com	mailto:erc@pconline.com	Open an e-mail window to send a message to the given user at the given domain.
news:newsgroup	news: linux.redhat.announce	Call up the news reader with the given newsgroup.
file:///directory/filename	file:///home/ericfj/startpage.html	Call up the given document locally.

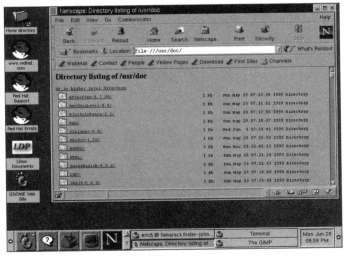

▶ Viewing a directory with Netscape.

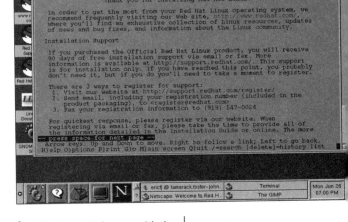

▶ Viewing a Web page with the text-mode program **lynx**.

Understanding E-mail Protocols: SMTP, POP, and IMAP

Like most network access, e-mail follows the client-server model. From an e-mail client — a program that reads e-mail messages — you connect to an e-mail server. Servers hold your messages and enable you to send messages to other users. The client programs connect to the servers using a number of standard protocols.

To send messages, just about every system supports SMTP, the Simple Mail Transport Protocol. Long a part of the UNIX and Linux program called **sendmail**, SMTP defines how you send messages. About 80 percent of all Internet e-mail gets sent by some version of **sendmail**, which goes to show how the UNIX and Linux model of open protocols really helps make things happen.

A completely different protocol defines how you can receive messages. The reason for this separation is mostly historical. Originally, UNIX placed your incoming mail in a file on disk and all the e-mail programs then read your mail from a file. As the Internet grew, you were no longer required to access files on disk to get your e-mail. Instead, you got your mail from the server using a network protocol. The most common protocols for receiving your e-mail messages include POP3 and IMAP4. POP3 stands for the Post Office Protocol version 3, and is widely available. IMAP4, short for Internet Message Access Protocol version 4, is less widely available but provides greater flexibility.

Linux provides servers for both protocols, **ipop3d** and **imapd** respectively. Even proprietary e-mail systems that run on PCs normally support SMTP and either POP3 or IMAP4. In most cases, you need to ask your Internet Service Provider or system administrator which protocols are supported at your site. To get e-mail, you need an account somewhere, whether on your local system or on an e-mail server run by an Internet service provider (ISP), or on a server on your organization's network. In all cases, you need a user name and password — on the mail server system — to get your e-mail.

Typically, when you get an e-mail account, you also get a password. This may be the same as your user name and password on your current Linux system or it may be different. In most cases, it's your user name and password for the e-mail server. If you use an ISP, then this will likely be your username and password with the ISP. You need to set this as the user name in the Identity subcategory under Mail and Newsgroups in Netscape's Preferences dialog box. When you actually try to download your e-mail, though, you'll be prompted to enter your password on the mail server.

Then you need the name of the system that acts as a mail server for your e-mail. Armed with this information, call up the Mail Servers subcategory under Mail and Newsgroups in Netscape's Preferences dialog. Fill in the information as shown on the facing page.

CROSS-REFERENCE

Chapter 13 covers how to get on the Internet and introduces ISPs.

248

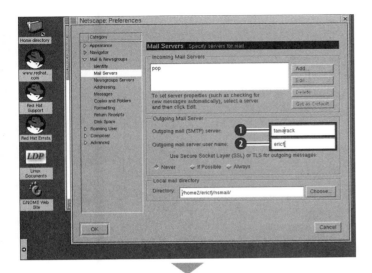

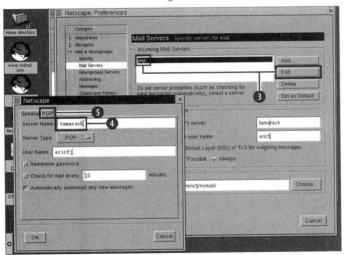

① *Fill in the name of the outgoing mail server. This is sometimes different from your incoming mail server.*

② *Fill in your user name on the outgoing mail server, usually the same as your current user name.*

③ *Select a POP server and click Edit.*

④ *In the separate dialog for POP servers, enter the server name.*

⑤ *The POP tab enables you to choose whether to leave the messages on the server.*

POP3 Servers

For POP3 e-mail servers, select the POP entry in the Incoming Mail Servers box in Netscape and click Edit. In the dialog that appears, enter the name of the POP3 e-mail server, along with your user name on that server. In the POP tab, you need to choose whether you want the messages left on the server. Leaving the messages on the server allows you to connect to the server from a number of sites, such as when travelling, and still see your e-mail messages. But, this can use up a lot of space on the server if you get a lot of messages. If you select to not leave the messages on the server, Netscape will download your messages to your Linux system and then delete the messages on the e-mail server. In either case, this is all you need to set up to be able to download your e-mail.

TAKE NOTE

FIGURING OUT E-MAIL SERVERS

You can find a mini-HOWTO document explaining more on e-mail servers at **http://www.sfu.ca/~yzhang/linux/qmail/index.html**. This can be a big help if you're a newcomer to Linux and want to set up a mail server.

FIND IT ONLINE

For more on IMAP, see **http://www.imap.org**.

Mailers and Mail-Checking Programs

Because Linux supports open standards for e-mail, there is a huge number of mail programs to choose from. You can stick with Netscape or use a different program.

In Netscape, call up the message window from the small toolbar and then ask Netscape to check for new messages or launch the new message window to enter in your own e-mail message.

In Netscape, click Get Msg to download your e-mail messages. Netscape will prompt you for your password if necessary. Once you have all your messages, you can compose a reply if needed, or click New Msg to start a new e-mail message.

In general, we find it easier to reply, if possible, because you don't have to type in the e-mail address. (You may have to edit the address, though, for those who mess up their reply address to defeat junk bulk e-mailers. Remove words like SPAM from the return address; for example, convert fred@nospam.bigfun.com to fred@bigfun.com.) You can also select Add Sender To Addressbook from the Message menu to add the sender to the Netscape address book. This helps you keep track of the people you frequently contact.

Once in your address book in Netscape, you can click Address when composing a message. Select the people you want to receive your e-mail message and then click the To or cc (carbon copy) buttons.

Continued

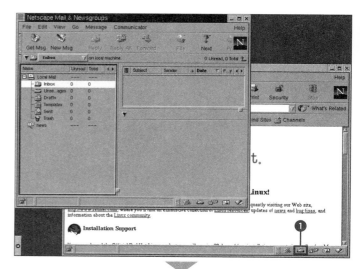

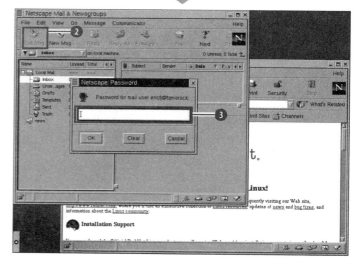

❶ Call up the Netscape message window from the toolbar.

❷ In the Netscape message window, click Get Msg to check for messages.

❸ Netscape prompts you for your password.

CROSS-REFERENCE

Chapter 8 covers the Netscape address book.

250

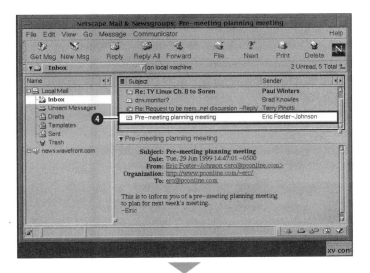

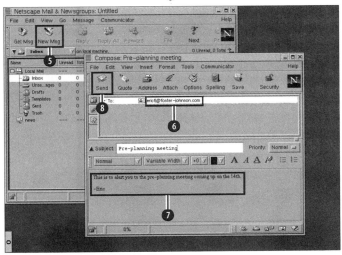

④ *Select a message to read it.*

⑤ *In the Netscape message window, click New Msg to start a message.*

⑥ *Enter the recipient's e-mail address.*

⑦ *Enter your message.*

⑧ *Click Send to send your message.*

TAKE NOTE

▶ USING SIGNATURE FILES

You'll often see pithy quotes, funny messages, and information on a person's employer, address, and so on placed at the end of e-mail messages. Instead of typing this information by hand with each message, most users set up a .signature file. A .signature file, so named because it usually resides in a file of that name in your home directory, is a file that gets appended to the end of every e-mail message you send.

You can set up a .signature file in Netscape from the Identity subcategory under the Mail and Newsgroups category in the Preferences dialog. Fill in the filename in the Signature File entry. Configure most other mail tools, such as **elm**, similarly to use a file named .signature in your home directory.

▶ CHECKING FOR E-MAIL

Linux provides a number of programs that just check for new e-mail and then alert you. Some play a sound, while others change a graphic on your screen. Many of the programs sport the name **biff** or some variant like **xbiff**. Biff was reportedly the name of a dog and according to UNIX legend, Biff barked at the mail deliverer, announcing new postal mail.

The **xbiff** program displays a small mailbox. If you have mail, the flag goes up. The program **xmailbox** acts similarly but shows a color mailbox. In the optional KDE desktop, you can run **kbiff**, which acts like **xmailbox** and **xbiff**.

FIND IT ONLINE

Hormel makes the real SPAM, as opposed to e-mail SPAM, at **http://www.spam.com**.

Mailers and Mail-Checking Programs *Continued*

Choosing a mail tool

Netscape isn't the only e-mail program that you can use. Linux supports hundreds more because it uses open e-mail standards. When choosing a mail tool, some things to think about include how many messages you expect to receive in a day, and how you manage your messages. You may, for example, create hundreds of mail folders for organizing your messages. If so, look at the capabilities of each tool for managing folders. You may need to be able to switch tools. In that case, look for the file format used to store the messages. If it is a text-based format, you should be able to migrate your messages to another tool.

If you install the optional KDE desktop, you can run **kmail**, shown on the facing page, to read your e-mail and send missives. If you're not using KDE, or perhaps not using a desktop environment at all, you may want to try **exmh**, a graphical mail tool built on top of the **mh** suite, which is short for mail handler. **mh** includes a number of command-line programs for handling mail, moving messages to folders and so on. As such, it fits well into the UNIX and Linux philosophy of many small tools each doing one task. **exmh**, shown on the facing page, sits on top of **mh** and provides a typical graphical e-mail client program.

Both **exmh** and **kmail** come with Red Hat Linux. If you want to search further for the e-mail program that meets your needs, we recommend **tkrat**, also called Ratatosk, a squirrel from Norse mythology. **tkrat**, shown on the facing page, is partially written in the Tcl/Tk scripting language. **tkrat** supports e-mail attachments, and so is one of the best graphical e-mail programs, many of which don't yet handle attachments very well.

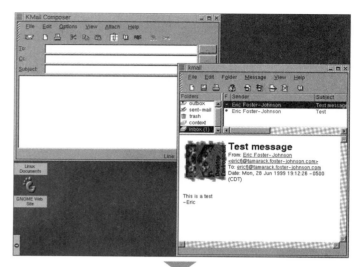

▶ The KDE **kmail** program.

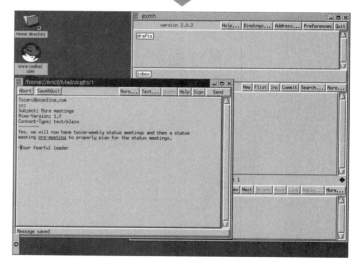

▶ The **exmh** mailer is a good choice if you don't run the GNOME or KDE desktops.

CROSS-REFERENCE

Chapter 5 covers the **vi** text editor.

252

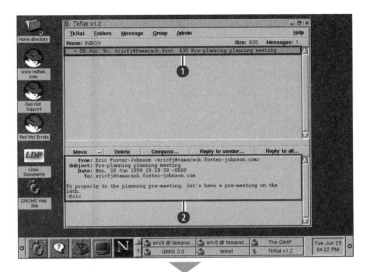

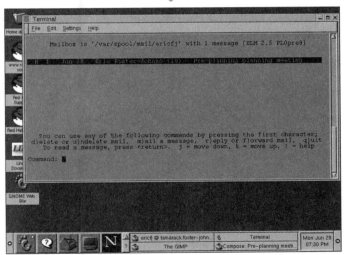

In addition to all these graphical e-mail tools, you can also run a number of text-based mail programs. The best of these is **elm**. **elm** provides one of the fastest and most efficient e-mail tools available. In fact, until Netscape improved its e-mail client, one of us used **elm** for years. **elm** works well supporting a large number of mail folders and a huge number of messages. Because it's a text-based program, **elm** launches a text editor for entering messages, defaulting to **vi**. **elm** also comes with Red Hat Linux.

If you're very new to Linux and UNIX systems, a very easy to learn mail program is called **pine**. **pine** provides a lot of menus and prompting, which helps new users.

And if all else fails, you can try the very basic **mail** program. Once considered state-of-art technology, **mail** sports a very primitive line-based interface. Unlike **elm** or **pine**, **mail** doesn't even use the full text terminal. Instead, it presents messages in a line-by-line format with very cryptic commands. Once the only program for reading mail on UNIX, we recommend you use **mail** only if all else fails.

TAKE NOTE

▶ **READING MAIL FROM EMACS**

emacs, the wonder editor, can also act as your mail tool. Start by selecting Read Mail from the Tools menu. Once started, you can read your e-mail from the familiar **emacs** interface. You can also send e-mail from **emacs**, of course.

---

❶ From the **tkrat** mailer, select messages in the top window.

❷ **tkrat** displays the message in the bottom window.

▶ You can run the **elm** mailer in any shell window. You don't need to run the X Window System.

FIND IT ONLINE

Find Ratatosk at
http://www.dtek.chalmers.se/~maf/ratatosk.

253

Transferring Files with FTP

One of the first tasks supported on the Internet was exchanging files. Using the File Transfer Protocol, or FTP, you can connect to remote systems, and download from and upload to them. To support the FTP protocol, Linux includes a client program that you can run called **ftp**. For **ftp** to work, though, the remote system must be running FTP server software. On Linux, this is run by the **in.ftpd** program, which handles FTP requests.

To use **ftp**, you run the command and pass it the name of a remote system. For example:

```
$ ftp tamarack
```

The remote system will prompt you for your user name and password. Once connected, you'll see the ftp prompt:

```
ftp>
```

At this prompt, you can enter any of the **ftp** commands listed in Table 14-2 on the facing page. The most common commands include cd, to change to a different directory on the remote system, get, to download a file, and put, to upload a file.

When transferring files with **ftp**, the remote system is typically called an FTP server. On UNIX or Linux systems, FTP servers often place files available for public access in a directory named **pub**. Due to security restrictions, you'll rarely have permission to upload files into system directories such as **/usr/bin**.

Enter **quit** at the **ftp** prompt to quit **ftp**.

Anonymous FTP

With the **ftp** command, you need an account on the remote system in order to exchange files. With anonymous FTP, you can access servers where you don't have an account. The vast majority of files downloaded from the Internet are downloaded via anonymous FTP. Here's what happens. First, an organization decides to provide the generous service of archiving files for others to download. Then, that site runs FTP server software, such as the Washington University FTP software that comes with Linux. Then, the site sets up a user account of anonymous — hence the name anonymous FTP. Oftentimes, you are prompted to provide your e-mail address as a password.

TAKE NOTE

MICROSOFT WINDOWS FTP

Microsoft Windows includes **ftp.exe**, a program that acts very much like the Linux ftp. Run this program from an MS-DOS prompt window, the Microsoft Windows equivalent of Linux shell windows. This is just the client program. To make a Windows system act as an FTP server, you need to install add-on software.

NETSCAPE AND FTP

You can download files via FTP from the Netscape Web browser, making Netscape an even handier tool. In Netscape, you can enter URLs, or Uniform Resource Locators, in the form of ftp:// to indicate an FTP server.

GRAPHICAL FTP

The GNOME desktop provides an **ftp** client program called **gFTP**. The connection dialog also provides a list of common anonymous FTP servers to connect to. Another handy **ftp** program is called **ncftp**, which provides for friendlier text-based **ftp** access.

CROSS-REFERENCE
Chapter 3 covers directories.

FIND IT ONLINE
A good download FTP site is **metalab.unc.edu**.

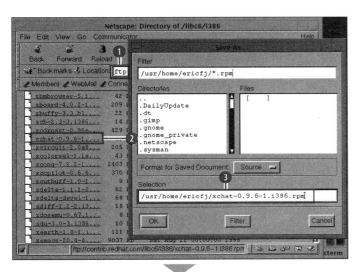

Table 14-2: FTP COMMANDS

Command	Usage
binary	Changes to binary transfer mode. You almost always want to use this mode.
open *hostname*	Opens connection to *hostname*.
get *filename*	Downloads *filename* from remote system.
mget *filenames*	Downloads multiple files from remote system. Supports wildcards like *.txt.
put *filename*	Uploads *filename* to remote system.
mput *filenames*	Uploads multiple files to remote system. Supports wildcards.

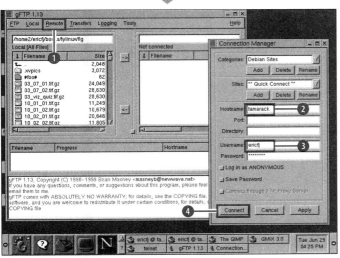

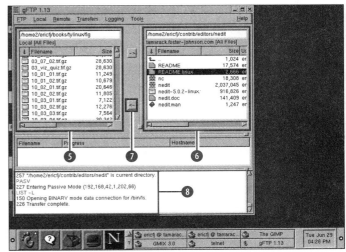

▶ *Using Netscape to view an FTP URL and directory, and then to save a file.*

❶ *Enter in an ftp:// link in Netscape to view a directory via FTP.*

❷ *Shift-click a filename to download the file.*

❸ *Enter the location and name to store the file on your local system.*

▶ *The gFTP connection manager window.*

❶ *Choose Connect from the Remote menu to establish a link in **gFTP**.*

❷ *Enter the hostname to connect.*

❸ *Enter your user name and password.*

❹ *Click Connect to establish the connection.*

▶ *gFTP's GUI window.*

❺ *Once you establish a connection, choose a location for the downloaded files in the left, local, window.*

❻ *Browse through the remote files on the right and select one for transferring.*

❼ *Click the ← button (think arrow) to transfer a file.*

❽ *Status messages appear below.*

Downloading Linux Software

This book comes with two CD-ROMs packed with Linux and other applications. But that's not all there is. There are thousands more applications available over the Internet. Many of these applications come in packages in the RPM format, making it very easy to download and install. Other packages come in different formats (RPM has not been adopted by all Linux distributions) and sometimes you get just the source code, which you have to compile yourself. This isn't that bad. We've found that RPMs sometimes don't work, but that compiling from the source usually does.

You can find quite a few prebuilt RPM packages. A great place to look for these packages is **http://www.rpmfind.net**, which indexes most RPM servers on the Internet, including the Red Hat set and the Red Hat contributed set.

RPM files are often segregated by the processor architecture: i386, SPARC, ARM, Alpha, and so on. So be sure to download binary packages for the proper system (i386 for Intel-compatible PCs). In addition, Linux distributions are moving from libc5, a version of the C programming standard library that most Linux applications use, to glibc2, also called libc6 or just plain glibc. Despite the confusing version numbers (glibc2 is a later version than libc5), with Red Hat 6.0 you want glibc2 packages. On many FTP servers, these packages are stored in a different directory than the libc5 packages.

If you can find RPM files for the packages you are interested in, life becomes a lot easier. That's because someone else went to the trouble to build the package. You can then install the package with the following command, run as root:

`# rpm -ihv filename.rpm`

Replace filename.rpm with the name of the RPM file you downloaded, such as **wine-990328-1_i386.rpm**. If

you are upgrading a package you've already installed, then use the **–U** option to **rpm**:

`# rpm -Uhv filename.rpm`

When you install from a RPM file, documentation typically goes into **/usr/doc** in a new subdirectory that is based on the package name. Use the following command to list all the files in an RPM file, along with the basic summary information:

`$ rpm -q -i -l -p filename.rpm | more`

This command can help you determine the name of the new command in the RPM file, and where it will get installed. You'll also see where all the support and configuration files get stored. You don't have to be root to run this command.

You won't find RPM files for all packages. Quite a few packages are compressed with the gzip program and usually sport filenames with a .gz or .tgz extension. If you download such a package, uncompress the file with the gunzip command:

`$ gunzip filename.gz`

Replace filename.gz with the name of the file you downloaded. The uncompress file will no longer have the .gz extension.

Typically, gzipped files are bundled with the tar command before being gzipped. Thus, you'll often find filenames ending in .tar.gz or .tgz indicating a tarred gzipped file. Run the **gunzip** command first to uncompress, then use **tar** to extract all the files:

`$ gunzip filename.tar.gz`
`$ tar xvof filename.tar`

Again, replace filename with the name of the file you downloaded. Once uncompressed and extracted, you should find a file named README or a close variant.

CROSS-REFERENCE

Chapter 2 covers the **rpm** command and Chapter 6 covers the **tar** command.

FIND IT ONLINE

The site **http://www.rpmfind.net** is a great place to find RPM files.

You should read this file. The file should introduce the package and often provides installation instructions. Sometimes a separate file named INSTALL describes how to install the package.

If the package comes as source code, you'll need to compile it. To do this, you must have the C compiler, cc (**egcs** or **gcc**), and **make** commands available. You should always install these when you install Linux. You may also need special libraries or other packages to build the package you downloaded.

TAKE NOTE

▶ **DEALING WITH RPM DEPENDENCIES**

Sometimes RPM files require other packages, too. In that case, you need to find the proper RPM file and install it first. If you see an error message like the following, you need to download another package:

```
error: failed dependencies:
libglide2x.so is needed by q3test-
1.05-glibc-9
```

▶ **CHECK BEFORE DOWNLOADING**

And, before you go to the trouble of downloading a package, it's a good idea to see if you already have it. Run the following command:

```
$ rpm -qa | grep name
```

Replace name with the name of the package, or a subset of the name if you don't know the full name.

Table 14-3: LINUX DOWNLOAD SITES

Site	Holds
http://www.redhat.com/mirrors.html	Red Hat mirror site listing. Check for FTP sites closer to you than Red Hat's overloaded main site.
ftp://contrib.redhat.com/libc6/i386/	Contributed packages for Intel-based Red Hat systems.
ftp://rhcn.redhat.com/	Red Hat Contrib Network, which is different from the contributed packages collection, also at Red Hat's site.
http://www.rpmfind.net	Central archive of Red Hat RPM files and contributed applications from many sources.
http://linux.davecentral.com	Good download site, especially for office applications.
http://www.linuxberg.com	Site holding many Linux applications, and mirror sites on many continents, from the Tucows folks.
http://metalab.unc.edu	Home of most free Linux source code; formerly called sunsite.
http://www.linuxgames.com	Many games for Linux; holds information and links to download sites.

Internet Relay Chat

The Internet Relay Chat, or IRC, enables you to engage in real-time conversations with other users over the Internet. In this type of chatting, you type in messages for others to read, and follow the printed conversation in a chat window. Messages from other users appear in the main window. The messages appear just about as fast as you type them in, which can lead to fast and furious discussions.

To make this work, you need to run an IRC client program and connect to an IRC server. The client and server communicate using the IRC protocol. This means you can select from a variety of clients and servers. In typical usage, you connect to one IRC server. Other users connect to the same IRC server. Still more users connect to other IRC servers that are part of the same IRC system. These servers communicate with each other, propagating all the messages to all connected users. This provides for a fairly robust system where the failure of one server only brings down a small portion of the conversation.

Sometimes, organizations that host IRC servers sponsor chat events. For example, you may get a chance to chat with television personalities.

When connected to an IRC server, you can select from the many available channels. Usually, each channel is devoted to a particular topic, such as Linux or the Perl scripting language. IRC channel names start with a pound sign (#), such as #linux or #irchelp.

The main GNOME chat interface is provided by a program named **xchat**. You can start **xchat** from the Internet menu from the task bar, or enter the **xchat** command into a shell.

When **xchat** starts up, you'll see a server list from which you can select servers and channels. You'll also see the main **xchat** interface. Even though you see a graphical interface, IRC is really a text-based protocol.

So, you'll enter a number of commands directly into the window. These IRC commands start with a /, such as /HELP to get a list of commands. (You can also ask for help on a particular command, such as /HELP JOIN for very brief information on joining channels.)

> **TAKE NOTE**
>
> ▶ **OTHER CHAT CLIENTS**
> Other chat clients on Linux include ircii, available on the AnotherLevel menus, and ksirc, which is part of the optional KDE desktop.
>
> ▶ **ANSWERING QUESTIONS**
> You can find a lot of help on chatting and IRC at **http://www.irchelp.org**. This is a great resource for newcomers to the chat field. It has lists of IRC server sites, channels, software downloads, and frequently asked questions, also called FAQs.
>
> ▶ **SEEKING OTHERS**
> In addition to IRC, there are several other chatting protocols. A related protocol is called ICQ, or I Seek You. You can download ICQ clients from **http://www.icq.com**.

Trying to be polite

With users all over the world participating in chats, you need to be extra polite when conversing. If everyone jumps in all at once, the chat will devolve into a mess of messages, all competing for your attention. Users will often end messages with o, short for over, which radio operators use to signify being done with a message. Before starting to converse, watch the conversation for a while and see how it flows. You'll do best trying to fit in with the way the group operates.

> **SHORTCUT**
> Launch **xchat** from the Internet menu on the GNOME taskbar.

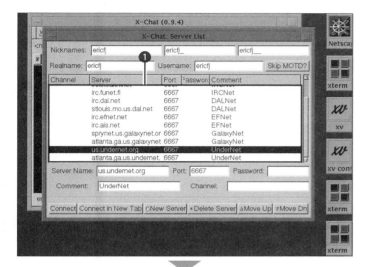

Table 14-4: MAIN IRC SITES

Site	Holds
http://www.efnet.net	Large site holds over 12,000 channels
http://www.undernet.org	Another large site with servers spanning three continents
http://www.mn.us. undernet.org	Local Undernet site in Minneapolis, Minnesota
http://www.dal.net	Another large chat network

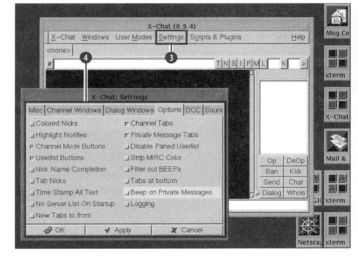

① *Select IRC servers and channels from the **xchat** server list window.*

② *Enter your messages and commands in the main **xchat** window.*

③ *Configure **xchat** by calling up dialogs from the Settings menu.*

④ *From the Setup menu, you can control how **xchat** works with the Settings dialog.*

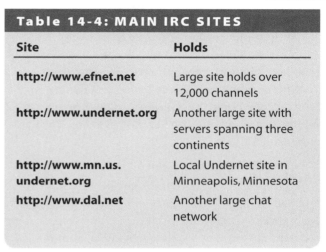

FIND IT ONLINE

For more on xchat, see
http://www.xchat.linuxpower.org.

259

Logging on to Remote Systems

The Linux shells give you a powerful tool, but just on your Linux system. True to its UNIX roots though, Linux also enables you to log on to remote systems connected on your network.

Run the **telnet** program to log on to a remote system. Of course, you must have an account on the remote system or you won't be able to log in. The basic command follows:

```
$ telnet hostname
```

Replace hostname with the name of the remote system you want to access. **telnet** will prompt you for your user name and password — on the remote system. Your account on your Linux system may differ from the remote account. You can also pass an IP address of the remote machine, as discussed in Chapter 15. If you just run **telnet** alone, or from the Red Hat menus on the GNOME desktop, you'll get a **telnet** prompt. At that prompt, use the open command with the name of the remote system:

```
$ telnet
telnet> open tamarack
```

If you have an account on the remote system, it doesn't matter how far away the system is located, so long as a network connects your system and the remote system. For example, many Internet service providers run Linux and give users **telnet** access. **telnet** access opens a security hole, though, so many companies use firewall software to prevent **telnet** access.

rlogin provides an alternative to **telnet**. Originally developed as part of the UNIX system created at the University of California at Berkeley, BSD UNIX included a number of r — or remote — tools including **rlogin**, **rcp** for copying, and **rsh** for executing shell commands on remote systems.

Like **telnet**, **rlogin** also takes the name or network address of the remote system. For example:

```
$ rlogin tamarack
```

Also like **telnet**, you need an account on the remote system. Unlike **telnet** though, **rlogin** defaults to using your current user name, so it just prompts you for your password on the remote system. If your user name on the remote system doesn't match your user name on your current system, pass the –l option as shown here:

```
$ rlogin -l fred tamarack
```

This command tells **rlogin** that the user name on the remote system tamarack is fred.

TAKE NOTE

▶ MICROSOFT WINDOWS TELNET

Microsoft Windows also includes a Telnet program, telnet.exe, which you can launch from the Run choice on the Start menu. Tera term is a great free Telnet program for Microsoft Windows that also includes a Windows CE version. Get Tera term from **http://www.tucows.com**.

▶ RLOGIN SECURITY

One of the holes in security has been that you can create a file of trusted users and those users could run **rlogin** without entering in a password at all. Avoid this feature, or use Kerberos authentication as described in the man **rlogin** command. You can also run **SSH** (secure shell), which is supported by many shell servers.

CROSS-REFERENCE
Chapter 3 covers Linux shell commands.

260

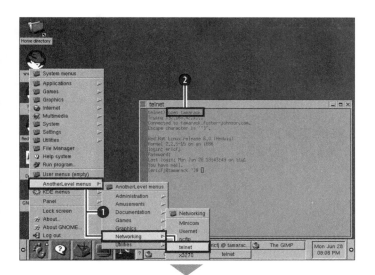

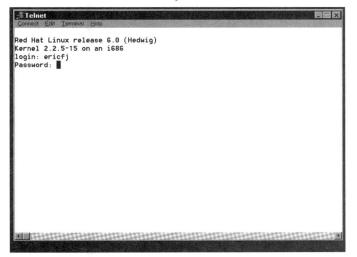

1 Select Networking from the AnotherLevel menus and launch **telnet**.

2 In the **telnet** window that appears, type **open** and the system name at the telnet> prompt.

▶ Run telnet.exe to launch the Microsoft Windows Telnet.

Listing 14-1: RUNNING TELNET

```
$ telnet tamarack
Trying 192.168.42.1...
Connected to tamarack.foster-johnson.com.
Escape character is '^]'.

Red Hat Linux release 6.0 (Hedwig)
Kernel 2.2.5-15 on an i686
login: ericfj
Password:
Last login: Mon Jun 28 20:07:58 from
tamarack
You have mail.
[ericfj@tamarack ~]$
```
▶ Using **telnet** to access a remote system.

Listing 14-2: RUNNING RLOGIN

```
$ rlogin tamarack
Password:
Last login: Tue Jun 29 16:31:18 from
tamarack
You have mail.
[ericfj@tamarack ~]$
[ericfj@tamarack ~]$ uname -m
i686
[ericfj@tamarack ~]$ exit
logout
rlogin: connection closed.
$
```
▶ You can also use **rlogin**. On many systems, though, **rlogin** access is disabled for security reasons.

FIND IT ONLINE

For more on BSD UNIX, see **http://www.freebsd.org**.

Reading the News

Long before every home — let alone every refrigerator — was connected to the Internet, the Usenet sprang up and provided a public forum for users worldwide to exchange messages. Unlike e-mail, Usenet news messages get sent to all readers worldwide. As you'd expect, this results in a lot of data.

News servers transmitted megabytes of data every day. Every night (saving long distance charges), UNIX systems would connect to other systems over phone lines and exchange the e-mail and public messages for the Usenet news. Now these messages are transferred using the Internet and the Network News Transport Protocol, or NNTP. Often called discussion groups, the Usenet news consists of thousands of newsgroups, individual areas of discussion, and discussion topics on just about everything imaginable — and then some.

Like your Linux file system and network hostnames, the Usenet news is divided up in a hierarchy. At the top sit top-level areas such as comp for discussions related to computers, and rec for recreational issues. There are also top-level groups for specific geographic areas, such as mn for Minnesota-related discussions.

Under these top-level groups are specific groups, organized around topics. The newsgroup names are separated by periods. For example, the newsgroup **linux.redhat.announce** covers announcements related to Red Hat's Linux distribution. Topics range the gamut from **alt.buddha.short.fat.guy** to **rec.recipes. vegetarian**. And, yes, there are plenty of newsgroups devoted to pictures of women. The vast majority of messages, though, are devoted to computing subjects, spanning the range from hardware setup and configuration to detailed programming issues. In general, the more specific and detailed the newsgroup, the more useful the information you'll get.

Because there are so many groups and messages — the daily traffic is far too large to read in one day (gigabytes) — you typically subscribe to only the groups in which you are most interested. To do this, newsreading programs present you with a list of newsgroups and you choose which to read.

Each group you subscribe to contains a number of messages, sometimes in the thousands. Like e-mail, each message has a subject line, which is helpful in determining whether you want to read the message.

To read the news, you need three things:

▶ A system that will act as a news or NNTP server
▶ A network connection to that system
▶ Software that can read the news

Typically, your Internet service provider acts as a news server. You just need to know the name of the system, which is usually news or news.*domain*.com, where domain gets replaced with your ISP's domain name.

For software, there are quite a few options available. Just about every newsreading program for UNIX works on Linux. Netscape includes newsreading software, so a good program to start with is Netscape, especially if you use it for Web browsing and e-mail.

Continued

CROSS-REFERENCE

Appendix B provides a list of Linux-related newsgroups.

FIND IT ONLINE

Newsgroups provide a lot of Linux support. For more support options, see **http://www.linuxcare.com**.

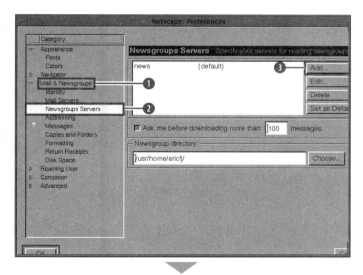

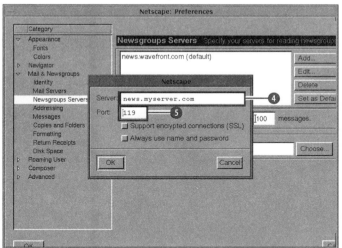

READ IT WITH A GRAIN OF SALT

Anyone — and we mean anyone — can post messages. Many times, employees of a company will post favorable messages for their company's products — but under user accounts that look like they are not part of the company. Users may fake their location, creating fake but official-looking announcements. Other times, you find wild claims, and frequently you find bad advice from people who don't know what they are doing. Sit back, relax, and just be sure to treat all messages — and we mean all — skeptically. Be especially wary around April 1, April Fool's Day, when there are a lot of hoaxes on the Internet.

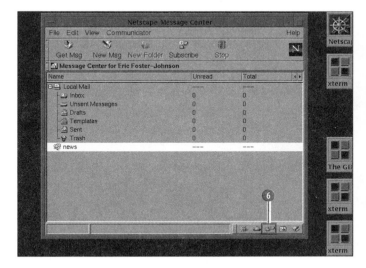

① *In the Netscape Preferences dialog, select the Mail & Newsgroups category.*

② *Select the Newsgroup Servers subcategory.*

③ *Click Add to add a news server.*

④ *In the Add Server dialog in Netscape, enter the hostname of your news server.*

⑤ *You normally don't need to edit the port number.*

⑥ *Call up the newsgroups window from the Netscape toolbar. From here, you can subscribe to groups and read the news.*

Reading the News
Continued

Subscribing to newsgroups

To read the news with Netscape, first call up the Netscape Message Center window. From there, click Subscribe to get a list of all the newsgroups. Select the ones you want to read. The list takes a long time to generate and the Netscape interface can be confusing. Remember that newsgroups are stored in a hierarchy. So, to read computer-related newsgroups, you need to expand the comp hierarchy to see all the newsgroups under comp. You then have to expand the **os** group under comp to see the **comp.os.linux** entry. Finally, expand **the comp.os.linux** to see all the groups under **comp.os.linux**, including **comp.os.linux.announce**. This isn't all that intuitive for a newcomer.

Beside each group is a small dot that you can select to subscribe to the group. In Netscape, subscribing means that the main messages window presents a list that includes that group and enables you to select it. Don't worry, you can change which groups you subscribe to at any time.

Later on, you can click the New tab in the subscribing window to see all newsgroups that have appeared since you last checked. It's worthwhile to try this once every month or two.

Reading messages

Once you've selected the groups to subscribe to, you can start reading messages. From the main Netscape Message Center window, you can expand the entry for a particular news server to see all the groups to which you are subscribed. Again, this takes some time. Netscape checks the news server and then marks the group name bold if there are messages available. Click the group name to see the list of messages.

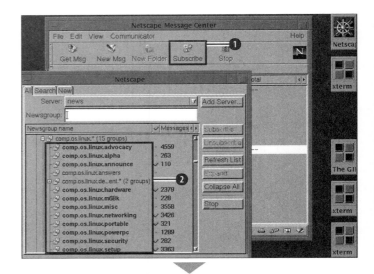

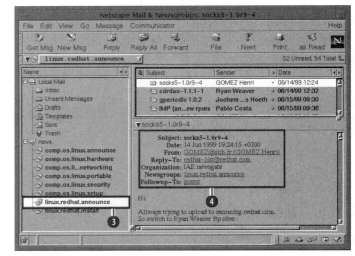

❶ In the Netscape Message Center window, click Subscribe to get a dialog listing all the newsgroups.

❷ Select the groups to which you want to subscribe.

❸ Select a newsgroup to read.

❹ Netscape displays the first message in the group.

CROSS-REFERENCE

Chapter 5 covers **emacs**.

264

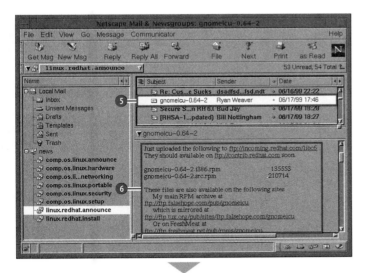

From the Netscape View menu, you can choose how to sort the messages, by subject, by date, by thread, and so on. We recommend by subject or by thread. Sorting by subject places all related messages together. Sorting by thread places the first message at the top of a hierarchical list. You expand the list to see responses. You expand on the responses to see the responses to the responses.

Other newsreaders

In addition to Netscape, there is a wide array of choices for newsreading programs. Red Hat Linux ships with **trn**, **tin**, and **slrn**, which are all text-based newsreaders. The optional KDE desktop includes **krn**, a graphical newsreader. Another, more basic, graphical newsreader is **xrn**.

In addition, there are a number of newsreading packages available on the Internet, such as **nn** or **vnews**.

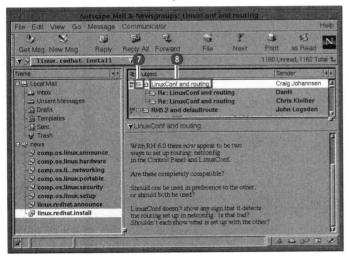

> **TAKE NOTE**
>
> ▶ **READING THE NEWS WITH EMACS**
>
> Because **emacs** can read e-mail, it's only a small step to reading news, too. Look on the Tools menu to set this up. Once running, you can read the news and post new messages from within the **emacs** windows.

⑤ Select a message to read from the message list.

⑥ Netscape shows the message below the list.

⑦ Click the icon to expand a thread of messages.

⑧ Select a message to read it.

> **FIND IT ONLINE**
>
> Important Linux announcements appear in the **comp.os.linux.announce** newsgroup.

Posting Messages to Newsgroups

Reading messages is only half the fun. You can also post your own messages. This is especially useful should you experience some problem that you cannot solve on your own. Most Linux support, in fact, occurs over the newsgroups and special mailing lists.

To post a message in Netscape, go to the news group in which you want to post and click New Msg. In the window that appears, enter your message and when you're done, click Send. The interface is almost exactly the same as that for composing e-mail messages.

Every message you post is sent to readers worldwide. Because of this, you probably don't want to ask about things that only apply to your hometown, such as directions to a store that sells Quake for Linux.

If you experience a problem with Linux or your hardware, posting a message is a great way to get help. When doing this, though, be as specific as possible. A message stating Linux doesn't work will likely not get you any helpful responses. A message providing more detail, for example, that you seem to be experiencing problems with Red Hat Linux 6.0 on a Pentium II chip and an Adaptec SCSI interface card, is likely to get better responses. The more information you provide about your problem, the better.

You should also be mindful about U.S.-centric messages. For example, it's just common courtesy that when listing prices you specify the country, too, such as $1,000 (U.S.) instead of just $1,000. Other countries name their currency the dollar, too.

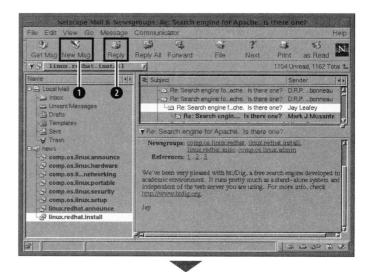

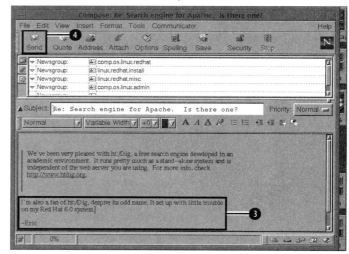

❶ Click New Msg in Netscape to post a message to the current newsgroup.

❷ Click Reply instead to post a message that replies to the current message.

❸ Enter your new message in the Netscape Compose window.

❹ Click Send when you're done.

CROSS-REFERENCE

Chapter 4 covers other ways to find help on Linux.

266

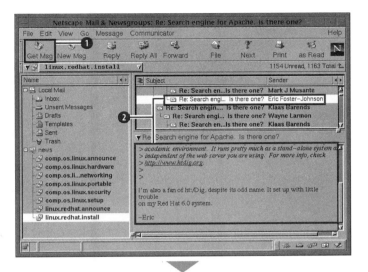

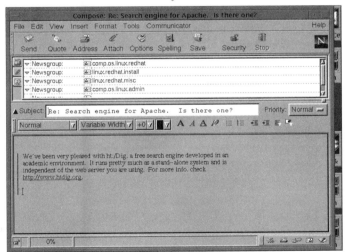

❶ *Click Get Msg to request an update from the news server.*

❷ *You should see your message in the window.*

▶ *When replying to a message, it's usually in bad taste to post to multiple groups, as shown here. You'll be accused of spreading SPAM.*

TAKE NOTE

▶ **NETIQUETTE**

Everything you post to the Usenet news gets sent around the world. Furthermore, archive services such as Deja News store your messages for years. So, avoid writing anything you'll be embarrassed by later. It's also a good idea to be polite. In normal conversation, people can see your facial expressions and body language, as well as hear your tone of voice. The written word generally doesn't convey these things. Furthermore, many readers aren't native English speakers. Thus, you want to carefully phrase your messages and should avoid things like dripping sarcasm.

▶ **ALLOW SOME TIME FOR RESPONSES**

It may take a while for other users to see your message and post a response, so be patient. Sometimes you have to wait a few days, but generally, you should see a response within 24 hours. The clearer and more specific you are in your message, the more likely you are to get a good response. For example, include the version of Linux that you run, the distribution, such as Red Hat, and any other pertinent data.

FIND IT ONLINE

Deja News, at **http://www.deja.com**, archives a lot of past messages, which you can search.

Personal Workbook

Q&A

1 Can you send e-mail messages from Linux?

_____

_____

_____

2 What applications can you use to log in to remote systems over a network?

_____

_____

_____

3 Can you log in to a Linux system from a Microsoft Windows system? If you can, the which program can you use?

_____

_____

_____

4 Can you read the Usenet news from **emacs**?

_____

_____

_____

5 Can you read e-mail from **emacs**?

_____

_____

_____

6 You've downloaded a file that ends in .gz. Which program do you use to uncompress the file?

_____

_____

_____

7 Which program can you use to participate in an online chat?

_____

_____

_____

8 Before you can read e-mail messages from Netscape, what do you need to do?

_____

_____

_____

ANSWERS: PAGE 341

EXTRA PRACTICE

1. Contact your Internet Service Provider to determine the name of the news server. Then, set up a newsreader such as Netscape to read the news. Take a look at the huge list of newsgroups available.

2. Subscribe to a newsgroup. Check over any messages that look interesting. Remember not to take what people post as the absolute truth. There's a lot of good information on Usenet news, but also a lot of incorrect information.

3. Check out all the archives available on the Internet from **http://www.rpmfind.net**. Look for updates to some of the current programs you run.

4. Download a RPM file and install it.

REAL-WORLD APPLICATIONS

✔ Using Usenet news raises a lot of issues. There's clearly pornography and offensive material in the daily message stream. Is this something your organization can deal with? How about restricting access? This may also cause problems related to freedom of expression. Talk this over with others in your organization.

✔ You're faced with some balky hardware, a network card, that you cannot get working on Linux. Compose a question to post to the Usenet news. Make sure that you include the version of Linux you're running, as well as the make and model of the network card. Also, mention that you have read the how-to documents and still have a problem. Now post the message.

Visual Quiz

How you can tell Netscape to display the Red Hat Linux home page?

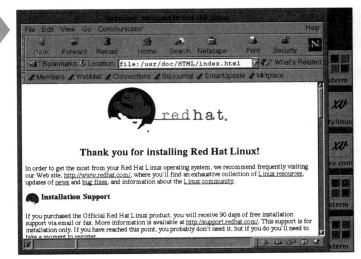

CHAPTER 15

MASTER
THESE
SKILLS

▶ Linux Networking
▶ Setting Up Your Network Card
▶ Starting Network Services
▶ Testing Your Network
▶ Sharing Files with Samba
▶ Sharing Files with NFS

Local Area Networking

Up to now, we've discussed a number of network tools that you can use with dial-up links to the Internet. This chapter expands that into local area networking.

Typically, your local area network will start with network adapter cards that you place in your PCs. Each computer requires at least one adapter card, or an interface built in the system board. Then, you wire your computers together based on a certain networking scheme. Most local area networking today uses 10 or 100Base-T twisted-pair cabling. The 10 stands for 10 megabits per second, or Mbps. The 100 stands for 100 Mbps. With this type of interface, you normally connect a twisted-pair cable to your computer and stick the other end in a network *hub*. Hubs are small boxes with two, four, eight, sixteen, or more ports. You can also connect hubs together, extending the reach of your network. For about $100 to $200, you can purchase off-the-shelf kits that include a hub, all the necessary cables, and a number of networking adapter cards — typically, two. Linux supports quite a few network adapter cards, but it is always a good idea to check first. Older styles of Ethernet networking include thicknet coaxial cable and thinnet, or 10Base-2 cabling.

Basic Ethernet networking on Linux uses the Internet Protocol, or IP. A protocol is merely an agreed upon way to communicate. The whole reason the Internet works is that various vendors — some willing, some brought in kicking and screaming — support a common set of protocols that enable computers to communicate with IP sites at the bottom of a layered cake of protocols. Layered on top of IP is a number of other protocols, including TCP, the Transmission Control Protocol, and UDP, the User Datagram Protocol. Most network services are built on top of TCP or UDP, which, in turn, are built on top of IP. Hence, you see names such as TCP/IP. A service such as HTTP, the Hypertext Transfer Protocol, drives the World Wide Web and uses TCP/IP as its underlying communications scheme. On top of TCP/IP, HTTP defines a set of messages for Web browsers to obtain Web pages. In addition to TCP/IP, other networking protocol families include IPX used by Novell NetWare and NetBIOS/NetBEUI used by Microsoft Windows.

In the tasks that follow, we show how to set up your computer to work on a local area network.

Linux Networking

Most Internet protocols follow a client-server model for simplicity. A client, such as your Web browser, requests something from a server. In this model, servers generally sit passively, awaiting requests from clients.

Using the Internet family of protocols, each system on a network must have an IP address. This address is a sequence of four bytes that uniquely names your system on the Internet or your local area network. The general form is something similar to 192.168.1.42, where the four-byte number is divided into its component parts. The dot notation shown here is used throughout discussions of networking.

When you run a networking program to establish a link to another system, that program requires the IP address of the target system. Because IP addresses are hard to remember, most users only need to provide a system's hostname, such as **www.linux.org**. The Domain Name Service, or DNS, converts the hostname, such as **www.linux.org**, into an IP address, such as 198.182.196.56, so that a program may connect.

The Internet is a collection of networks, so part of the IP address tells routers which network to send a message to. The rest of the IP address identifies the system on the local network.

IP addresses are assigned to organizations in ranges based on the four bytes that make up an Internet address. A certain part of the IP address identifies the organization, and the rest of the address identifies an individual machine within that organization. Depending on the size of the organization, you get a different class of addresses. A very large organization, for example, can register for a class A address, in which they get one number, say 3, and all the addresses that start with 3.x.x.x (with a few exceptions for specially

reserved addresses). With a class A address, you can set up 16,777,214 different systems on the network, far more than most companies require. Class A addresses start with a number between 1 and 127. Class A addresses are no longer available.

Class B addresses provide a smaller range in which the first two numbers of the IP address represent the organization. Class B addresses provide 65,534 different systems within the organization, making these far more common.

The next level down is a large jump. Class C addresses use three bytes to identify the network, leaving room for only 254 hosts on each class C network (0 and 255 are reserved addresses). There are also special stopgap addressing schemes that provide for networks in between class A, B, and C sizes.

CROSS-REFERENCE

Chapter 13 covers how to get on the Internet.

What you need to get

To set up a home network, you need a network adapter in each computer that you want on the network. You also need the proper cabling for the type of network, and if you use 10 or 100Base-T networking, you need to get a network hub. You can generally buy a kit containing a small four- to eight-port hub, two networking adapter cards, and two cables for about $200.

You need to ensure that the cables are long enough to reach between your systems and the hub. Many users place the hub in a closet somewhere in their house. All the systems have to be connected to the hub, and the cables must be long enough to reach. If you've turned a bedroom into an office, then that makes a good location for the hub. If one computer is located upstairs and one downstairs, then you may have some complex wiring to install in your house. For new construction, many builders offer to install network cables, especially UTP (unshielded twisted-pair) 10 and 100Base-T cables, while the house is built, saving you the hassle from installing them later.

There are also other networking schemes that transmit a signal over your existing phone lines. This is very helpful should you need to connect systems over a longer distance or a tougher location for wiring. Other alternatives include wireless networking. As of this writing, though, wireless networking is too expensive and too slow for most users. As the technology progresses, however, you should be able to avoid all the hassles of network wiring.

Almost all network hardware vendors write special drivers to make their products work with Microsoft Windows. Few vendors provide any sort of support for Linux (Linksys is one that does). So, before buying anything, check the Linux compatibility lists at

http://metalab.unc.edu/LDP/HOWTO/Ethernet-HOWTO.html.

Table 15-1: IP CLASS RANGES (NOT COUNTING RESERVED ADDRESSES)

Class	Ranges From	To
A	1.0.0.0	126.255.255.255
B	128.0.0.0	191.255.255.255
C	192.0.0.0	223.255.255.255

FIND IT ONLINE

For more on the classes of Internet addresses, see http://www.icann.org.

Setting Up Your Network Card

To get your Linux system on a local network, you need to set up a supported network card. The very best way to do this is when you install Red Hat Linux. During the installation, the Red Hat installation program autodetects most network cards and automatically sets up things for you, including dynamically loaded modules for your particular card, and other startup scripts to enable networking. During this process, you need to provide some information about your network and your Linux system.

One of the first things you must do is assign your system an IP address. You can assign this statically, or use DHCP or BOOTP to get the IP address at run-time. If in doubt, select static assignment and provide a number yourself, if you're setting up your own network. Otherwise, ask your system administrator.

When you dial into an Internet service provider, the provider dynamically assigns your system an IP address from the pool of addresses the provider owns. When you sign up for a cable modem, you may get a static IP address in which your cable provider assigns you an IP address from its pool.

It's only when you try to network the machines you have at home or in the office that you need to worry about assigning your systems IP addresses. While each system on the network needs an IP address, there are private ranges left for small organizations to use internally — which are perfect for home use.

In addition to the IP address, you need to provide the Red Hat setup program the name of your system, along with a full domain name. The hostname can be any name you like and are likely to remember. You'll use this hostname with most network commands when accessing your machine over your network.

For the domain, use a registered name, such as oualline.com, if you have one. If not, you can make up a name, such as bigfun.com.

You'll also be asked for a netmask. If you use a private class C IP address, such as 192.168.42.1, the netmask is 255.255.255.0. The setup program automatically determines the rest of the information.

From all this, you should have a network-ready system when Linux boots up after the install. Look in the /etc/hosts file and you should see the IP address and hostname you set up. The **uname –n** command should also report your hostname.

You can check the status of the network interfaces with the **ifconfig -a** command. You can also look in /proc/net/dev. Both list each network interface on your system.

Your first network card is called eth0, short for the first (starting at 0) Ethernet interface. If you add a second network card, its interface is called eth1, and so on. We've worked with servers running four Ethernet cards. The PPP interface is **ppp** and the special loopback-testing interface is **lo**.

Continued

TAKE NOTE

SAFE PRIVATE ADDRESSES

The Internet addressing scheme discussed here provides for a number of addresses that are considered private. Anyone can use these addresses without having to go through the trouble to apply for a class A, B, or C address family. So, these addresses, listed in Table 15-2, are perfect for home networks. There's one catch, though; you cannot use these addresses to get on the Internet.

CROSS-REFERENCE

Chapter 13's discussion of cable modems covers multiple IP addresses for one system.

Note that your Linux system may have more than one IP address at a time. With another networking interface, such as a PPP dial-up connection, you can have a local area network and get on the Internet.

CHOOSING NAMES

Now, if you're just a cog in a large enterprise, your system may get a name in the format of eng2051 or some other easy-to-remember name. On your own networks, though, you can pick any names you like. Some people like to keep hostnames to a theme, such as movie monsters (godzilla, rodan, gamera), or Norse deities (thor, heimdall), or place names (nicollet, tamarack), for example. It's good to plan the names and IP addresses in advance and write them down.

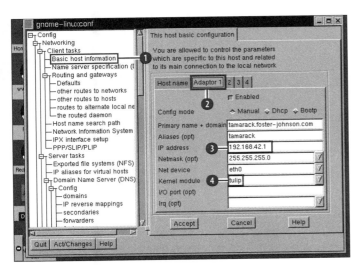

❶ Select Config ➪ Networking ➪ Client tasks ➪ Basic host information in **linuxconf**.

❷ Click Adaptor 1 for the first Ethernet adapter card.

❸ Enter your IP address.

❹ You need to pick the kernel module that is to drive your network adapter card. Most match up to the card or the chip on the card.

Table 15-2: PRIVATE IP ADDRESSES

Address Range	Type
10.0.0.0	Class A
172.16.0.0 through 172.31.0.0	Class B
192.168.1.0 through 192.168.255.0	Class C

Listing 15-1: RUNNING IFCONFIG

```
$ /sbin/ifconfig -a
eth0 Link encap:Ethernet HWaddr
00:A0:CC:26:60:C4
 inet addr:192.168.42.1 Bcast:
 192.168.42.255 Mask:255.255.255.0
 UP BROADCAST RUNNING MULTICAST
 MTU:1500 Metric:1
 RX packets:0 errors:0 dropped:0
 overruns:0 frame:0
 TX packets:48569 errors:0 dropped:0
 overruns:0 carrier:0
 collisions:0 txqueuelen:100
 Interrupt:10 Base address:0x1000

lo Link encap:Local Loopback
 inet addr:127.0.0.1 Mask:255.0.0.0
 UP LOOPBACK RUNNING MTU:3924
 Metric:1
 RX packets:16285 errors:0 dropped:0
 overruns:0 frame:0
 TX packets:16285 errors:0 dropped:0
 overruns:0 carrier:0
 collisions:0 txqueuelen:0
```

▶ *You can see the status of your installed network devices with the /sbin/ifconfig –a command. You can use other **ifconfig** options to enable or disable the network card, as well as to change the card settings.*

FIND IT ONLINE

See **http://metalab.unc.edu/LDP/HOWTO/ Ethernet-HOWTO.html** for more on how to set up Ethernet networking.

275

Setting Up Your Network Card
Continued

Adding routes

When a network packet gets sent, Linux needs to choose which interface to send the packet over, that is, which network card, PPP dial-up modem, and so on that you may have installed in your system. Because you may have more than one interface to the outside world, Linux keeps a table of routing information to tell it which IP addresses of remote systems are available from which networking interface. For example, if you use a modem for dial-up access to the Internet and an Ethernet adapter card for a local area network, Linux needs to know that packets for local systems should go out the Ethernet card and packets for the Internet should go out over the modem. Linux does this by consulting its routing table.

If all the systems on your local network use the same class of IP addresses, such as the class C addresses 192.168.42.x, then your routes should be set up by Linux without problem. If you need to connect to systems using wildly different IP addresses, even if they are on the same network hubs, then you may need to add a route to get to what is technically considered to be on a different network from the IP point of view.

The **netstat –r** command, as shown on the facing page, lists the current routing table. The **route** command, without any parameters, does, too.

The **route** command — run as root — adds routing information to a routing table kept by Linux. The basic syntax for adding a route is:

```
# route add -net IPaddr dev eth0
```

This command adds a route to a given network IP address (ending in a zero) for the device (dev) eth0, the first Ethernet interface. Note that this form of the route command differs from many UNIX versions. For example:

```
# route add —net 192.168.42.0 \
  metric 1 dev eth0
```

You can also set up a route to a particular host using **–host** instead of **–net**. You pass the actual IP address of the system with the **–host** option, as opposed to the network address (ending in 0) with the **–net** option.

TAKE NOTE

▶ **CONFIGURING ROUTES WITH LINUXCONF**

If you don't like the command-line interface of the **route** command, and if you didn't set things up when you installed Linux, you can use the graphical **linuxconf** program to set up routes. Because this is complicated, you should know the basic commands as well. But you can perform most of these tasks from **linuxconf**.

In the main **linuxconf** selection window, open up Networking and then Routing and gateways. The online help for topics such as default routes is quite helpful. It gives a description of what a route is, along with information to determine whether it applies to your network.

Listing 15-2: CHECKING /ETC/HOSTS

```
$ more /etc/hosts
127.0.0.1 localhost
192.168.42.1 tamarack.bigfun.com tamarack
```
▶ *The /etc/hosts file provides a simple way to list the machines on your network and the IP address for those machines.*

CROSS-REFERENCE
Chapter 2 has more on **linuxconf**.

Listing 15-3: CHECKING THE ROUTES

```
$ netstat -r
Kernel IP routing table
Destination Gateway Flags Iface
192.168.42.1 * UH eth0
192.168.42.0 192.168.42.1 UG eth0
192.168.42.0 * U eth0
127.0.0.0 * U lo
```

▶ *The **netstat –r** command, with output shown here in edited format, provides information on the Linux routing table. You can see the interface, such as eth0, associated with each route.*

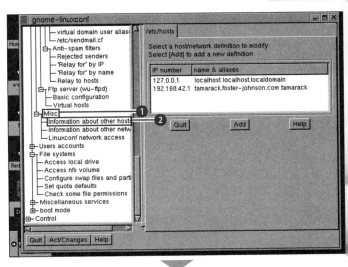

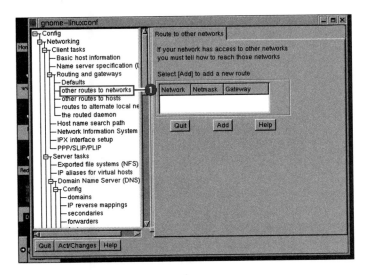

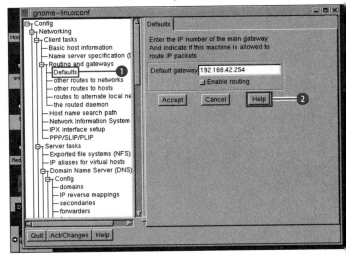

❶ *Choose other routes to networks in **linuxconf** to set up special routing.*

❷ *Select Misc under Networking in **linuxconf**.*

❸ *Select information about other hosts to see the /etc/hosts information.*

❹ *Click Defaults in the Routing and gateways section of **linuxconf**.*

❺ *Click Help to see the online help.*

FIND IT ONLINE

See **http://www.linux.com/howto/ Intranet-Server-HOWTO.html** for more on configuring networks.

Starting Network Services

This UNIX and Linux model has server programs—called *daemons*—running in the background and providing network services. Typically, a program handles a single protocol and hence a single service. For example, **httpd** handles requests for the Hypertext Transfer Protocol—that is, Web pages. Another daemon, **in.telnetd**, handles remote login requests that come in using the telnet protocol. You'll note that most of these daemons sport a name ending in d.

In most cases, a special networking daemon called **inetd** listens for incoming connections. When a connection arrives for a given service, **inetd** starts the proper program to handle that service. The main way Linux differentiates these services is by port numbers. Port numbers are like radio station frequencies, to request a given service, such as file transfers or e-mail, you tune in to the proper port number. These numbers are established in advance and hardwired into most network programs. For example, when you want to download a file, you run the **ftp** command. The **ftp** command knows that 20 and 21 are port numbers reserved for FTP. On the receiving (server) side, **inetd** launches the ftp daemon program **in.ftpd** to handle incoming requests.

The mapping between services and port numbers is defined in /etc/services. Take a look at this file and you'll see quite a few available services, along with their port numbers. **inetd** is configured from a file named /etc/inetd.conf. This file tells **inetd** which port numbers it should listen on, and which command to start for a connection on a given port. That said, the easiest way to start network services is to set them up when you install Red Hat Linux.

This is so much easier because you are prompted for which network services you want to start and the Red Hat installation program takes care of the rest. If you didn't set this up when you installed Linux, don't despair, you can still run **linuxconf**.

linuxconf is a wonder tool that enables you to configure quite a lot about your system, particularly for networking as shown in this chapter. Fire up **linxuconf** and open the Networking section, where there is a plethora of options.

CROSS-REFERENCE

Chapter 16 covers running **httpd** from **inetd** or on its own.

Table 15-3: COMMON PORT NUMBERS AND SERVICES

Port	Service
20, 21	FTP, File Transfer Protocol
23	Telnet (remote logins)
25	SMTP, Simple Mail Transport Protocol (sending e-mail)
80	HTTP, Hypertext Transport Protocol (Web pages)
98	linuxconf Web access port number
110	POP3, Post Office Protocol version 3 (picking up your e-mail messages)
119	NNTP, the network news transport protocol

Listing 15-4: EXAMINING /ETC/SERVICES

```
ftp-data 20/tcp
ftp 21/tcp
telnet 23/tcp
smtp 25/tcp
www 80/tcp # WorldWideWeb HTTP
pop-3 110/tcp # POP version 3
nntp 119/tcp # USENET News Trans Proto
snmp 161/udp # Simple Net Mgmt Proto
snmp-trap 162/udp # Traps for SNMP
xdmcp 177/tcp # X login proto
irc 194/tcp # Internet Relay Chat
```

▶ *You can find out about quite a few protocols by looking in /etc/services.*

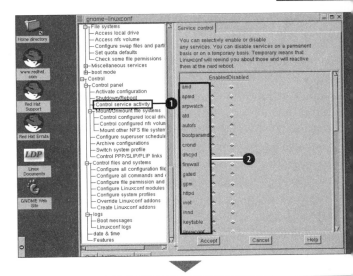

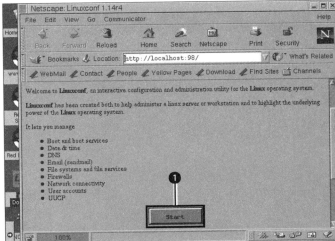

❶ *Select Control ⇨ Control panel ⇨ Control service activity from **linuxconf**.*

❷ *Choose which network services to start and stop.*

▶ *From the **linuxconf** Web interface, click Start to enter the protected configuration area.*

FIND IT ONLINE

Charles Spurgeon offers a great Ethernet tutorial at http://wwwhost.ots.utexas.edu/ethernet/ethernet-home.html.

279

Testing Your Network

Once you think you have your network setup, you should test it. Networking is fraught with errors, problems, and more problems, as most any system administrator will tell you. So, the first thing to do is check your system's connectivity with other systems.

Linux includes a number of commands that help you test out your network. Run the **ping** program to test network connectivity. **ping** sends out a set of messages to a remote system, and then waits for those messages to get echoed back. (When a system receives a ping message, it is supposed to send it back.) If no message comes back, you obviously have a network problem, either on your system, the remote system, or the network in-between. **ping** also times the packets, so you can see whether things are too slow as well.

The basic syntax for **ping** is:

```
$ ping hostname
```

Replace *hostname* with the name of the system you want to check. You can pass the IP address of the remote host instead of the hostname, if you want. If things go well, you'll start seeing line after line of output as shown in Listing 15-5. By default, **ping** runs forever. You need to press **Ctrl+C** to stop it. You can also **ping** a special hostname called localhost, which is shorthand for your local system, to see how fast **ping** can be without going over the network.

When working with **ping** or other commands that take a hostname, your system may have problems converting the hostname to the IP address that the networking commands really use. If you see errors that the hostname is unknown, then you likely have this problem.

You can pass an IP address to **ping** instead of a hostname. With this, you can still check the network connectivity to another system, so long as you know that system's IP address. Once you verify network connectivity, you can work on the hostnames.

Another program, called **traceroute**, works very well at tracking down routine problems, as well as helping to pinpoint the location of network breakdowns.

The syntax for **traceroute** is similar to ping:

```
$ /usr/sbin/traceroute hostname
```

You can also pass an IP address instead of a hostname. **traceroute** shows all the network hops to get from point A — your system — to point B — the target system.

The optional KDE desktop includes a handy program called **knu** (KDE network utilities) that combines **traceroute** and **ping** with a graphical user interface.

TAKE NOTE

LOOKING UP HOST NAMES

Almost all networking commands take in hostnames or IP addresses. Under the hood, all these commands require the IP address. This means that most commands attempt to look up a hostname and get back its IP address. The two primary ways to convert hostnames to IP addresses range from the simple entries in the /etc/hosts file to running the Domain Name Service, or DNS. When you connect to the Internet, you will likely access DNS for name lookups. But, on your local area network, the /etc/hosts method often works fine.

SHORTCUT
Use the **nslookup** command to help diagnose DNS problems.

Listing 15-5: PINGING A REMOTE SYSTEM

```
$ ping tamarack
PING tamarack.forster-johnson.com (192.168.42.1): 56 data bytes
64 bytes from 192.168.14.164: icmp_seq=0 ttl=64 time=0.4 ms
64 bytes from 192.168.14.164: icmp_seq=1 ttl=64 time=0.4 ms

-- overkill.globalmt.com ping statistics --
2 packets transmitted, 2 packets received, 0% packet loss
round-trip min/avg/max = 0.4/0.4/0.4 ms
```
▶ **ping** tells you how fast the remote system returns its packets. This example shows good network connectivity. Kill **ping** by pressing **Ctrl+C**.

Listing 15-6: A PING FAILURE

```
$ ping www.idgbooks.com
PING www.idgbooks.com (206.175.162.15):
 56 data bytes
```
▶ When **ping** cannot connect to a remote system, you often see the line with 56 data bytes as shown here. **ping** seems to wait forever for a response to its packets.

Listing 15-7: STOPPING PING

```
$ ping www.idgbooks.com
PING www.idgbooks.com (206.175.162.15):
 56 data bytes

-- www.idgbooks.com ping statistics --
17 packets transmitted, 0 packets
 received, 100% packet loss
```
▶ When **ping** cannot connect to a remote system and seems to hang, stop it by pressing **Ctrl+C**. **ping** will then print statistics.

Listing 15-8: TRACING A ROUTE

```
$ /usr/sbin/traceroute www.idgbooks.com
traceroute to www.idgbooks.com (206.175.162.15), 30 hops max,
 40 byte packets
 1 * * *
28 * * *
29 * * *
30 * * *
```
▶ Use **traceroute** to trace the route from one system to another.

FIND IT ONLINE

Find the KDE network monitor at **http://rpmfind.net/ linux/RPM/contrib/libc6/i386/X11_KDE_Applications_ Networking.html.**

Sharing Files with Samba

The Samba suite of applications enables your Linux system to act as a Microsoft Windows file and print server, potentially saving you lots of money in Microsoft license fees and the cost of Windows NT Server. You can also use Samba as a bridge between your UNIX, Linux, and Microsoft Windows systems.

When you install Red Hat Linux, you should choose to install Samba, which is also called smb. You can then tell Linux to run smb services on start up. If you do this, you are most of the way toward getting everything up and running.

The next step is to configure Samba for your environment. The main Samba configuration file is /etc/smb.conf. You need to edit this file as root. Without configuring this, you'll see a network share named MYGROUP that does not allow much access.

The **smb.conf** file has different sections for areas of service, including user home directories and printing, as well as other items that you can control.

One of the first things to change in this file is the workgroup, which defaults to:

```
workgroup = MYGROUP
```

You may want a more descriptive name, especially an NT domain name.

In the **/etc/smb.conf** file, you also set up whether your Linux system is to act as a Microsoft Windows printer, or whether you just want to serve up files.

You can name the NT system that acts as a primary domain controller, and you can lock out certain systems from accessing your server, along with quite a few other options.

All of this is discussed in the online manual page for smb.conf, which you should read carefully, particularly noting the security and performance issues. This online manual page is quite detailed; you should spend some time with it to avoid messing up your network.

To help map Linux user names and Microsoft Windows user names — which may differ — you can add entries to the file /etc/smbusers. This file contains entries for Linux user names and the matching Microsoft Windows names in this format:

```
ericfj = efoster-johnson
```

In this case, the Linux user name is ericfj and the Microsoft Windows name for the same user is efoster-johnson.

Don't be confused by the use of UNIX in the Samba documentation and configuration files. Linux and UNIX are the same from the perspective of Samba, as UNIX and Linux mostly work alike.

When everything is set up, Microsoft Windows users should be able to access files on the Linux system and print through Linux.

TAKE NOTE

FRIENDLY FRONTENDS
Run the **linuxconf** program to configure Samba.

SAMBA LOG FILES
The default configuration under Red Hat Linux places Samba log files in /var/log/samba.

ENCRYPTED PASSWORDS
Microsoft has done a lot to obscure the changes it makes to the SMB protocol to lock out Samba. Check the Samba home page for details. You may also need to enable encrypted passwords in the **linuxconf** window and make Registry changes on your NT systems. See the Samba online documentation for details.

Accessing Microsoft Windows disks from Linux

The **smbclient** program enables you to access files on Microsoft Windows 95 or Windows NT servers from Linux systems. To run this program, you need, at the very least, the name of a network share you want to access. You can find these names on a Microsoft Windows system by looking in the Network Neighborhood. The basic format is:

```
$ smbclient '\\server\share'
```

Replace *server* with the name of a Microsoft Windows server and *share* with the name of a directory or share on that server. To avoid shell issues with the backslash — a special character in Linux — we always put the name in quotes.

Once connected, **smbclient** will ask for your password and then present you with the following prompt:

```
smb: \>
```

From this prompt, you can enter commands such as **ls** or **dir** to see directory listings and **cd** to change directories. You can use **put** or **mput** (multiple put) to copy files from your Linux system to the Microsoft Windows server. The **get** and **mget** commands copy files from the Microsoft Windows system to your local Linux system.

The **smbmount** command enables you to mount SMB file systems in your Linux system so that the Microsoft Windows SMB disk appears like any other Linux disk. See the online manual information for more, as this soon gets very complex.

Listing 15-9: USING SMBCLIENT

```
$ smbclient '\\ntserver\Users'
Added interface ip=192.168.32.174
```

```
bcast=192.168.32.255 nmask=255.255.255.0
Server time is Tue May 25 12:48:15 1999
Timezone is UTC-5.0
Password:
Domain=[BIGFUN] OS=[Windows NT 4.0]
Server=[NT LAN Manager 4.0]
security=user
smb: \>
```

▶ *When you run **smbclient**, you'll be prompted for your password. Once logged on, you'll see the smb: \> prompt.*

Listing 15-10: GETTING HELP IN SMBCLIENT

```
smb: \ericfj\> help
ls dir lcd cd pwd

get mget put mput rename

more mask del rm mkdir

md rmdir rd pq prompt

recurse translate lowercase print printmode

queue qinfo cancel quit q

exit newer archive tar blocksize

tarmode setmode help ? !
```

▶ *The **help** or **?** commands list all the commands that you can enter.*

Listing 15-11: GETTING HELP ON SPECIFIC COMMANDS

```
smb: \ericfj\> help mget
HELP mget:
 <mask> get all the matching files
```
You can ask for help on a particular command.

CROSS-REFERENCE
Chapter 11 discusses working with Microsoft Windows and Chapter 14 covers the **ftp** command.

FIND IT ONLINE
The Samba home page is **http://www.samba.org**.

Sharing Files with NFS

With NFS, the Network File System, you can mount remote disks that appear, as if by magic, to be part of the directory hierarchy under the Linux root directory. You can also export your Linux disks to other systems, which they can transparently mount. For example, you may want to have all user home directories, normally placed under /home, to come from one centrally located disk. That way, all users can log on to all systems and still see the same home directory with all their files.

To mount a remote file system, use the **mount** command, much like you would for CD-ROMs. Instead of passing a device file, though, you pass the server and directory that you want to mount. The basic format is the server's hostname, a colon (:), and the name of the directory on the server. For example:

```
# mount tamarack:/realhome /home
```

This command mounts the /realhome directory from the host named tamarack under /home on the current system. This states that home directories really reside on a disk on machine tamarack, but that you will transparently see those files from the current system. Only root can run the **mount** command.

You can add special options to the **mount** command. One option is the type (–t nfs), which tells **mount** that this is an NFS mount. (The **mount** command usually figures this out from the colon in the name passed on the command line.) The online manual page for **mount** lists a plethora of other options to control access and usage of the mounted file system. A good example option is –o, which you can use to change the block size and speed up NFS. The following command adjusts the block sizes for reading and writing from 1K to 8K:

```
# mount –o wsize=8192,rsize=8192 \
```

Once you mount a file system, you can access the files through the normal commands discussed in Chapter 3, such as **ls**, **cp**, **rm**, and so on.

To unmount an NFS-mounted file system, use the **umount** command:

```
# umount /home
```

With most NFS mounts, you want to establish these mounts each time Linux boots up. To do that, edit the /etc/fstab file. The file /etc/fstab lists which file systems to mount and under what permissions. For example, your system can mount a disk as read-only if you don't want anyone changing files on the disk. The basic format, continuing with the same example, is:

```
tamarack:/realhome /home nfs
```

You can also add options, to mount the file system as read-only, set timeouts, and so on, as described in the online manual entry for **nfs**.

The **mount –a** command mounts all file systems described in the **/etc/fstab** file. Linux issues this command when it boots up, mounting all the file systems you set up.

The file **/etc/mtab** holds the list of all mounted file systems. You can look at this file to determine what Linux thinks is currently mounted (very helpful if you experience problems). For example:

```
tamarack: /realhome /home nfs rw 0 0
```

This shows that /realhome from machine tamarack is mounted with read-write (rw) access via the NFS protocol on the /home directory.

CROSS-REFERENCE
Chapter 2 covers more on mounting disks.

FIND IT ONLINE
See Hummingbird at http//www.hummingbird.com.

TAKE NOTE

SETTING UP FROM LINUXCONF

You can set up NFS from the **linuxconf** interface, which is a lot easier than entering data directly into the **/etc/fstab** file.

To mount remote disks, choose Access nfs volume from the File systems area in **linuxconf**. To export disks, look in Networking (not File systems) and then check under Server tasks.

EXPORTING YOUR LINUX DISKS

On the server side, you control which file systems can be exported by editing entries in the file /etc/exports. Remote systems can only mount the file systems named in this file as directories. From this file, you can set up options to control which machines can mount the file system, and restrict the access.

THE NFS SERVER

Your system serves up file systems via NFS through a program named **nfsd**, short for NFS daemon (or server). You must set this program to run when Linux boots up, or your system will not export file systems via NFS.

NFS AND UNIX

Just about every UNIX system supports NFS.

NFS FOR MICROSOFT WINDOWS

NFS is more common in the UNIX and Linux arena than in Microsoft Windows. But, you can purchase NFS software for Microsoft Windows from vendors such as Hummingbird.

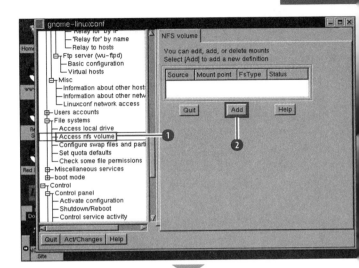

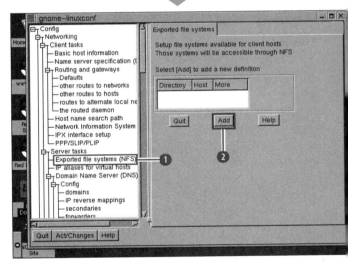

❶ Choose Access nfs volume from the File systems area in **linuxconf** to mount remote disks via NFS.

❷ Select Add to enter the mount information into the window.

❶ Select Exported file systems (NFS) from Server tasks under Networking in **linuxconf** to set up file systems to export.

❷ Select Add and enter the directory to export along with the other requested information in the window.

Personal Workbook

Q&A

1 All systems on the network must have what sort of address?

2 What format do these addresses have?

3 Name two ways for Linux systems to share files with Microsoft Windows systems over a network.

4 Can a Linux system act as a Microsoft Windows file and print server?

5 Can you set up and configure your networking during your Linux installation or do you have to wait until later?

6 If you didn't configure your network when you installed Linux are you stuck?

7 What is the name of the magical program that provides a graphical interface to configuring most of Linux networking?

8 To mount a remote disk via NFS, what command do you run?

ANSWERS: PAGE 342

EXTRA PRACTICE

1. Check the routing table for your Linux system with the **netstat –r** and **route** commands.

2. Enable **linuxconf** to run over a Web link on port 98 so that you can configure your system remotely via the Web.

3. Determine whether your organization or Internet service provider has a class A, B, or C network address. After you've looked, ask your administrators. Many newer assignments get a blended style of network address, due to the huge gaps between the sizes of the class A, B, and C addressing. As the Internet runs out of IP addresses, we'll see more of the special combinations until IPv6 is widely adopted and gives us some breathing room.

REAL-WORLD APPLICATIONS

✓ Your system administrator — through bitter experience — doesn't trust any graphical frontends on administration commands, and so won't touch **linuxconf**. Explain to your reluctant administrator that Linux does, indeed, support most of the same networking commands that most versions of UNIX run. Begin by discussing the **netstat**, **route**, and **ifconfig** commands.

✓ You are thinking of buying an Ethernet card, perhaps as part of a home networking kit that includes a cheap 10 or 100Base-T network hub. Check the Ethernet How-To document online under **/usr/doc/ HOWTO** or on the Web at **http://www.linux.com/ howto/Ethernet-HOWTO.html** to learn which network adapter cards work best with Linux.

Visual Quiz

Which file system shown here is served up by Samba?

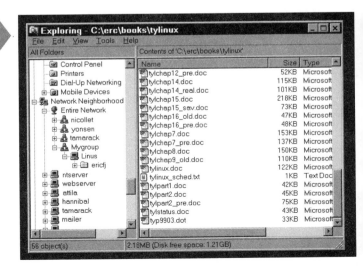

CHAPTER 16

MASTER
THESE
SKILLS

▶ **Setting Up Apache**
▶ **Starting Apache**
▶ **Creating a Top-Level Web Page**
▶ **Setting Up a Search Engine**

Setting Up Your Own Web Server

The world's most popular Web server is free and comes with Linux. Called Apache, this Web server shows up on Internet surveys as the number one Web server, with more installed Internet sites than commercial products from companies such as Microsoft.

A Web server is a program that runs on a server system that feeds up Web pages and other documents to browsers such as Netscape Navigator. At its most basic level, that's all a Web server does. A Web browser requests a particular file and the Web server sends it off.

Web browsers identify documents based on the URL, or Universal Resource Locator, that you type in. For example, **http://www.idgbooks.com/** identifies the main IDG Books Worldwide Web site. Your Web browser uses the URL to determine which system it should connect to and what document on the system to request. The Web server then responds by sending back the requested document or an error message. The data gets sent back via the Hypertext Transport Protocol, or HTTP, one of many network protocols supported by most Web browsers.

Of course, there's a lot more to that and to the World Wide Web and Apache. For starters, Apache enables you to run Common Gateway Interface, or CGI, scripts. A CGI script often handles search requests, online transactions, and other data-entry forms. Most CGI scripts, though, are quite slow. That's because each script starts a new process and usually reloads the Perl interpreter because Perl is the scripting language most used for CGI scripts. Apache helps this situation by providing something called mod_perl that dramatically speeds up CGI scripts.

The mod_perl module is part of a general set of modules that Apache supports. Apache was designed by the Apache Group to be extended by add-on modules. By programming to the Apache API, you can extend the Web server in new and interesting ways. Apache add-ons provide for secure transactions, performance statistics, and alternate forms of authentication.

This capability for writing add-ons is one reason why Apache is so popular.

The name Apache comes from the history of the project. Originally designed as a set of patches to the freeware National Center for Supercomputing Applications, or NCSA, httpd 1.3 Web server, in 1995, Apache got its name because it was "a patchy" server. It has no relationship to the native people from the Southwest U.S.A.

Setting Up Apache

The easiest thing about Apache is that it may already be set up for you. If you installed the Apache RPM file when you installed Linux, then it should be already configured to start up. To test this, set your Web browser, such as Netscape Navigator, to view the URL **http://localhost/**. If all works out, you should see a document similar to that shown on the facing page.

If you see this document, then you'll see a link to the online Apache documentation. That forms a good start to finding out more information on Apache. One thing to watch out, though, is that the Red Hat installation of Apache differs from the default locations described in the Apache manuals. Red Hat chose to spread out some of the Apache files into different directories.

You configure Apache by editing a number of configuration text files stored in a directory named /etc/httpd/conf. These files allow you to control who (or what machines) can access the Web server, as well as controlling what files and directories are available.

Unless you're an experienced Webmaster, most of the configuration options are pure gibberish. Luckily, you don't have to know a lot about Web servers to get Apache up and running. This is most appropriate, though, for an internal or intranet Web server. If you're going to place a Web server on the Internet — using Apache or any other server software — then you should get up to speed on Web server security. Otherwise, you may end up exposing key company data to the world.

Web servers present a directory structure to the world that is much like a file system. Through URLs, you can request files or directories from the Web server. This directory structure starts at some top-level directory, but, for security reasons, almost never your true root directory. When you present a URL such as **http://localhost/**, it returns the document root, that is, the top-level directory on machine localhost, an alias for your Linux system. This will either be a listing of the document root directory, or a file named index.html stored in the document root directory. The name index.html is a magical name that Apache uses when you request a directory. This may take some getting used to. URLs usually map to files, and Apache dutifully serves up those files. It's only when a URL maps to a directory that you need to worry about the magical index.html file. If a file named index.html resides in the directory, Apache presents that file. Otherwise, it presents a listing or an error if you have not set up permissions to list the directory. (This is configurable, of course.)

As part of the configuration, you specify which directory Apache should treat as its document root, which defaults to /home/httpd/html/.

Continued

TAKE NOTE

▶ HTTPD

The Apache program name is **httpd**, short for Hypertext Transport Protocol daemon (or server). You won't find a program named Apache or apache.

CROSS-REFERENCE

Chapter 14 covers Netscape Navigator. Chapter 13 covers cable modems.

Table 16-1: APACHE FILES AND DIRECTORIES

Location	Holds
/usr/sbin/httpd	The Apache Web server program
/etc/httpd/conf/	Apache configuration directory
/etc/httpd	Apache support directory, links to modules and logs
/var/log/httpd	Apache logs
/home/httpd/	Top-level directory for Apache, the server root
/home/httpd/html/	Top-level directory for HTML Web documents
/home/httpd/cgi-bin/	Default location to store CGI scripts
/usr/include/apache/	Include files for Apache module writers
/usr/lib/apache/	Shared libraries for Apache module writers
/usr/lib/linuxconf/	Linuxconf files to configure Apache

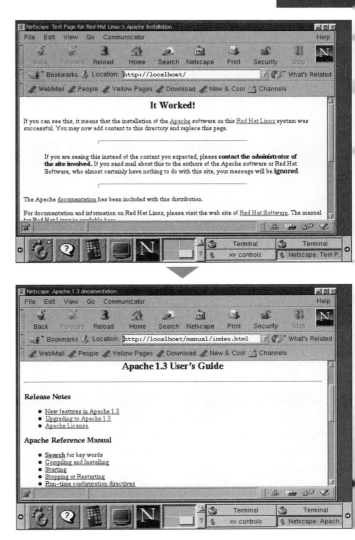

▶ To test whether Apache is running OK, set a Web browser to **http://localhost/**.

▶ From the top-level page, you can call up the Apache manual, as shown here, which is quite useful.

FIND IT ONLINE

See **https://www.seifried.org/lasg/** for the Linux Administration Security guide.

291

Setting Up Apache
Continued

To configure Apache, you need to edit the file httpd.conf stored by default in /etc/httpd/conf. For users of previous releases of Apache, note that with Apache 1.3.4, the three configurations files, access.conf, httpd.conf, and srm.conf, were merged into just the single file, httpd.conf.

The httpd.conf file holds the basic configuration values for Apache. This file contains a lot of comments, indicated by a # at the start of the line, and then a set of keys with values. The values that you define control the key settings. For example, the Port key defaults to the value 80:

```
Port 80
```

This means that Apache should listen in on TCP/IP port 80, which is the default for Web servers worldwide. Other common values are 81, 88, 8000, and 8080. In many cases, firewall software filters out some or all of these ports. Unless you have a good reason, keep Apache at port 80.

The ServerRoot key lists the location of the Apache configuration files, and defaults to /etc/httpd.

The MaxClients key controls the maximum number of client connections allowed at any one time. This value defaults to 150, which you may want to increase if users complain they are being locked out of the Web server.

Next, you need to control what files and directories are available to Web site users.

The tables on the facing page show some of the main values.

After determining what files are available, you need to control access to those files. For example, you'll see an entry similar to the following in httpd.conf:

```
<Directory /home/httpd/html>
```

This starts the access controls on the DocumentRoot directory previously mentioned. Each Directory entry controls who can access a given directory and what these users can do. The settings continue until the </Directory> line.

User home pages typically have a URL of /~username, such as **http://localhost/~ericfj** for user ericfj (using the localhost name for the Web server for now).

To set this up, ensure that the UserDir setting in the httpd.conf file holds the following value:

```
UserDir  public_html
```

This means that the directory for each user's Web pages will be named public_html.

Once you ensure that this is set up, the next step is to tell each user how to create his or her own home page. Based on the UserDir setting, each user needs to create a subdirectory in their home directory named public_html. Each user also has to deal with special permission issues to enable the Web server to access the files. Run the following commands from a user home directory:

CROSS-REFERENCE
"Creating a Top-Level Web Page," later in this chapter, has more discussion on Web documents.

FIND IT ONLINE
The Apache online manuals are at **http://localhost/manual/index.html** on your local system.

```
$ mkdir public_html
$ chmod 775 ~ public_html
```

This opens a user's home directory to the world.

Now, users can add HTML files to their public_html directory. The files directly in this directory correspond to the top level of the Web tree for that user. For example, a file named linux.htm under the public_html directory for user ericfj would result in a URL of **http://localhost/~ericfj/linux.htm.**

To create the true home page for the user, create a file named index.html inside the public_html directory.

You're not limited to one directory. You can create subdirectories under public_html to help organize Web pages. For example, you may want to keep files relating to the projects you're working on under a directory named projects. Create this directory under public_html and then reference the files in that directory, such as next_release.html with a URL similar to **http://localhost/~ericfj/projects/next_release.html.**

Table 16-2: CONFIGURATION VALUES IN HTTPD.CONF

Setting	Description
Port 80	The port Apache listens to for incoming connections
ServerRoot / etc/httpd	Directory where Apache configuration files are stored
PidFile /var/run/ httpd.pid	Filename to store the process ID of the master Apache process
StartServers 10	Number of servers to start up when Apache begins; impacts performance
MaxClients 150	Maximum number of connections allowed at any one time

Table 16-3: FILE-RELATED CONFIGURATION VALUES IN HTTPD.CONF

Setting	Description
DocumentRoot /home/ httpd/html	Top-level directory for Web documents.
UserDir public_html	Name of subdirectory in your home directory to use for Web documents.
AccessFileName .htaccess	If in a directory, controls who can access the files.
ScriptAlias /cgi-bin/ / home/httpd/cgi-bin/	Aliases CGI scripts in the URL /cgi-bin to really be stored in the directory /home/httpd/cgi-bin.
AddHandler cgi-script .cgi	Uncommenting this enables Apache to support CGI scripts. By default, this is commented out.
DirectoryIndex index.html index.shtml index.cgi	Sets which files are used if a client requests a directory URL instead of a filename. By default, index.html is served up, if that file exists in the directory.

Starting Apache

This may seem dumb, but before trying to start Apache, see whether it is already running. Use the **ps ax** command and search for **httpd** with the **grep** command, as shown in Listing 16-1. If you find **httpd**, chances are Apache is already started. Only if you change the configuration do you need to restart Apache. Furthermore, if Apache is running now, it should restart whenever you boot the system. That's another handy task that is performed by the Red Hat installation programs.

Even so, at some point you'll need to stop and restart Apache. Remember that the Apache program is **httpd**. When you run the **ps ax** command, you'll likely find many copies of **httpd**. What you want to do is kill the master copy of **httpd**, the one that can stop all the others for you.

To completely kill Apache, run the following command as root:

```
# /etc/rc.d/init.d/httpd stop
```

This is the preferred command. You can also try the following command, which is documented in the Apache manuals:

```
# kill -TERM `cat /var/run/httpd.pid`
```

This kills off Apache. The **kill** command sends the TERM signal, short for terminate, to the process ID stored in the file /var/run/httpd.pid. This holds the ID of the master **httpd** process. At any given time, you may have a number of **httpd** copies running. (This is one reason why Apache stores its master process ID.) This command tells the Apache master process to kill off all child processes and then to exit itself. Many times, though, you just want Apache to reread its configuration files. In that case, run the following command as root:

```
# /etc/rc.d/init.d/httpd restart
You can also run this command:# kill -HUP
`cat /var/run/httpd.pid`
```

This command sends the HUP (hang up) signal to the master Apache process. Apache then kills off all child **httpd** copies, rereads its configuration files, and restarts.

An even nicer command is to send the USR1 signal, again as root:

```
# kill -USR1 `cat /var/run/httpd.pid`
```

This command lets children of the master process continue until they naturally die, and then Apache restarts them using the changed configuration. As usual, Apache rereads the configuration files.

During any of these commands, you can monitor the process of the shutdown or restart operation by viewing the Apache log files. By default, these are stored in /var/log/httpd/error_log. You can view this with the following command:

```
# tail -f /var/log/httpd/error_log
```

The **tail** command prints out the final 10 lines of a file. The –f option tells **tail** to run forever, and it will print out all new lines as they are logged. That way, you can see, in real-time, what Apache is doing.

To start Apache, use a command similar to the following:

```
# /etc/rc.d/init.d/httpd start
You can also run the manual command that
follows:# /usr/sbin/httpd -f \
    /etc/httpd/conf/httpd.conf
```

You need to tell the **httpd** command where to find the **httpd.conf** file, with the –f option. When Linux boots up, **httpd** should start automatically.

CROSS-REFERENCE

Chapter 3 covers the **grep** command and Chapter 16 details networking.

TAKE NOTE

▶ INETD VERSUS A POOL OF PROCESSES

The standard networking daemon — or server process — on Linux and UNIX is called inetd, the Internet daemon. This server listens for outside connections for a number of services and then launches the proper program in response. For example, with an incoming request to log in remotely via telnet, inetd launches the telnet daemon, **in.telnetd**. You can have **inetd** launch a copy of **httpd** every time a Web request comes in. This approach is relatively easy to set up, but it does not scale well. This is one area where you may want to tune Apache.

To control this, set the ServerType key in the **httpd.conf** file to inetd or standalone. In standalone mode, Apache runs automatically. See the online Apache manuals for more on tuning Apache.

▶ APACHE MUST WRITE TO ITS DIRECTORY

On startup, the **httpd** program writes out its process ID to a file named **httpd.pid**. You can use this process ID to kill the Web server. The problem is that if you mount the Web directories as read-only (oftentimes used to ensure Web pages won't be changed without permission), then **httpd** may fail. It needs to write to the disk to store the **httpd.pid** file. We got bit by this one when we mounted /usr/local, which is often used to store Apache, as read-only and all of a sudden the Web server didn't work. You should not face this problem if you leave the default location for this file, /var/run/httpd.pid, alone. Whichever file system holds /var should be mounted read-write.

Listing 16-1: CHECKING WHETHER APACHE IS RUNNING

```
$ ps ax| grep httpd
  286  ?  S     0:00 httpd
  292  ?  S     0:00 httpd
  293  ?  S     0:00 httpd
  294  ?  S     0:00 httpd
  295  ?  S     0:00 httpd
  296  ?  S     0:00 httpd
  297  ?  S     0:00 httpd
  298  ?  S     0:00 httpd
  299  ?  S     0:00 httpd
  300  ?  S     0:00 httpd
  301  ?  S     0:00 httpd
 2824  ?  S     0:00 grep httpd
```
▶ *This command tells you how many copies of httpd, if any, are running. If you see even one, not counting the **grep** command, chances are Apache is up and running OK.*

Listing 16-2: KILLING APACHE

```
# # /etc/rc.d/init.d/httpd stop

Shutting down httpd:      [  OK  ]
# ps ax| grep httpd
28543  ?  S     0:00 grep httpd
```
▶ *After killing Apache, you should not see any **httpd** processes in the process output from the **ps** command.*

FIND IT ONLINE

Tips for tuning Apache are located at **http://localhost/ manual/misc/perf-tuning.html** on your local system.

295

Creating a Top-Level Web Page

When you connect to your local Web server, that is, to the URL **http://localhost/**, Apache creates a default page for you. Seeing this page is proof that things are working OK, but you'll likely want to change that page to something else. For example, if you're creating an internal Web site for documents from your department, this top-level page should identify the Web server as being for your department and also contain links to the major topics you plan to provide. Top-level Web pages, whether for an organization or for yourself, should introduce the topic that you want to cover. Most top-level pages are made up of links to Web pages deeper within the site.

You want your top-level Web page to draw users to your site and to direct them to relevant information. This raises the big issue of what exactly you want your Web page to do. It's easy to get lost in all the cool Web tricks that you can use and end up with a page that provides no value to users, who will then avoid your page like the plague.

Web pages are formatted in HTML, or Hypertext Markup Language. Whenever you see a filename ending in either .html or .htm, chances are it's an HTML file. HTML provides for a set of formatting tags — all in text. Edit HTML files with any text editor, or with Netscape Composer, an HTML editor that comes with Netscape. HTML uses these tags to indicate elements in the document. The basic syntax is *<tag>* to indicate the start of a tagged area and *</tag>* the end. For example, to mark text bold, use <b> to start and </b> to end:

```
This is normal <b>this is bold</b>.
```

which displays as:
This is normal **this is bold**.

Place an HTML document between the <html> and </html> tags. After <html>, start a header section with <head>. About the only thing you place in this section is <title>, which provides text shown in the window manager title bar. After the header, enclose the main text in the document with a <body> tag.

To make a link, use the following as a guide:

```
<A HREF="url">text</A>
```

Replace url with the actual URL you want to link to. Replace text with the actual words you want displayed. (Avoid click here.) For example:

```
<A HREF="http://www.idgbooks.com">
IDG Books</A>
```

This creates a link to the IDG Books Worldwide, Inc. Web site and displays the text IDG Books in the document. Most Web browsers underline this text to indicate that it's a link.

Continued

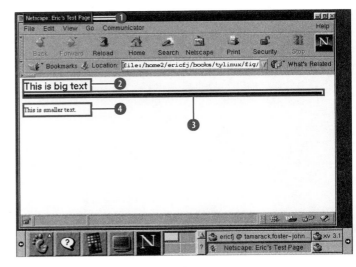

❶ The <title> tag sets the title.
❷ The large text, made larger by the <font> tag.
❸ A horizontal rule.
❹ Normal text.

SHORTCUT
You can edit HTML files with Netscape Composer in place of a text editor.

296

Table 16-4: COMMON HTML ELEMENTS

Tag	Example	Usage
<html>	<html></html>	Encloses an entire HTML document.
<head>	<head></head>	Encloses the document header and usually a <title>.
<title>	<title>My Home</title>	Lists text to place in Web browser title bar.
<body>	<body bgcolor=#FFFFFF text=#000>	Encloses main part of document.
<h1>	<h1>Important</h1>	Top-level (level 1) heading.
<h2>	<h2>Less Important</h2>	Level 2 subheading. You can go to H6 for a level 6 subheading.
<b>	<b>This is bold</b>	Marks text as bold.
<i>	<i>This is italics</i>	Marks text as italic.
<code>	<code>This is fixed width</code>	Marks text in a fixed-width font.
<p>	<p>Hello.</p>	Indicates a paragraph.
 	 	Break (uses less vertical space than a <p>).
<hr>	<hr size=5 align=center noshade>	Creates a horizontal rule (line).
<a>	<A href="http://foo.com">text</a>	Creates an anchor, a hypertext link in this case.
<font>	<font face=helvetica,arial size=6>	Changes the font. Note the normal (Helvetica) and Windows (Arial) font names.

Listing 16-3: A SAMPLE HTML FILE

```
<html>
<head>
<title>Eric's Test Page</title></head>

<BODY BGCOLOR=#FFFFFF TEXT=#000>
<font face=helvetica,arial size=6>
This is big text
</font>
<br>
<hr SIZE=5 ALIGN=CENTER NOSHADE>
<p>This is smaller text.</p>
</body>
</html>
```

▶ *The following creates a simple HTML file that you can serve up from Apache.*

TAKE NOTE

▶ **XML**

XML, or eXtensible Markup Language, forms the follow-on to HTML. XML is a lot like HTML and uses very similar tags. But, where HTML provides tags directly related to document formatting, XML offers greater flexibility to define your own tags. When converting HTML to XML, you need to ensure that you use the proper ending tags for things such as paragraphs, where HTML does not require the ending tag.

FIND IT ONLINE

See **htp://www.w3.org/TR/REC-html40/** for a full listing of HTML tags.

Creating a Top-Level Web Page
Continued

Following the document root

The top-level Web page used by Apache is /home/httpd/html/index.html. This is the file that you need to edit to create your own top-level page. From that page, you can link to other local pages using the <A> tag. You can create a full URL such as **http://www.idgbooks.com**, or a local URL naming a file in the local Web directory or in a subdirectory. For example, linux/install.html or support.html are both local — or relative — URLs that refer to a position in the file system relative to the current document.

This can take some getting used to. The default document root, or virtual root directory, is /home/httpd/html. Any file in this directory has a root-based URL, such as **http://localhost/support.html.** This URL — based on the default configuration described here — links to a file named support.html inside the /home/httpd/html directory. How do we know it resides in the /home/httpd/html directory? Because that directory is the document root in the Apache configuration files.

Recall that user home pages are located in a subdirectory named public_html in their home directories. For example, the home page for user ericfj is /home/ericfj/public_html/index.html. You can create subdirectories of /home/http/html for purposes other than user home pages. For instance, you may want to have separate directories for each part of your organization, such as software developers, quality assurance engineers, and product supporters.

Table 16-5 provides examples in mapping URLs to the default Apache document root. If you change this configuration, you'll need to update the table. The whole reason for this odd mapping is to enable your Web page to present a virtual root that you anchor anywhere you want in the Linux file system (but that defaults to /home/http/html). You are in control of what users can and cannot see from Web browsers. This is mostly a security issue, but it is also related to the organization you want for your Web pages.

Another key issue with organization lies in the use of *relative links*. Once a Web browser has called up your top-level Web page, say http://localhost/, then other Web documents in the same directory can be accessed by links to just the file name. For example:

```
<A HREF="linux.html">
Information on Linux</A>
```

This link refers to the file /home/httpd/html/linux.html. How do we know that? Because the link is relative to the calling Web page, /home/httpd/html/index.html in this case (our top-level Web page).

Relative links can also go down into subdirectories. This enables you to start at one top-level location and create a whole hierarchy of Web pages, all of which refer to each other through relative links. This saves you a lot of typing, and makes it much easier to move the Web pages to a different location. You may just want to move the whole directory tree down one directory, or move the whole thing to a different Web server. In all these cases, relative links help.

CROSS-REFERENCE
Appendix B lists books on HTML and XML.

FIND IT ONLINE
The main Apache page is located at
http://www.apache.org.

Table 16-5: MAPPING URLS TO FILES

URL	File	Notes
http://localhost/	/home/httpd/html/index.html	Directory
http://localhost/index.html	/home/httpd/html/index.html	Names the index.html file directly instead of relying on the mapping between a directory name and the magic filename index.html
http://localhost/support.html	/home/httpd/html/support.html	Regular document in a directory
http://localhost/linux/hardware.html	/home/httpd/html/ linux/ hardware.html	Regular document in a directory
http://localhost/linux/	/home/httpd/html/ linux/index.html	Special document for a directory, in this case a subdirectory
http://localhost/~ericfj/	/home/ericfj/public_html/index.html	Home page for user ericfj
http://localhost/~ericfj/linux.html	/home/ ericfj/public_html/linux.html	Web document (HTML file) in the directory for user ericfj's home Web pages
/~ericfj/	/home/ericfj/public_html/index.html	Home page for user ericfj

TAKE NOTE

COPYING IS SINCERE FLATTERY

One of the best ways to get going with HTML is to find a Web page that you like and copy its format. For internal Web pages, you'll never get in trouble doing this, but avoid copying copyrighted material for a Web page to be placed on the Internet. In many cases, it's better to simply study the HTML techniques used by others. For example, if you want a multicolumn Web page, find a site that presents a good-looking multicolumn Web page and see how that site uses the HTML <TABLE> tag to set up the columns. Note that some sites cheat and use images for most everything, which is not very efficient, especially for users who view your site from dial-up lines.

WEB SERVER NAMES MAY DIFFER BASED ON ACCESS

If you dial in to a network, you may have to use the full domain name of a system, such as **http://tamarack.foster-johnson.com** instead of a local network name such as http://tamarack. Thus, all the Web pages with links containing the local host name — http://tamarack in this case — in the link might be invalid depending on how users access your network. We found this really hits Windows users hard. Why should you worry? Because users running on Windows machines can point their Web browsers at your copy of the Apache Web server running on Linux.

Setting Up a Search Engine

htdig, or ht:/Dig as it is officially known, provides a search engine for your Web server. **htdig** isn't set up to compete against Lycos, AltaVista, or other massive Web search engines. Instead, **htdig** provides the means for users to search your site.

To use **htdig**, you first need to download it from the Web, as **htdig** does not come with Red Hat Linux. At first we thought we were lucky that the **htdig** home page sports a nice binary RPM file that we could install. It didn't work on Red Hat Linux, so you'll need to build **htdig** from its sources. This isn't that hard, so long as you installed the C and C++ compilers when you installed Linux.

Building htdig

To build **htdig**, first download the source (abbreviated as src) RPM file (htdig-3.1.2-0glibc.src.rpm) and run the following command as root:

```
# rpm —rebuild htdig-3.1.2-0glibc.src.rpm
```

This command should build the program from its sources and then build a binary RPM file from the sources. This binary file will be stored in /usr/src/redhat/RPMS/i386/. In this case, the file will be named htdig-3.1.2-0glibc.i386.rpm. You can then install this binary RPM with the following commands, again run as root:

```
# cd /usr/src/redhat/RPMS/i386/
# rpm —ihv htdig-3.1.2-0glibc.i386.rpm
```

Configuring htdig

By default, the htdig configuration file is installed in /etc/htdig/htdig.conf. Edit this file as root and look for start_url. Change this to your top-level Web page, such as http://localhost/:

```
start_url: http://localhost/
```

Now, you need to build the search database of all the documents linked by start_url. This requires a two-step process. First, run the **htdig** program:

```
# /usr/sbin/htdig
```

Then run **htmerge** when **htdig** finishes:

```
# /usr/sbin/htmerge
```

When that's done, you have an index database of your site. The next step is to set up Web-based searching. This enables users to enter a phrase to search for in a Web form. From **Netscape**, call up the following URL: **http://localhost/search.html**. Enter your query as shown on the facing page. You should be in business.

Find documentation on **htdig** in the **htdoc** subdirectory with the **htdig** source code.

CROSS-REFERENCE

Chapter 2 covers the **rpm** command.

TAKE NOTE

WATCH YOUR DISK SPACE

To speed searches, **htdig** stores index files on your system, which can grow quite large. According to the **htdig** home page, you should multiply the number of documents by 12,000 to get approximately the amount of bytes that will be used by the word list indices. By default, the database appears in /var/lib/htdig/db. You can change that in the configuration file.

CUSTOMIZING THE FORMS

You can then customize the standard search form used by **htdig**, named /home/httpd/html/search. html. When **htdig** searches, it builds a Web page of the results from a number of pieces. First, **htdig** places the contents of the file /var/lib/htdiog/ common/header.html into the output Web page. This enables you to place a navigation bar or logo at the top of every Web page. At the end of the output, **htdig** appends the contents of the footer.html file in the same directory, again, so that you can provide a consistent look for your Web pages.

HTDIG INDEXES FROM LINKS

Htdig starts with the start_url you configure and then indexes all Web documents linked from there that are still part of your site (you can change that, too, in the configuration file). If you don't link to a Web page, such as your user home page, then **htdig** won't find it.

OTHER SEARCH ENGINES

Glimpse and its Web frontend called Webglimpse, forms another search engine that uses different technology. You can download Glimpse from **http://webglimpse.net**.

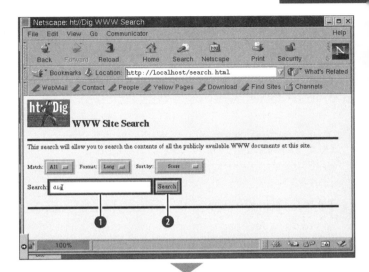

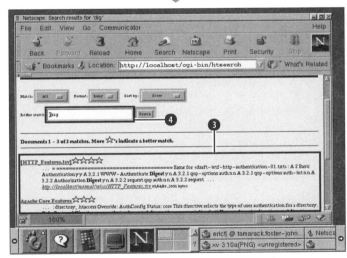

① Enter your search criteria in the **htdig** form.

② Click Search to start the search.

③ The search results appear in a list, along with the HTML header and footer you created.

④ You can refine the search if you didn't get the results you wanted.

FIND IT ONLINE

The ht:/Dig home page is **http://www.htdig.org**.

301

Personal Workbook

Q&A

1 Does Linux come with a Web server?

_____

_____

_____

2 If you installed the Apache packages, what do you need to do to get Apache up and running the first time?

_____

_____

_____

3 What URL should you type in Netscape to determine whether Apache is running?

_____

_____

_____

4 What does the <b> tag do in HTML?

_____

_____

_____

5 Which programs can you use to view Web pages?

_____

_____

_____

6 Which programs can you use to edit HTML files?

_____

_____

_____

7 What is the *document root?*

_____

_____

_____

8 Which programs can you use to set up a Web search engine?

_____

_____

_____

ANSWERS: PAGE 343

302

EXTRA PRACTICE

1. Start the Netscape Web browser and point it to **http://localhost** to see if Apache is running on your system.

2. Check out the online manual page for **httpd**. Now check out the online Apache manuals in HTML format from a Web browser.

3. Calculate how much disk space **htdig** will use for storing its index of your Web documents. Now, run **htdig** and **htmerge**, and then verify the amount of disk space actually used.

4. Do a Web search for other Web indexing or searching tools.

5. Set up your own personal home page on your Linux Web site.

REAL-WORLD APPLICATIONS

✔ Explain to another user exactly how the URLs for your local Web site map to the actual files on disk. Then, go further and explain the use of the magical index.html files for URLs that map to directories.

✔ Discuss whether you want Apache to run in standalone or **inetd** mode. As part of this, read the online manual page for **inetd**.

✔ You have a top-level Web page that doesn't link to all the pages underneath. Rather than changing the layout of your Web pages, look in the comments in the htdig.conf configuration file to see if **htdig** can index all these pages, even though the top-level page doesn't link to all branches in the tree. Also check the online **htdig** documentation.

Visual Quiz

What sort of Web page is shown here? Hint: Look at the URL.

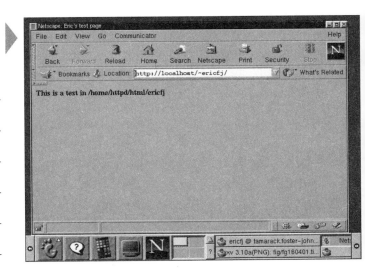

CHAPTER 17

MASTER THESE SKILLS

▶ Understanding How the Kernel Works

▶ Creating a Custom Kernel

▶ Build Details

▶ The LILO Configuration File

▶ The Care and Feeding of Modules

▶ Configuring a Kernel

Advanced System Configuration

Linux is a very powerful and flexible system. It can be used for a variety of different things. For example, it can serve as a small office server, a firewall, or a Web server.

To get the most out of your system, you need to configure it to fit your needs. In this chapter, we go through the steps for configuring your kernel and some of the advanced features that you can play with.

One of the nice things about Linux is that text files control almost the entire configuration process. Propriety operating systems such as Microsoft Windows tend to hide configurations in a binary, propriety database (that is, the registry). With Linux, everything is open.

Linux is designed to run on a variety of different systems. You can run it on a 386 with 8MB of memory, or you can run it on a quad Pentium III with 2GB of memory. You can run it as a stand-alone personal machine, or as a huge, company-wide database system.

Linux can be configured to do a number of amazing things. For example, you can configure your network card to respond to a variety of different network addresses. (This is called *IP aliasing*). This lets one machine look like many, which is useful when you are trying to serve Web pages as www.eatatjoes.com, www.buyahouse.com, and www.bookrestore.com.

Another area in which configuration comes to play is when Linux is used as a firewall. A *firewall* is a machine that protects a company's internal network from the outside world. It has two network interfaces, one for inside the company and one for the outside world. Its job is to pass messages between the two interfaces, making sure that nothing bad gets in from the outside. Because what's "bad" is determined by the system administrator, the configuration for the message-passing rules can be quite extensive. But it all starts when you configure the kernel.

The tools for configuring your kernel are quite simple to use. All you have to do is select the options and modules that you want. There's where the problem comes in. You see there are a lot of options. So many that they are organized into 30 different categories.

Fortunately there's an extensive help system that comes with the kernel configuration program. If you have an idea of what you want, this will help you get it.

Understanding How the Kernel Works

To properly configure and tune your kernel you need to know how it works. The operating system consists of three major parts. There's the main kernel with its core operating system and device drivers. Then there are the modules, which can be added at run-time to the kernel. Modules include items such as sound drivers and other device drivers that are not needed to load the initial kernel. Finally, there are daemons, which are called Services on Microsoft Windows NT. These are programs such as **routed** and **mountd** that run in the background and perform operating system functions such as handling TCP routing and NFS requests.

In the following tasks, we look in detail at the various ways of loading and configuring different parts of the kernel.

How Linux starts

The first part of Linux to be loaded and run is the kernel. The kernel performs a variety of initialization tasks and then starts the program **init**. This program examines the file /etc/inittab to see what needs to be done. This tells **init** to begin by executing the script /etc/rc.d/rc.sysinit. This script executes the commands needed to get a minimal system running.

Next **init** executes the script /etc/rc.d/rc, which, in turn, executes all the scripts in the /etc/rc.d/rc*run-level*.d directory. (Linux uses the run-level number to control what services and functions are available. Run-level 3 is normal; run-level 1 is single-user mode; and so on.)

The scripts in the /etc/rc.d/rc*run-level*.d directory starts daemons and load modules. They perform configuration and other initialization tasks.

Finally, after all the scripts have been processed, Linux is fully operational.

PNP devices

Plug and Play (PNP) devices are designed to be configured by the operating system. They advertise a list of possible configurations and the OS tells them which to use.

The Linux kernel does understand Plug and Play devices and configures them, but this support is extremely limited. Most Plug and Play devices are handled by a utility named **isapnp**, which enables you to also configure the devices. After the device is configured by **isapnp** you can load a device driver module for it and use your Plug and Play hardware. This tool is run by scripts that are placed in the /etc/rc.d directory. For complete details, see the task on PNP devices later in this chapter.

PCMCIA cards

Laptops contain slots for devices called PCMCIA cards. These cards can be inserted and removed while the system is running. The PCMCIA slots are monitored by the **cardmgr** program (automatically started at boot time out of /etc/rc.d). When it detects that a card has been inserted it loads the device driver for the card and initializes it using a script in the directory /etc/pcmcia.

CROSS-REFERENCE

Chapter 7 shows you how to use run-level 5 to start an X Window graphical login screen.

Load order

Boot loader (LILO, LOADLINE, etc.)
└──► **init**
        └──► **rc.sysinit**
                *Runs **isapnp** to configure PnP
                devices (if any).*
        └──► **/etc/rc.d/rc**runlevel**.d**
                *These scripts initialize things,
                load modules as necessary,
                and start daemons.*
                └──► **cardmgr**
                        *Watches the PCMCIAslots and loads
                        the driver modules for any devices
                        present at boot time or inserted later.*

                        *Run scripts in **/etc/pcmcia** as
                        needed to initialize the device.*

This diagram shows the major components used by
Linux when it starts up.

Table 17-1: KEY KERNEL FILES AND DIRECTORIES

File	Purpose
/etc/rc.d/init.d	Initialization scripts
/etc/pcmcia	PCMCIA configuration file and startup scripts
/etc/sysconfig/network	Network configuration files and startup scripts
/lib/modules/*kernel-version*	Location of loadable kernel modules

TAKE NOTE

▶ **REQUIRED PACKAGES**

This is a list of packages that must be installed for
kernel compilation:
- ▶ kernel-headers-version.i386.rpm
- ▶ kernel-source-version.i386.rpm
- ▶ egcs-version.rpm
- ▶ make-version.i386.rpm
- ▶ bin86-version.i386.rpm
- ▶ glibc-devel-version.i386.rpm

These packages supply tools and other files that
are needed by the kernel configuration and compilation process. (-version refers to a version number
that changes with each new release of the software.)

SHORTCUT

For PCMCIA, think People Can't Memorize Computer
Industry Acronyms.

Creating a Custom Kernel

The previous Take Note lists the packages that must be installed before you can build a kernel. The kernel sources are placed in the directory /usr/src/linux.

Configuration

To configure the kernel, login as root and start an X session. Go to the /usr/src/linux directory and execute the command:

```
# make xconfig
```

This starts a GUI that enables you to configure the kernel. (The settings for specific options are discussed in subsequent tasks.) When you are finished configuring the kernel, click Save and Exit to exit the configuration utility.

The next step is to make the kernel. There are two sets of commands needed to make the kernel, depending on how you plan on booting your new kernel. These commands are in Listings 17-1 and 17-2.

These are the two methods for booting your kernel:

▶ Put the system on a floppy.
▶ Use LILO to boot the kernel.

In the tasks below, we discuss how to use both these methods.

Putting the system on a floppy

Booting with an experimental kernel is easy when you boot off a floppy. To boot experimental kernels, put the floppy in and you boot the kernel. Remove the disk and you don't boot the kernel. Very simple.

To create a bootable floppy, put a disk in drive A and execute the script in Listing 17-1.

Using LILO to boot the kernel

The LILO loader is much more flexible than a floppy. Not only can you load the kernel, but you can also specify boot parameters. (For example, if you want to boot in single-user mode, enter **linux S** at the LILO prompt.)

LILO is smart enough to boot Microsoft Windows and other operating systems. In general, it's a much easier way to go if you don't mind modifying your boot sector.

The script in Listing 17-2 builds and installs an experimental kernel named /boot/vmlinuz.exp. The LILO configuration in Listing 17-3 gives this kernel the name exp. So to boot your normal Linux, enter **linux** at the LILO prompt; to boot the new kernel, enter **exp**. (Also for Microsoft Windows use "dos".)

Advanced System Configuration

being changed. In the entire history of Linux, there have been only three such numbers: 0, 1, and 2.)

The kernel version number is important because it's used for many things, such as the selection of the directory used for module storage and other version-dependent information.

Listing 17-1: LINUX-LILO.SH — BUILD SCRIPT FOR LINUX WITH LILO

```
#!/bin/sh -x
make dep
make clean

make

make bzImage

make modules
make modules_install


/bin/cp arch/i386/boot/bzImage
/boot/vmlinuz.exp
/sbin/lilo
```

Listing 17-2: LINUX-FLOPPY.SH — SCRIPT TO BUILD LINUX AND WRITE IT TO A FLOPPY

```
#!/bin/sh -x
make dep
make clean

make

make modules
make modules_install

make zImage
make zdisk
```

Listing 17-3: /ETC/LILO.CONF — LILO CONFIGURATION FILE

```
# Note: Comments begin with #
#(LILO ignores them)
boot=/dev/fd0
map=/boot/map
install=/boot/boot.b
prompt
timeout=50


#————————————————
# Definition of the first operating system.
# This is a linux system named "linux"
# with a root disk on partition /dev/hdc1
#
# Note the root needs to
# be set to your linux root
# partition.
#
image=/boot/vmlinuz-2.0.32
        label=linux
        root=/dev/hdc1
        read-only


#————————————————
# Definition of the second operating system
# This is a linux system named "exp"
# (The experimental linux system)
# Root, again is /dev/hdc1
image=/boot/vmlinuz.exp
        label=exp
        root=/dev/hdc1
        read-only
#————————————————
# Definition of the third operating system
# This is a system of type "other" (i.e.
# Microsoft Windows) and is named
# "dos".
other=/dev/hda1
        label=dos
        table=/dev/had
```

Build Details

This task goes through the build scripts in detail explaining each command that's used to build the kernel.

To build a new kernel, first we clear away binaries created by the old one:

```
# make clean
```

Because the **make** program does not handle items such as options or configuration changes, clearing away binaries ensures that we compile everything, just to be on the safe side.

Next, we update the dependencies. (This is a list indicating which bottom-level files each top-level file uses.)

```
# make dep
```

Now we actually compile the kernel:

```
# make bzImage
```

The next two commands create any loadable modules and installs them in /lib/modules/*os_version* (where *os_version* is the version number of the kernel):

```
# make modules
# make modules_install
```

Floppy only commands

Now the scripts diverge. If we are making a floppy, we need a kernel that we can stick on a disk, so we need to create a compressed image:

```
# make zImage
```

Next we put the compressed image on floppy. Put a floppy in drive A and execute the command:

```
# make zdisk
```

The system is now ready for booting. To start the system, just insert the floppy and reboot.

Creating a LILO-loadable kernel

The **make** command (listed above) builds the basic kernel. Unfortunately, the basic kernel is a little too big for LILO to handle. We need to make a compressed kernel for LILO. This is accomplished with the command:

```
# make bzImage
```

The result is put in the file /usr/src/linux/arch/i386/boot/bzImage. The kernels that LILO boots are placed in the directory /boot, so we put the kernel in that directory with a copy command (**cp**):

```
# cp arch/i386/boot/bzImage \
/boot/vmlinuz.exp
```

If you haven't done so already, edit the /etc/lilo.conf configuration file to include the entry for the exp system. Then tell LILO about the new kernel using the command:

```
# lilo
```

Note: You must run **lilo** each time you change the kernel. That's because it needs to know the sector numbers of every block in the file, so each time you change anything, rerun **lilo**.

Making the experimental kernel the default

After you test your new kernel to ensure that it works, you may want to make it the default. To do that, just copy your experimental kernel to the default name:

```
# cp /boot/vmlinuz.exp /boot/vmlinuz
```

Because you've made a change to the kernel, you need to run LILO again:

```
# lilo
```

FIND IT ONLINE

Information on building a kernel and kernel configuration can be found in /usr/src/linux/ Documentation.

Listing 17-4: SAMPLE BUILD OF A LILO-LOADABLE KERNEL

```
+ make dep
make[1]: Entering directory `/usr/src/linux-2.2.3/arch/i386/boot'
make[1]: Nothing to be done for `dep'.
make[1]: Leaving directory `/usr/src/linux-2.2.3/arch/i386/boot'
scripts/mkdep init/*.c > .depend


.......

gcc -Wall -Wstrict-prototypes -O2 -fomit-frame-pointer -o tools/build tools/build.c -
I/usr/src/linux-2.2.3/include
objcopy -O binary -R .note -R .comment -S compressed/vmlinux compressed/vmlinux.out
tools/build bootsect setup compressed/vmlinux.out CURRENT > bzImage
Root device is (3, 5)
Boot sector 512 bytes.
Setup is 3524 bytes.
System is 497 kB
make[1]: Leaving directory `/usr/src/linux-2.2.3/arch/i386/boot'
+ cp arch/i386/boot/bzImage /boot/vmlinuz.exp
+ lilo
Added linux *
Added exp
Added dos
Added diag
#
```

Listing 17-5: SAMPLE BUILD OF A FLOPPY-BASED KERNEL

```
+ make dep
make[1]: Entering directory `/usr/src/linux-2.2.3/arch/i386/boot'
make[1]: Nothing to be done for `dep'.


.....

Root device is (3, 5)
Boot sector 512 bytes.
Setup is 3524 bytes.
System is 497 kB
dd bs=8192 if=bzImage of=/dev/fd0
62+1 records in
62+1 records out
make[1]: Leaving directory `/usr/src/linux-2.2.3/arch/i386/boot'
+ /usr/sbin/rdev -R /dev/fd0 1
+ /usr/sbin/rdev -s /dev/fd0 /dev/hdc1
#
```

The LILO Configuration File

The LILO loader uses the file /etc/lilo.conf to tell it which operating systems are out there. Listing 17-3 is a typical LILO configuration file.

The first few lines are

```
boot=/dev/hda
map=/boot/map
install=/boot/boot.b
prompt
```

Leave these alone unless you know what you are doing. (If you want to know the details, see /usr/doc/lilo-21.)

The next line:

```
timeout=50
```

tells LILO how many seconds to wait before booting the default operating system. You'll see a LILO: prompt for that long. In that time, you can start typing the name of another operating system to boot, or press Tab to see the full list of available systems. With the timeout, you need type nothing; after the given timeout, **lilo** boots the default operating system.

The next section contains entries for each bootable operating system. The Linux entry looks similar to this:

```
image=/boot/vmlinuz-2.2.3-5
       label=linux
       root=/dev/hda5
       read-only
```

This tells LILO that the operating system is an "image" file named /boot/vmlinuz-2.2.3-5, that the LILO name for this system is linux, that the root partition is /dev/hda5, and that it is to be initially mounted read-only.

For Microsoft Windows, the LILO entry is

```
other=/dev/hda1
       label=dos
       table=/dev/hda
```

This entry tells LILO that we have a non-Linux operating system (type = other), that the name of this entry is dos, and that the operating system is located on the active partition of the first hard drive (/dev/hda).

LILO supports more than just Linux and Microsoft Windows, though. The other type can work for additional operating systems, such as Be OS:

```
other=/dev/hda1
       label=beos
       table=/dev/hda
```

In this case, Be OS is loaded on /dev/hda1, the first partition of the first IDE hard drive.

FIND IT ONLINE
The scripts presented here can be found at
http://www.oualline.com/linux.

Global options

These options affect the entire LILO configuration and should appear at the beginning of the file.

boot=*device* This is where the boot record is to be written. Typical devices are the first floppy (/dev/fd0) and the first hard drive (/dev/hda). If you have another multisystem loader (such as the one that comes with Windows NT) you can put this on the Linux partition and point your fancy loader at it.
delay=*time* This is the amount of time to delay before booting the default image. You can set this to 0. In this case, the default image boots immediately unless you hold down Shift while booting.
default=*name* Specify the name of the default boot image.
linear Generate more efficient linear disk addresses.
lock If this option is present, and you specify an operating system, that system will become "locked in." In other words, the last specified system is the default if this option is present.

Per system options

LILO can boot multiple systems. These options affect only the system being booted.

label=*name* The name of the system.
image=*file* The name of the Linux kernel to boot.
other=*device* The name of a non-Linux operating system to boot.(Such as MS-DOS, Windows 98, or Windows NT.)
read-only This option is needed on almost all Linux systems. It causes the root file system (/) to be initially mounted. (Linux will quickly check the fiel system and if it's OK remount it read/write.)
append If your Linux kernel needs command-line parameters, this command will append them to the command line at boot time. The command append=S for the label linux will boot as the system linux S.
password=*word* Protect the image with a password.

The Care and Feeding of Modules

Modules are kernel device drivers or other kernel features that can be loaded and unloaded separately from the main kernel. To see what modules are loaded, use the command:

```
$ /sbin/lsmod
```

Modules can be manually loaded by the **insmod** and **modprobe** commands. The difference between the two is that **insmod** tries to load a single module, whereas **modprobe** will load a module and all the supporting modules that the top-level module needs. Unless you really know what you are doing, use the **modprobe** command.

These commands are usually run automatically by the scripts in /etc/rc.d/init.d at boot time and by the **cardmgr** daemon when a PCMCIA card is inserted. Unless you are debugging a kernel configuration you probably will never run this program.

The **rmmod** command removes modules.

In addition to **insmod** and **rmmod**, there is the kernel thread called kmod. This is an internal kernel process that examines each system request that may require a module. If a request comes in that requires a module that is not loaded, kmod calls **modprobe** to load it.

By default **modload** and **modprobe** look for modules in the directory tree /lib/modules/2.2.3-15 (2.2-3.15 is the current kernel version number).

Modules for PCMCIA devices are loaded by **cardmgr**. These modules are located in the directory /lib/modules/2.2.3-5/pcmcia.

Recompiling the kernel will not recompile these modules. To compile your PCMCIA modules, go to the directory /usr/src/linux/pcmcia-cs-3.0.9 and execute the commands:

```
# ./Configure
# make
# make install
```

Plug and Play devices

The kernel or the **isapnp** utility can configure Plug and Play devices. Because the kernel support is weak and not that good, you probably want to use **isapnp**. Another advantage of using the **isapnp** utility is that you can control the resources yourself. Also, you should understand the functioning of this utility because the sound configuration tool **sndconfig** uses it to configure your sound card.

The Plug and Play (PNP) system was designed to fix the problems associated with configuring devices. Before PNP, you had to set jumpers on the device to control things such as the I/O address and interrupt number. If you accidentally configured two boards to use the same number, problems arose.

With the PNP system, boards let the operating system know how many I/O addresses and interrupts they require. The operating system then tells them which settings to use. If the operating system is working properly, it will tell each device to use settings that do not conflict.

The utility **pnpdump** writes out the configuration information for each PNP device on the system. The format of this file is designed to be used as the input of the **isapnp** program.

So, to create a ./etc/isapnp.conf for your system, first run **pnpdump** to create the file. Then edit the result to uncomment the entries you want. Finally, run **isapnp** to configure the device.

Most of the entries are self-explanatory. The key entry is the (ACT Y) line. If this is commented out, **isapnp** will check the configuration, but will not set it. Make sure you uncomment this line or your configuration will not be set.

Advanced System Configuration

Listing 17-6: OUTPUT OF LSMOD

```
Module Size Used by
smc91c92_cs 9392 1
ds 5740 2 [smc91c92_cs]
i82365 21892 2
pcmcia_core 39688 0 [smc91c92_cs ds i82365]
nls_iso8859-1 2020 1 (autoclean)
nls_cp437 3548 1 (autoclean)
```

Listing 17-7: OUTPUT OF PNPDUMP (ABBREVIATED) AND THE INPUT TO ISAPNP.

```
#
# For details of this file format, see
isapnp.conf(5)
#
#
# Trying port address 0203
# Board 1 has serial identifier e5 ff ff ff
ff 70 00 8c 0e

# (DEBUG)
(READPORT 0x0203)
(ISOLATE)
(IDENTIFY *)
```

Board information follows:

```
# Card 1: (serial identifier e5 ff ff ff ff
70 00 8c 0e)
# CTL0070 Serial No -1 [checksum e5]
# Version 1.0, Vendor version 1.0
# ANSI string —>Creative ViBRA16C PnP<—
#
# Logical device id CTL0001
#
# Edit the entries below to uncomment out
the configuration required.
# Note that only the first value of any
range is given, this may be changed if
required
```

```
# Don't forget to uncomment the activate
(ACT Y) when happy

(CONFIGURE CTL0070/-1 (LD 0
# ANSI string —>Audio<—

# (INT 0 (IRQ 5 (MODE +E)))
# First DMA channel 1.
# 8 bit DMA only
# Logical device is not a bus master
# DMA may execute in count by byte mode
# DMA may not execute in count by word mode
# DMA channel speed in compatible mode
# (DMA 0 (CHANNEL 1))
```

Lots of configuration choices follow. The choices end with the line:

```
# End dependent functions
# (ACT Y)
))
) #
```

Uncomment the (ACT Y) line or nothing will happen when **isapnp** is run. The file ends with:

```
# Returns all cards to the "Wait for Key"
state
(WAITFORKEY)
```

Configuring a Kernel

To configure your kernel, run the X-based configuration program using the command:

```
# cd /usr/src/linux
# make xconfig
```

There is a text-based GUI configuration tool (**make menuconfig**) and a command-line-based configuration (**make config**). These require a lot of typing and take longer than the X configuration utility.

The X kernel configuration program displays a window listing the various configuration groups. In the sections below, we discuss the features of these groups.

Some of the Linux device drivers are mature and stable. Others are experimental and may be incomplete or nonfunctional. The Code maturity level options lets you decide whether you want to stick with what's known to work, or whether you want to be adventurous. If you select Prompt for development and/or incomplete code/drivers, the configuration program will let you try the experimental code. If you select n for this option, all experimental driver options are disabled.

The configuration program identifies some experimental drivers as experimental; others it does not.

The processor type and features option enables you to configure the kernel to best use your processor. The processor type is used for optimization. Select the wrong processor type and your kernel will still run, only it will be a little bit slow.

The Math emulation option turns on floating-point emulation for 386 and some 486 processors that do not have a floating-point unit. Leave this option off unless you have one of the ancient machines.

The Linux kernel can support multiprocessor motherboards. If you have one of these, turn on Symmetric multiprocessing support.

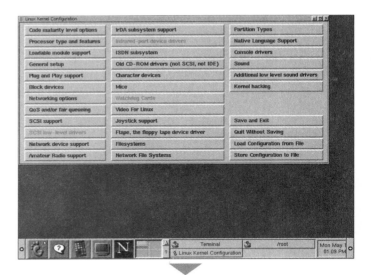

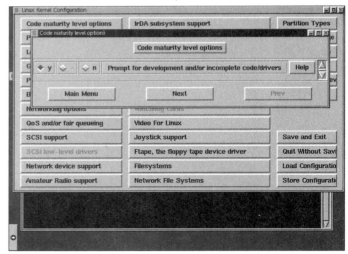

▶ **xconfig** Main screen ▏ ▶ Code maturity level options

CROSS-REFERENCE

Chapters 13, 14, and 15 have more coverage of networking.

FIND IT ONLINE

For more on SMB networking, see
http://www.samba.org.

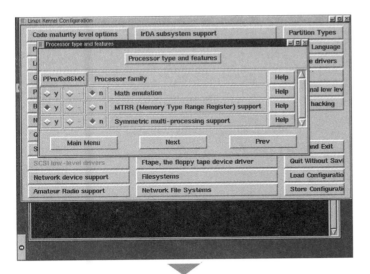

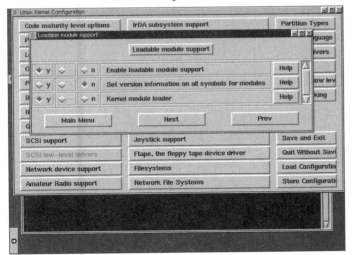

▶ *Processor type information* | ▶ *Loadable module support*

If you have an advanced Pentium chip, you can enable MTRR support. This uses the MTRR register on the processor to improve graphics speed.

Device drivers come in two flavors. There are those that are compiled into the kernel and those that are loaded in the kernel as modules.

Some drivers, such as the basic IDE disk driver and video driver, must be compiled in the kernel. Others such as those for Plug and Play devices (such as sound cards) and PCMCIA devices must be modules. For most devices it doesn't matter.

The advantage of loadable modules is that you can load and unload them as needed without stopping the kernel. Also, if you define a module for a device driver for hardware that's not present, the device driver will automatically unload itself when it discovers it's not needed.

The disadvantage of loadable device drivers is that you have to make sure that they get loaded at the proper time. Most of the time, the Linux startup scripts or the kernel module thread (kmod) do this for you, but sometimes you have to tweak the files in /etc/rc.d/init.d to get things to load right.

In general, you want to use loadable device drivers (modules) whenever possible.

Because loadable module support is stable and extremely useful, enable it.

Modules can be "branded" with a version number. This prevents modules from one kernel being loaded into another. This is a useful safety measure, but it prevents loading third-party modules in your kernel. The Kernel module loader lets the kernel request modules. By enabling this, you avoid loading a lot of modules manually.

Continued

Configuring a Kernel
Continued

General setup

This section of the kernel setup enables you to set a number of general options. The first, Networking support should be enabled, unless you are running in a really strange environment. Even if you are running a standalone system with no network card, enable this option. (Some Linux programs talk to other programs on the same system using the network.)

On most motherboards, there are two kinds of expansion slots: the older ISA slot and the newer PCI slot. Unless you have a very old motherboard without PCI slots, enable PCI support.

One thing you'll notice as you get more into Linux is that Linux gets much better performance out of the hardware than does Microsoft Windows. This also means that Linux stresses the hardware more. As a result of this, the Linux people are always finding bugs and performance bottlenecks with the hardware. Also they aren't shy about calling buggy hardware "brain damaged."

The PCI access mode, PCI quirks, and PCI bridge optimization options are designed to get around hardware strangeness.

The MCA and SGI support options support unusual bus systems. Leave these off unless you have an unusual system.

There are a number of different options concerning various kernel services, including System V IPC, BSD Process Accounting, and Sysctl support. Leave these on because many different programs use them.

The Linux kernel is designed to run a variety of different programs. Most programs use a format called ELF so you must select that. The other binary formats

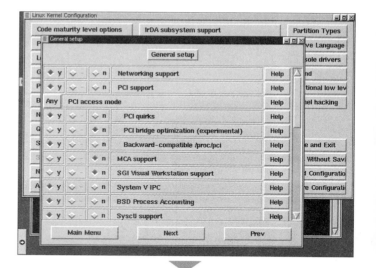

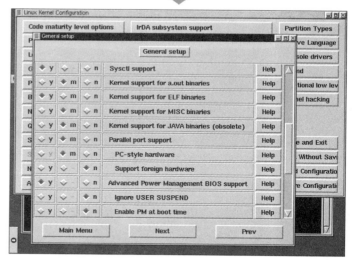

▶ *General setup part 1* | ▶ *General setup part 2*

318

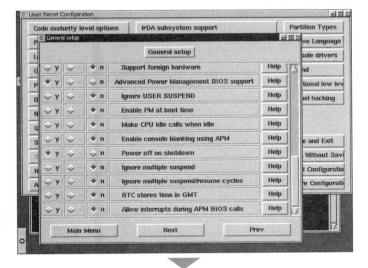

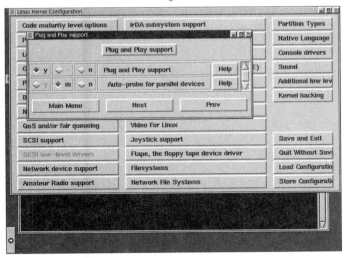

▶ *General setup part 3* | ▶ *Plug and Play support*

can be made modules. When you try and run a program in one of these formats (say a.out), the kernel will detect the format, load the module to support the format, and then run the binary.

The next set of options concerns the parallel port. If you want to use a printer or other parallel device, you need to select this driver.

The last section concerns Advanced Power Management (APM). These options control not only whether your system recognizes APM, but also which services it takes advantage of. This option is of particular interest to laptop users.

The program **apmd** is a daemon that should be installed if you are using the APM system. It monitors battery levels and screams if you are running out of power.

Plug and Play support

That Linux presents an option to configure Plug and Play options might lead you to think that it can actually do it. Actually, this option enables Plug and Play on a very limited set of boards.

These boards include some sound cards and devices that connect to the parallel port and that can identify themselves as using it. (Things like parallel port tape and disk drives.)

For real Plug and Play control use the utilities **pnpdump** and **isapnp** as discussed in the preceding section.

Continued

319

Configuring a Kernel
Continued

Block devices

A block device must be read and written one block at a time. (The other types of devices are called character devices because you can read and write one character at a time on them.) Disks, CD-ROMS, and magnetic tapes are all block devices. This section contains the usual set of options to work around buggy hardware such as the CMD640 chipset.

There are some special devices as well. The first is the Loopback device. This "device" lets you treat a file as a partition. For example, if you have a CD-ROM writer, there's software that creates an image of your CD-ROM. With this device you could "mount" that file as a file system. But unless you are doing clever things with the file system, this option is not for you.

The Network block device is an experimental device for using block devices on a network, such as a remote tape drive. Because this is experimental, don't enable it unless you are really adventurous and want to have fun trying to get it to work properly.

RAID

The Multiple device driver enables grouping multiple disks into a single device. This is also called RAID, sort of. (RAID is short for Redundant Array of Inexpensive Disks and it uses multiple disks to devise a way to recover from disk errors.) Actually, this is a software grouping that can be used with RAID or any other disk grouping.

In linear mode, the disks are just concatenated to each other. This forms one large disk, but gives you no performance improvement. In this mode, if you write a file to disk, it will probably occupy one physical drive.

On the other hand with RAID-0, each block is written to a different disk, improving disk speed tremendously.

RAID-1 provides mirroring. This means that the same data is written to at least two different disks. Very useful if a disk crashes, but the redundancy costs a lot.

RAID-4 and RAID-5 use multiple disks, with parity to provide for redundancy.

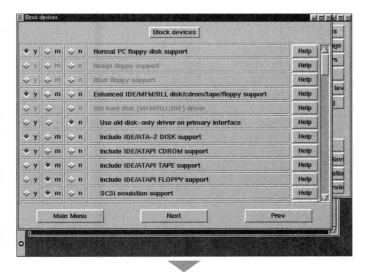

All of the RAID options require the use of external tools to configure the disk array. (Check out the package raidtools-0.90-1.i386.rpm.) The online documentation file /usr/doc/HOWTO/mini/Software-RAID describes the tools and how to use them.

If you are new to Linux, first get the system running without RAID. Then, after you are sure you know how things work, enable RAID.

Parallel port IDE

There are a number of devices that connect to the parallel port, including disks such as the SyQuest drives and tapes such as HP Surestore products. To use these you need Parallel port IDE device support enabled.

Unfortunately, manufacturers couldn't agree on a standard for communication over the parallel port, which means you need to select the protocol specific to your device. Check out the file /usr/src/linux/Documentation/paride.txt to learn whether it has information on your particular device.

Continued

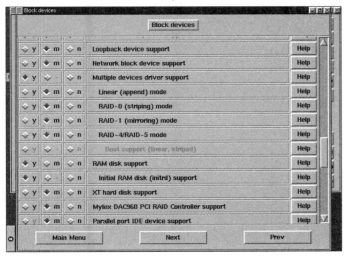

▶ *Block Devices part 1* | ▶ *Block Devices part 2*

Configuring a Kernel

Continued

Networking options

The Linux kernel is extremely flexible when it comes to networking. It can do things most other systems, even UNIX systems, find impossible.

There are some key features in this section that you should note. You should enable the basic services such as Unix domain sockets and TCP/IP networking. If you have two network cards, enable Routing as well. Most of the other options apply to advanced networking. If you're new to Linux, you can leave these off. (And if you're smart enough to need the advanced options, you're smart enough to know what they are.)

There are a few advanced options to look at. For example, Linux can be configured as a firewall. A firewall is a machine with two network cards. One connects to the Internet and the other to an internal network. The firewall machine can be configured to only allow "good" network traffic to pass through it, keeping the hackers out.

One particularly interesting firewall feature is IP masquerading, which enables the firewall machine to rewrite each outgoing packet to make it appear as if it came from the firewall itself. Incoming packets are similarly rerouted when they come in. This is extremely useful if you have a home network and are on a cable modem. Your cable company wants to charge you for each machine you have. With IP masquerading, you appear as one machine no matter how many machines are at home. (See Chapter 13 for information on using cable modems.)

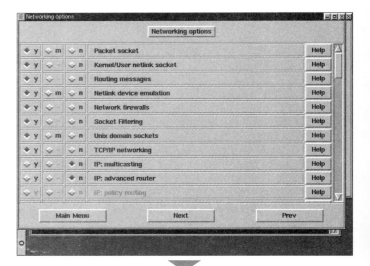

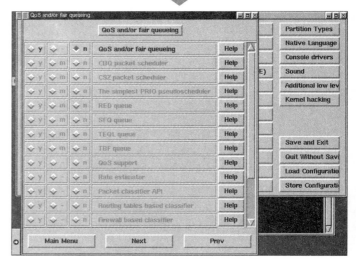

▶ Networking options   ▶ Queuing options

322

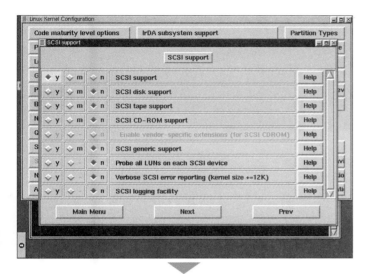

Another interesting feature is IP aliasing. This enables a single network card to respond to multiple addresses. This is useful if you want to provide Web services for multiple names. For example, you can use it to configure a system that displays a different home page for www.mycompany.com and www.yourcompany.com. This option is also useful for people with cable modems.

QoS and/or fair queuing

On a heavily loaded network, you can configure Linux to decide which packet gets sent next using a variety of sophisticated algorithms. However, for home use turn the QoS and/or fair queuing off. You don't have enough packets to make it useful.

SCSI support/SCSI low-level drivers

If you have SCSI devices, you need to tell Linux which ones to support. You also need to tell it which SCSI controller cards are in your system.

Continued

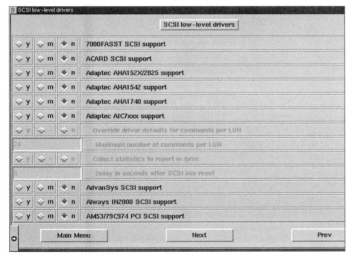

▶ *SCSI support*   │ ▶ *Low-level SCSI driver*

Configuring a Kernel
Continued

Network device support

This section lets you define the network cards you have in your system. Linux's network probe routine stops after it finds the first Ethernet card. Thus, if you have more than one network card, you need to define the second network card as a module. (See Chapter 13 for details.)

There are some non-Ethernet devices to consider as well. The PPP device enables you to communicate with other machines over a modem. This is the most popular way of communicating with an Internet service provider.

The PLIP device enables using a parallel cable as a network device. (However, with the cost of cables so high and the cost of network cards so low, you may just want to use Ethernet instead.)

Amateur radio support

If you are into packet radio and have a radio device connected to your system, you define it here.

IrDA subsystem support

Most laptops and PDAs come with an infrared (IrDA) port. In this section, you tell Linux how to use that port. If you want IrDA, you need to define the protocol being used, as well as some options. Check the file /usr/src/linux/Documentation/networking/irda for information on which options will work with your device.

Infrared-port device drivers

In this section, you define exactly which infrared hardware you have.

ISDN subsystem

ISDN was the phone company's attempt to get into the high-speed communications market. Unfortunately, it's

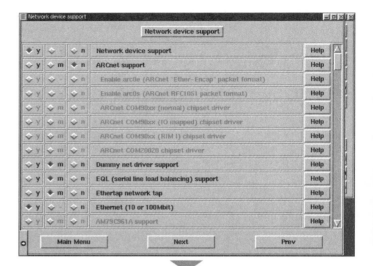

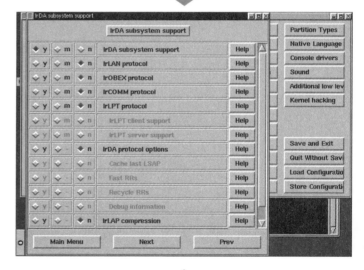

▶ *Network device support* | ▶ *IrDA support*

324

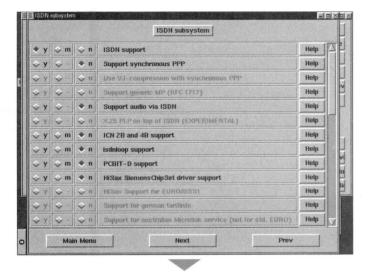

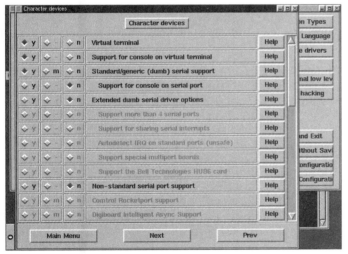

▶ *ISDN subsystem* | ▶ *Character devices*

overpriced and not used very much. Products such as cable modems and DSL have taken over the market.

However, if you do have an ISDN modem, you define it here.

Almost all new CD-ROM devices use either the IDE or SCSI protocol. In the old days, however, each CD-ROM came with it's own custom controller. If you have one of these, you can select the Linux driver for it here.

Character devices

Character devices can be read and written one character at a time. Devices such as the console, serial ports, mice, and parallel port are character devices.

Linux supports some unusual character devices, including a large number of serial boards, which support multiple serial controllers and the access to your machine nvram through the /dev/nvram driver.

One of the more interesting types of device is the Watchdog Timer. This device is used to keep a system running no matter what. A program starts by opening the device and performing some initialization. After that, it must tickle the time by writing to it every so often. If the timer notices that too much time has passed since the last tickle, it resets the system.

Other unusual devices include the system's real-time clock and the Double Talk speech card.

Mice

There are a large number of specialized mouse cards available, such as the PS/2 mouse interface. If you have one of them, you specify it here. (This section does not contain drivers for the simple serial mouse.)

Continued

325

Configuring a Kernel
Continued

Watchdog cards

If you have a watchdog card, enable watchdog support in the Character devices section and select the actual board from this configuration section.

Video for Linux

This configuration section configures Linux for video capture and video overlay hardware. These devices require special tools that are not supplied with Red Hat. See the files in /usr/src/linux/Documentation/video4linux for details.

Joystick support

Here is where you define the joysticks that are connected to your system.

Floppy tape device driver

A floppy tape (ftape) is a tape drive that is connected to your floppy controller. HP and Iomega make several such tapes. This section enables you to define the driver for your tape drive.

File systems

Properly operating systems have one problem in common: they think that the format they use for their file system is the best and they won't talk to any other file system. (Actually, that's not quite true. Some OSs have grudgingly put MS-DOS file system support in their kernel.)

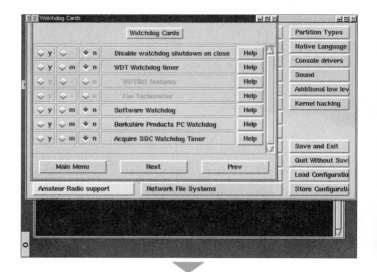

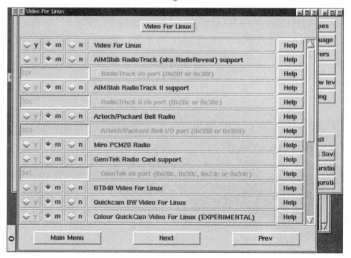

▶ *Watchdog cards*   ▶ *Video for Linux*

326

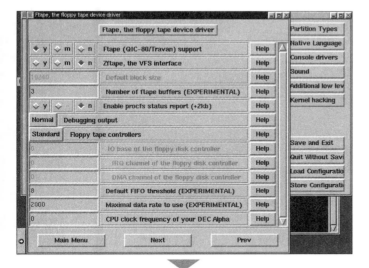

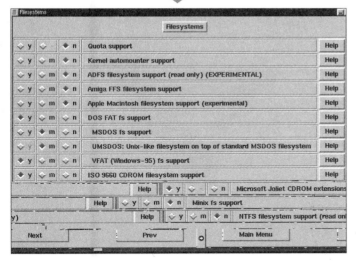

▶ *Ftape support*　　　▶ *File systems*

Linux is open source, so lots of people have put lots of different file systems support in it. Among the different types of disks that Linux can handle are

ADFS	Acorn systems-based machine.
efs2	Second extended fs support; the Linux native format.
FAT	Microsoft MS-DOS.
FFS	Amiga file system.
HFS	Apple Macintosh.
HPFS	OS/2.
Joliet	Microsoft's extension of the CD-ROM standard so that you can use long names on the CD-ROM.
ISO 9660	The standard CD-ROM format.
Minix	A UNIX-like operating system that was the basis of Linux.
QNX	QNX 4 operating system.
NTFS	Microsoft Windows NT.
ROM	Similar to a RAM disk, but read only.
SYSV	System V based UNIX systems; includes SCO, Xenix, and Coherent.
UFS	BSD-derived UNIX systems, including SunOS, Solaris, FreeBSD, NetBSD, OpenBSD, and NeXTStep.
UMSDOS	A hack to let you use UNIX filenames on an MS-DOS partition (stay away from this one).
VFAT	Microsoft Windows 95 and Windows –98.

In addition to these disk file systems, there are a couple of special file systems that can be configured.

The first is /proc. This is a very useful file system that contains lots of information about the running system. Always enable it.

The second is /dev/pts, which is a file system for handling pseudo ttys (terminals). Enable this as well.

Continued

327

Configuring a Kernel
Continued

Network file systems

Because Linux is an open-source product, it can talk to lots of different types of file servers. (It can also be a server for lots of different types of file systems, but that's handled by daemons, and not the kernel.)

For each type of server that you want Linux to use, you need to enable the driver in this section. Drivers are included for:

Coda   An advanced version of NFS
NFS   The standard UNIX file service
SMB   Microsoft Windows-based servers
NCP   NetWare servers

Partition types

Linux supports the Microsoft standard disk labels by default. If you want support for other types of disks, enable them here.

Native language support

Microsoft file systems provide for native language support. What that means is that the character codes in the file names must be translated through a "code page" before they are displayed. There is a different code page for each language.

In this section, you can select which code page you want available for translation.

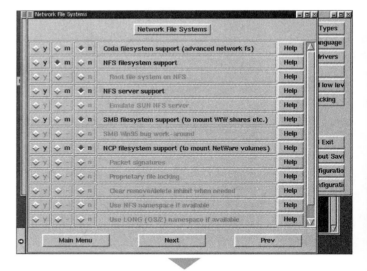

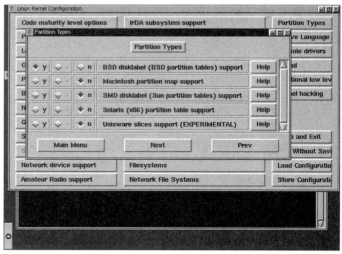

▶ *Network file systems* | ▶ *Partition types*

328

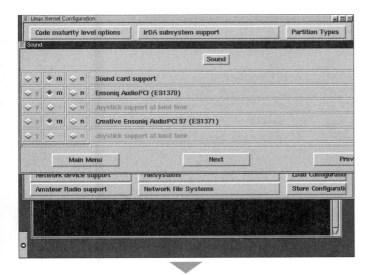

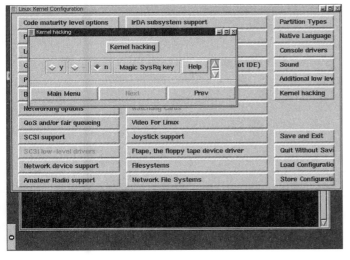

▶ Sound | ▶ Kernel hacking

Console drivers

These drivers handle the console screen. Because most people immediately start the X Window System, they don't need fancy console support. Just leave the defaults set for this section.

This section is designed for people who are running a Linux "farm" containing lots of machines. Normally, you control the system using a keyboard and monitor. These options let you actually run a system using a serial line instead. Although not useful to the person with one machine, it is extremely useful to the person trying to control 50 Linux machines from a central location.

Sound/additional low-level sound drivers

Red Hat supplies the **soundcfg** utility discussed in Chapter 10, which does a much better job of configuring the sound system than you can do here. Just leave everything set to m for module and use **soundcfg** to set things up.

Kernel hacking

If you are playing with the kernel, enable the Magic SysRq key. Most people should leave this disabled.

Personal Workbook

Q&A

1 How do you start the kernel configuration program?

_____

_____

_____

2 What commands are needed to compile the kernel and put it on a floppy disk?

_____

_____

_____

3 What is _LILO?_

_____

_____

_____

4 Why do you need to rerun **lilo** each time you change the kernel?

_____

_____

_____

5 What is a _firewall?_

_____

_____

_____

6 What is a _partition?_ What partition types does Linux support?

_____

_____

_____

7 What does the **lsmod** command do?

_____

_____

_____

8 If you have two or more types of network cards, why must you use modules?

_____

_____

_____

_____

ANSWERS: PAGE 343

EXTRA PRACTICE

1. Compile an experimental kernel and boot it off a floppy disk.

2. Use **/sbin/lsmod** to find out which modules are loaded. Go to /lib/modules to locate the binaries for these modules. Go to /usr/src/linux to locate the source for these modules.

3. Enable IP aliasing and setup your system for two network addresses.

4. Configure your Linux system for a tape drive Then read Chapter 6 and use the tape to backup your system.

5. Checkout the kernel documentation in /usr/src/linux/Documentation.

6. Try to create the smallest kernel possible.

REAL-WORLD APPLICATIONS

✔ A small ISP uses Linux as a Web server. Linux comes with an excellent server (Apache) as well as many different text-manipulation tools to make Web management easy. By using IP aliasing, the server can handle many different domain names. This means that a number of customers can all have their own sites hosted on this one server.

✔ Linux has been used in the movie industry to do computer animation. Hundreds of machines were configured with a small, efficient operating system — Linux. The Linux systems were configured so that they used a serial port for a console. This meant that they could be administered from a central system.

Visual Quiz

You have a Zip drive connected to your SCSI bus. What options do you need to turn on to use it?

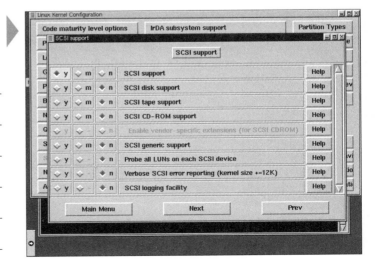

Appendix A: Personal Workbook Answers

Chapter 1

see page 4

1 Does your existing system have any data on it that you value?

A: Yes.

2 When was the last time you made a backup?

A: For most people: Too long ago.

3 How many partitions does Linux require?

A: Two: One for the file system and one for swapping.

4 Where can they be located?

A: On any disk drive.

5 How many partitions does Microsoft Windows require?

A: One.

6 Where must they be located?

A: On the first disk drive, in fact, on the first partition of the first drive.

7 What is *FIPS?*

A: FIPS: First Interactive Partition Splitter. It is a program that lets you split your Microsoft Windows partition in two. (The Linux install can then split the new, free partition into the two partitions that it needs.)

8 What is *LILO?*

A: LILO: The LInux LOader. It is an operating system loader that enables you to select which operating system to run. (For example, you may want to choose between Windows 98 and Linux at boot time.)

Visual Quiz

Q: How would you configure this partition as the Linux file system?

A: Set the mount point to /, leave the size alone, set the type to Linux file system, and check the Growable box.

Chapter 2

see page 24

1 What two commands can you use to shutdown Linux?

A: **halt** and **reboot**

2 How do you start the windowing system?

A: **startx**

3 What must you do before you use your CD-ROM?

A: Mount it or use **linuxconf** to tell Linux to mount it automatically at bootup.

Appendix A: Personal Workbook Answers

4 **Can Linux read and write Microsoft Windows partitions? Can Microsoft Windows read Linux partitions?**

A: Linux can read/write Microsoft Windows partitions. Microsoft won't read/write Linux partitions.

5 **What's *root* and why should you avoid using it?**

A: root is the superuser account. It lets you do anything you want to the system. Because normal protections that prevent you from damaging the system do not affect root, you should avoid using it whenever possible. You can do most anything you want to with a user account and remain protected against stupidity.

6 **What does the Red Hat Linux equivalent of the Start button look like?**

A: A foot. The origin of the icon is interesting. There was actually a logo contest and Tigert's foot won by a large margin. Why is anyone's guess. Our guess is that the origin has something to do with all the Microsoft Windows users kicking their machine.

7 **How do you start a terminal window?**

A: Click the terminal icon.

8 **What is a *pager* and how do you use it?**

A: The pager is a very small display of the various display pages available to the user. Clicking one of the panes of the pager switches pages.

Visual Quiz

Q: **How would you fill out the blanks to the left for a user named Steve Oualline, account name steveo?**

A: Fill in the form with the following values:

Login name	steveo
Full name	Steve Oualline
group (opt)	Leave blank
Supplemental groups	Leave blank
Home directory (opt)	Leave blank
Command interpreter (opt)	Leave alone (/bin/bash)
User ID (opt)	Leave blank

Press Accept after the form is complete.

Chapter 3

see page 40

1 **Does Linux lock you into one command shell?**

A: No, you can run any of a variety of shells; bash is the default Linux shell.

2 **How can you tell which shell is your default?**

A: Try the following command:
```
$ echo $SHELL
```

3 **Which commands can you use to view files?**

A: Any of the following should help: `more`, `less`, `cat`, `head`, `tail`. In later chapters, you learn about `vi` and `emacs`, too.

4 **Which command can you use to change your default shell?**

A: Try `chsh` or call up the About Myself choice from the GNOME System menu and change your shell from there.

5 **What is an *alias*?**

A: An alias provides a name — the alias — that refers to another command. You can, for example, alias type (a DOS command) for the Linux command cat.

6 **What is the magic syntax for the first line of a bash shell script?**

A: #!/bin/bash

7 **What does this do?**

A: Tells your shell which program to launch to run the shell script.

Appendix A: Personal Workbook Answers

(8) Name one of the files executed by bash when it starts up.

A: /etc/profile, $HOME/.bash_profile or $HOME/.profile (for login shells); $HOME/.bashrc (for interactive shells); $ENV; .bash_logout (on logout).

Visual Quiz

Q: What command is running here?

A: top

Chapter 4

see page 68

(1) What do the following commands do?

```
$ man man
$ info info
```

A: The first gets the man page on the man command. The second gets the info file on the info command.

(2) When you use the info command's search feature, you can stop the search with either Ctrl+G or Enter. What's the difference between these two commands?

A: Ctrl+G aborts the command and returns the cursor to where the search starts. The Enter command ends the search and leaves the cursor where it is.

(3) How many times must you run groff before you get a good output file? How many times must you run tex to get a good output file?

A: groff, once; TeX, twice.

(4) How would you view a file named pam.ps.gz? How would you print it?

A: Use gunzip to decompress it, then use gv to view it.

(5) How would you find all the files in /usr/doc that contain the word LILO?

A: find /usr/doc —type f —exec fgrep LILO {} /dev/null \;

(6) Which command would you use to list the names of all the HTML files on the CD-ROM?

A: find /mnt/cdrom —type f —name "*.html" —print

(7) You are running a program and you get an error message that you've never seen before. After searching all the documentation and not finding any help, what can you do?

A: Take a look at the source.

(8) You've just installed your system and for some reason the man —k command doesn't work. What might be the trouble?

A: You many need to run the makewhatis command. (Or you can wait a day and let Linux run it automatically.)

Visual Quiz

Q: The viewer shows only the middle of the page. How would you view the top of the page? The bottom? How would you view the next page?

A: Move the small box to the top to view the top. Move it to the bottom to view the bottom. Press PgDn to move down a page.

Chapter 5

see page 86

(1) Which command exits vi?

A: Try :q or ZZ.

(2) Which command exits emacs?

A: Ctrl+x Ctrl+c

(3) How do you search for text in vi?

A: Use the forward slash (/) and enter the text you are interested in. Use a question mark (?) for a reverse search.

335

Appendix A: Personal Workbook Answers

4 **How do you search for text in emacs?**

A: Ctrl+s starts a forward search, Ctrl+r a backwards search.

5 **How do you get out of insert mode in vi?**

A: Press Escape.

6 **What can you use to check the spelling of words in a file?**

A: ispell.

7 **How can you call this from emacs?**

A: Choose the Spell submenu under the Edit menu and select the Check Buffer choice.

8 **Which commands can you use to read online manual pages with vi?**

A: `$ man subject | ul -i >tmp.txt`
`$ vi tmp.txt`

Visual Quiz

Q: **Which editor is shown here?**

A: emacs.

Chapter 6

see page 120

1 **What does the v option in the command:**
`tar cvf /dev/nst0 /home/sdo`

mean?

A: v means verbose. The name of the files are printed as the archive is created.

2 **How do you get a table of contents of a tape using tar?**

A: `tar tf /dev/nst0`

3 **What's the difference between a tape file and a disk file?**

A: A disk file has a name and can be any size from 0 bytes to 2GB. A tape file is a section of tape. Tape files have a number and their size must be a multiple of the physical block size of the tape.

4 **Which option to tar turns on compression?**

A: `-- gzip`

5 **The following commands are used to back up two different directories.**

```
$ mt -f /dev/nftape rewind
$ tar cf /dev/nftape ./first
$ tar cf /dev/nftape ./second
```

How would you extract all the files in the directory "second"?

A:
```
$ mt -f /dev/nftape rewind
$ mt -f /dev/nftape fsf 1
$ tar xvf /dev/nftape
```

6 **A system administrator decided to use the following two commands to position the tape at the beginning of the second tape file. But he did something wrong. What?**

```
$ mt -f /dev/ftape rewind
$ mt -f /dev/ftape fsf 1
```

A: Because he used the rewinding device, the fsf command spaced the tape forward one file, then closed it, causing it to rewind.

7 **If you write a compressed archive and try to read it without the -- gzip option, will it work?**

A: No.

Appendix A: Personal Workbook Answers

8 Why should you avoid the cpio program?

A: The tape format is not commonly used and because there are several options to **cpio** that affect the tape format, it's not even compatible with itself. To read a **cpio** archive you must not only know that it was written by **cpio**, but also what options were used to write it.

Visual Quiz

Q: What command is being scheduled and when will it run?

A: The `clean-root.sh` command is scheduled to run at 1:00 every Monday (1), Wednesday (3), and Friday (5).

Chapter 7

see page 140

1 What does GNOME stand for?

A: GNU Network Object Model Environment.

2 Name two different window managers.

A: fvwm95 and Enlightenment. There's also fvwm2, kwm, WindowMaker, and many others.

3 Can different window managers be run under the GNOME desktop?

A: Yes. Window managers should support the GNOME extensions, though. So far, only Enlightenment and WindowMaker do.

4 Can you set up a screen saver?

A: You bet.

5 What can you use to get a graphical login screen?

A: XDM, gdm, kdm, and all variants of the X Display Manager.

6 What is the default run-level for Red Hat Linux?

A: 3.

7 How do you set the screen background?

A: You can set this from the GNOME configuration tool window.

8 If you set the screen background and cannot see it, what is the likely cause?

A: The window manager's virtual desktop screens are likely covering up your screen background.

Visual Quiz

Q: What window manager is running in this picture?

A: KDE's kwm.

Chapter 8

see page 160

1 Critics attack the lack of applications on Linux. Does Microsoft Office run on Linux?

A: Not as of this writing, but this may change in the future.

2 Can you get any office suites that are written for Linux?

A: Absolutely. Look at StarOffice and Applixware for two commercial suites.

3 Name two free Linux word processors.

A: PatheticWriter, KWord, GWP, Maxwell, AbiWord. You can also get free personal use licenses for StarOffice and WordPerfect.

4 Can Linux send faxes?

A: Yes. You just need a modem that supports fax protocols.

Appendix A: Personal Workbook Answers

5 **Which programs can you use to create budgets, crunch numbers, and otherwise perform calculations on Linux?**

A: Try the gnumeric spreadsheet for starters. The KOffice package also has a spreadsheet. There are quite a few other choices, too.

6 **Can you play Microsoft Windows AVI files on Linux?**

A: Yes, with a variety of tools. We have found problems in that the tools don't support all the latest codecs used on Windows.

7 **How can you get the ee image-viewing program to display a set of thumbnail images?**

A: Hold down the rightmost mouse button and then select the list view.

8 **Can you display Adobe Acrobat PDF files on Linux?**

A: Yes, with Adobe's acroread or with xpdf.

Visual Quiz

Q: **What can you use to convert Microsoft Word files to HTML?**

A: You can try Microsoft Word's lame HTML output. We've found that mswordview on Linux does a lot better job of converting to HTML.

Chapter 9

see page 182

1 **When you run a graphical desktop, can you get access to a Linux shell?**

A: Yes. Click on the icon that looks like a TV on the GNOME task bar and you'll see.

2 **Name three different shell window programs.**

A: xterm, nxterm, gnome-terminal and kvt.

3 **Which mouse button do you normally use to select text?**

A: The leftmost button.

4 **Does text need to be copied to a clipboard before it can be pasted?**

A: No. X uses an active select and paste mechanism.

5 **Which mouse button do you normally use for pasting text?**

A: The middle button.

6 **How much text does a triple-click select?**

A: Generally, a triple-click selects an entire line. This is not supported in all applications, though.

7 **Can you run a clipboard program on Linux?**

A: Yes. Try xclipboard.

8 **How can you make nxterm run a program other than your shell?**

A: Try a command such as the following:
```
$ nxterm —e rlogin foo
```
Everything after the —e is taken to be the program to run in place of your shell. In this case, the command to run is the `rlogin` command.

Visual Quiz

Q: **How would you change fonts from this nxterm window?**

A: Hold down Ctrl and the rightmost mouse button, and then select a font from the pop-up menu.

Appendix A: Personal Workbook Answers

Chapter 10

see page 192

1 **Can Linux systems play sounds or do you have to run Windows?**

A: Linux can play sounds in most file formats.

2 **What command do you use to play Windows .wav sound files?**

A: Try the play command:
```
$ play filename.wav
```

3 **How about Sun .au sound files?**

A: The `play` command works for these, too.

4 **Can you play audio CDs in Linux?**

A: Yes, from a variety of programs. Try gtcd, the GNOME CD-playing program, or xplaycd.

5 **Does Red Hat Linux come with utilities to play MP3 files?**

A: Yes, it includes xmms. The version with Red Hat 6.0, though, has proven problematic, so you may want to upgrade, or use mpg123 (included with Linux) or freeamp (available on the Internet), instead.

6 **What does MP3 stand for, anyway?**

A: MPEG-2 Level 3. MPEG is short for the Motion Picture Experts Group.

7 **How can you convert a sound file from one format to another?**

A: The sox program converts files between sound formats.

8 **Which command do you use to mix audio sources together?**

A: The xmixer and gmixer programs can do this.

Visual Quiz

Q: How could you increase the treble volume using the program show here?

A: You could adjust the treble volume gmix window.

Chapter 11

see page 202

1 **What program can you use to copy files to a floppy disk?**

A: Use mcopy with DOS-formatted floppies; cp if you mount the floppy.

2 **What program can you use to copy files from a floppy disk to your Linux hard disk?**

A: Use mcopy with DOS-formatted floppies; cp if you mount the floppy.

3 **What is the device filename for the A: drive?**

A: /dev/fd0

4 **What do you need to know to format a floppy drive?**

A: Location (A: or B:), capacity (such as 1.44MB), physical size (3.5-inch or 5.25-inch), and which file system you want to put on the floppy.

5 **Can Linux support the long format Windows file names on floppy disks?**

A: Yes.

6 **Where is the typical location for mounting floppy disks?**

A: /mnt/floppy

7 **What does DOSEMU do?**

A: Runs DOS programs under Linux.

Appendix A: Personal Workbook Answers

8 **What can you use to run Windows applications under Linux?**

A: WINE.

Visual Quiz

Q: What type of commands could you enter at this prompt?

A: DOS commands.

Chapter 12

see page 212

1 **Linux comes from boring UNIX with zillions of cryptic commands. Can you run any games or have any fun on Linux?**

A: Absolutely.

2 **If you feel like killing and maiming, can you run games such as Doom and Heretic on Linux?**

A: Yes. You can also get Quake for Linux, which is available commercially as well as on the Internet.

3 **Are these games easy to set up?**

A: Not exactly. We had problems with most of the high-end games.

4 **Can you start the freeciv program from the GNOME desktop taskbar menus?**

A: Yes, when you install freeciv, it includes entries on the AnotherLevel menus.

5 **Freeciv requires at least two programs to run. Name them.**

A: The two programs are civserver and civclient.

6 **Can you play freeciv with your friends?**

A: Yes. When you run civclient, you can specify a different server on the network. All your friends need to be connected to that network, too.

7 **Is there a commercial version of the game Civilization that you can purchase for Linux?**

A: Yes.

8 **What other games are there for Linux? Are some available from the GNOME taskbar?**

A: There's a host of games available with the GNOME and KDE desktops.

Visual Quiz

Q: OK, you see a creature in the Doom window. What do you do?

A: Shoot it.

Chapter 13

see page 222

1 **What protocol is used for connecting to the Internet using a modem?**

A: PPP.

2 **Why do most Internet Service Providers (ISPs) use two different protocols for mail: one for sending, and one for receiving?**

A: The sending protocol: SMTP (Simple Mail Transfer Protocol) is designed for machines which are always on and connected to the Internet. The ISP server is always on and connected. This protocol doesn't work for machines that connect occasionally such as personal computers, so another protocol has been devised to access stored mail. This protocol is POP (Post Office Protocol) and it's successor IMAP (Internet Mail Access Protocol) and is used to fetch stored mail off a server's machine.

Appendix A: Personal Workbook Answers

❸ Define *IP aliasing?*

A: IP aliasing is where a network interface is configured to respond to more than one IP address.

❹ Define *IP masquerading?*

A: This is where messages from machines behind the firewall are rewritten by the Linux firewall to appear as if they come from the Linux box. They "masquerade" as the Linux machine's messages. This is useful for systems where you want your internal network to look like a single machine to the outside world.

❺ Define *chat script?* **Where does linuxconfig put chat scripts?**

A: A chat script is the input to the program "chat." This program is used to perform the initial connection from the local machine to the Internet service provider using a modem. The chat scripts, by default, live in /etc/sysconfig/network-scripts.

❻ Describe *DHCP.*

A: DHCP is a protocol used by Linux and other systems to get an IP address from a central server.

❼ Define *routing.* **How can you view the current routing tables?**

A: When a computer has multiple network interfaces, it must decide which one to use when it sends a message out. This process is called routing. The system will also take messages coming in from one network interface or machines on another network and pass them on. This is also part of routing.
The routing tables can be listed using the command **/sbin/route**.

❽ What is a *default route?*

A: A default route is used when the system can't figure out where to send a message. A typical use for a default route is where you are connected to the Internet by a PPP connection. In that case, you want your default route to be the PPP interface. The idea is that if your machine doesn't know where the system you want to talk to is located, you should ship the packet off to your ISP and let them figure out where it goes.

Visual Quiz

Q: How would you configure the Ethernet device named "eth0" for an internal, private network system named "Linus", with a fixed IP address?

A: Answer: Fill in

Primary name + domain =	Linus
Alias	Blank
IP address	192.168.0.1 (Or another address reserved for a private network.)
Netmask	Blank (defaults)
Net device	eth0

Chapter 14

see page 240

❶ Can you send e-mail messages from Linux?

A: Yes.

❷ What applications can you use to log into remote systems over a network?

A: You can use telnet and rlogin.

❸ Can you log into a Linux system from a Microsoft Windows system? If you can, which program can you use?

A: Yes. Use telnet.exe. Or, download Tera Term, a much better free telnet program for Windows.

❹ Can you read the Usenet news from emacs?

A: Yes.

Appendix A: Personal Workbook Answers

5 **Can you read e-mail from emacs?**

A: Yes. Emacs can do most anything.

6 **You've downloaded a file that ends in .gz. Which program do you use to uncompress the file?**

A: Run gunzip. Chances are you'll need to run tar to extract the set of files from the archive you just uncompressed with gunzip.

7 **Which program can you use to participate in an online chat?**

A: Try xchat for IRC chatting. There's a number of other programs available, too, if you don't like xchat.

8 **Before you can read e-mail messages from Netscape, what do you need to do?**

A: You need to configure Netscape so that it knows your mail server's name or IP address and your e-mail address (essentially, your user name on the e-mail server). When you ask for e-mail, Netscape will prompt you for your password.

Visual Quiz

Q: How you can tell Netscape to display the Red Hat Linux home page?

A: Type in **http://www.redhat.com** in the entry marked Location. You can also click the link marked *www. redhat.com*.

Chapter 15

see page 270

1 **All systems on the network must have what sort of address?**

A: An IP or Internet Protocol, address.

2 **What format do these addresses have?**

A: Four bytes with a dotted notation such as 192.168.42.1.

3 **Name two ways for Linux systems to share files with Microsoft Windows systems over a network.**

A: You can share files with NFS and Samba. You can also use ftp.exe to exchange files with a Linux system set up with an FTP server.

4 **Can a Linux system act as a Microsoft Windows file and print server?**

A: Yes.

5 **Can you set up and configure your networking during your Linux installation or do you have to wait until later?**

A: You can do it at installation time.

6 **If you didn't configure your network when you installed Linux are you stuck?**

A: No, you can configure networking at any time. It's just easier to do it at installation time.

7 **What is the name of the magical program that provides a graphical interface to configuring most of Linux networking?**

A: linuxconf

8 **To mount a remote disk via NFS, what command do you run?**

A: The mount command.

Visual Quiz

Q: Which file system shown here is served up by Samba?

A: You cannot tell, and that's the whole point, but at least one Samba server is likely to be the server Linus, which has the Mygroup default share name from the Samba configuration files.

Appendix A: Personal Workbook Answers

Chapter 16

see page 288

1 Does Linux come with a Web server?

A: Yes, it includes Apache, the number one Web server on the Internet.

2 If you installed the Apache packages, what do you need to do to get Apache up and running the first time?

A: Chances are it's already running. You should edit the configuration files in /etc/httpd/conf, though.

3 What URL should you type in Netscape to determine whether Apache is running?

A: Try the following URL: **http://localhost/.**

4 What does the <b> tag do in HTML?

A: It starts a section of bold text.

5 Which programs can you use to view Web pages?

A: A Web browser such as Netscape Navigator. You can also use a text-mode browser such as lynx.

6 Which programs can you use to edit HTML files?

A: Any text editor will do. There are also special programs for editing HTML.

7 What is the *document root?*

A: The document root, listed with the DocumentRoot directive in the Apache configuration files, is a directory that maps to the top-level directory available from your Web server. For security reasons, you don't want to allow Web viewers access to your real root directory, /.

8 Which programs can you use to set up a Web search engine?

A: We recommend ht://Dig, a great search engine that's easy to set up.

Visual Quiz

Q: What sort of Web page is shown here? Hint: Look at the URL.

A: A user's home page, as indicated by the tilde (~) in the URL.

Chapter 17

see page 304

1 How do you start the kernel configuration program?

A: `cd /usr/src/linux; make xconfig.`

2 What commands are needed to compile the kernel and put it on a floppy disk?

A: See Listing 17-5.

3 What is *LILO?*

A: The Linux Loader. It is a program run at boot time that enables you to select which system you want to boot.

4 Why do you need to rerun lilo each time you change the kernel?

A: Because lilo needs to know which disk blocks are used by a kernel file. (It knows nothing about file systems.) When you change the file, you change its location on disk and lilo loses it.

5 What is a *firewall?*

A: A machine with one network connection to the outside world and one to the inside network whose job it is to filter data coming in so that nothing bad gets through.

6 What is a *partition?* What partition types does Linux support?

A: A partition is a section of a disk. It can be the entire disk or just a piece of one. Linux supports Linux partitions (called ext2), MS-DOS partitions, OS/2, and many different types of file systems.

Appendix A: Personal Workbook Answers

7 **What does the** `lsmod` **command do?**

A: It lists the modules that are currently loaded.

8 **If you have two or more types of network cards, why must you use modules?**

A: The "smart" built-in network system stops looking for a built-in network card after it finds the first one. Modules look for the card each time they are loaded.

Visual Quiz

Q: You have a Zip drive connected to your SCSI bus. What options do you need to turn on to use it?

A: Turn on SCSI Support and SCSI disk support.

Appendix B:
Finding Out More

In This Appendix

- ► Linux Web resources
- ► Newsgroups
- ► General books
- ► Other Linux books
- ► UNIX books
- ► Magazines

Because Linux continues under active development, there are a number of places to which you can turn in your quest to find out more. In this Appendix, we review some of the main areas, including Web pages, books, and magazines.

Linux Web resources

Linux grew up around the Internet. With Linux developers and users spread all over the planet, it's no wonder that there are thousands of Linux-related Web resources. The next few tables list a number of places that you can check on the Internet for Linux information or software.

Table B-1 lists some of the main sites from which you can download Linux software.

TABLE B-1: LINUX SOFTWARE SITES

Site	Holds
http://www.redhat.com	Main Red Hat site.
http://www.redhat.com/mirrors.html	Red Hat mirror site listing. Check for FTP sites closer to you than Red Hat's overloaded main site.
ftp://contrib.redhat.com/libc6/i386/	Contributed packages for Intel-based Red Hat systems.
ftp://rhcn.redhat.com/	Red Hat Contrib Network, which is different from the contributed packages collection, also at Red Hat's site.
http://www.rpmfind.net	Central archive of Red Hat RPM files and contributed applications from many sources.
http://linux.davecentral.com	Good download site, especially for office applications.

Continued

APPENDIX B: FINDING OUT MORE

Table B-1: (CONTINUED)

Site	Holds
http://www.rpm.org	Home of sources for the **rpm** command itself.
http://www.linuxberg.com	Site holding many Linux applications, and mirror sites on many continents, from the Tucows folks.
http://www.kernel.org/mirrors	Location for mirror sites holding Linux kernels. When a new kernel comes out, you can download it from a site listed here.
http://metalab.unc.edu	Home of most free Linux source code; formerly called sunsite.
http://www.gnome.org	Home of GNOME desktop software.
http://www.kde.org	Home of KDE desktop software.
http://koffice.kde.org	Home of KDE Office software.
http://www.linuxgames.com	Many games for Linux; holds information and links to download sites.

Because Linux includes so many packages, it is often more convenient to get a CD-ROM containing software than it is to download applications one at a time. Unless you have a high-speed connection to the Internet, it's often much cheaper to purchase a CD-ROM with software. Table B-2 lists a number of sites with which we've done business.

Table B-2: SITES OFFERING SOFTWARE Cd-ROMs

Site	Vendor
http://www.cdrom.com	Home of Walnut Creek, which offers quite a few CD-ROMs of source code and applications.
http://www.cheapbytes.com	Source for less expensive CD-ROMs, including Red Hat Linux.
http://www.redhat.com	Official source for Red Hat CD-ROMs.

Important developments in Linux seem to happen nearly every day. Vendors announce products, free project teams announce upgrades, security problems get discovered and people react passionately to other large vendors, especially Microsoft.

The two best information sites by far are **http://slashdot.org** and **http://freshmeat.net**. Slashdot, or /. for those in the know, provides a daily news summary of the most important events for Linux and other operating system users. Slashdot covers Linux, Be OS, cryptography, general science, advances in computing hardware, science fiction, the latest efforts of Microsoft, and quite a lot of editorials on various topics. You'll also find fun things, such as links to the User Friendly comic strip, and fun and often bizarre Web pages, such as the dancing hamsters and *Star Wars* movies made by filming action figures using stop-motion photography. One thing to watch out for, though, is the infamous Slashdot effect. This occurs when the highly popular Slashdot Web site mentions an interesting link, which causes far too many readers to try that link, which causes the poor site mentioned on Slashdot to tip over due to the increased load. For really popular sites, you may want to wait a few days and then try to access the sites.

Despite the off-putting name, freshmeat.net offers a single site that contains just about every announcement of free software upgrades and patches. Every day you'll see a list of new applications upgraded. Most items in the list include a short description and links to the software, and often links to the application's home page.

Table B-3 lists a number of useful information sites.

Table B-3: LINUX INFORMATION SITES

Site	Holds
http://slashdot.org	Great source of technical news on Linux and other topics.
http://www.linuxtoday.com	Linux Today provides daily Linux news, as you'd guess from its name.
http://www.lwn.net/daily	Daily news page of *Linux Weekly News*.
http://linuxjournal.com	Home of *Linux Journal* magazine, another great source for information.
http://linux.org	Main Linux portal site that contains many links.
http://linux.com	Portal site for VA Linux Systems.
http://www.linux-howto.com	Linux HOW-TO documents.
http://www.pconline.com/~erc/linux.htm	Includes a background on Linux and information on a lot of good applications, Linux distributions, and so on. Maintained by one of this book's authors.
http://www.linuxapps.com	Lists zillions of Linux applications, sorted by category.
http://www.xnet.com/~blatura/linapps.shtml	The Web Wanderer's List of Linux Applications.
http://www.redhat.com/linux-info/linux-app-list/linapps.html	Red Hat list of Linux applications.
http://freshmeat.net	Lists the latest versions of free software programs as they come out.
http://news.com	Mainstream technology news site, covers Linux more and more.
http://www.happypenguin.org/news	Linux Game Tome News.
http://www.xdt.com/ar/linux-snd	Linux MIDI and Sound information pages.

APPENDIX B: FINDING OUT MORE

Newsgroups

The Usenet news, introduced in Chapter 14, includes quite a few groups that are devoted to the discussion of Linux and related issues. Some of the most useful Linux groups are listed in Table B-4.

Branching out from Linux, Table B-5 lists a number of groups that we also find useful, each covering different areas of computing related to our Linux usage.

Table B-4: USEFUL LINUX NEWSGROUPS

Group	Covers
comp.os.linux.hardware	Hardware issues with Linux with workarounds to many problems
comp.os.linux.announce	Announcements of import to the Linux community, mostly new software releases
linux.redhat.announce	Announcements regarding the Red Hat Linux distribution and lots of noise
linux.samba.announce	Announcements regarding the Samba Windows SMB networking package
linux.redhat.install	Help with installing Red Hat Linux
linux.redhat.sparc	Issues for users running Red Hat Linux on Sun SPARC systems
comp.os.linux.networking	Covers Linux networking
comp.os.linux.setup	Covers setup issues with Linux
linux.wine.users	Newsgroup for users of the WINE Microsoft Windows emulator

Table B-5: OTHER USEFUL NEWSGROUPS

Group	Covers
comp.lang.perl.announce	Announcements regarding the Perl scripting language
comp.lang.tcl.announce	Announcements regarding the Tcl/Tk scripting language
comp.lang.java.announce	Announcements regarding the Java programming language
comp.windows.x.announce	Announcements related to the X Window System, used for Linux graphics
comp.sys.laptops	General laptop issues; includes many Linux-related messages
comp.protocols.ppp	Covers the Point-to-Point Protocol, used for dial-up networking
comp.protocols.smb	Covers the Microsoft SMB protocol, used by Samba, discussed in Chapter 15
linux.samba.announce	Announcements on Samba
comp.protocols.snmp	Covers the Simple Network Management Protocol, often used to help manage servers
gnu.misc.discuss	Rants and raves on free software, often obscure

General books

We've found the following books, on a variety of topics, useful.

Mastering Regular Expressions by Jeffrey E. F. Friedl, O'Reilly, 1997. This book delves into quite a lot of detail on regular expressions, used with the **grep** command covered in Chapter 3. Most text editors also support regular expressions, as do scripting languages like Perl and Tcl.

Artist's Guide to The GIMP, by Michael J. Hammel, SSC, 1998. The GIMP image-editing program provides one of the applications available on Linux — for free. This is quite a detailed application, one that cries out for a book such as this to explain its inner workings.

Other Linux books

No one book can tell you everything there is to know about Linux. We recommend these other books to help your journey.

The Linux Network, by Fred Butzen and Christopher Hilton, M&T Books, 1998. An excellent book for getting started with networking, it goes much further than part 3 of the book you are reading now.

Linux: Configuration and Installation, by Patrick Volkerding, Kevin Reichard, and Eric Foster-Johnson, M&T Books, 1998. More bias showing. While this book covers a slightly different Linux distribution — Slackware — it provides in depth information about configuring XFree86, the program that provides the X Window System for Linux. You'll also find more on hardware issues, shell scripts, and C/C++ programming on Linux.

UNIX books

Although Linux isn't the same as UNIX, it shares many concepts. The following UNIX books are helpful.

UNIX Programming Tools, by Eric Foster-Johnson, M&T Books, 1997. This book covers the commands you need to run to compile, edit, debug, and maintain programs. If you're familiar with programming on one platform, such as Microsoft Windows, and want to learn about programming on Linux, this book can help. Even though it focuses on UNIX, the basic commands are the same for Linux and UNX.

UNIX in Plain English, by Kevin Reichard and Eric Foster-Johnson, M&T Books, 1999. A command reference to UNIX commands, most of which work the same on Linux. Includes special notes for Linux-specific issues and covers hundreds of commands.

Teach Yourself UNIX, 4th Edition, by Kevin Reichard and Eric Foster-Johnson, IDG Books, 1999. This book has a long section on shells and commands, providing greater background on the UNIX and Linux command lines. If you want to know more about the shell and programming commands, this is the book for you.

UNIX Administrator's Guide to the X Window System, by Eric Foster-Johnson and Kevin Reichard, M&T Books, 1994. This book covers the X Window System — how to configure it and how to deal with its many obscure commands. If you want more information on the topics presented in Chapter 7, this is the perfect follow-on book because it covers X resource files, the X Display Manager (xdm), and more.

Samba: Integrating UNIX and Windows, by John Blair and the Samba Team, SSC, 1998. This is just about the only book on Samba available. If you plan on replacing Windows NT servers with Linux systems, you should get this book.

Magazines

If you want to follow Linux developments, we recommend the Linux Journal. You can find subscription information on the Web at **http://www2.linuxjournal.com**.

Appendix C:
DOS to Linux Command Reference

DOS to Linux Command Reference

DOS Command	Linux Command
ATTRIB	chmod
CD	cd
CHDIR	chdir
CLS	clear
COPY	cp
DATE	date
DEL	rm
DELTREE	rm –r
DIR	ls
ERASE	rm
FIND	grep, fgrep, egrep
HELP	man
MD	mkdir
MKDIR	mkdir
PROMPT	prompt="string"
REN	mv
TIME	date
TYPE	cat
XCOPY	cp

Other differences
In addition, note the following:

▶ **Drive letters** — Microsoft Windows uses a different letter for each different disk "drive." Linux makes additional drives a seamless part of the file system through the use of the **mount** command. Linux uses drive letters with the mtools commands described in Chapter 11.

▶ **Directory Separator** — Microsoft Windows uses backslash (\) to separate directory components. Example: C:\WINDOWS\SYSTEM\MFC.DLL. Most Linux shells, however, treat the backslash as a special character.

▶ Linux uses forward slash (/). For example: /usr/Sam/file.txt.

351

Appendix D:
What's on the CD-ROM

This book teaches you the basics of Linux, but it wouldn't be complete without including Linux itself. So, two CD-ROMs packed to the gills with Linux software accompany the book. We chose Red Hat Linux because it's one of the easiest Linux distributions to install and set up.

The CD-ROMs contain Red Hat Linux 6.1 and the software we describe in this book. It also includes Internet access programs to enable you to download extra software, including Corel's WordPerfect. WordPerfect is not part of Red Hat Linux, but you can download it from the Internet.

Some of the highlights of this release of Linux include

▶ The GNOME desktop, discussed in Chapters 7, 8, and 9. This new suite of desktop applications puts a much friendlier face on top of Linux and works very well for newcomers.
▶ The alternative KDE desktop, also covered in Chapters 7, 8, and 9. We recommend installing both.
▶ Netscape Communicator, a full-blown Web browsing, e-mail, and newsreading program.
▶ The Apache Web server, the number one Web server for Internet sites. See Chapter 15 for more on Apache.
▶ Tools to get online, as discussed in Chapter 13.
▶ Software development tools, including C, C++, Perl, Python, Tcl/Tk, and the Kaffe Java development kit.

Exploring the CD-ROM

After installing Red Hat Linux, you may want to install other packages that you didn't install the first time. You can run the installation program again, selecting an upgrade rather than a full installation, or you can look for the RPM, or Red Hat Package Manager, files directly. You can find the full set of RPM files in the RedHat/RPMS directory on the first CD-ROM.

You can learn more about each RPM file using the **rpminfo** script developed in Chapter 3. The packages can be installed with the **rpm** command.

To access the CD-ROM after installing Linux, you must first mount it using the mount command. Run the following as root:

`# mount /mnt/cdrom`

You also probably want to look through the directories on the CD-ROM to discover more of what's available.

Upgrading Linux

Linux continues under active development. Just about every day, ten or so packages are released with new versions. Sometimes, you see bug fixes. Other times, you find major upgrades. In either case, Linux isn't a static operating system, so you'll want to get on the Internet and look for new and better versions, especially if you are facing problems.

Appendix B lists a number of good sites for downloading Linux software. Two of the best include **http://www.redhat.com/mirrors.html**, which lists the sites worldwide that offer copies of the files on Red Hat's overloaded servers (these are called mirror sites and you'll want to choose the site that is closest to your location), and **http:// www.rpmfind.net**, which is a great resource for finding RPM packages.

Index

Index

Index

Index

Index

Index

Index

Index

Index

Index

Index

Index

Index

Index

Index

Index

MS-DOS
    C: drive directory location, 43
    commands, profile file, 65
    file system, 31, 326–327
    file system, mounting, 206
    FIPS program, 12
    floppy disks, 204
    game files, 214
    Linux command-line advantages over, 41
    partitions, 10, 30–31
    removing carriage returns from files, 106
mswordview, 164
mt command, 124
mtools programs, 204–205
multimedia. *See Also* **sound**
    audio, 196, 214
    desktop applications, 176–177
    video, 326
multiple windows, 186–187
multiuser play, 216
music, 196, 214
mutt, 223
mv command, 48

N

n command, 90
name server (DNS) configuration. *See* **Domain Name**
    Server
names
    accounts, 32
    edit a file, 104–105
    fonts, 186–187
    names, lists of, 107
    network, 275
    printer, 36
    reading man pages, 106

    removing carriage returns from MS-DOS files, 106
    reordering list, 107
    Samba, 282
    script, 61
    tape drives, 122, 124–125
    trimming blanks off ends of lines, 106–107
    write-protected files, 107
naming conventions
    CD-ROM, 8
    disks, 10
National Center for Supercomputing Applications
    (NCSA), 289
native language support, 328
navigating
    GNU info files, 76
    help screen, 92
    installation GUI, 17
    PostScript files, 78
ncftp, 254
NCP, 328
nedit text editor, 114–115
NetBIOS/NetBEUI, 271
NetBSD, 327
netmask, 274
Netscape Composer, 296
Netscape Navigator
    Apache test, 290
    configuring, 230–231, 242–245
    described, 241, 289
    FTP, 254
    HTML, 70
    posting newsgroup messages, 266
    viewing Web Pages, 246–247
Netscape Preferences dialog
    Mail & Newsgroups category, 263
netstat –r command, 276
NetWare (Novell), 271, 328
network adapter cards, 271, 273
network addresses, 305
network administrator, 224

Index

Index

Index

Index

Index

Index

Index

Index

Index

Index

Index

Index

xanim, 10
xbiff, 251
xbiff program, 251
xchat program, 258
xclock program, 144, 148–149
Xdefaults, 148
xdm, 156
Xenix, 327
xfontsel program, 186
XFree86, 21, 144
xglobe, 216
Xi Graphics, 144
xloadimage command, 154–155
xman command, 74
xmessage program, 169
XML, 297
xpdf RPM file, 164
xplanet, 216
xplaycd, 199
xsetroot command, 154
XTerm, 148–149
    described, 184–185
Xtns, 177

Y

Yamaha FM synthesizers, 195

Z

zcat command, 80–81
zgrep function, 80–81
ZZ command, 96

GNU General Public License

Version 2, June 1991
Copyright © 1989, 1991 Free Software Foundation, Inc.
59 Temple Place - Suite 330, Boston, MA 02111-1307, USA
Everyone is permitted to copy and distribute verbatim copies of this license document, but changing it is not allowed.

Preamble

The licenses for most software are designed to take away your freedom to share and change it. By contrast, the GNU General Public License is intended to guarantee your freedom to share and change free software—to make sure the software is free for all its users. This General Public License applies to most of the Free Software Foundation's software and to any other program whose authors commit to using it. (Some other Free Software Foundation software is covered by the GNU Library General Public License instead.) You can apply it to your programs, too.

When we speak of free software, we are referring to freedom, not price. Our General Public Licenses are designed to make sure that you have the freedom to distribute copies of free software (and charge for this service if you wish), that you receive source code or can get it if you want it, that you can change the software or use pieces of it in new free programs; and that you know you can do these things.

To protect your rights, we need to make restrictions that forbid anyone to deny you these rights or to ask you to surrender the rights. These restrictions translate to certain responsibilities for you if you distribute copies of the software, or if you modify it.

For example, if you distribute copies of such a program, whether gratis or for a fee, you must give the recipients all the rights that you have. You must make sure that they, too, receive or can get the source code. And you must show them these terms so they know their rights.

We protect your rights with two steps: (1) copyright the software, and (2) offer you this license which gives you legal permission to copy, distribute and/or modify the software.

Also, for each author's protection and ours, we want to make certain that everyone understands that there is no warranty for this free software. If the software is modified by someone else and passed on, we want its recipients to know that what they have is not the original, so that any problems introduced by others will not reflect on the original authors' reputations.

Finally, any free program is threatened constantly by software patents. We wish to avoid the danger that redistributors of a free program will individually obtain patent licenses, in effect making the program proprietary. To prevent this, we have made it clear that any patent must be licensed for everyone's free use or not licensed at all.

The precise terms and conditions for copying, distribution and modification follow.

Terms and Conditions for Copying, Distribution, and Modification

0. This License applies to any program or other work which contains a notice placed by the copyright holder saying it may be distributed under the terms of this General Public License. The "Program", below, refers to any such program or work, and a "work based on the Program" means either the Program or any derivative work under copyright law: that is to say, a work containing the Program or a portion of it, either verbatim or with modifications and/or translated into another language. (Hereinafter, translation is included without limitation in the term "modification".) Each licensee is addressed as "you".

GNU General Public License

Activities other than copying, distribution and modification are not covered by this License; they are outside its scope. The act of running the Program is not restricted, and the output from the Program is covered only if its contents constitute a work based on the Program (independent of having been made by running the Program). Whether that is true depends on what the Program does.

1. You may copy and distribute verbatim copies of the Program's source code as you receive it, in any medium, provided that you conspicuously and appropriately publish on each copy an appropriate copyright notice and disclaimer of warranty; keep intact all the notices that refer to this License and to the absence of any warranty; and give any other recipients of the Program a copy of this License along with the Program.

   You may charge a fee for the physical act of transferring a copy, and you may at your option offer warranty protection in exchange for a fee.

2. You may modify your copy or copies of the Program or any portion of it, thus forming a work based on the Program, and copy and distribute such modifications or work under the terms of Section 1 above, provided that you also meet all of these conditions:

   a) You must cause the modified files to carry prominent notices stating that you changed the files and the date of any change.

   b) You must cause any work that you distribute or publish, that in whole or in part contains or is derived from the Program or any part thereof, to be licensed as a whole at no charge to all third parties under the terms of this License.

   c) If the modified program normally reads commands interactively when run, you must cause it, when started running for such interactive use in the most ordinary way, to print or display an announcement including an appropriate copyright notice and a notice that there is no warranty (or else, saying that you provide a warranty) and that users may redistribute the program under these conditions, and telling the user how to view a copy of this License. (Exception: if the Program itself is interactive but does not normally print such an announcement, your work based on the Program is not required to print an announcement.)

   These requirements apply to the modified work as a whole. If identifiable sections of that work are not derived from the Program, and can be reasonably considered independent and separate works in themselves, then this License, and its terms, do not apply to those sections when you distribute them as separate works. But when you distribute the same sections as part of a whole which is a work based on the Program, the distribution of the whole must be on the terms of this License, whose permissions for other licensees extend to the entire whole, and thus to each and every part regardless of who wrote it.

   Thus, it is not the intent of this section to claim rights or contest your rights to work written entirely by you; rather, the intent is to exercise the right to control the distribution of derivative or collective works based on the Program.

   In addition, mere aggregation of another work not based on the Program with the Program (or with a work based on the Program) on a volume of a storage or distribution medium does not bring the other work under the scope of this License.

3. You may copy and distribute the Program (or a work based on it, under Section 2) in object code or executable form under the terms of Sections 1 and 2 above provided that you also do one of the following:

   a) Accompany it with the complete corresponding machine-readable source code, which must be distributed under the terms of Sections 1 and 2 above on a medium customarily used for software interchange; or,

   b) Accompany it with a written offer, valid for at least three years, to give any third party, for a charge no more than your cost of physically performing source distribution, a complete machine-readable copy of the corresponding source code, to be distributed under the terms of Sections 1 and 2

GNU General Public License

above on a medium customarily used for software interchange; or,

c) Accompany it with the information you received as to the offer to distribute corresponding source code. (This alternative is allowed only for noncommercial distribution and only if you received the program in object code or executable form with such an offer, in accord with Subsection b above.)

The source code for a work means the preferred form of the work for making modifications to it. For an executable work, complete source code means all the source code for all modules it contains, plus any associated interface definition files, plus the scripts used to control compilation and installation of the executable. However, as a special exception, the source code distributed need not include anything that is normally distributed (in either source or binary form) with the major components (compiler, kernel, and so on) of the operating system on which the executable runs, unless that component itself accompanies the executable.

If distribution of executable or object code is made by offering access to copy from a designated place, then offering equivalent access to copy the source code from the same place counts as distribution of the source code, even though third parties are not compelled to copy the source along with the object code.

4. You may not copy, modify, sublicense, or distribute the Program except as expressly provided under this License. Any attempt otherwise to copy, modify, sublicense or distribute the Program is void, and will automatically terminate your rights under this License. However, parties who have received copies, or rights, from you under this License will not have their licenses terminated so long as such parties remain in full compliance.

5. You are not required to accept this License, since you have not signed it. However, nothing else grants you permission to modify or distribute the Program or its derivative works. These actions are prohibited by law if you do not accept this License. Therefore, by modifying or distributing the Program (or any work based on the Program), you indicate your acceptance of this License to do so, and all its terms and conditions for copying, distributing or modifying the Program or works based on it.

6. Each time you redistribute the Program (or any work based on the Program), the recipient automatically receives a license from the original licensor to copy, distribute or modify the Program subject to these terms and conditions. You may not impose any further restrictions on the recipients' exercise of the rights granted herein. You are not responsible for enforcing compliance by third parties to this License.

7. If, as a consequence of a court judgment or allegation of patent infringement or for any other reason (not limited to patent issues), conditions are imposed on you (whether by court order, agreement or otherwise) that contradict the conditions of this License, they do not excuse you from the conditions of this License. If you cannot distribute so as to satisfy simultaneously your obligations under this License and any other pertinent obligations, then as a consequence you may not distribute the Program at all. For example, if a patent license would not permit royalty-free redistribution of the Program by all those who receive copies directly or indirectly through you, then the only way you could satisfy both it and this License would be to refrain entirely from distribution of the Program.

If any portion of this section is held invalid or unenforceable under any particular circumstance, the balance of the section is intended to apply and the section as a whole is intended to apply in other circumstances.

It is not the purpose of this section to induce you to infringe any patents or other property right claims or to contest validity of any such claims; this section has the sole purpose of protecting the integrity of the free software distribution system, which is implemented by public license practices. Many people have made generous contributions to the wide range of software distributed through that system in reliance on

GNU General Public License

consistent application of that system; it is up to the author/donor to decide if he or she is willing to distribute software through any other system and a licensee cannot impose that choice.

This section is intended to make thoroughly clear what is believed to be a consequence of the rest of this License.

8. If the distribution and/or use of the Program is restricted in certain countries either by patents or by copyrighted interfaces, the original copyright holder who places the Program under this License may add an explicit geographical distribution limitation excluding those countries, so that distribution is permitted only in or among countries not thus excluded. In such case, this License incorporates the limitation as if written in the body of this License.

9. The Free Software Foundation may publish revised and/or new versions of the General Public License from time to time. Such new versions will be similar in spirit to the present version, but may differ in detail to address new problems or concerns.

Each version is given a distinguishing version number. If the Program specifies a version number of this License which applies to it and "any later version", you have the option of following the terms and conditions either of that version or of any later version published by the Free Software Foundation. If the Program does not specify a version number of this License, you may choose any version ever published by the Free Software Foundation.

10. If you wish to incorporate parts of the Program into other free programs whose distribution conditions are different, write to the author to ask for permission. For software which is copyrighted by the Free Software Foundation, write to the Free Software Foundation; we sometimes make exceptions for this. Our decision will be guided by the two goals of preserving the free status of all derivatives of our free software and of promoting the sharing and reuse of software generally.

No Warranty

11. BECAUSE THE PROGRAM IS LICENSED FREE OF CHARGE, THERE IS NO WARRANTY FOR THE PROGRAM, TO THE EXTENT PERMITTED BY APPLICABLE LAW. EXCEPT WHEN OTHERWISE STATED IN WRITING THE COPYRIGHT HOLDERS AND/OR OTHER PARTIES PROVIDE THE PROGRAM "AS IS" WITHOUT WARRANTY OF ANY KIND, EITHER EXPRESSED OR IMPLIED, INCLUDING, BUT NOT LIMITED TO, THE IMPLIED WARRANTIES OF MERCHANTABILITY AND FITNESS FOR A PARTICULAR PURPOSE. THE ENTIRE RISK AS TO THE QUALITY AND PERFORMANCE OF THE PROGRAM IS WITH YOU. SHOULD THE PROGRAM PROVE DEFECTIVE, YOU ASSUME THE COST OF ALL NECESSARY SERVICING, REPAIR OR CORRECTION.

12. IN NO EVENT UNLESS REQUIRED BY APPLICABLE LAW OR AGREED TO IN WRITING WILL ANY COPYRIGHT HOLDER, OR ANY OTHER PARTY WHO MAY MODIFY AND/OR REDISTRIBUTE THE PROGRAM AS PERMITTED ABOVE, BE LIABLE TO YOU FOR DAMAGES, INCLUDING ANY GENERAL, SPECIAL, INCIDENTAL OR CONSEQUENTIAL DAMAGES ARISING OUT OF THE USE OR INABILITY TO USE THE PROGRAM (INCLUDING BUT NOT LIMITED TO LOSS OF DATA OR DATA BEING RENDERED INACCURATE OR LOSSES SUSTAINED BY YOU OR THIRD PARTIES OR A FAILURE OF THE PROGRAM TO OPERATE WITH ANY OTHER PROGRAMS), EVEN IF SUCH HOLDER OR OTHER PARTY HAS BEEN ADVISED OF THE POSSIBILITY OF SUCH DAMAGES.

End Of Terms And Conditions

CD-ROM
Installation Instructions

Installing Linux

The first step in installing Linux is to read and understand Chapter 1, which describes the installation process. Linux is a complete operating system and tool set. It requires more than typing **A:SETUP** to get it running. If you understand and properly plan the installation process, you only have to install it once.

Before you start you'll have to do some preparation, such as inventorying your hardware. While Linux supports most PC configurations, it's a good idea to list all the hardware in your system, so that you can make the right choices when installing.

After the planning is done, as described in Chapter 1, the actual installation should go smoothly. The CD-ROM is a special bootable CD. So, if your CD-ROM drive supports booting from the CD, you can load the CD-ROM, reboot, and go. If not, you need to make a Linux boot disk, which isn't too difficult. In either case, follow the instructions in Chapter 1 (including those for making boot disks).